Paradoxes of Desegregation

Paradoxes of Desegregation

African American Struggles for Educational Equity
in Charleston, South Carolina, 1926–1972

R. Scott Baker

University of South Carolina Press

© 2006 University of South Carolina

Published by the University of South Carolina Press
Columbia, South Carolina 29208

www.sc.edu/uscpress

Manufactured in the United States of America

21 20 19 18 17 16 15 14 13   10 9 8 7 6 5 4 3 2

Library of Congress Cataloging-in-Publication Data

Baker, R. Scott, 1956–
  Paradoxes of desegregation : African American struggles for educational equity in
Charleston, South Carolina, 1926–1972 / R. Scott Baker.
    p. cm.
  Includes bibliographical references and index.
  ISBN-13: 978-1-57003-632-3 (cloth : alk. paper)
  ISBN-10: 1-57003-632-2 (cloth : alk. paper)
  1. School integration—South Carolina. 2. College integration—South Carolina.
3. Segregation in education—South Carolina. 4. African American political activists—
South Carolina. I. Title.
  LC214.22.S6B35 2006
  379.2'6309757915—dc22

                                                                    2006005500

For Beth, with love

History, despite its wrenching pain,
cannot be unlived, but if faced
with courage, need not be lived again.

—Maya Angelou
On the Pulse of Morning

CONTENTS

ILLUSTRATIONS AND TABLES

Illustrations

Tables

ACKNOWLEDGMENTS

Many people brought this book into print. I would like to thank Jeanne Hahn, Tom Rainey, Allan Nasser, David Marr, and their colleagues at the Evergreen State College. I was very fortunate to work with Reed Ueda at Tufts University, who introduced me to the history of American education. I remain indebted to Ellen Condliffe Lagemann for encouraging me to write a dissertation about *Brown* and to Douglass M. Sloan for teaching me how to tell a story. Wayne J. Urban is an important mentor.

Many years ago, when I began this project, African American students, teachers, and activists in South Carolina patiently answered my questions and politely educated a naive northerner. I am especially grateful to Millicent Brown, who desegregated the Charleston Public Schools in 1963, and to Eugene Hunt, Lois Simms, Marjorie Howard, Viola Duvall, George and Hermine Stanyard, Lucille Whipper, Frederick Cook, and J. Michael Graves, who did so much to make desegregation a possibility. Fred Moore and Cecil J. Williams offered insights and images.

Archivists in Atlanta, Charleston, Columbia, Orangeburg, Washington, D.C., New York, and elsewhere tolerated endless questions about boxes, shelf lists, and documents as they helped me track down elusive sources. Thanks to Oliver Smalls, College of Charleston; Sherman E. Pyatt, Avery Research Center; Thomas Townsend, Charleston County, Office of Archives and Records; Elizabeth C. West and Herb Hartstook, Caroliniana Library; Aimee Berry James, South Carolina State University; and Jeffery M. Flannery, Library of Congress Manuscript Division.

Robert Rosen took time from his busy law practice to talk with me about his own experience at Rivers High School in 1963 and the history of desegregation in Charleston. He graciously provided me with documents. Ruth Cook and Lois Simms allowed me to examine their personal collections.

I owe a great debt to my colleagues at Wake Forest University, especially Patricia M. Cunningham, Robert H. Evans, Joseph O. Milner, Loraine M. Stewart, and Deans Paul D. Escott, Deborah L. Best, and Gordon A. Melson. Robin H. Hawkins and her staff provided expert assistance in preparing the manuscript.

Students at Wake Forest, Kristin Bennett, Jeff Morgan, Brett Summers, Rob Warfield, Joy Batista, Kristen Morrison, Paul Singleton, Kelly Dean, Sara Fischer,

Stephanie Howard, Betsy Browder, Amy Talley, Anne Ward, and Christine
Bigelow listened to ideas, read drafts, and reminded me that I had something to
say. I am especially grateful to Katherine E. Baird, Melanie A. Fehrenbacher, and
Kate Kemmerer for their careful reading of the manuscript.

Alex Moore skillfully steered the manuscript through the review process at
the University of South Carolina Press. Karen Beidel, Jonathan Haupt, and others at the press transformed a manuscript into a book.

Most of all, I want to thank my parents, Jean and Robinson Baker; my wife,
Beth Thompson; and our children, Davis, Palmer, and Luke, whose love and
encouragement made this book possible.

INTRODUCTION

"No southern state," wrote Robert Coles, "can match South Carolina's ability to resist the claims of black people without becoming an object of national scorn." As Orval Faubus, Ross Barnett, and George Wallace defied the courts, incited violence, and invited federal intervention, "South Carolina remained relatively untouched and unnoticed, managed and run, though, by exceptionally clever and cool political leaders who long ago learned how to dress up the rankest kind of hate and exploitation in those lovely, old, 'fine-appearing' clothes that go under the name of 'southern gentility.'" While much has been written about the most dramatic and violent battles over school and university desegregation in the South, what deserves scrutiny is not simply the massive resistance that collapsed but the educational evasions that endure. Beginning in the 1940s officials in South Carolina responded to black demands for educational access and equality by rationalizing restrictions that could no longer be sanctioned by law, institutionalizing a new, more sophisticated system of white supremacy that has come to govern educational arrangements in the region.[1]

The African American struggle for equality and access in South Carolina did not produce the kind of theater that was staged in other parts of the region, but during the middle decades of the twentieth century the state was one of the most important educational battlegrounds in the South, the site of NAACP campaigns to equalize teachers' salaries, desegregate higher education, and eliminate state-sanctioned segregation in the public schools. This study tells the story of the African American educational activists who joined with the NAACP and made these campaigns possible. It is a story that begins not just in the NAACP's New York offices, as important as litigation would become, but also in schools and colleges that generations of institution building had done so much to develop. As NAACP lawyers crafted legal strategies for challenging the constitutionality of state-imposed segregation, black educators sowed the seeds of the struggle for equality and access. I have explored the history of four African American educational institutions in South Carolina that were at the center of this struggle: the school at Society Corner, a rural elementary school on James Island; Burke Industrial School in Charleston, a combination vocational and academic high school; Charleston's Avery Normal Institute, a private college-preparatory institution; and South Carolina State College, the African American land-grant college

in Orangeburg. Unlike other historians of black education, I attribute the growing power of these institutions not simply to the initiative of African American
parents, teachers, and students but also to the combined effects of educational
activism and NAACP litigation.[2]

The history of these institutions illuminates the transformation of African
American education during the middle decades of the twentieth century and
highlights the significant and still largely unexplored role that black educational
activists played in the NAACP's legal campaign against segregated education. In
South Carolina this campaign took off in the 1930s as the initiatives of African
American teachers combined with political and economic currents to promote
the educational advancement of more and more students. As young African
Americans were pushed out of the workforce by the collapse of youth labor
markets and pulled into schools and colleges by federal education programs, the
number of black students who graduated from high school and college in South
Carolina and other southern states tripled between 1935 and 1945. Growing
enrollment and rising demand for more advanced academic training formed an
indispensable, and still unrecognized, foundation for NAACP legal challenges in
education.

As activist students and teachers joined African American educational aspirations with the NAACP's nascent legal program, two movements—one southern, local, and educational; the other northern, national, and legal—coalesced.
During the 1940s and 1950s local activism and NAACP litigation brought contending visions of black advancement to the surface and fueled conflicts
between activists, who wanted to desegregate white institutions, and accommodationists, who favored the construction of a parallel system of black schools and
colleges. Conflicts over educational access and institutional development persisted, but litigation and local activism forced state and local officials to increase
sharply funding for black education, generating resources that accelerated the
institutional development of Burke Industrial School and South Carolina State
College, where teachers, professors, and administrators prepared student
activists to realize new educational possibilities.[3]

As African Americans tried to realize these possibilities, South Carolina's
clever political leadership adopted new barriers to black access. Scholars continue to lavish attention on the politics of massive resistance, but surprisingly little attention has been devoted to the new educational policies and practices that
were adopted as authorities were forced to eliminate caste restrictions and segregation statutes. This resistance did not begin or crystallize after *Brown v. Board
of Education* (1954) as Michael J. Klarman, Derrick Bell, and others argue. Rather
it emerged in the 1940s and was developed, refined, and institutionalized in the
decades that followed.[4]

In many respects South Carolina is an ideal place to examine this historical process. Perhaps more so than any other southern state, South Carolina was governed by an exceptionally stable, shrewd, and unified generation of political and educational leaders, who came to prominence in the 1930s and 1940s and led the state into the 1960s. These men, James F. Byrnes, David W. Robinson, L. Marion Gressette, and William C. McCall—like those who promoted segregation as a solution to the region's racial problem in the beginning of the twentieth century—were moderates, not extremists. As demagogues in other states defied the courts, educational and political authorities in South Carolina sought legally defensible solutions to the problems posed by black demands for equality and access. Local activism, litigation, and federal court orders forced authorities to eliminate state-imposed racial classifications, but because there was no clear conception of educational equality to be enforced, federal judges, including one of the NAACP's most important allies on the federal bench, J. Waties Waring, deferred to state and local officials, leaving it to them to determine just what equal protection in education meant. As the long and highly contested process of creating a new system of public education moved from the courts to the General Assembly, officials used their control of education to construct a more rational educational order that has proved to be more durable than the segregated caste system it replaced. In the pages that follow I argue that, while a combination of African American activism and NAACP litigation eliminated caste constraints and segregation laws, officials in South Carolina responded to demands for equality and access by institutionalizing a more rational, legally defensible, and durable system of white supremacy in education.[5]

This new architecture of public education grew out of decades of conflict between determined black activists and attorneys and South Carolina's clever political leadership. As growing numbers of black students sought access to high schools, colleges, and universities, authorities constructed a parallel system of black schools and colleges that was designed to contain black aspirations in segregated institutions. At the same time they adopted standardized tests to restrict black access to white schools, colleges, universities, and the professions. Working with educational experts at the Educational Testing Service (ETS), state and local authorities found in standardized examinations what Michael Foucault calls "a whole type of power" and used this power to exploit African American educational disadvantages constructed by generations of exclusion, discrimination, and segregation. Standardized tests were institutionalized, I argue, to limit black access to white institutions and the professions and to confine the overwhelming majority of African Americans to separate, if increasingly equal, schools and colleges. As massive resistance gave way to more rational and durable evasions in the 1950s and 1960s, educational authorities in other southern states followed

South Carolina's lead, institutionalizing educational policies and practices that continue to govern educational arrangements in the region.[6]

The history of school and university desegregation in South Carolina not only illuminates the new educational order that replaced the segregated caste system but also offers an opportunity to examine the paradoxical and problematic effects of a half-century of standardized testing on African Americans and black educational institutions. Unlike the caste constraints they replaced, standardized tests did not restrict the access of advantaged African Americans, heirs of the state's black elite, but they remain legally defensible barriers for most African Americans. As new, more rational restrictions replaced those once required by law, the legacies of caste—and the class divisions that developed within African American communities during segregation—shaped educational and economic outcomes. While access to broader educational and employment opportunities promoted the advancement of advantaged blacks, most African Americans— handicapped by the legacies of poverty, exclusion, and discrimination—were not prepared to compete with whites and were consigned to institutions that lost vitality as they became segregated by class as well as race. Desegregation, I argue, has been both a triumph and a tragedy, expanding opportunities for advantaged blacks without ending the isolation of most African Americans.

These paradoxical educational and institutional outcomes have deep roots in southern history. When black educational activists and the NAACP began challenging South Carolina's caste system of education in the late 1930s, 90 percent of African Americans lived in poverty. Historical work on African American class formation is sparse, but it is clear that as blacks were disenfranchised, barred from occupations, and driven behind a widening and hardening color line, education became the main form of stratification in southern African American communities. According to David Levering Lewis, "E. Franklin Frazier's black bourgeoisie carved out tolerable educational enclaves" and used them to facilitate the intergenerational transmission of class status. In South Carolina the most significant of such enclaves was Charleston's Avery Normal Institute. Like other private black schools in the South, Avery offered access to higher education and the professions at a time when northern philanthropists and southern educators restricted those opportunities. As Avery prepared teachers and professionals and enhanced the mobility of literate African Americans, the school divided Charleston's class- and color-conscious black elite from most African Americans in the lowcountry, whose isolation sustained allegiances to African American folk cultures well into the twentieth century.[7]

These class and cultural divisions lingered as a generation of African American teachers made elementary schools agents of uplift in the Jim Crow South. In chapter 1, I use the school at Society Corner on James Island, South Carolina, to examine where the generation of African American students who participated in NAACP legal challenges came from, what they brought with them, and how their early schooling shaped the limits and possibilities of campaigns for equality and access in the decades to come. During the 1930s, Society Corner was the kind of inadequately funded and overcrowded rural elementary school that most of the region's 2.5 million African American school children attended. As the local economy contracted, the school's head teacher, Mamie Garvin Fields, used New Deal resources to sustain the advancement of more and more students. Poverty, parental illiteracy, and inadequate funding prevented most students from persisting in school, but during the Depression, the number of black students who graduated from Society Corner and other elementary schools in South Carolina doubled. Encouraged by Fields and her colleagues, more and more of these graduates moved to Charleston to pursue a secondary education.

While the struggle for equality and access grew out of rural elementary schools, it gathered strength and momentum at Charleston's Burke Industrial School. As young blacks were pushed out of the labor force by the collapse of the local youth labor market and pulled into schools by New Deal education programs, the number of African Americans who graduated from Burke and other black high schools in the South tripled between 1935 and 1945. Burke was designed to train what Charleston school superintendent A. B. Rhett called "cooks, maids, and delivery boys," but in chapter 2, I show how resourceful African American educators, many of whom had been hired because of spectacular increases in enrollment, oriented the school toward the liberal arts and college preparation. Growing demand for more advanced training fueled early challenges to an educational system that limited African American access to higher education and the professions. In the late 1930s—unable to find work and excluded from white colleges and universities—high school and college graduates in Charleston, Orangeburg, and Columbia challenged caste constraints in education and became part of what NAACP special counsel Charles H. Houston called "the first signs of a mass movement."[8]

In Charleston, as in other southern cities, early attempts to launch this movement faltered. Black students were eager to challenge educational authorities in federal court, but Houston and his protégé Thurgood Marshall had trouble enlisting the support of the city's black elite, which remained as interested in sustaining the prestige of Avery Institute as improving the black public schools. In South Carolina, as elsewhere in the South, the NAACP was unable to extend the legal precedents it established in higher-education cases in Maryland and Missouri in 1936 and 1938.

The first systematic challenge to the caste system in the South came in the early 1940s, when activist educators joined with the NAACP in a campaign to equalize the salaries of white and black teachers. Throughout the region school officials maintained caste salary schedules that prevented the best black teacher from earning as much as the worst white. While local activism, NAACP litigation, and court orders forced officials to eliminate separate and unequal pay scales in Charleston and Columbia, in 1945 the South Carolina General Assembly adopted the National Teacher Examinations (NTE) and began using test scores to determine salaries. The new salary system, I argue in chapter 3, did not so much repudiate white supremacy as raise it to a more sophisticated level. Charleston's talented tenth, heirs of the city's black elite who graduated from private schools and colleges, earned scores and salaries that exceeded those of many whites. Most black teachers, however, handicapped by the legacies of poverty and inadequately funded schools and colleges, earned test scores and salaries that were well below those of most whites. The results of the salary campaign offer an early indication of how the elimination of caste restrictions heightened the importance of class, offering benefits to black elites without fundamentally changing the subordinate status of most African Americans. As other southern states followed South Carolina's lead and adopted the NTE in the 1950s and 1960s, teacher testing became part of the new, more legally defensible and durable educational order that replaced the caste system in the South.

As officials institutionalized new, more rational barriers to black equality, the resources generated by the salary campaign combined with political and economic currents to promote African American educational advancement. By the middle of the 1940s the growing number of teachers, students, and African American veterans swelled enrollment in black colleges in the state and the region. Encouraged by activist teachers, dozens of African Americans applied for admission to colleges and universities in South Carolina in the 1940s, reviving the campaign in higher education that had stalled during World War II.

Growing demand for more advanced training brought to the surface contending visions of black educational advancement. In chapter 4, I examine the new architecture of public higher education that emerged out of conflicts among African American educators, the NAACP, and state and local officials during the 1940s. After educational authorities responded to black demands for admission to the University of South Carolina Law School by constructing a separate legal program at South Carolina State College in 1947, Thurgood Marshall tried to persuade black educators and students to boycott what he feared would become "a monument to the perpetuation of segregation." As the separate law school in South Carolina—as well as those in North Carolina, Missouri, Texas, Louisiana, and Florida—embedded segregation ever more deeply in an unequal system of public higher education, African American law professors trained attorneys who were instrumental in desegregating schools, colleges, and universities during the 1960s.[9]

Much of what these lawyers accomplished depended on the activism of the African American students who staged a series of school strikes and boycotts in the late 1940s to dramatize severe overcrowding in black high schools. The first act of what Adam Fairclough has called "a two act play," the wave of student activism that swept through the South after World War II, pushed the NAACP to challenge directly the constitutionality of state-imposed segregation in public education. The first challenge came in South Carolina and was heard in Charleston in 1951. Although the U.S. District Court's ruling in *Briggs v. Elliott* upheld the state's school-segregation laws, I show in chapter 5 that this litigation forced the state to fund a $75 million school-equalization program and improve facilities at Burke and other black high schools. The political and educational resources generated by the campaign to desegregate schools helped teachers at Burke strengthen academic courses and extracurricular programs that prepared students to realize educational possibilities created by a generation of activism, litigation, and court rulings.[10]

The Supreme Court's affirmation of the democratic possibilities of public education in *Brown* invigorated black activists, as I show in chapter 6. With the law on their side thousands of southern African Americans, including hundreds in South Carolina's largest cities and towns, petitioned school boards to reorganize the public schools on a nondiscriminatory basis. Across the state dozens of black teachers publicly proclaimed their support for integration. At South Carolina State College the entire student body staged a week-long boycott of classes to show their support for desegregation, and a dozen black students in Columbia applied for admission to the University of South Carolina. In the first demonstration of black political power in the state since Reconstruction, African American voters in Charleston blocked passage of a school bond that local activists charged was designed to prolong segregation.

African American attempts to create desegregated educational institutions where whites and blacks might share power and resources on equal terms unleashed a wave of retaliation and repression. As state officials retaliated against African American teachers, students, and professors who stood up for desegregation, educational authorities insulated white educational institutions by adopting tests rationalizing restrictions that could no longer be sanctioned by law. Massive resistance deferred desegregation, but, as I argue in chapter 7, it was only part of a broader, more sophisticated effort to limit black access that began well before 1956. Faced with the prospect of dozens of State College law-school graduates gaining admission to the South Carolina bar and joining the NAACP's legal campaign, the legislature established in 1948 new requirements that restricted African American access to the legal profession. Similar policies were adopted in Florida, Alabama, Mississippi, and Georgia. Two weeks after the *Brown* decision in May 1954, the University of South Carolina became the first public institution of higher education in the South to require that all undergraduate applicants submit standardized entrance-examination scores. As officials in North Carolina, Texas, Virginia, Florida, Georgia, and Mississippi followed what university president Donald S. Russell called South Carolina's "pioneering pol-icy," examinations designed by the ETS created durable barriers to access for most African Americans. After black parents, teachers, and students petitioned for the desegregation of public schools, David W. Robinson helped officials ex-pand testing and tracking in primary and secondary schools arguing that "this difference in achievement between the races may be our last line of defense." While Robinson and his colleagues recognized that advantaged African Ameri-cans would qualify for admission, they saw that public-school placement tests, college-entrance examinations, and professional-licensure tests could be used legally to exclude most African Americans from white institutions.[11]

As officials institutionalized more rational barriers to access and equality, high-school and college students at Burke and State College used new forms of protest to realize the educational possibilities created by *Brown*. The product of a generation of institutional development in black schools and colleges, the direct-action demonstrations that began in the spring of 1960 and continued through the summer of 1963 were a necessary condition to the elimination of segregation in public education. Acting on lessons learned in classes and skills developed in extracurricular activities at Burke and State College, students organized and led sit-ins, boycotts, and marches that stirred the NAACP, which revived its desegregation efforts and raised the political and economic costs of continued segregation. In chapter 8, I explore how the activism that flowed out of black schools and colleges combined with NAACP litigation, pressure from the Kennedy administration, and court orders to force the desegregation of Clemson College, the University of South Carolina, and the Charleston public schools. In 1963 South Carolina became the last southern state to desegregate public education.

As African Americans crossed the color line, state and local officials drew on policies and practices developed in the 1940s and 1950s to construct more-defensible forms of separation based on class as well as race. Desegregation became an enduring reality, but the educational order that was established in the 1940s and 1950s and refined in the 1960s made class, not caste, and resi-dence, not race, the new arbiters of educational access and opportunity. In chap-ter 9, I explore the paradoxical effects of desegregation in South Carolina. Class did not become more important than race, but advantaged African Americans realized the most significant gains in an educational order where restrictions had been rationalized. While the most affluent, educated, and ambitious African Americans gained access to the most prestigious institutions and the most valu-able programs within them, a majority of African American students, limited by the legacies of discrimination, became increasingly isolated in institutions that lost vitality as they became segregated by class as well as race. The educational policies and practices that authorities in South Carolina institutionalized in response to black demands for equality and access promoted the advancement of advantaged blacks, but left most African American students behind. The chapters that follow examine the historical origins and contradictory consequences of the new, more sophisticated system of white supremacy that has come to define southern public education in the twenty-first century.

Paradoxes of Desegregation

ONE

Mamie Fields and the School at Society Corner, 1926–1938

When Mamie Garvin Fields arrived at the school at Society Corner in 1926, she found two "dilapidated buildings in the middle of some woods." Educational authorities in Charleston County, South Carolina, "had let the schools run down terribly," and parents who could afford it sent their children to a private African American Presbyterian school rather than one of the four public schools: Cut Bridge, Society Corner, Sol Legare, and Three Trees. Isolated, overcrowded, and inadequately funded, Society Corner, like almost all rural black schools in the South, lacked rudimentary instructional equipment and supplies. The white school supervisor, Aubrey Welch, considered books and desks "extras, durn extras." Students had to "kneel on the floor and use the benches to write on." When Fields and her colleagues asked for books, Welch told her that black students wouldn't read books "if they had em" and that she "didn't need no dictionary. Never had none in there." School officials didn't care if children attended school, but African American teachers went out and found the school-age children "no matter how big the classes got."[1]

As enrollment at Society Corner grew, Walter White, acting executive secretary of the National Association for the Advancement of Colored People (NAACP), retained a young Harvard law-school graduate, Nathan Ross Margold, to devise a legal strategy for challenging the constitutionality of state-imposed segregation in the South. While scholars have lavished attention on the report Margold submitted to the NAACP in 1931, the origins of the African American struggle for equality and access lie not simply in the NAACP's New York offices, but also in rural African American elementary schools such as Society Corner, where teachers sowed the seeds of the struggle against segregation and discrimination.[2]

The school at Society Corner provides a way of understanding where this struggle began. Located on James Island, one of the many islands that surround Charleston, Society Corner was the kind of rural African American elementary school that most of the South's 2.5 million black children attended in the 1930s. While poverty prevented most students from persisting through elementary school, the scarcity of work, New Deal relief and education programs, and the initiatives of black teachers fueled educational advancement. During the Depression the number of black students who graduated from Society Corner and other elementary schools in South Carolina doubled. Fields's lesson plans and the classroom observations of social scientists who visited black schools in the rural South illustrate how African American teachers transmitted scholastic knowledge and skills to young people who grew up in a folk culture that retained strong affinities to West African traditions, customs, and practices. These affinities—and the poverty, parental illiteracy, and isolation that sustained them—circumscribed what students learned even as Fields nurtured and the New Deal supported aspirations that propelled growing numbers of students into high school in Charleston and other southern cities. Tracing African American students through Society Corner allows us to understand where the black students who fueled NAACP legal challenges came from, what they brought with them, and how their early schooling shaped the limits and possibilities of campaigns for educational equality and access in the decades to come.[3]

Mamie Garvin Fields personifies the generation of teachers who made educational institutions agents of uplift in the Jim Crow South. Like many of the black teachers who were at the forefront of African American educational advancement, Fields grew up in a "better-off family" that "came out of slavery with education." Born in Charleston in 1888, she was the youngest child of literate parents. At the age of three she enrolled in Miss Anna Izzard's School, one of the many private elementary schools that African American women in Charleston established before blacks secured positions in the city's public schools in 1920. When she was six, Fields entered the publicly funded and severely overcrowded Shaw School. Although she led her class through Shaw, the dark-skinned Fields did not follow in the footsteps of her lighter-skinned siblings and attend the city's most prestigious private high school, Avery Normal Institute. "Back then, honors [at Avery] were always given to mulatto children. Colored people at Avery discriminated against dark-skinned children. It didn't matter what you did if you were dark."[4]

Instead Mamie won a scholarship to Claflin, a private Methodist college in Orangeburg, South Carolina, which was founded by abolitionists in 1869. Claflin was one of the many educational institutions that created what James Leloudis calls "bridge[s] between the freedom struggles of the late nineteenth and those of the mid-twentieth [centuries]." Flourishing at Claflin, Fields studied the liberal arts with a faculty that included southern blacks as well as northern whites from well-to-do abolitionist families. Her most important course was pedagogy. During her practice teaching, she was encouraged to "get to know the community, the adults as well as children, and try to help the community as a whole." Her professors knew that Claflin graduates would not teach in "ideal schools," and she learned "what to do with 125 children, by yourself in a one-room school, for example; how to divide that crowd into groups and supervise all at one time; how to make the schoolroom attractive for the pupils, no matter what the conditions were." Earning a high-school diploma and a teaching license in 1908, Fields taught in rural African American schools in South Carolina during the early decades of the twentieth century.[5]

While whites enjoyed access to publicly funded colleges and professional-development programs, most black teachers had to create their own private voluntary networks for continuing education. As African Americans were disenfranchised, and the region's teaching force was feminized, wrote Glenda Elizabeth Gilmore, African American women created "vast voluntary networks" that made teachers "motivators of black citizens."[6]

Fields's education continued through the National Federation of Colored Women's Clubs, where she learned that uplift required bridging the gap between the scholastic culture of the school and the folk culture that surrounded it. "Those of us fortunate enough to have an education must share it," Mary Church Terrell told a large audience at the A.M.E. Zion Church in Charleston in the 1920s. "We must go into our communities and improve them." Fields was also influenced by Mary McLeod Bethune, the founder of Bethune-Cookman College, whom Fields met in the 1920s. Bethune inspired teachers, Fields recalls, telling them that "uplift in the South is up to us." Teachers had a duty to improve their schools and "organize a PTA." Reminding Fields of lessons she had learned at Claflin, Bethune spoke of the need to "reach outside the school. She didn't wait for parents to send the children. She went out and got them. And if something was holding the children back, she took that as her business too." Fields and her colleagues learned how to extract concessions from reluctant school officials as they raised significant sums from impoverished African American parents. Drawing on her training at Claflin, the skills she honed during more than a decade of teaching in rural South Carolina, and lessons she learned in the federation, Fields began improving Society Corner.[7]

There was certainly much to improve. During Reconstruction, political power allowed African Americans in South Carolina to secure a roughly equitable share of school funds, but as black access to the ballot was restricted, J. Morgan Kousser has shown, white elites in South Carolina and other southern states "increased discrimination in the only important service that government provided—education." Discriminatory appropriations were legalized by an 1896 South Carolina statute that allowed local school boards to appropriate funds "for the best interests of the school district, according to the judgment of the board of trustees." Without access to the franchise, there was little African

Americans could do to prevent school boards from diverting a larger and larger share of school funds to white educational institutions. "South Carolina's public school system is notable for its deliberate and continued discrimination against Negro schools," African American historian Asa Gordon wrote in the *Crisis* in 1927. "The discrimination which has always been pronounced is growing." By the time Fields began teaching at Society Corner in 1926, educational authorities in Charleston County spent $343,942 on white schools, more than five times what was appropriated on black schools. As a participant observer in Sunflower County, Mississippi, in the early 1930s, anthropologist Hortense Powdermaker found that whites used their control of public education "to influence the rate of [African American] acculturation."[8]

Separate and increasingly unequal schools and colleges limited acculturation. Educational authorities acknowledged that blacks needed some schooling, enough to be healthy and productive tenants and laborers, but they believed that broader opportunities would unsettle a social order built on black subordination. "The withholding of education from the southern Negro," wrote NAACP special counsel Charles Houston in 1937, "is deliberate and based on a program of exploitation. Ignorance makes this exploitation easier both on the plantation and in the city industries." Authorities accommodated black students in schools where inadequate funding, overcrowding, decrepit facilities, and the absence of books and equipment made teaching and learning problematic. "There is a great reluctance to spend money for Negro education," Yale psychologist John Dollard wrote after spending a year in Indianola, Mississippi, in 1935. "It is really the fervor of Negro belief in education as a means of advancement that has been responsible for much of the development."[9]

Keen observers such as Dollard understood that the systematic underfinancing of these institutions was only part of the story of African American education. As blacks were driven to the margins of southern life and forced to turn inward, they built a network of schools and colleges that played a crucial role in advancing the race. Black women, especially those associated with the club movement, were at the center of this institution building. Fusing what Neil R. McMillen has called "self-help and prudent agitation," teachers rallied communities behind the improvement of an institution that after the turn of the century offered one of the few ways of transcending the poverty, isolation, and oppression that defined so much of black life in the rural South. "This is grueling pioneer work," Powdermaker wrote, "and only a few have the necessary persistence, drive, acumen, and realism to carry it forward."[10]

What made this pioneer work so problematic was not simply the rundown facilities, the lack of books and supplies, or the many ways whites wore black teachers down, but also grinding poverty, widespread illiteracy, and a folk culture that retained powerful affinities to West African ways of life. When Fields began teaching at Society Corner, more than 80 percent of James Island's three thousand residents were African American. The black islanders, she recalled, were more prosperous and less isolated than African Americans on the more remote Edisto, Johns, Wadmalaw, and Yonges Islands. Sherman's Special Field Order no. 15 of 1865 reserved for the freed people "the islands from Charleston south, and the abandoned rice fields along the rivers for thirty miles back from the sea," but by 1930, federal manuscript census data shows, few blacks on James Island owned their own land. Almost all parents and children worked as laborers on truck farms that defined the island's agricultural economy, earning meager incomes that barely approached subsistence levels. Many African American families rented "cabins" that the census bureau valued at two dollars. "Doors and windows," the 1938 Works Progress *Guide* noted, "are often painted blue to keep away spirits."[11]

On James Island, as elsewhere in the Black Belt, most parents had little formal schooling. Census data shows that in 1930 more than one-third of the African American parents of school-age children on James Island could not read or write. When Fisk University sociologist Charles S. Johnson studied 612 African American families in rural Macon County, Alabama, during the late 1920s, residents told him that adults "didn't go to school in them days, like they [children] do now." Those who were literate could "read and write feebly. With counting and figuring they are much better." Children came of age in households without newspapers, magazines, or books. "Reading and writing," Johnson found, "are not a serious part of the routine of daily life for either adults or children."[12]

James Island was connected to Charleston by a low drawbridge, but well into the twentieth century, most of the island's black residents remained isolated from the main currents of American culture. Travel was difficult. The dirt roads were narrow, and "on hurricane and high tide days," Fields recalled, the island's many waterways overflowed, making Society Corner accessible only by small flatboats called battoes. "Cut off from the mainland," wrote historian Charles Joyner, "generations of Sea Islanders preserved their cultural heritage, reflecting both continuity with Africa and creativity in the New World." During Fields's tenure at Society Corner, the anthropologist Melville Herskovits documented the specific ways in which geographical isolation in the lowcountry led black residents to retain African languages, folktales, religious practices, polygamous mating patterns, and social organizations. They syncretized these retentions into a distinct African American folk culture. Many residents of James Island spoke Gullah, a Creole language with its own vocabulary, syntax, and sounds. "When people spoke fast and in rhythm," Fields wrote, "it didn't sound much like English." During the 1940s Fields served as an interpreter and guide for Fisk College linguist Lorenzo D. Turner, who found in "the vocabulary of the Negroes thousands of West African words as well as survivals in syntax, inflections, sound, and intonation."[13]

Teaching at Society Corner, then, required acculturating an impoverished African American population whose isolation sustained a distinct folk culture. "The average Negro youth," Johnson wrote after interviewing scores of black children in southern Louisiana in 1940, "is born into this Negro folk culture, receives his earliest conditioning in it, and is introduced into ever widening aspects of his life through his family." Before entering school "he learns the folk idiom, sings its songs, enjoys and understands its jokes, grasps the suggested meanings, and manipulates its concepts and appreciates its values." As Gullah culture provided what Lawrence W. Levine calls a source of "identity, sustenance, and survival," it divided many of the islanders from teachers such as Fields, whose education enhanced social mobility and acculturation.[14]

As much as white resistance wore Fields down, so too did conflicts between her uplift philosophy and the folk culture of many of the island's residents. At the heart of these conflicts were different worldviews, differences between blacks who, like Fields, "did things in a modern way, believed in education, dressed properly, were progressive, and wanted to own property" and those who, Fields believed, "were not interested in uplifting conditions." As Fields began improving Society Corner, she tried to persuade those who lived around the school to improve their places "if they were not well kept." Some did, but others told her "this ain't the we land." In other cases she fought with parents who refused to send their children to school. Hostility toward schooling was receding, but some African American parents did not believe that their children should be bothered with "no schoolin." Many, perhaps most, of these children did not enroll because their parents could not afford it, but African American indifference toward schooling was cultural as well as economic. On James Island, as elsewhere in the rural South, not all African Americans shared Fields's belief in progress.[15]

The attitudes of some islanders toward education confirmed the prejudices of Charleston's famed "Negro Aristocracy," who, Fields recalled, were always talking about what people on the islands "wouldn't do for progress. [Black] people in Charleston could make you sick always talking the county down." Fields's colleague Septima Clark, an Avery graduate who taught at the Promise Land School on Johns Island in the early twentieth century, believed that "many cared little about improving themselves," and at least initially Clark regarded her students as "superstitious, sexually promiscuous, and primitive." When Fields tried to include Society Corner students in an Emancipation Day Parade, organizers at Burke Industrial School in Charleston told her that the parade was "not for the schools in the county." Advantaged African Americans tried to shield their children from what W. E. B. Du Bois called the "largely untrained and ignorant, and frequently diseased, dirty, and noisy" children of the black masses. Sometimes, Fields recalled, "black people could draw you back as much as any of the white folks."[16]

These cultural divisions persisted, but they did not prevent Fields from improving the school. As much as inadequate funding, poverty, and intraracial cultural conflict defined the outer reality of Society Corner, Fields made it clear they did not control its inner spirit. Commuting to Society Corner from her home on President Street in Charleston—where she lived with her husband, Bob, and their sons—Fields arrived in a Model T Ford. She "let people know that Mrs. Fields wouldn't have just anything at her school." Improvements came not only from her determination and resourcefulness but also from her association with individuals and organizations in Charleston, especially the federation. Relying on what she could find in the local community, Fields outwitted the trustees, who rarely visited the school. Rejecting the county's offer to paint the school a "muddy black, for black people," she enlisted the help of a local black contractor, J. Arthur Brown Sr., who painted the school with cheerful colors and installed new windows. The children whitewashed trees, marked a path with stones, and planted "sea muckle" as a hedge around the schoolyard. When the trustees in Charleston closed the Shaw School, Fields acquired the used desks and had them transported to Society Corner so that students would not have to kneel on the floor. The point of these efforts, she wrote, wasn't "just decorating." The point was "progress. I wanted the school to look like a place where the parents would want to send the children, and where the children would want to come themselves."[17]

Black folk culture on James Island was strong, but so too was the black belief in the power and promise of education. "The faith of the present-day Negroes is much like the faith of those Americans who set up the public school system," Powdermaker wrote in 1939. In Mississippi many African Americans believed that "if illiteracy were removed, poverty and social disadvantage would vanish with it." Much of the progress that occurred at Society Corner was the result of the parent-teacher association (PTA) that Fields organized with the help of Alice LaSaine, the African American supervisor of schools in Charleston County. As James D. Anderson and Vanessa Siddle Walker have shown, these associations were part of a long tradition of black self-help in education, an institutional expression of the faith African Americans placed in schooling. PTA members in Sunflower County were "indefatigable in their efforts to maintain and improve the schools," Powdermaker noted. Parents made "severe sacrifices" to expand opportunities for their children. In South Carolina "the colored folk are willing to give of their time and money to secure better school conditions," wrote one educational official in 1927. During the 1941–1942 school year, twelve hundred African American PTAs in the state raised more than $50,000, a considerable sum given the limited incomes of most parents.[18]

Drawing on a Bookerite philosophy that informed much of the work of African American teachers during this period, Fields appealed to parents for contributions: "for the boys and girls of James Island, your boys, your girls, give them a chance. Cast down your buckets where you are." Like colleagues in other communities, Fields developed a keen eye for "school projects in the junk that other people would throw away." With the help of PTA members, Fields divided Society Corner into three departments. Part of a broader pattern of institutional development in African American communities that was spearheaded by black women associated with the federation, the initiative of African American teachers and the contributions of land, labor, and income from PTA members were instrumental in creating a viable system of universal education in the rural South. "This significantly improved structure of opportunity at the elementary level," Anderson has shown, "enabled black southerners to alter radically their patterns of school enrollment and attendance."[19]

As Fields and her PTA "kept right on doing with only what we could find in the community," Depression-era state and federal programs supplemented the initiatives of teachers and parents, providing resources that supported the schooling of more and more students. "Before the Depression," Fields wrote, "it was private individuals, churches, lodges, and so forth who helped with most of the social work the teachers did." The contraction of the local economy brought new publicly funded social work to black schools. Discrimination stalked African Americans in every New Deal endeavor, but black parents and students reaped significant long-term benefits. The New Deal supported African American education by channeling funds into schools, and it also helped blacks through relief and public-works programs. As minimum-wage requirements and Works Progress Administration (WPA) employment provided parents with income to support their children's schooling, the Federal Emergency Relief Administration (FERA) funded the employment of new teachers; the WPA paid for hot lunches at school, and the National Youth Administration (NYA) offered grants that allowed more students to persist in school.[20]

While federal measures were important, so too were state initiatives. Although South Carolina passed a compulsory-attendance law in 1917, early efforts, Fields recalled, "didn't mean much." The agricultural crisis of the 1920s and 1930s brought a new attentiveness to the issue of school attendance. In 1937 the South Carolina legislature appropriated $76,000 for the salaries of "attendance teachers" in each of the state's forty-six counties. According to Fields, this put the "government, authority, and the law behind our effort to bring children [into the school]." While the days when overseers rode up to school and dismissed the children because they were needed to plant or harvest crops were passing, getting children to attend meant prodding the truant officer, challenging powerful planters, and educating parents. Most families on James Island, she wrote, "worked for somebody." Because most parents earned meager incomes, children "went to work young and became truant that way." Fields told the truant officer which children were not attending school, but he was "in with the

owner of the King Plantation and didn't bother with children v
there." After Fields convinced one parent, Jim Euree, that it would
buy clothing and supplies for his children than go to jail, Euree's
with Fields's help, began to attend school. Planters on James Island
continued to believe that "the children's work was [a] good 'education' ror w....
they grew bigger." Still, the enforcement of a statute that required school attendance for children between the ages of seven and sixteen, one state official
noted in 1941, "has been an important contributing factor in increasing enrollment and holding children in school longer."[21]

New Deal employment policies and programs provided parents with income
that helped more students attend school. After Fields read about federal minimum-wage requirements in the newspaper, she immediately let her PTA know,
and it served as a "'radio broadcast' for people in the neighborhood." The next
morning parents confronted the planter, Mr. Rivers, telling him "the wages gone
up. When you gon'start to pay us? We teachuh tell us last night." When he resisted, Julia Chisholm, whose daughter was one of Fields's best students, told
him "we reed it weself in depeepuh." Rivers eventually relented and began paying his workers more than fifty cents a day. Prevailing wage scales for African
Americans remained well below those of whites, but minimum-wage requirements and WPA employment created what Harvard Sitkoff called "an economic
floor for the whole black community in the 1930s, rivaling both agriculture and
domestic service as the chief source of Negro income." African Americans in the
rural South were less likely to secure WPA jobs than whites, but by 1938 blacks
in South Carolina composed more than one-third of the agency's workforce.
The New Deal did not eliminate discrimination, but it did provide resources
that helped more black children attend school.[22]

WPA-funded health and nutrition programs spurred local educational authorities to finance "extras" and "social work" that offered incentives to attend
school. At Claflin, Fields learned how to build a cafeteria. During her early years
at Society Corner, students brought jars of soup they heated on the woodstove
for a hot lunch at noon. The WPA funded the purchase of cooking utensils and
equipment and paid the salary of a cook, Mrs. Bertha Allen. Impressed by the
cafeteria at Society Corner, the county nurse pressed the trustee, Aubery Welch,
to build a kitchen. PTA members brought vegetables to the school and helped
Allen prepare meals that Fields supplemented with "day old bread" and "bones"
acquired from grocers in the city. Hot lunches at Society Corner provided an
important source of nutrition for students. The combination of black initiative
and New Deal funding, Fields wrote, created the first school cafeteria on the
island and improved the diet of residents. In Mississippi, Powdermaker found,
"the lunches served at the schools not only improve health, deportment, and
school work, but also act as an incentive toward regular attendance."[23]

Athletics, art, music, and literacy programs made possible by the WPA also stimulated enrollment. Federal funding brought an athletics teacher, Robert Johnson, to James Island, and he divided his time between the island's four elementary schools. Using a court constructed by PTA members, Johnson built up a basketball program, which was especially popular among boys, who were less likely to attend school than girls. The WPA also paid the salaries of music and art teachers, who helped to instruct the growing number of students attending school. Another initiative was state and federal funding for adult literacy classes, which helped Fields teach parents and older children during the evenings. "Some of the men who attended literacy classes at Society Corner," Fields noted, were members of the PTA, and by attending classes and becoming literate they "set an example for children." During the 1930s thirty thousand African Americans in South Carolina and four hundred thousand blacks in the United States learned how to read and write through the WPA. This literacy program was one of the New Deal's most enduring contributions because the children of literate parents were considerably more likely to attend school than the children of parents who could not read or write. Employment, nutrition, and education programs brought tangible social and economic improvements that supported the schooling of black children.[24]

For African Americans the most significant New Deal education program was the National Youth Administration (NYA). Established by executive order in 1935 to combat the problem of youth unemployment, the program funded part-time jobs for school, college, and graduate students between the ages of sixteen and twenty-four so they could continue their education. The NYA also funded employment for students who were out of school. Aubrey Williams, who directed the program, created a Division of Negro Affairs within the NYA, and appointed Mary McLeod Bethune to lead it. Bethune convinced Williams to name African Americans to NYA advisory boards in every southern state. The most influential member of Roosevelt's "Black Cabinet," Bethune's friendship with Eleanor Roosevelt brought access to the Oval Office, where she met regularly with the president, telling him that blacks had been "taking crumbs for a long time. The time has come when we want some white meat." As Bethune gained Roosevelt's support, she pressed African Americans who administered the NYA in the South to "get as many [black] students" into the program as possible.[25]

Still, enrolling students from rural elementary schools such as Society Corner required information and determination. "We often had to maneuver and push to get projects," Fields recalled. In Charleston the first obstacle was knowledge, since local officials told African Americans only what "they wanted you to know. We had to hear our own 'broadcasts,' often from our national organizations." Fields first heard about the NYA at a federation meeting in New York, where Mrs. Roosevelt explained "how to work it through the federation and the schools. Even if a child was past sixteen the NYA would allow him to stay in school and take a little job at the same time." Fields "couldn't wait to tell her students," especially those who had begun school late. However, when she returned to Charleston and tried to enroll them, she encountered resistance from parents who did not believe that the program was "for we," and from local officials who were "always planning a way to hold colored people back." Determined to secure NYA grants for her most promising students, Fields traveled to Orangeburg and met with the African American NYA state director, John Burgess, who sent the enrollment forms directly to Bethune's office in Washington. Even then, Fields had to spend hours convincing local administrators to enroll black students in the county. "You see," she recalled, local authorities wanted "those children staying in the fields to work for nothing much."[26]

NYA grants helped thousands of African American students to persist in school well beyond the age that most black parents had been able to afford, altering enrollment and attendance patterns. "Having the special teachers and the possibility of jobs for youth," Fields recalled, "kept many children in school who mightn't have wanted to come in any other way." Throughout the South, "the $15 and $20 monthly [NYA] checks meant real salvation," Bethune wrote, bringing "the light of training to thousands of Negroes whose own economic resources would have held them in darkness, ignorance, and dependence." For the ten Society Corner students who were enrolled in the program in 1935, NYA grants provided the margin of support that allowed these young people to remain in school. As teachers at schools on James Island "saw how I was getting the program, they had to have it too," Fields wrote. "Plenty of people began to find out that the relief projects were 'fo'we,' just like they were for the white folks." By 1938 the NYA paid almost $270,000 to more than eight thousand black students in South Carolina, who were among the more than three hundred thousand African Americans who participated in the program throughout the country before it was dismantled by southern conservatives in Congress in 1943.[27]

NYA stipends and federal funding for new teachers drew more and more students into the school. The Federal Emergency Relief Administration (FERA) sent millions of dollars to teachers in southern states and as the number of African American educators employed in thirteen southern states grew from 43,852 in 1930 to 64,431 in 1940, teaching became one of the few occupations where opportunities for African Americans expanded during the Depression. When Fields arrived at Society Corner in 1926, she taught one hundred students by herself, but by 1938 she had two full-time colleagues, Thelma Simmons and Edith Caldwell Blunt, as well as special teachers in athletics, art, and music. These new colleagues allowed Fields to divide the 188 students who were enrolled by 1938 into three departments: first and second graders with Edith

Caldwell in the cottage, third and fourth graders with Thelma Simmons on one side of Society Corner, and fifth, sixth, and seventh graders with Fields on the other side of the school. Grading Society Corner helped Fields and her colleagues to avoid the chaos and confusion that plagued ungraded schools in the rural South, where overwhelmed educators tried simultaneously to teach one hundred or more students in different grades. By grading the school and organizing special programs, Fields and her colleagues were able to devote more attention to individual students, especially the most promising students. "As bad as the depression was," Fields recalled, "yet still it brought us some progress."[28]

At Society Corner, as elsewhere, progress was the product of political, economic, and educational currents that produced sharp and sustained increases in African American enrollment. The New Deal did not narrow disparities between white and black schools, Gunnar Myrdal found, but it did "improve" black schools, "increase educational benefits," and raise African Americans' share of "public services." Building on the initiatives of black parents and teachers, compensating for the scarcity of work and income, and stimulating the aspirations of students, the New Deal helped more and more students realize educational opportunities that a generation of African American institution building had done so much to create. At Society Corner and other elementary schools in South Carolina, the number of black students enrolled doubled between 1930 and 1941.[29]

Which brings us, then, to the schoolhouse door and a series of questions about what was taught in rural African American schools, how it was taught, and what students did and did not learn. Fields's lesson plans and the observations of social scientists who visited rural African American schools in the 1930s allow us to look inside classrooms and examine the pedagogies that Fields and her colleagues used to teach reading, writing, and counting. Fusing an African American uplift philosophy with John Dewey's progressivism, Fields crafted lessons that began with students' experience and used books, stories, songs, and assignments to extend that experience. After the appointment of Caldwell and Simmons, Fields taught fifth, sixth, and seventh grades at Society Corner. As head teacher, or principal, she also planned a daily schedule and wrote a detailed curriculum for the entire school. Students in the early grades were given an "opportunity to grow" at the same time that Fields and her colleagues set "higher standards" for the increasing number of students who persisted into the upper grades. As Fields transmitted scholastic knowledge and skills, she taught students that literacy, unlike freedom or the franchise, "is something that no one can take away from you." Fighting "the battle of the book," she acquired texts that brought young people into contact with egalitarian ideas and prepared them to be American citizens.[30]

During the 1930s more than a third of the students at Society Corner and other rural elementary schools in the South were enrolled in the first or second grade. As table 1 shows, the school day at Society Corner was divided into ten- to thirty-minute periods, beginning with conversation, inspection, and devotions at 9:00, followed by number work, word drills, reading, writing, language, and other activities. In the afternoon students had a story hour, recess, silent reading, phonics drill, and a lecture before dismissal at 1:30. Fields wanted these students to learn how to count, read, and write numbers, to become familiar with foot and inch, dime and nickel, and pint and quart, and to know the days of the week. In teaching arithmetic, most teachers, she warned, "try to do too much and are not thorough." Instruction began with drills on counting, using rhymes such as "1, 2, buckle my shoe," and "1, 2, 3 little Indians." Students loved "unison work," she recalled. In math Fields urged her colleagues to "focus on concrete objects" and to have students count such things as the number of children in the room or the number of desks. Students were expected to master counting and learn concepts before they were taught how to write numbers or symbols. "If a student hesitates," she told her colleagues, "quickly help them, before a guess forms in his mind. Help him be accurate, [but] don't make these facts too formal."[31]

Another sixty-nine pupils, 36 percent of the student body, were enrolled in third and fourth grades on one side of the school, and Fields wanted these students to attain "higher standards of achievement." The surviving lesson-plan books for these grades are less detailed, but they do show that in math, the objectives

Table 1 *School at Society Corner, First and Second Grade Schedule, 1937–1938*

Time	Daily Schedule
9:00–9:10	Conversation, Inspection, and Devotions
9:10–9:30	Number Work
9:30–9:45	Word Drills
9:45–10:00	Short Recess
10:00–10:30	Reading
10:30–10:45	Writing
10:45–11:00	Language
11:00–11:30	Music, Handicraft, and Games
11:30–12:00	Story Hour
12:00–12:30	Recess
12:30–12:45	Silent Reading
12:45–1:00	Writing Numbers
1:00–1:15	Card Drill Phonics
1:15–1:30	Dismissal and Lectures

Source: Mamie Garvin Fields, School Planners, Box 7, Folder 2, Mamie Garvin Fields Collection, Avery Research Center, College of Charleston, Charleston, South Carolina.

included being able "to read and write numbers to 10,000, mastery of multipli-
cation tables and the ability to use the four fundamental operations with speed
and accuracy." She believed that "oral work should always precede written work.
The pencil is only used to help the mind solve some problem." In math and
other subjects teachers were encouraged to speak "to the children in a conver-
sational tone."[32]

By 1937 forty-nine pupils, 25 percent of the student body, were enrolled in
fifth, sixth, and seventh grades. Fields's roll book shows that they studied standard subjects—English, math, geography, and history. The most detailed lessons
in her papers contain information about the curriculum in a fifth-grade history
course. Using Harry F. Estill's *The Beginner's History of Our Country* (1919),
Fields covered familiar ground: Columbus, Magellan, Sir Walter Raleigh, and
Pocahontas, among other topics. Unlike lessons in the earlier grades, history lessons were drawn largely from textbooks and were taught in a more formal manner. In geography seventh graders completed a project, "Our United States," that
examined the occupations of African Americans in cities and states.[33]

To teach these lessons African American educators had to fight what Fields
called "the battle of the book." Well into the twentieth century books remained
scarce in black households and schools. "I'm sure I would have read many books
in my childhood had they been available," recalled Benjamin Mays, who grew
up in rural South Carolina at the turn of the century. "They were not. Not in
the Brickhouse School, not in my home, not in the community." You could
"teach the children songs by rote," Fields wrote, "but to teach them how to read
you needed books." When she arrived at Society Corner, "we had none at all." As
school officials "dared black children" to learn to read, Fields acquired a dictionary here and a set of books there. Many of these books were not appropriate for
elementary students. "It's Socrates and Demosthenes, it's novels not suited for
children, and all broken books with the pages falling out." In 1937 the state began
to provide textbooks, but children had to "rent them in the fall and turn them
back in the spring." Few parents could afford the rental fees, and because there
were never enough books to go around, most students "had to look on." African
American teachers "never got a new book to give out." The state provision of
used textbooks, as degrading as it was, meant that whites and blacks read the
same texts. Powdermaker argued that "as the younger generation" was "nour-
ished on intellectual fare much more like that of the whites," they developed
similar attitudes. "The colored child at school may read the same history book
that white children read, telling of accomplishments by other nations in other
times. Geography broadens his world."[34]

Exposing African Americans to a wider world required teaching students
how to read and speak the English language. Because most students brought a
second language, Gullah, to Society Corner, English was taught in all classes.

"Language," Fields wrote, "is the one tool that we must use everyday in and out of work hours. Reading is the key which unlocks the treasure house of knowledge, and language is the talisman by which alone we may transmit this treasure into forms of use and value." First graders recited poems, told stories, learned punctuation and capitalization, and wrote their names and addresses. Second graders worked to build sentences, master capitals, abbreviate, and memorize the spelling of words. Much of this was taught through unison work and drill. Games were also used to teach proper speech. One game, "Somebody and I," was designed to help "pupils form the habit of saying I saw, instead of I see," and to get them to substitute "Mary and I, for me and Mary." By the end of the second grade students were expected to be able to recite a poem, present and dramatize a story to the class, and read an original composition. More advanced students read "The Oil Merchant" and were assigned comprehension questions on Ali Baba. Fields came to understand and appreciate that Gullah was a language with its own syntax and grammar, but, like many of her colleagues, she believed that "progress" required students to use "proper English." Alma Shokes, who taught at Cut Bridge School on James Island, recalled that "we endeavored to acculturate those children through spelling bees, speaking contests, and operettas."[35]

Lessons in racial pride and self-respect were woven through the curriculum. No black teacher could succeed unless she instilled in students what the larger society tried to deny: a sense of black identity and dignity. "We had to do more than teach reading, writing, and arithmetic," recalled Shokes, expressing sentiments echoed in the oral testimony of many black educators. "All the teachers had a hard time, as it was, trying to make each child understand that he was somebody," wrote Fields. At Society Corner this meant challenging parents who taught their children to "lower their eyes, curtsy and shuffle, and hang your head" when they encountered a "superior person." In the classroom students would "shuffle to beg my pardon" as they approached her desk to ask a question. Such "manners," Fields noted, "didn't help these black children come up in the world. [They] kept us in our place. They conditioned us in old South ways." Fields threatened to punish students who behaved this way, but parents did not necessarily approve. "Oh, how I had to fight with some of the people on James Island." Teaching what Fields called "proud ways" also meant countering the many ways whites tried "to degrade the Negro. I always tried to oppose that." After one student was ridiculed by a group of whites, she told him and his classmates "black isn't a cuss." Asking students to name all the beautiful things that were black, she declared "you are black and glad of it." In Georgia, Arthur Raper found that "a Negro school teacher in the rural community who can instill a feeling of self-respect and confidence into Negro children is doing work of the first importance."[36]

As Fields taught racial pride and self-respect, she prepared students for citizenship; "never mind if many Negroes couldn't vote yet." For her, teaching students that they were "as good as anybody" meant showing them that they were American citizens. In the early grades pupils learned the words to "America the Beautiful" and the Pledge of Allegiance. When she taught in Sumter County in the early twentieth century, Fields had to fight to get an American flag for her classroom so students would understand that "my school was in the United States, after all, and not [in] the Confederacy." Acting on lessons she learned from Bethune, Fields also established a "citizenship department" at Society Corner even though most African American adults believed that voting was "white folks business" and only thirty of the island's three thousand black residents were registered to vote. Lessons on the structure of government and the courts were designed to induct schoolchildren into American political culture.[37]

What made this induction and the process of transmitting scholastic knowledge and skills so problematic was not simply inadequate funding or overcrowding, as much as they limited, but the poverty that prevented most black students from consistently attending school. On James Island, as elsewhere, economic exigencies forced black children into the labor force at an early age. "We always had a hard time with school attendance," Fields recalled. Almost all black families subsisted on low and irregular incomes, and few parents could forgo a working child's contribution to family income or afford books, supplies, and presentable clothing. In rural Georgia "any work, be it ever so little, meant too frequently no school," Raper wrote. "I started school when I was eight or nine, but I didn't get to go much," one frustrated seventeen-year-old from Madison County, Alabama, told Johnson. "I had to work most of the time." Congressman John Lewis, who grew up in rural Alabama, recalled that "when there was work to be done in the fields that came first. It was a Southern tradition, just part of a way of life." Even when children were not working, the lack of presentable clothing kept students out of school. When parents did not have clothing for all their children, they tended to send females to school. One parent told Fields: "I will send Rosa, but Leon, ee ain'got no shoe or ee ain got no shut." Fields's roll book shows that measles, tonsillitis, typhoid fever, and other health problems also curtailed attendance. Robert A. Margo's econometric analysis confirms what every contemporary observer emphasized, that poverty prevented most students from consistently attending school.[38]

Because work and survival remained so much more urgent than schooling, most students were unable to persist through elementary school. During the 1937–1938 school year average daily attendance at Society Corner was 58 percent with students attending an average of 75 of the 138 days the school was in session. In Macon County, Alabama, Johnson found that "attendance fluctuates by months to such an extent as to keep the school work seriously disorganized, and render impossible very consistent learning on the part of the children." As table 2 indicates, most students at Society Corner did not regularly advance from one grade to the next. In 1938, only 109, or 57.9 percent, of the students at Society Corner were promoted. As anthropologists Mary A. Twining and Keith E. Baird have noted, these attendance and promotion patterns "prolonged a period of cultural indoctrination and social initiation into Sea Island folkways undistracted by the acculturative inducements to mainstream values and conduct which public school normally provides." It was common for students to spend two years in first grade, three years in second grade, and so on. Most students were overaged, "retarded" in 1930s parlance, two, three, or more years behind.[39]

For most black students educational advancement awaited fundamental improvements in the social and economic conditions of African American life. As students at Society Corner "fell behind," Fields recalled, most became "too ashamed" to be with others, and "the big little boys," who were twice as likely as girls to be overaged, "wouldn't attend school with the younger smaller children." By the time most young people reached the age of twelve or thirteen, they stopped attending school altogether. Using enrollment data from the 1933–1934 school year, Howard University education professor Doxey Wilkerson estimated that for every 100 Negro pupils who entered the first grade in eighteen southern states, 56 remained in school by the fourth grade, 45 by the fifth grade, and 26 by the seventh grade. Because white families had higher incomes, higher rates of parental literacy, and access to better schools, African American educational attainment remained well below that of whites. Wilkerson estimated that more than five times as many whites as blacks were enrolled in seventh grade.[40]

Poverty remained a powerful obstacle to African American educational progress, but during the 1930s political, economic, and educational currents swept

Table 2 *Enrollment and Promotion, School at Society Corner, 1937–1938*

Enrollment		Promoted	
Grade	Enrollment	Number	Percent
1	45	30	66
2	25	20	80
3	37	18	49
4	32	11	33
5	16	10	62
6	17	10	59
7	16	10	62

Source: Mamie Garvin Fields, School Planners, Box 7, Folder 2, Mamie Garvin Fields Collection, Avery Research Center, College of Charleston, Charleston, South Carolina.

growing numbers of black students through elementary school, setting in motion a significant and sustained rise in African American educational attainment. With fewer and fewer crops to plant or harvest, with financial support from the federal government, and with incentives to attend school, more and more African Americans, especially those of literate, landowning parents, attended school consistently enough to be promoted. During the 1930s the proportion of blacks between the ages of ten and fifteen who were gainful workers fell. Ambrose Caliver, a specialist in African American schooling at the U.S. Office of Education, found that because of the "inability of older children to find work, schools are holding pupils longer." Blacks remained far more likely to drop out of school than whites, but federal minimum-wage requirements, WPA jobs, and NYA grants provided the margin of support that helped more and more blacks to persist in school. "The colored children of the state are gradually remaining in school through the higher grades," the supervisor of Negro schools in South Carolina, J. B. Felton, wrote in 1942. "The number enrolled in seventh grade is twice the size it was 11 years ago." Unable to work, supported by the New Deal, and pushed forward by teachers and parents who wanted a better life for children, nine students graduated from Society Corner in April 1938, part of a cohort of African American elementary-school graduates that was larger—twice as large—as the one that preceded it.[41]

What did students who graduated from Society Corner and other rural elementary schools learn? How successful were African American teachers at transmitting scholastic knowledge and skills? How literate were these students? "In view of the achievement testing that pervaded schools by the 1930s," wrote Carl Kaestle in his authoritative study of literacy in twentieth-century America, "one would expect that our knowledge about the history of literacy skills would be familiar and precise. On the contrary, there is little historical work on the subject and the sources are riddled with problems." These problems are evident in the contradictory portraits that social scientists have painted of what African American students in the rural South knew about scholastic subjects.[42]

Most of the social scientists who observed rural ungraded elementary schools were stunned by how little African American students knew about American history, politics, and culture. At one ungraded school in Sunflower County, Mississippi, Powdermaker found that "none of the students has any real comprehension of his lessons. One gets the impression that the children feel that this is all very dull, but better than working." In Georgia "at a one-teacher school west of the river in Macon County," Raper was stunned that "a child by the name Booker T. Washington Williams" did not know "for whom he was named." Myrdal visited a class in "an old Rosenwald School in a rural county outside Atlanta in 1938." The Swedish observer could hardly believe that students could not identify the president, England, or Europe. When he asked students what the

Constitution was and what it meant to them, "all remained in solemn silence until the bright boy helped us out, informing us that it was a 'newspaper in Atlanta.'"[43]

These were observations of ungraded schools, but where students were divided into grades, as they were at Society Corner, it is likely that they learned more. Myrdal acknowledged that the school outside Atlanta was not necessarily "typical," and other observers reached different conclusions. Johnson's account of Brooks Elementary School in East Feliciana Parish, Louisiana, thirty miles from Baton Rouge, illustrated how a "resourceful and intelligent teacher" employed progressive educational practices to promote learning. The study of cotton was used to teach reading and writing, and Johnson concluded that "in this school the children learn, and this is reflected in their speech, manner, and general alertness." At another school in rural Ouachita Parish, eighty miles east of Shreveport, Louisiana, Estille Massey Riddle observed classes at the Mineral Springs School in 1934 as part of her Rosenwald Fund–sponsored study of an "all Negro community." Young people in one class stumbled on questions about Magellan and Columbus, but in another, Riddle saw students engaged in a discussion of early modern Europe. During one history class the teacher asked: "Why do we have this period of Reformation? What caused Christianity to stand, brave or scary men? How can we reform our community rights here in Mineral Springs? A good discussion followed." As the class compared Charlemagne to Huey Long, the students were "enthusiastic and spontaneous" and asked "thought provoking questions."[44]

Students at Society Corner probably had discussions like those that Riddle documented in Louisiana, but the grades of students in Fields's fifth-grade history class suggest that students' grasp of American history was tentative. During the 1937–1938 school year, the grades in history ranged from ten to seventy, with a class average of thirty-five. These were, of course, pre-grade-inflation marks, but students' comprehension of American history was clearly restricted by the limited schooling of most parents, linguistic patterns, and isolation. Because the educational attainment of nearly all black parents remained below that of their children, few could reinforce lessons that were taught in school. The fact that students at Society Corner had to learn a second language complicated the task of teaching American history, and Johnson argued that this inhibited understanding of school subjects. "Just as the subtleties of Negro speech may escape one with life-long experience in communicating the standard English language," he wrote, "so may the concepts and word meanings of formal written language escape the understanding of those of the Negro youth whose experience has been limited to manipulation and transmitting folk idioms." As the curriculum at Society Corner became more academic and more distant from students' experience, isolation—what Myrdal called African Americans' "extreme lack of contact with mainstream American civilization"—left gaps in most students' comprehension of school subjects. These gaps created a powerful intergenerational drag on what future generations of African American students learned in school.[45]

As incomplete as the transmission of scholastic knowledge was, African American teachers nurtured and the New Deal supported aspirations that propelled increasing numbers of rural African American elementary-school graduates into high schools in Charleston and other southern cities. During the early decades of the twentieth century, southern educational authorities constructed a system of secondary schooling for whites in the rural South, but in South Carolina, as elsewhere in the region, most black high schools were located in cities. While public support for the schooling of African Americans in rural Charleston County, as in two hundred other counties in the region, ended at the seventh grade, African American teachers, Alma Shokes recalled, "did everything we could to motivate boys and girls to continue their education." Using the same kind of initiative that improved schools on James Island, Fields and her colleagues encouraged their best students to move to Charleston and pursue an education at Burke Industrial School, the only publicly supported secondary school for African Americans in the rural South Carolina lowcountry. Marjorie Howard, who taught at Burke, recalls that "teachers saw promising students in the low country, and made sure that they had a place to board in the city." One of Fields's most talented graduates, Laura Jackson, lived with her former teacher in Charleston and attended Burke. By the late 1930s growing numbers of black students who graduated from rural elementary schools swelled secondary enrollments in Charleston, Baltimore, Washington, Richmond, Atlanta, Jackson, New Orleans, and other southern cities. As much as inadequate funding, poverty, and isolation limited, Mamie Fields and her colleagues sowed the seeds of a struggle for educational equality and access that emerged in southern cities in the late 1930s.[46]

TWO

"The First Signs of a Mass Movement," 1938–1945

"All the colored principals have been told more than once not to admit children from outside the city," Superintendent A. B. Rhett told the Charleston school board in February 1942. During the late 1930s and early 1940s educational authorities used Public Works Administration (PWA) funds to construct new high schools for whites in and around Charleston, but until 1950, Burke remained the only public African American secondary school in Charleston County accessible to most students in the South Carolina lowcountry. As growing numbers of students graduated from rural elementary schools and entered Burke, Rhett instructed the school's principal, William Henry Grayson, to "follow [the] buses [and] furnish the superintendent with the names of the pupils getting off, and dismiss children who were from outside the city." In spite of Rhett's attempts to restrict access, increasing numbers of black students from Charleston County enrolled at Burke with the tacit encouragement of Grayson and the school's faculty.[1]

While the African American struggle for equality and access grew out of rural elementary schools such as Society Corner, it gathered strength and momentum in urban secondary schools such as Burke. By the late 1930s students who migrated to Burke from the rural lowcountry were only one of the streams of students who swelled the school's enrollment. Young African Americans who were pushed out of the labor force by the collapse of the local youth-labor market, were pulled into schools by New Deal education programs, and the number of black students who graduated from African American high schools in the South, including Burke tripled between 1935 and 1945. Rising educational attainment and growing demand for more advanced training fueled challenges to an educational system that limited African American access to higher education and the professions. Unable to find work and excluded from white colleges and universities high-school and college graduates in Charleston and Columbia were striking at caste constraints in education by the late 1930s. They became part of what NAACP special counsel Charles H. Houston called "the first signs of a mass movement."[2]

The obstacles student activists and the NAACP encountered as they tried to organize legal campaigns in South Carolina illustrate why this movement faltered even as Houston and his colleagues won significant legal victories in Maryland and Missouri in 1936 and 1938. Student and faculty activists were eager to challenge school officials in federal court, but the exclusion of African Americans from state-supported graduate and professional programs in the half century after 1877 left the state without a local African American attorney who would assist the NAACP. Acts of assertion in the Palmetto State grew in the late 1930s, but many black leaders were skeptical that litigation was an effective way to improve educational institutions. Accustomed to collaborating with whites rather than confronting them in federal court, class- and color-conscious black elites in Charleston remained more interested in sustaining the prestige of private institutions than in improving the black public schools. These local problems compounded obstacles that the NAACP's small, financially hard-pressed legal staff faced as it struggled to extend legal precedents established in border states into South Carolina.

At Burke educational change came not through the courts but through the petitions of Parent-Teacher Association (PTA) leaders and the initiatives of black teachers. Inspired by the example of students, emboldened by NAACP's early legal victories, and motivated by the political and economic currents set in motion by American involvement in World War II, African American parents, students, and teachers made Burke a battleground during the war, as African Americans pressed for broader educational opportunities and school officials struggled to restrict them. Although PTA petitions extracted only modest concessions from educational authorities, who remained firmly committed to using the schools to buttress white supremacy and black subordination, rising enrollment at Burke led to the appointment of college-educated teachers who seized on these concessions to lay the groundwork for a generation of institutional development at the school.

The African American students who moved to Charleston to attend Burke entered a city where a patina of paternalism obscured a savage system of white supremacy. Steeped in what V. S. Naipaul calls a "religion of the past," the city's close-knit and self-consciously aristocratic white leadership lived in antebellum mansions that overlooked Fort Sumter. These patricians prided themselves on their "good relations with Negroes," but as Charleston industrialized and modernized and as the black population grew to 45 percent of the city's residents by 1940, segregation institutionalized white supremacy and prescribed in ever greater detail "the Negroes'" separate and subordinate place in Charleston's social order. "The commanding fact," William Watts Ball, editor of the

Charleston News and Courier, wrote in 1940, "is that separation of the races grows. The separation in living, in industries, and therefore in associations or contacts, has widened and hardened."[3]

Unlike racial extremists who believed that white supremacy should be maintained by any means necessary, the paternalistic conservatives who led Charleston into the twentieth century were not opposed to "Negro Progress." Whites and blacks should be kept apart, but segregation, they asserted, would allow each race to develop its own culture, institutions, and leadership to its highest potential. However, educational authorities provided blacks with few opportunities to develop that potential, and during the early decades of the twentieth century African Americans were driven from occupations they had long held. By 1940 two of every three black adults in the city worked as domestic servants or laborers. As segregation constrained, it created opportunities for an African American elite that educated its children in private schools and colleges. In 1938 the Works Progress *Guide* found that there were "many well-educated prosperous Negroes in various professions and businesses." While the city's black aristocracy, one observer noted, "owned rare old mahogany furniture and lived in their homes for several generations," the vast majority of African Americans in Charleston, a 1937 survey reported, lived in "congested and unsanitary surroundings and often in dire poverty."[4]

This class and caste structure was, in large part, a product of public education. In Charleston, as elsewhere, public schools and colleges rationalized and reproduced white supremacy and black subordination. Expenditures for public education rose sharply during the 1920s, but so too did the disparities between white and black schools. In those parts of the South where the proportion of blacks was high and expenditures for African American schools were low, whites derived substantial benefits from segregation. South Carolina state law permitted school officials to allocate funds "in the best interests of the district," and the trustees responded to growing demand for public education among the city's German, Irish, Italian, and Jewish voters by appropriating a greater and greater share of school funds to white institutions. By 1940 white students in Charleston enjoyed access to five elementary schools, a junior high school, three high schools, and three institutions of higher education. As a result, the median educational attainment of whites in the city approached the national median, and exceeded that of blacks by more than three years. Disenfranchisement, bars on black employment in business, commerce, industry, and state and local government, and access to educational opportunities in schools, colleges, museums, libraries, and parks fueled the social and economic advancement of almost all whites. In 1940, 70 percent of the city's white workforce was employed in professional, managerial, clerical, or skilled blue-collar jobs, compared to 14 percent of black workers. "Because such a large part of total urban income is retained by whites," Myrdal wrote, "the white population in the urban South is not appreciably worse off than the urban population in the North—in spite of the greater general poverty in the region."[5]

As separate and increasingly unequal schools and colleges promoted the advancement of whites, the systematic shortchanging of Burke Industrial School constrained blacks. Built on a dumping ground in 1910 with substantial support from the Peabody and Slater Funds, Burke, like other black secondary schools established in the early decades of the twentieth century, was based on the Hampton-Tuskegee model. Burke's curriculum emphasized vocational and mechanical training through courses in cooking and laundry for girls and painting and bricklaying for boys. After a NAACP-sponsored campaign brought the appointment of black teachers to Burke's faculty in 1920, African American leaders pressed officials to upgrade the school. Secondary grades were added in the early 1920s, but in 1925 school superintendent A. B. Rhett refused to allow the teaching of French and Latin. Born into a prominent Charleston family in 1877, Rhett was educated at the High School and College of Charleston. After earning bachelor's and master's degrees from the University of Virginia, he returned to Charleston and was appointed superintendent in 1911. Imbued with what one school-board member called "the old traditions of Charleston," Rhett remained a staunch opponent of the academic training of African Americans during his long tenure as superintendent. Like his colleagues in other southern cities, Rhett believed that blacks should be prepared for "jobs that are available under present conditions" a policy that would make Burke graduates "self-supporting" and benefit "not only the Negroes but the white people of the city." In 1939 Rhett secured federal funds to establish new vocational courses at Burke "to supply cooks, maids, and delivery boys."[6]

African American students and teachers showed little interest in such training, but inadequate funding and the board's opposition to an academic curriculum limited the education that Burke students received. Convinced that permanent improvements to the school's campus would attract "an overwhelming flood of students from the county" and "unlimited enrollment," the board cobbled together portable classrooms and temporary structures, creating a facility that one observer called a "pitiful apology for its supposed purpose." In 1936 per-pupil spending on students in the city's three white high schools was three times that of per-pupil spending at Burke. Student-teacher ratios were 30 percent larger at Burke than in the white secondary schools. Burke did not offer the foreign-language or social-science courses that were required for admission to private black colleges in the South. "What we are furnishing the colored schools," Rhett told the trustees in 1937, "is meager."[7]

A generation of visitors commented on the fact that Burke was a high school in name only. Burke was "supposed to be the high school," but African American

historian Asa Gordon wrote that "the real high school for the city is a
school, Avery Institute." Like other southern cities, Charleston had two
American school systems: public schools that were designed to train African
Americans for "Negro jobs" and a network of private educational institutions
that prepared children of the black elite for college and the professions. Because
southern school boards diverted a larger and larger share of school funds to
white institutions, "E. Franklin Frazier's black bourgeoisie," wrote David Levering Lewis, sent its children to exclusive educational "enclaves" that were connected to churches, colleges, and northern missionary societies. Private schools
in Atlanta, Charleston, New Orleans, Greensboro, Savannah, and elsewhere prepared the majority of African American high-school graduates into the 1930s,
and facilitated the intergenerational transmission of class status. As northern
philanthropic support for private black high schools in the South waned, African American leaders turned to whites for financial assistance. Applauding the
accomplishments of institutions that saved school officials substantial sums,
whites helped save private schools that they believed showed how segregation
allowed blacks to build institutions to their highest potential. While Avery's survival preserved black access to colleges and the professions, it also created a basis
for collaboration between white and black elites that inhibited African American activism and reduced the pressure that the city's black elite exerted on the
school board to improve Burke.[8]

"The saying in Charleston," wrote American Missionary Association (AMA)
executive secretary F. Lee Brownlee, "is that everyone who can read and write has
a private school usually in the elementary grades, in a private house." Charleston
had several well-subscribed elementary schools and three private high schools,
Avery, Immaculate Conception, and Laing School. Avery Normal Institute was
the city's oldest, most prestigious, and most significant African American educational institution. Founded by the AMA in 1866, Avery assumed much of the
burden of black secondary education well into the twentieth century. The school
remained firmly committed to the liberal arts during a time when northern
philanthropists and southern educators embraced vocational models of black
education. "The curriculum was set along New England classical lines," Brownlee wrote, "and has so remained to the present day." Unlike Burke, the school
offered classes in French and Latin, as well as English, history, the sciences, and
mathematics.[9]

At Avery, as at other exclusive African American schools in the South, "social
class governs a much wider area of the child's training than do Negro-white con-
trols," Allison Davis and John Dollard wrote in their study of Natchez, Mississippi, and New Orleans, Louisiana. Like other private schools, Avery played a
key role in the transmission of class status within the black community. Myrdal
argued that because "capitalist business and wealth mean so relatively little"

among African Americans, "education and professional training mean so relatively much, as criteria for attaining upper class status." In Charleston few African Americans could afford tuition, and Avery drew its students from families
headed by parents whose income, educational attainment, and occupational status were well above those of most African Americans. These family-background
characteristics, Avery's liberal-arts curriculum, and a close-knit network of religious, voluntary, and neighborhood affiliations produced patterns of African
American achievement that rivaled those of whites. Top black colleges "vied" for
Avery graduates, who, the AMA noted, won an "unusual percentage of college
scholarship awards." The school "sent an enormous proportion of students to
Fisk." By 1940 Avery had trained three of four black teachers in the county, four
of the local school principals, and a majority of the city's black doctors and
businessmen.[10]

Even as schooling became more important in determining class, the connection between status and skin color was never completely severed. As Avery's
exclusivity promoted excellence in education, it perpetuated class and color divisions within the black community. These divisions had deep roots in Charleston,
where admission to schools, churches, cemeteries, and voluntary associations was
determined by one's pigmentation, the straightness of one's hair, and one's ances-
try. Critics charged that Avery did much to perpetuate color consciousness. During the early years of its existence, students at the school were chosen according
to the "blueness" of their blood. When the AMA attempted to appoint the dark-
skinned William Pickens as principal in 1915, Averyites protested so strongly
that a lighter-skinned candidate, Benjamin Cox, was hired. As Edmund L.
Drago's rich history of Avery shows, the children of the city's "Negro Aristocracy" dominated the school, winning a "lion's share of awards and honors."
African American historian Lewis K. McMillan wrote that Avery "was shot
through with the spirit of caste and class based merely upon the mechanics of
color." Because Averyites were "indifferent to the plight of the Negro masses," he
argued, the school "separated rather than unified the city's black population."
McMillan's colleague at South Carolina State College, Asa Gordon, detected a
"growing group consciousness" in Charleston in the late 1920s, but he also
found that many of the school's graduates continued to believe in "the value of
blue-blood. Their dissatisfaction with the present arrangement in the South is
not rooted in their belief in democracy, but in their conviction that the caste system as now organized, fails to recognize all the aristocrats."[11]

This aristocratic ethos troubled the AMA. "It is hard for an organization
which was created to destroy caste," association officials conceded, "to have to
admit that Avery has not escaped the temptations of aristocracy." Brownlee
believed that the school produced students who "have the point of view of the
old blue-blooded South and contain a great proportion of Caucasian blood.

Highly developed caste is among them. Some were slave-owners." He argued that "in the struggle of minority groups for equal rights and the privileges of citizenship, an aristocracy which divides the group within itself is costly."[12]

The struggle to save Avery created patterns of collaboration between the city's white and black leaders. During the 1920s and 1930s Avery's survival increasingly depended on tuition and the private financial support of local whites and blacks. "Each year," Principal Benjamin Cox's daughter Anna remembered, "the contribution of the AMA decreased and the quota raised by Avery increased." Determined to preserve an institution that offered the best opportunity for college-preparatory and professional training in the city, Cox, who served as principal between 1916 and 1936, raised tuition and organized fund-raising campaigns. Students pressed their parents for contributions, and Cox solicited donations from local black churches. In 1925 an administrative council was formed, and during the financial crises of the decade the local board raised thousands of dollars annually, allowing the school to survive. Composed of prominent alumni and leading black businessmen with ties to the city's patricians, the council nurtured relationships with prominent whites. After addressing the White Minister's Union in 1926, Cox wrote that "one of the most gratifying signs of progress is the interest which our neighbors are taking in the work of Avery Institute." Arthur J. Clement Jr., an Avery graduate and businessman who served on the council, recalled that "the well-trained singing of these students and their sense of decorum combined to loosen the purses of many visitors." In 1930 Cox arranged a benefit concert by Charleston's white philharmonic orchestra that raised money for the school.[13]

Cox used these resources to improve Avery, and under his leadership it became one of the best black high schools in the South. When the AMA closed a school in Capahosic, Virginia, Cox obtained books from that institution, and J. Michael Graves, who graduated from Avery in the 1930s, remembers that the library "resembled that of a small liberal arts college." Cox strengthened the faculty, sending older teachers to northern universities in the summer to sharpen their skills and recruiting some of the school's top graduates, who returned to teach after earning bachelor's degrees from private black colleges. He also purchased laboratory equipment that was used to modernize the science curriculum. During the 1930s enrollment remained above four hundred students, including more than two hundred in the school's secondary and normal program. In 1934 Avery was one of five black high schools in the state, four of which were private, to earn accreditation from the Southern Association of Secondary Schools and Colleges. The following year, the supervisor of Negro schools in South Carolina, W. A. Schiffley, called Avery's teacher-training program "the best in the state." Even critics such as McMillan acknowledged that Avery graduates "confronted white Charleston with the embodied proof of what the Negro can become. Their accomplishments provoked admiration and respect. What leadership the Negro in Charleston has had, Avery has provided it."[14]

By the 1930s this leadership was out of step with egalitarian currents of the era, and the AMA and the NAACP pressed Averyites to assume greater responsibility for improving the public-school system. Brownlee was increasingly critical of Avery. L. Howard Bennett, who was appointed principal in 1941, recalled that the AMA thought "as long as the black elite had Avery Institute, this leadership would not put pressure on the city of Charleston to improve the public system." The AMA believed that Avery should promote collective advancement rather than transmit class status and color consciousness. Brownlee charged that black parents in Charleston "sent their children to Avery thus draining away the best leadership from agitation for the public schools." He wanted the city's black elite to "agitate" for improvements in the public system and build what he called a "people's movement." NAACP officials in New York shared these sentiments. When the director of branches, Robert Bagnell, tried to arrange a meeting with local NAACP members, he was told that "the so-called leading Negroes [are] frankly not interested." After visiting the city, Bagnell criticized black leaders for "their complacent satisfaction" and their tendency "to gain favor with the mighty and beg favors of them."[15]

As national organizations pushed Charleston's black elite to assume more responsibility for improving conditions in the public schools, economic currents swept unprecedented numbers of black students into Burke. By the late 1930s students from outside the city were joined by increasing numbers of young blacks who were pushed out of the workforce by the collapse of the local labor market. Charles S. Johnson argued that urbanization, mechanization, and the increased participation of women and rural migrants in the labor force, "placed white and Negro workers more acutely in competition for the same jobs, with the result that white workers were frequently given preference." This was especially true in "city, county, and state work where political influence can grant favors to voters and receive votes in return." By the late 1930s Myrdal found that in southern cities unemployment was "much more widespread" among blacks than whites and that "young workers are suffering from unemployment much more than others." African American youth were particularly hard-hit, displaced because they were young and because they were black. "The most significant factor in the education of Negro children in the South in recent years," wrote Horace Mann Bond in 1935, "has been the rapid rate at which these children have been withdrawn from employment. If children attend school today in the South, it is principally because there is no employment to which they might be assigned."[16]

While the collapse of the city's youth-labor market pushed young black workers out of the labor force, National Youth Administration (NYA) grants

helped hundreds of African American students in Charleston enroll in high
school. After the requirement that recipients come from families who were on
relief was dropped, many NYA grants went to black students who attended private schools, but Burke students also benefited. "Hundreds of our best students
would not have been able to continue their high school education without these
grants," one African American educator wrote. The twenty-five Burke students
who received stipends in 1936 created an NYA club at the school, and in the
city as in the county, NYA aid provided the margin of support that allowed
more and more students to attend school.[17]

The scarcity of jobs and the availability of NYA assistance produced dramatic
increases in African American high-school enrollment. When J. C. Newbold,
state agent of Negro schools in North Carolina, surveyed urban school superintendents in the South in 1933, he reported that "Negro pupils are entering school
earlier than in former years and remaining in school for a longer period." In
Charleston 253 students graduated from Burke's elementary program in 1938,
and 218, an unprecedented number, entered the high school. The following
year, Rhett informed the board that there would be another "large increase in
enrollment because of the unusual number of pupils being promoted from the
elementary school to the high school." As high-school enrollment at Burke grew
from 377 in 1935 to 911 in 1939, Rhett told the board that, unless it established
separate morning and afternoon sessions at the school, "it will be necessary to
provide more classrooms. The cheapest way of doing this is to bring in additional temporary portable classrooms." In Baltimore, Washington, Richmond,
Atlanta, and New Orleans, school officials faced similar problems as they tried
to accommodate African American high-school populations that tripled during
the 1930s. "Southern city schools," wrote W. E. B. Du Bois in 1935, "are crowded
to the point of suffocation. The Booker T. Washington High School in Atlanta
built for 1,000 has 3,000 attending in double daily sessions."[18]

The recession of 1937–1938, the continuing displacement of black workers,
and the refusal of local authorities to employ blacks in white-collar WPA jobs
left young African Americans with little else to do but attend school. During the
1930s the number of African Americans who graduated from high school rose
sharply, growing to thirty thousand by 1940, more than three times what it had
been a decade before. In towns in the Mississippi Delta, Powdermaker wrote,
the development of black "abilities" was not matched by the growth of "opportunities." While schooling "dressed up blacks," Dollard argued, "they have no
or little professional place to go." Houston believed that "one of the greatest
tragedies of the Depression has been the humiliation and suffering which public
authorities have inflicted upon trained Negroes forcing them to accept menial
low-pay jobs as an alternative to starvation." Depression-era black leaders in
Charleston recalled that no African Americans were employed in "white-collar

WPA jobs," a memory confirmed by Steiner, who found that beyond teaching, "the proportion of Negroes" in professional and managerial jobs was "negligible." As African Americans were driven out of skilled jobs in New Orleans, historian Charles B. Rousseve wrote that young African Americans were becoming "more interested in higher education."[19]

One of Houston's most important contributions to the legal campaign was in seeing that these young people could fuel challenges to the segregated caste system. As African American college enrollment rose from ten thousand in 1930 to thirty-six thousand in 1938, Houston argued that growing demand for access to colleges and universities could impress on "the opposition that what we have is a real program sweeping up from ground influence and popular demand." Following his appointment as NAACP special counsel in 1935, Houston traveled widely through the South "to explain and convert the public to the [NAACP's] program." He spent considerable time in South Carolina and visited Charleston and Columbia on several occasions. Speaking at black churches, visiting black schools and colleges, and meeting with local NAACP leaders, Houston encouraged students to "grasp and cling to every bit of educational opportunity and clamor for more." As the number of African American college graduates rose to 4,440 in 1938, four times what it had been a decade before, black aspirations collided with caste constraints.[20]

The first collision occurred in Maryland, when nine members of the African American fraternity Alpha Phi Alpha applied for admission to the University of Maryland. Fraternity members raised several hundred dollars and, acting independently of the NAACP's national office, retained an attorney and convinced Donald Murray to apply for admission to the University of Maryland Law School. After Murray filed his application, Houston took charge of the litigation. In 1936 the court ordered the state to "furnish equality of treatment now" and admit Murray to the university's law school. After the Maryland Court of Appeals affirmed the decision, "the local [NAACP] branches around the country started referring cases to the national office." As a generation of young people saw that change was possible, black students in Virginia, the Carolinas, Tennessee, Kentucky, Georgia, Texas, and Arkansas pressed for access to graduate and professional programs. "The first signs of a mass movement are beginning to appear," Houston wrote in 1935.[21]

In South Carolina educators encouraged students to join this movement. "I have been advised by J. Andrew Simmons, Principal of Booker T. Washington High School and Mr. C. A. Johnson, supervisor of Negro Public Schools [in Columbia]," wrote Morehouse College graduate Charles Bailey, in a letter to the NAACP in April 1938. "I have a [plan] under consideration which the National Association for the Advancement of Colored People might be interested." Two months later two Burke graduates appeared before the Charleston school board,

success of Murray v. U Maryland Law (1936) [handwritten marginalia] telling the trustees that the education they had received had not prepared then to "discharge their functions in the community" and asking that the "board provide by some means a college education for Negroes." In January 1939 Burke graduate J. D. Roper challenged the exclusion of black students from the municipally supported College of Charleston and asked the school board to pay his "college tuition" at South Carolina State in Orangeburg, the only public institution of higher education in the state that admitted African Americans. In May 1939 J. C. Prioleau, a Claflin College graduate, sought admission to the State Medical College in Charleston.[22]

The most promising of these challenges was Charles Bailey's application for admission to the University of South Carolina in Columbia. After conferring with Houston, Bailey informed law-school dean J. N. Frierson of his "desire to apply for admission to the School of Law of the University of South Carolina." Bailey acknowledged that "if South Carolina had a scholarship law providing adequate scholarships for Negro citizens to study law outside of the state, I would apply for such a scholarship." In the 1920s West Virginia and Missouri began providing scholarships for African Americans to pursue graduate and professional study in other states, and—following NAACP legal challenges in the 1930s—Maryland, Virginia, Tennessee, and Kentucky followed suit. Like most southern states, however, South Carolina did not fund such scholarships, and in April 1938 Bailey informed university officials "I hereby apply for admission to the state university school of law, the only law school maintained in South Carolina at public expense." Houston believed that Bailey's case might "reestablish the right of Negro citizens to attend the State University just the same as they did during Reconstruction days. From the time President Hayes recalled federal troops from South Carolina there has been no known Negroes in state universities in the Deep South."[23]

As Bailey waited for the NAACP to act, Houston convinced the Supreme Court that out-of-state scholarships were unconstitutional. Like Donald Murray, Lloyd Gaines wanted to study law in his native state, and he worked with Houston to seek admission to the University of Missouri Law School. The state of Missouri responded to Gaines's application by offering him two options: application to the publicly supported Lincoln University, where the state claimed it would establish a new separate law school for African Americans, or a state-funded scholarship to study law outside the state. Houston appealed lower-court rulings upholding the constitutionality of these options. In December 1938 Chief Justice Charles Evans Hughes wrote in *Missouri ex. rel. Gaines v. Canada* that "the basic consideration is what opportunities Missouri itself furnishes to white students and denies to Negroes solely upon the ground of color. The admissibility of laws separating the races in the enjoyment of privileges afforded by the State rests wholly upon the quality of the privileges which the laws give to the ups within the State." Following the Court's ruling in *Gaines*, rshall wrote that "South Carolina is going to be a difficult state to e] believe that we should nevertheless do so if it is possible. We ase against the University of South Carolina for admission to the

Educational and political leaders in South Carolina were well aware of the NAACP's legal campaign, and after the *Gaines* decision, they acknowledged that something would have to be done. In a letter to the NAACP, the president of South Carolina State College, Miller F. Whittaker, wrote that "our state legislature is in session, and they have been calling me three or four times a week, not only on the graduate question, but also on our current appropriation." Bailey continued to press university officials for action on his application, and in January 1939 the speaker of the South Carolina House of Representatives, Solomon Blatt, who also served on the University of South Carolina board of trustees, sponsored legislation to establish a separate law school for African American students at South Carolina State in Orangeburg. "We know of no other way to meet this than to establish a chair of law at the state Colored college," Blatt declared. Marshall told White that "the legislature of the State of South Carolina should be warned that any effort to establish a make shift graduate school will only lead to litigation."[25]

Blatt's bill passed the House, but after it stalled in the South Carolina Senate, opposition mounted. As African Americans in South Carolina began challenging white supremacy in new ways, white resistance to educational change stiffened. Some senators supported a plan that would have required prospective students to secure recommendations from two state legislators as part of the application process, but members of the House opposed the plan. *News and Courier* editor William Watts Ball argued that "the way out of the wilderness" was to close the law school at the university and privatize legal education in the state. "Separate colleges have got to be provided," Ball wrote. "Otherwise the white people will turn to private and church colleges." Bailey's application provoked what Ball called "deep resentment." He published a letter to the editor from "Rustic," who advocated "using Hitlerian methods to squelch the negro and put him back in his place," which the author asserted, was in "the cotton field and not the courts of law." Richmond newspaper editor Virginus Dabney reported that "there was talk" in the Deep South that educational authorities would "refuse to do anything and [that] the practical effect of the court's ruling [in *Gaines*] might be virtually nil."[26]

Houston and his colleagues did not think that Missouri or other southern states could afford to construct separate law schools for African Americans, but in 1939 the Missouri legislature appropriated $200,000 for African American graduate and professional education. As officials in Missouri prepared to open a new separate law school for African Americans at Lincoln, NAACP leaders discussed whether or not Gaines should enroll. Walter White argued that "[it] is most definitely not our function to advise Gaines to go to a jim-crow law school." Guy Johnson, a professor at the University of North Carolina, agreed, noting that "the most obvious result of the *Gaines* case is the extension of segregation into graduate and professional work for Negroes in the South. Once they are set up they [African Americans] will acquire a vested interest which will make a change in fundamental policy all the more difficult." Marshall complained that those who supported the "Jim Crow University were sell[ing] the race down the river." When prospective students tried to register at Lincoln in September 1939, they were greeted with pickets that stated "Don't Be a Traitor to Your Race," and "Stay Away From this School it is Inferior." Although thirty black students enrolled, Lloyd Gaines mysteriously disappeared, forcing the NAACP to withdraw a complaint charging that the program at Lincoln was not equal to the University of Missouri Law School. The case ended in "disarray."[27]

The prospect of a similar educational outcome in South Carolina dampened the NAACP's enthusiasm for Bailey's case. Like most of the requests the NAACP received in the late 1930s and early 1940s, Bailey's application did not lead to litigation. After Houston resigned as special counsel and returned to his law practice in Washington in 1938, Marshall had difficulty keeping up with all of the requests for assistance that flowed into the national office. While Bailey remained eager to challenge the state in court, W. Lewis Burke and William C. Hine have shown that in the late 1930s "there was not a single black lawyer in Charleston, Columbia, or Greenville," and Marshall was unable to locate a local attorney "who would help us." By 1940, two years after he applied to the law school, Bailey had grown impatient, telling Marshall that "had I been in possession of sufficient money, I would not have waited for the NAACP to act." In June 1940 Marshall urged Bailey to "bear with us, the only thing that has been holding your case up is the fact that there are so many other items in our campaign to secure educational equality." Lacking time, local legal support, and money, Marshall wrote in 1941 that, "due to limitations of staff and funds," the NAACP had to "refuse a number of worthy cases." *Murray* and *Gaines* were powerful precedents, but in South Carolina, as in most southern states, black activists and the NAACP were unable to capitalize on them during the late 1930s and early 1940s. Bailey's case languished, leaving the growing number of black college graduates in South Carolina with no opportunities for graduate and professional education.[28]

Different problems arose in Charleston when black students and activist members of the local chapter of the NAACP pressed Houston and Marshall to make the Supreme Court's *Gaines* decision "operative" in the city. On January 24, 1939, the same day J. D. Roper asked the school board to pay his college tuition, Kenneth Hughes, rector of Charleston's most exclusive African American church, St. Mark's Episcopal, wrote Houston telling him that members of the local branch of the NAACP planned to discuss "the significance of this decision" at their next meeting. Hughes informed Houston that black students were "barred" from the College of Charleston. "There is also no accredited high school. Negroes in search of a high school education must pay tuition at Avery Institute." How, Hughes asked, "may we break these bars down? I realize that I ask quite a lot, but this matter means everything to us. Will you please help us all you can?"[29]

The national office was clearly interested in Charleston. Hughes's letter was marked "important," and within a week Houston had informed Hughes that "Negroes can make application to the city college and notify the board of education that unless the Negro high school is improved Negroes will apply to the white high school. The city cannot force you to continue applying [to] and paying tuition at Avery Institute." Houston urged Hughes to complete "a comparative study of white and black high schools and organize a committee to meet with school officials. We have not had a case where the Negro school was set aside the white school, being inferior in degree. But we might as well crack that whenever the people are ready."[30]

In spite of Houston's bold response the Charleston branch of the NAACP was not ready to challenge local educational authorities in federal court. The local NAACP chapter, like others in the region, was disorganized and dysfunctional. "I have spoken throughout the South," Houston told Roy Wilkins in 1935, and "I know the general feeling is that the association is out of touch with the people." After attending a meeting in Atlanta in 1937, Houston informed Walter White that "we must do something about the branches." Ralph Bunche found that the southern branches were controlled by "an exclusive, often class and color snobbish, self-appointed Negro upper class group." Bunche's research assistant, Wilhelmina Jackson, wrote that Charleston branch president Dr. William Miller was "an intellectual snob, a word-monger without equal." During Jackson's visit to Charleston in 1940, only twelve members attended the association's monthly meeting. "I can put nothing before the house," Miller told the national office, because "the house isn't there." The chapter's membership was "dilatory, lethargic, and noncommittal," and the election of branch officers was "postponed twice." After meeting with "the leading and the 'leadingest' Negroes in Charleston," Thurgood Marshall wrote that "everyone is too busy to take on leadership of the branch. Negroes as a whole are militant, [but] they lack leadership." Charleston, he concluded, "must be worked on." Marshall's assessment confirmed the AMA's view that the city's black elite was too busy sustaining Avery to take responsibility for improving the city's African American public schools.[31]

As concerned as the city's black leadership was with Avery's survival, the problems that activists and NAACP attorneys faced were not, however, simply local. Kenneth Hughes's letter to Houston outlined educational and legal issues that the NAACP had been unable to crack. In 1935 Marshall challenged the exclusion of blacks from high schools in Baltimore County, Maryland. As in Charleston, educational officials in Baltimore County operated high schools for whites, but none for fifteen hundred high-school-aged African Americans. Black students in the county who passed an examination were permitted to enroll at Frederick Douglass High School in the city of Baltimore, but only one-third of those who took the exam passed. Marshall argued that the high failure rate was the result of inadequate and unequal facilities in the county's black elementary schools; however, in 1937 the Maryland Court of Appeals held that "incidental differences and inequalities" that resulted from officials' efforts to "meet practical problems" were not unconstitutional. The decision led the NAACP to view secondary-school cases skeptically. The NAACP's victories in *Murray* and *Gaines* showed southern school officials that adjustments would have to be made. However, during the 1940s, when the NAACP won no major legal victories in secondary-school or higher-education cases, the improvement of African American high schools depended not simply on the NAACP but also on how assertive local black activists were in pressing for change and how successful southern school officials were at limiting it. As the challenges of the 1930s created a new era in the African American struggle for access, they also signaled a new phase in white resistance to black equality in education. This resistance did not, as Michael J. Klarman has argued, begin or crystallize after *Brown v. Board of Education* in 1954.[32]

Local activists and national NAACP leaders were unable to organize legal campaigns in Columbia and Charleston, but the tempo of African American educational activism quickened in the late 1930s and early 1940s. Emboldened by the ferment of the New Deal, the example of students, the NAACP's early legal victories, and the political and economic currents set in motion by American involvement in World War II, black leaders in Charleston became more assertive and insistent. During the war the federal government invested more than $100 million in local military and naval installations, transforming Charleston from a sleepy southern town into a booming, overcrowded, and racially charged industrial metropolis. Thousands of African Americans from the rural lowcountry moved to the city in search of jobs. Wartime wages helped growing numbers of black students attend Burke, where enrollment rose from 911 in 1939 to 1,500 in 1945. Rising enrollment highlighted Burke's limitations and made the school a battleground, the site of continuous contests between African Americans who pressed for broader opportunities and school officials who sought to limit them. In a series of petitions, letters, and appearances before the school board, African American leaders linked black patriotism and sacrifice in the war to the need for improvements in Burke's physical plant and curriculum. In Charleston access to industrial jobs and higher education was part of the campaign for the Double V, against fascism abroad and against racism, discrimination, and segregation at home. As significant as the growing assertiveness of African Americans was, these polite protests brought only modest concessions from a school board that remained firmly committed to using the schools to reinforce white supremacy and black subordination.[33]

Nowhere was this resistance more evident than in the school board's refusal to train African Americans for skilled industrial jobs at the Charleston Naval Shipyard. In Charleston, as in Norfolk and Mobile, African Americans saw the war as an opportunity to secure well-paying skilled industrial jobs. After school officials received federal funds for national defense classes in 1940, they established training programs for machinists, ship fitters, welders, and sheet-metal workers at Murray Vocational School. By March 1941, 270 young white men were enrolled in day and evening classes at the school. In 1942 the board used federal funds to establish a preaviation-cadet training program at the High School of Charleston and officer-training courses at the College of Charleston and the Citadel. In spite of the growing need for skilled workers at the local shipyard, Rhett created new courses in woodworking, food preparation, and child care at Burke. As labor shortages developed, leaders of the Negro Community Council urged the board to train blacks for skilled jobs so Charleston could remain "an effective defense area," but the board applied for federal funds to support a program at Burke in automobile cleaning, greasing, and tire repairing. The following May, the government rejected this application. "The government suggests," Rhett told the board, "that applications should be made for equipment to train colored men for work in the Navy Yard." Federal officials repeatedly urged the board to train African Americans for skilled jobs at the naval shipyard, and in January 1944 provided equipment for a sheet-metal course at Burke as well as funds to pay the salary of an instructor. However, after Rhett expressed concerns about whether there would be "many openings for colored people in the sheet metal line," the course was discontinued in early 1945.[34]

Because of persistent pressure from local black leaders and the federal government, African Americans secured a permanent foothold at the Charleston Naval Shipyard and other military installations, but Rhett's opposition to training programs at Burke helped keep African Americans at the bottom of the occupational hierarchy. Between 1940 and 1943 only five hundred of the four thousand trainees in federally funded vocational courses in Charleston were African American. After A. Philip Randolph threatened to march on Washington in 1941, the Fair Employment Practices Commission began investigating complaints of discrimination, but Myrdal found that southern officials used "token employment of Negroes in custodial and other menial jobs as evidence of non-discrimination." By March 1944 African Americans composed 28 percent of the twenty-five thousand workers at the Charleston Naval Shipyard, but the vast majority remained in unskilled and semiskilled jobs. In spite of dramatic industrial expansion in the region during the war, more than three times as many whites as blacks held skilled blue-collar jobs in the South by 1950. The war created new employment opportunities for blacks in the city, and labor shortages and wartime wages narrowed racial earnings ratios in the city, but because the benefits of industrialization went chiefly to whites, white parents had more resources to support their children's schooling through high school. In 1945 five times as many whites as blacks graduated from high school.[35]

African Americans also contested advantages that white students enjoyed in Charleston's high schools. Although higher wartime wages helped increasing numbers of students to enroll in and graduate from Burke, the lack of an accredited high school remained a serious obstacle to African American educational advancement. In 1931 the Southern Association of Secondary Schools and Colleges began accrediting African American high schools on the same basis as white schools, and accreditation standards pushed recalcitrant southern school officials to improve black secondary schools. Graduates of high schools that were accredited by the Southern Association were admitted "without examination" to colleges. While the High School of Charleston (for boys) was accredited by the Southern Association, and the curriculum of Memminger (for girls) was "closely correlated" with college-entrance requirements, Burke was not accredited. As the number of students who graduated from Burke rose, African Americans waged a sustained campaign to accredit the school. "After our children have spent years meeting the requirements of the curriculum at Burke," a 1939 petition from the Colored PTA Council declared, "they find it impossible to enter higher institutions without repeating two years of work that they have not had because of a lack of facilities."[36]

Convinced that improvements at Burke would attract more students, jeopardize the board's ability to finance improvements in white schools and colleges, and sharpen economic competition between whites and blacks, the board rejected demands for accreditation. To meet Southern Association standards, the board needed to complete several costly improvements to Burke's physical plant and curriculum, and school officials told PTA leaders that "money is not available for improvements" at Burke. The trustees used the savings to strengthen the white schools, widening the gap between the educational opportunities available to white and black students.[37]

As important as financial considerations were, the board's opposition to accreditation was also based on the fact that schooling increased the likelihood of African American employment in higher-status and higher-paying occupations.

For African Americans in the Deep South, a high school education was "a portal to middle-class status," Dollard wrote, "and facilitation or retardation at this point plays a great role in tightening or loosening caste and class boundaries." By 1940 African Americans who graduated from high school were more likely to go to college than whites. "A much smaller proportion of all Negroes than of whites goes to college," Myrdal found, "but once Negroes have attained high school graduation, they have a slightly better chance of going to college [than whites]." By opposing accreditation, school officials restricted opportunities at a time when large-scale federal investment in the local economy was loosening caste boundaries. As Charleston's economy grew and as employment options for African Americans expanded, unequal opportunities in secondary schools became all the more important to the maintenance of white supremacy. Certainly, the Charleston school board did not want to prepare Burke graduates to become better competitors with whites for jobs. "The general interest in keeping the Negro down to preserve the caste order," Myrdal wrote, "is intact in cities too."[38]

Although pressure for accreditation from blacks and sympathetic whites grew during the war, in 1945 the trustees announced that accreditation was "premature because of a lack of facilities at Burke." Separate and unequal schools for black students were too important to the maintenance of white supremacy for the board to do anything more than grant modest concessions to black demands for better educational programs. During the summer of 1945 Avery alumnus and businessman Robert F. Morrison and other black leaders met with school officials. The board, however, continued to oppose improvements in the school's physical plant that would have allowed it to secure accreditation from the Southern Association and become a fully accredited institution that prepared students for admission to the region's best black colleges. Instead, school officials sought accreditation under less demanding and less costly state standards, and Burke, like most African American schools in the South, was not accredited by the Southern Association. (By 1946 the Southern Association had accredited 1,833 white schools and 163 black schools.) Even after Burke was accredited by the state, Burke students attended a school that was worth a fraction of what the city's white high schools were, enrolled in classes where student-teacher ratios were significantly higher, and had access to fewer science labs and library books, inequities that compounded the social and economic disadvantages that students brought to the school. "The intent of whites who controlled the school board" recalled Lonnie Hamilton, who graduated from Burke in 1947, "was to keep you from getting knowledge and power."[39]

That intention, recent scholarship suggests, was never fully realized. Although Burke remained an unaccredited, overcrowded, and inadequately financed industrial school, African American petitions and protests extracted concessions from the school board that black teachers seized on to lay the groundwork for a generation of institutional development at Burke. In 1939 the board responded to PTA petitions by adding social-science and foreign-language courses to Burke's curriculum and adopting a policy of appointing only college graduates to Burke's faculty. Led by Burke principal William Henry Grayson, black teachers, many of whom had graduated from Avery and gone on to earn degrees from leading colleges and universities, strengthened the curriculum, created new extracurricular programs, and prepared growing numbers of Burke students for college. Well into the twentieth century African Americans contested white supremacy not simply in front of the school board but also inside schools.[40]

Historians are just beginning to appreciate how significant schools were as sites of black resistance, where African Americans created an evasive and oppositional culture that propelled growing numbers of black students forward in spite of white opposition. Few historians have seen the work of teachers as political, but as Robin D. G. Kelley has argued, we need to expand our definition of politics and explore in greater detail "spaces" where African Americans "expressed their opposition to white supremacy. For southern blacks in the age of Jim Crow," Kelley has written, "politics was the many battles to roll back constraints, to exercise power over, or to create space within, the institutions and social relationships that dominated their lives." This definition of politics helps us see how the initiative of black teachers created space inside the most important public African American institution in the South. African American educators did not overtly challenge white supremacy, but as Adam Fairclough noted, by "insisting on the sanctity of knowledge and the innate humanity of black children, [they] performed political work of the most far-reaching kind."[41]

The initiatives of Burke's faculty were part of a long history of African American autonomy in situations that were ostensibly controlled by whites. Just as slaves carved out human space within a system that sought to deny their humanity, African American teachers created avenues of advancement in segregated schools that were designed to limit achievement. Certainly, inadequate funding, overcrowding, and the lack of accreditation handicapped black students and teachers at the school, but it did not paralyze them, in part because the board exercised little direct supervision over what occurred inside Burke. There is considerable evidence that the Charleston school board, like others in the South, had little knowledge of what actually went on inside the school. "As far as their teaching is concerned," Myrdal wrote, black teachers are "more independent than appears." Students and teachers recall that Rhett rarely visited Burke, and the Negro school supervisor, F. M. Wamsley, was ineffectual and unaware. As the board's resistance to accreditation shows, school officials controlled the outer reality of Burke, but in significant ways black teachers and administrators claimed parts of Burke as black space.[42]

Educational authorities monitored African American schools through the principal, and the man the school board trusted to run Burke was William Henry Grayson. A descendant of one of Charleston's leading black families, Grayson graduated from Avery in 1924 and went on to earn degrees from Fisk University and Teachers College at Columbia University. Returning to Charleston, Grayson served as principal of the Simonton Elementary School between 1932 and 1939, where he earned the respect of black parents and school officials. In October 1938 the Simonton PTA praised Grayson's "progressive ideas and his ability to put them into operation through the cooperation of his faculty." Rhett was impressed by his leadership, and in 1939 Grayson was appointed principal of Burke.[43]

Grayson was critical of Avery's exclusivity and wanted Burke to unite African Americans of all classes and colors. He saw many talented students from disadvantaged families who were not being helped by Avery, and he believed he could reach them through Burke. Grayson "believed in educating the entire child," recalled Eugene Hunt, who taught English at Burke between 1941 and 1972. "He had to be a skillful administrator," Hunt noted, "because there wasn't much sympathy or support for the idea of giving black students the opportunity to get a full education. The prevailing attitude was that black students had no need for intellectual development."[44]

Without directly challenging the board's authority Grayson found ways to improve Burke. Rhett continued to believe that "the great bulk of the pupils should have that [vocational] training rather than college preparatory training," but his attempts to develop "the trade side of the school" were compromised by the shortage of vocational teachers during the war. Although the local draft board began to "carefully consider" deferments for teachers, many vocational teachers found higher-paying jobs at military and naval installations or were drafted, and the board was unable to fill carpentry and painting positions in the school's vocational department in 1943 and 1944. Grayson used this shortage to increase the number of teachers who taught academic subjects.[45]

The new board's policy of appointing college-educated teachers and the shortage of vocational teachers helped Grayson to orient Burke toward the liberal arts and college preparation. Burke's faculty changed rather dramatically between 1937 and 1941. In 1937 only twelve of the school's thirty-one teachers, or 38 percent, had bachelor's degrees, well below the 75 percent of black high-school teachers who had B.A.'s in the South as a whole. By 1941 the faculty had grown to forty-one; one had a master's degree, and thirty-seven had bachelor's degrees. By 1942 Burke's faculty included graduates of Atlanta University, Teachers College of Columbia University, Fisk University, Howard University, the Juilliard School of Music, the University of Pennsylvania, and Talladega College. By

1942, 85 percent of the school's faculty taught academic subjects: English, math, science, and history. In spite of Rhett's continued promotion of vocational training, Viola Duvall, a Howard University graduate who began teaching at Burke in 1941, recalled that "most students at Burke pursued an academic curriculum." A random sample of one hundred Burke student transcripts from the 1942–1943 school year confirms what James D. Anderson, Faustine Jones, and David S. Cecelski have shown: most black students took three or four academic subjects and one vocational subject.[46]

During the 1940s a cadre of college-educated faculty members—Frederick Cook, Viola Duvall, Eugene Hunt, Marjorie Howard, Sarah Greene Oglesby, and Malissa Smith—laid the groundwork for a generation of institutional development at the school. These teachers changed the tenor of the school, and Burke began to take on a more academic orientation. Although the board refused to support accreditation, during Grayson's administration, Hunt recalled, "there was a drive to raise standards." Academic training gave teachers a sense of the kind of preparation students needed, and teachers modeled their courses at Burke after ones they had taken in college. "We knew what the requirements for college were," Duvall recalled. "We wanted to make sure that our young people could meet them." George Stanyard, a James Island native who moved to Charleston to attend Burke in 1941, remembered that "teachers knew what we needed to know. The courses were not as inferior as they would have been if we had left them to the powers that be." AMA executive secretary F. Lee Brownlee noted that Burke, "which had had rather inferior standards, has pushed into the senior high school area and is beginning to do excellent work." In 1944 Burke's curriculum received an A rating from the Southern Association of Secondary Schools and Colleges, an assessment that underscored the board's refusal to support the school's accreditation.[47]

As a new generation of black teachers strengthened the curriculum, they created in the most unmonitored social spaces of the school extracurricular programs, which held more students in high school and in the process taught them that African Americans were citizens who deserved the same rights and opportunities as whites. "We are trying, as teachers in a minority group," Grayson wrote in 1942, "to make our children proud of the contributions to America and the world by their race, and at the same time conscious of themselves as Americans." Like other black principals, Grayson understood that these extracurricular programs could, as David Tyack and his colleagues have noted, "give black students an understanding of the nature of an oppressive society, and a long term strategy for changing that society and their place in it." Far from leaving black students back and "adjusting black students to the bleak reality of limited opportunity," as Diane Ravitch has asserted, the democratic ideals of progressivism and the extracurricular activities they encouraged were essential tools in the educational advancement of students at Burke and other African American high schools in the South.[48]

During the 1940s extracurricular programs helped increase the percentage of students who persisted through high school. While better-paying jobs helped more parents to sustain their children's education into high school, the availability of jobs in Charleston's booming economy also drew students into the labor force, and Grayson and his colleagues recognized the need to create programs that increased Burke's holding power. "There was some difficulty in keeping some students in school [in the early 1940s] because it was so easy to get a job," Duvall recalled. Rhett saw vocational courses as a way of training "colored help," but Margaret Broadnax, who earned her master's degree at Columbia University's Teachers College, coordinated a vocational program that allowed students to work in the morning and attend school in the afternoon. African Americans who attended Burke in the 1940s remember that the program helped many students graduate. The board refused to hire music and drama teachers, but Grayson recruited liberal-arts graduates who created after-school programs that were extremely popular among students. Eugene Hunt was hired to teach English, but he also developed a chorus. Ernest Roper was recruited to teach science, but he also formed a string ensemble. Sarah Green Oglesby was an English teacher, but she also established a drama program. A place in Hunt's chorus, Roper's ensemble, or Oglesby's plays, recalled math teacher William Merriweather, was a "way of keeping older children in school."[49]

By the early 1940s extracurricular activities at Burke—such as the school bank, student government, and the school newspaper—were animated not simply by progressive educational ideas but also by the idealism of American war aims. Organized by students in math classes, the school bank was a vehicle for schooling students in the campaign for the Double V. After students sold two hundred dollars worth of defense stamps during the 1942 school year, James Gadsen wrote that "victory at home and abroad is the cry of Negroes all over America. So it is the cry of citizens of United Burke. Our Double 'V' means victory against all the ills of democracy. The citizens of United Burke, well schooled in democratic ways, will show that even colored men are part of a true democracy." During the war teachers prepared students for citizenship by exposing them to features of American democracy that African American adults were excluded from. Working with math teacher Marjorie Howard, Grayson established a student government, United Burke. Each homeroom represented a state and elected a representative to a student council or congress, which in turn elected a president and vice president. "Grayson was training students for citizenship in the United States," Howard recalled. Student government leaders were appointed to positions on the staff of the school newspaper, the *Parvenue,* another progressive program that faculty members established in the early 1940s. As students learned how to express their dissatisfaction with white supremacy and their determination to end it, these extracurricular programs, recalled Hermine Stanyard, who graduated from Burke in 1945, gave students "the courage they needed to fight for what was right."[50]

By strengthening the curriculum and creating new extracurricular activities, Burke's faculty and administration helped growing numbers of students graduate in spite of the board's refusal to accredit the school fully. "Teachers wanted a better life for you, and they worked hard to make that possible," recalled Nevada Heyward, who graduated from Burke in 1945. Challenged by young, college-educated teachers, engaged by new extracurricular programs, students graduated from Burke in growing numbers, from 33 in 1938 to 145 in 1945, a trend mirrored in other African American high schools in the region. Inadequate funding and overcrowding continued to restrict access to private black colleges, but a poll published in the *Parvenue* in 1945 reported that almost half of these graduates planned to attend college. Just as the graduates of Society Corner and other rural elementary schools highlighted Burke's limitations and fueled demands for change, the generation of African Americans who graduated from Burke and other African American high schools in the early 1940s highlighted the limitations of South Carolina's caste system of higher education.[51]

The activism of PTA leaders and the initiatives of African American educators made Burke an increasingly significant avenue of advancement in the 1940s, but there were certainly limits to what African American parents and teachers could accomplish in a city where whites retained unfettered control of public education. Black teachers could strengthen the curriculum by modeling their courses at Burke after ones taken in college, but they could not finance improvements in the school's physical plant that would have allowed it to become a fully accredited institution. While extracurricular programs increased the number of students who attended and graduated from Burke, African Americans did not have the power to eliminate the economic disparities that prevented most black students from persisting through high school. Nor could petitions and polite protests persuade the school board to raise the salaries of black teachers who, like their colleagues throughout the region, earned less than 60 percent of what comparably trained and experienced whites were paid. Changing this caste system required more than polite protest and educational initiative, and in the early 1940s a new generation of teachers at Burke, who favored a more activist interpretation of the uplift philosophy, turned to Thurgood Marshall, who was waging a legal campaign to equalize the salaries of white and black teachers in the South.[52]

THREE

Testing Equality, 1936–1946

The first systematic challenge to the southern caste system came in the late 1930s when activist educators joined with the NAACP in campaigns to equalize the salaries of white and black teachers. In Charleston, Columbia, and elsewhere in the region, school officials maintained caste salary schedules that prevented the best black teacher from earning as much as the worst white. The practice of paying comparably trained and experienced African American teachers less than whites saved southern school boards substantial sums and illustrated the NAACP's contention that segregation "as provided and administered" always resulted in inequality. Following his appointment as assistant special counsel in 1936, Thurgood Marshall secured the support of African American teachers who financed equalization suits that forced educational authorities in every southern state to eliminate separate and unequal pay schedules for white and black teachers.[1]

The most significant and durable response to African American demands for equal pay came in South Carolina, where educational authorities adopted standardized tests to maintain salary differentials that could no longer rest on race. As divisions between activist and accommodationist teachers in South Carolina delayed legal action, educational and political leaders found a way to evade equalization before the first salary case was heard in federal court in Charleston in 1944. Working with testing and measurement specialist Ben D. Wood, the state established a new system that based teacher pay on scores on the National Teacher Examinations (NTE).

Approved by the South Carolina Legislature in 1945, the new salary system did not so much repudiate white supremacy as raise it to a higher, more sophisticated level. Far from being an unequivocal victory, as some scholars have suggested, the results of the salary campaign were problematic and paradoxical, providing benefits to black elites without fundamentally altering the subordinate status of most black teachers. As new, more rational restrictions replaced those once sanctioned by law, the legacies of caste—and the class divisions that developed within the black caste—shaped educational and economic outcomes.

Advantaged African American teachers who graduated from private schools and colleges earned NTE scores and salaries that exceeded those of many whites, but most African Americans, hampered by generations of exclusion and discrimination, continued to earn less than almost all whites. South Carolina was the first state to adopt teacher testing, and the revenues generated by the state's use of the NTE helped the program survive. As other southern states followed South Carolina's lead and adopted these exams in the 1950s and 1960s, teacher testing became part of the new, more rational and durable educational order that replaced the caste system in the South.[2]

Separate and unequal salary schedules were a cornerstone of the southern system of caste education. Unlike most jobs, in which African Americans were paid less because they performed different and usually less-skilled work, black teachers faced what Gunnar Myrdal called "clear-cut and pronounced wage discrimination." Howard University professor Doxey Wilkerson found that "for every dollar in salary received by the average white teacher in 1935–1936, the average Negro teacher received only 61 cents." School officials claimed that African Americans deserved to be paid less because blacks were not as well trained as whites, but as Robert A. Margo has shown, more than 80 percent of this racial salary differential was the result of discrimination rather than differences in educational attainment or teaching experience. Discrimination saved southern school boards an estimated $26 million in 1941, reducing the burden of operating dual school systems. Raising the costs of operating the segregated system became one of the objectives of the salary campaign.[3]

Early attempts to challenge this discriminatory educational policy in court fizzled. African American educators in the South were committed to uplift and advancement, but most were reluctant to challenge their employers in court. Dependent on the good will of whites at a time when jobs were scarce and teacher-tenure laws weak, many teachers did not want to risk being fired. "I often heard the complaint," Myrdal wrote, "that teachers are too timid about identifying themselves with the association for fear of jeopardizing their jobs. Teachers are important in local [NAACP] associations, but they do not urge action." Charles H. Houston was unable to organize a salary campaign in Columbia in 1934 because African American teachers were "so cowed and afraid of incurring official displeasure" that no black teacher would step forward and serve as a plaintiff. The NAACP faced similar problems in North Carolina, where leaders of the state teachers' association opposed litigation and gave "no consideration to the rank and file." Eugene Hunt recalled that his older colleagues especially "thought we should be patient and reasonable and try to get the school board to change it [the salary schedule] voluntarily." Septima Clark, an Avery graduate who helped to organize the salary campaign in Columbia, South Carolina, wrote that "many of our Negro teachers" were opposed to litigation and

thought it was "foolish" to try to bring "the issue into the courts." Such deference reflected a deeper black reluctance to embrace the NAACP's legal program and confront authorities in federal court.[4]

The salary campaign did not take off until Marshall found ways to enlist the
support of skeptical black educators. The son of an elementary-school teacher
and a Pullman porter, Marshall was born on July 2, 1908, and grew up in relatively advantaged circumstances in Baltimore. After graduating from the city's
overcrowded Colored High and Training School in 1925, Marshall entered Lincoln University, a small, private, African American liberal-arts institution in
Chester, Pennsylvania. While Marshall was not a particularly diligent student, he
excelled as a debater and graduated with honors. Barred from the University of
Maryland Law School, which was located three blocks from his parents' home
on Druid Hill Avenue in Baltimore, Marshall pursued his legal studies at Howard
University in Washington. He flourished at Howard, finishing his first year at the
top of his class and securing a job as a student assistant in the law library. Marshall began working for Houston, who was dean of the law school, performing
research, checking citations, and learning how to think like a lawyer. After graduating from Howard in 1933, Marshall established a private practice in Baltimore
before Houston persuaded Walter White to hire his courageous, charismatic,
and determined protégé as assistant special counsel in 1936. According to Mark
V. Tushnet, while personal problems forced Houston to withdraw from the day-
to-day work of the legal campaign in the late 1930s, Houston found in Marshall
"a student who had the potential to surpass him." Even more than his mentor,
Marshall saw the need to cultivate alliances with black teachers, who formed the
core of most southern branches of the NAACP.[5]

Marshall believed that litigation could bring results where polite protests and
appeals to fairness and justice had failed, and in the late 1930s he persuaded
African American teachers and state teachers' organizations to finance challenges
to the caste system. "We first started off on the theory, and this was Margold's
theory, that if you made them [segregated schools] so expensive, segregation
would die of its own weight," Marshall recalled in an interview in the 1970s. In
the 1930s, however, the NAACP "didn't have any money. We didn't have anything to operate with. So I came up with the idea that the teachers could pay
for those [salary-equalization] cases, because it's their money," he remembered.
"They'll get [a salary] increase." Rising African American enrollment led school
officials to hire more and more teachers, and the number of black teachers
employed in thirteen southern states grew from forty-three thousand in 1930
to more than sixty-four thousand a decade later. While the salaries of black
teachers were well below those of whites, for the most part black educators
received regular paychecks, and during the Depression they were among the
race's more solvent citizens. In Maryland, Virginia, South Carolina, Texas,

Louisiana, and elsewhere, state and local African American educational associations financed salary-equalization suits.[6]

Working with educational activists in Maryland and Virginia, Marshall and his colleagues won important legal victories in 1939 and 1940. The campaign began in Maryland, where black teachers had been lobbying the legislature for salary increases for almost a decade. After negotiations broke down between Marshall and officials in Anne Arundel County, Maryland, the NAACP litigated. In *Mills v. Board of Education* Judge W. Calvin Chesnut ruled that salary differentials in the county were the result of unconstitutional racial discrimination, not differences in "professional attainments and efficiency." In Virginia teachers' organizations raised one thousand dollars to support a legal challenge in Norfolk. The first black plaintiff, Aline Black, was fired, but Norfolk Teachers' Association president Melvin O. Alston's case led the Fourth Circuit Court of Appeals to rule that Norfolk school officials "arbitrarily" discriminated against blacks, paying Alston $921 a year while comparably trained and experienced whites earned $1,200. "This is as clear a discrimination on the ground of race as could well be imagined," the court held, "and falls squarely within the inhibition of both the due process and equal protection clauses of the 14th Amendment." In October 1940 the U.S. Supreme Court refused to review the case.[7]

Mills and *Alston* prohibited discrimination "solely on account of race," but left the door open to new kinds of discrimination. As Judge Chesnut framed the issue in *Mills*, NAACP demands for equalization had to be weighed against the rights of individual teachers and the prerogatives of school officials, and he rejected the NAACP's plea for an injunction barring the Anne Arundel County Board of Education from paying any black teacher less than any white. African American teachers certainly had the right to "pursue their profession" without being subjected to unconstitutional racial discrimination, but school authorities were not prohibited from deciding whom to employ or from exercising their judgment as to "the respective amounts" to be paid to teachers on the basis of "individual qualifications, capacities, and abilities." Because there was no clear conception of educational equality to be enforced, court decisions in Maryland and Virginia only began the process of constructing new educational policies to replace caste arrangements.[8]

As the struggle for salary equalization in Maryland and Virginia shifted from the courts to the schools, school officials retaliated, firing dozens of black teachers and denying others salary increases through what the NAACP called "intimidation, chicanery, and trickery of almost every form imaginable." Myrdal found that *Mills* and *Alston* "have not persuaded southern school authorities to retreat from this illegal practice. Those having political power in the South have shown a firm determination to maintain these salary differentials in the Negro schools." In Norfolk the school superintendent told Marshall, "I will not be party to paying a nigger the same money I pay a white person." NAACP litigation provided black teachers with new ways of challenging racial discrimination, but educational authorities discovered new methods of perpetuating it. In a July 1941 memo to Walter White, Marshall wrote that school officials were trying to "evade the question since it is impossible to defeat these cases in court." The campaign, he argued, "is passing into the second and logical stage. The next step is to attack these rating systems whereby Negro teachers, for the most part, are rated lower than whites of equal standing." As the salary campaign moved from Maryland and Virginia into other southern states, the NAACP contested new salary schedules that based pay on school officials' evaluation of a teacher's attitude, personality, character, and other subjective criteria.

Unable to pay blacks less because of their race, white political and educational leaders turned to testing and measurement specialist Ben D. Wood for help in devising new ways of evaluating teachers and determining their pay. Wood had a major influence on the salary schedules that were created in response to NAACP litigation. His tireless advocacy of teacher testing during the 1940s illustrates the central role that educational experts and prestigious national testing organizations played in crafting the new, more rational, and legally defensible educational policies that replaced caste arrangements in southern education.

Born in Brownsville, Texas in 1894, Ben D. Wood was a central figure in the spread of standardized testing, developing exams in education, law, and medicine. After working as a statistician in "Negro intelligence research" during World War I, Wood studied under Edward Thorndike at Columbia's Teachers College, earning his Ph.D. in educational guidance in 1923. As Ellen Condliffe Lagemann has written, Wood was an essentialist who believed that the "ability to think was innate rather than acquired" and that "thinking was dependent on knowledge and knowledge on facts." This conception of intelligence shaped his view that teaching ability was based on knowledge of facts and his faith in "scientifically constructed" multiple-choice tests. Wood believed that standardized tests could provide a more valid and reliable measure of teaching ability than the existing system that granted the same certificates and pay to persons of vastly unequal ability.[10]

In the late 1930s Wood spearheaded a national effort to create what he called a meritocracy in teaching. Working with a group of influential northern school superintendents, Wood formed the National Committee on Teacher Examinations. In 1939 he secured a grant from the Carnegie Foundation to finance the construction and administration of a battery of exams that purported to measure the "mental ability" of teachers and their knowledge of liberal-arts subjects and professional information. It was a good time to begin such an effort, he believed. During the 1930s there was a surplus of teachers, and Wood argued that the NTE would allow superintendents to restrict employment to "educated persons." As originally conceived, the NTE was designed to aid in the process of teacher selection by providing school officials with an objective basis for "judging the standing of applicants."[11]

The National Committee on Teacher Examinations hoped to attract ten thousand candidates to the first test administration in March 1940, but because of questions about the NTE's validity and cost, fewer than four thousand candidates—almost 80 percent of whom were from the North—took the two-day battery of exams. Early critics raised questions that have plagued the NTE for more than half a century. John G. Pilley, a professor of education at Wellesley College, argued that the NTE's "authors have no grounds other than their intuition for claiming that the results of the examination provide any evidence of the ability to teach." Wood acknowledged that "objective examinations do not and cannot measure the total complex which we call teaching ability," but he warned against "the naive error of judging validity in terms of [the NTE's] correlation with available criteria of teaching ability." It is an argument that the proponents of teacher testing continue to make, because they have never been able to demonstrate clearly or convincingly that the NTE is a valid measure not simply of what teachers know but of the more important issue of how well they can make what they know accessible to students in a specific educational context.[12]

In spite of the support and financial backing of powerful individuals and organizations, use of the NTE remained limited during the 1940s. As the teacher surplus of the 1930s gave way to wartime shortages in the 1940s, the number of candidates taking the exams declined, threatening the program's existence. Unable to sustain the program with revenues generated by test administrations, the National Committee on Teacher Examinations had to obtain additional grants from the Carnegie Foundation to survive. It was in this context of financial duress that Wood shifted his attention to the South, where the NAACP's salary-equalization campaign created the kind of interest in the NTE that Wood had been unable to generate in the North.[13]

By forcing southern school boards to establish new salary schedules, NAACP litigation created opportunities for Wood to expand use of the fledgling NTE. After the court of appeals issued its *Alston* decision, letters poured into Wood's office as southern school officials scurried to create new methods of determining teacher pay. "They want and need help," Wood wrote to his colleague on the National Committee on Teacher Examinations, Philadelphia school superintendent A. J. Stoddard, in March 1941. While Wood worried about "getting mixed up in the racial problem," he was attracted to the possibility that thousands of teachers in the region might be required to take the exams, producing much-needed revenue for the teacher-testing program.[14]

Wood was careful to define the limitations of the NTE when he marketed the test in the North, but the purpose of the NTE was redefined to suit new southern needs. Created to improve the process of selecting new teachers, the NTE became a basis for determining salaries. Stoddard warned that the use of test scores to determine salaries had been tried in several cities and abandoned, but Wood wanted to capitalize on southern interest in the test. "There are," Wood told one school official in Georgia in 1941, "certain advantages in using exams in the certification procedure particularly with respect to a certain crucial problem."[15]

To expand use of the NTE Wood organized a series of conferences for "persons interested in using the NTE in the South." He wrote a "Certification-Salary Classification Plan for Use by Local Educational Authorities" that was widely disseminated and presented at meetings in Virginia, the Carolinas, Georgia, Florida, and Alabama in the spring of 1941. Worried that litigation might lead to "blanket equalization," he argued that the same certificates should not be "issued to persons of very unequal ability." Wood urged school authorities to resist NAACP demands for equal pay by establishing a system of "merit certification" that scaled salaries "in accordance with ability." Pleased that his plan had been "favorably received," Wood told Stoddard that superintendents "all the way from Norfolk to El Paso" felt that the NTE could "be of great assistance in working out a constructive solution to the problems brought to focus by the Norfolk [*Alston*] decision." In June 1941 Wood reported that educational authorities in Tulsa, Houston, Montgomery, Birmingham, Greenville, and Raleigh were using the NTE and that officials from Mobile, Memphis, New Orleans, Nashville, and Louisville "have shown interest and need to be contacted again."[16]

As the NAACP became increasingly successful at challenging crude merit systems, southern interest in the NTE grew. Acting on what they learned from Wood, educational authorities began adopting the NTE and using test scores to maintain racial salary differentials. In Newport News, Virginia, the NAACP found school officials were "giving tests to all teachers and basing individual salaries on the results of the tests." In Miami more than two hundred African American teachers and principals were "herded together in a cafeteria of one of the Negro schools where they sat from 9 AM until 12:30 on backless benches, with a temperature of 88 degrees, the light poor, and the supervisor pacing the length of the room peering at everyone's paper and trying to catch someone communicating." According to the white supervisor of black schools, Dan J. Conroy, the purpose of the tests was to "determine if the Negro teachers were worthy of salaries equal to those paid to white teachers." Encouraged by the response to his promotion of the exams, Wood informed the National Committee on Teacher Examinations that "it is very likely that other schools in the South may request administration of the exams with a similar end in view."[17]

While Wood persuaded school officials in more than a dozen southern cities to use the NTE, his greatest success came in South Carolina, where he convinced educational and political leaders to adopt a statewide salary system that based teacher pay, in part, on scores on the NTE. The third and final stage of the equalization campaign in South Carolina, Georgia, and Mississippi was delayed by accommodationist leaders of state teachers' organizations, who refused to support litigation. In South Carolina these delays gave educational authorities time to work with Wood and test teachers before NAACP litigation led educational and political leaders to adopt his proposed salary plan in 1945.[18]

Wood had a major impact on the results of the NAACP's salary-equalization campaign in South Carolina. "I prepared the way [for the use of the NTE in the state]," Wood recalled in an interview in the 1970s. "I worked with them for years." In the early 1940s he traveled to the state on several occasions in an effort to make "South Carolina the first state to put teaching on a basis of true professional selection." After meeting with local educational and political leaders and speaking publicly on the merits of the NTE, Wood believed that South Carolina provided "the best chance for [a] large-scale examination."[19]

His influence is evident in a report written by a special legislative committee that was appointed to investigate the salary issue after the court of appeals issued its *Alston* decision. The committee was chaired by David W. Robinson, a prominent Columbia attorney, who became the chief architect of the new, more sophisticated system of white supremacy that was institutionalized in South Carolina. Born in North Carolina in 1899, Robinson earned his bachelor's degree at Roanoke College and master's and law degrees from the University of South Carolina in 1921. The following year he completed a year of graduate study at Harvard Law School. In addition to teaching at the University of South Carolina and practicing law, Robinson served on numerous state and national boards and became a leader of the South Carolina Bar Association.[20]

After meeting with Wood, the all-white committee, which included members of the legislature and leading school and university educators, issued a report that called for the adoption of a new salary system that based teacher pay, in part, on scores on the NTE. The existing system of certification was inadequate, the committee argued, because it gave "little real evidence of a teacher's value" and did not account for "wide variation" in the quality of teacher-training programs in the state. While 80 percent of the black teachers and 90 percent of the white teachers held first-grade certificates, Robinson argued that "the state board cannot justify paying, through state salary supplements, a first-grade white teacher $90 per month and a first-grade Negro teacher $50 per month. If the case were presented to a federal court now, it would issue an injunction." Drawing on a plan drafted by Wood, the committee recommended that the legislature adopt a steeply scaled salary schedule that based pay in large part on "a comprehensive and objective system of examinations." The report stated that the decision to use the exams was based on the fact that "they can be scored objectively and impartially and their use would not be subject to the accusation that they were used for the purpose of discrimination."[21]

The NTE offered a way out of the dilemmas posed by the salary campaign because it provided an ostensibly objective basis for claims that African American teachers were inferior to whites. If school officials created a single-salary schedule that based pay on educational qualifications and teaching experience, as the NAACP urged, African American teachers could, as one school official noted, "prove themselves superior to whites." As the educational attainment of black teachers rose in the 1930s and 1940s, school officials worried that the educational qualifications and salaries of African Americans might soon exceed those of whites. Authorities continued to argue that black teachers should be paid lower salaries because their training was inferior, but this contention made the state vulnerable to NAACP demands for the equalization of separate facilities and even desegregation. The NTE allowed school officials to avoid these problems and, by judging white and black teachers against the same test norm and maintaining wide disparities in public education, to ensure that most African Americans would earn lower salaries than most whites. Rather than providing what Wood and the legislative committee called an "impartial" means of determining pay, the NTE dressed up discrimination in a more rational form and became an important means through which it was perpetuated.[22]

However interested the committee was in "objectivity and impartiality," when Robinson and his colleagues tried to sell the plan to local educational and political leaders, they encountered stiff opposition. Columbia school superintendent A. G. Flora worried that the NTE "will enable Negro teachers to prove themselves better than some white teachers." William C. McCall, director of the University of South Carolina Testing Bureau, "soothed" Flora's concerns "by pointing out to him that the exam service would be available and usable to prove anytime that the mass of Negro teachers are far below the average white teachers." After Robinson informed Wood of similar reservations among members of the legislature, Wood wrote that on previous administrations of the test, the average score of blacks was "at the lower fifth percentile of whites." Robinson also expressed concerns about the constitutionality of using tests to determine salaries, and Wood responded by stating that "at least a few of the lower salary group will clearly qualify for increases so that increases can be publicized to show the absence of discrimination." In spite of these assurances the legislature remained unwilling to abolish a salary system that saved the state almost $3 million a year. Convinced that the legislature would not adopt the new salary plan until the committee presented more specific evidence, state officials decided to test a sample group of white and black teachers.[23]

As state educational officials prepared to test teachers, African American activists organized a legal campaign that challenged the Charleston school board's salary schedule. Litigation was delayed by what one activist called the refusal of the leadership of the state teachers' organization "to act upon the demands of its members." In 1941, Joseph Murray, a leader of the state NAACP conference, informed Marshall that African American teachers "have become pretty well organized. Teachers will be glad to contribute liberally to a fund to promote such a cause [litigation]." That year members of the Palmetto State Teachers Association (PSTA) voted to appropriate $1,200 to support legal action at their annual meeting. Teachers reaffirmed their support for a salary drive the following year, but Modjeska Simkins, a former teacher in Columbia who was secretary of the state conference, charged that "the High Command in the PSTA" stood as "a buffer between the underpaid classroom teacher and the powers that conspire to keep them so."[24]

By 1943 pressure from activists who favored a more confrontational approach pushed the PSTA leadership to appropriate funds for a salary campaign in South Carolina. After a joint committee of NAACP and PSTA leaders retained Harold Boulware, a Howard University–trained attorney, as local counsel, state NAACP president James Hinton and high-school principal J. Andrew Simmons began searching for a plaintiff. A graduate of Immaculate Conception, Avery Institute, Fisk, and Columbia University, Simmons was one of the black teachers in the state who favored a more activist interpretation of the uplift philosophy. During his tenure as principal of Simonton School in Charleston in the early 1930s, Simmons encouraged teachers to register and vote, and most of the school faculty belonged to the local chapter of the NAACP. After the school board launched an investigation of his political activities, he resigned and pursued a master's degree at Columbia University. His 1935 thesis recommended that "the salaries of Negro teachers be brought more nearly on par with that of white teachers." Returning to South Carolina, Simmons was appointed principal of Booker T. Washington High School in Columbia, and under his leadership the school became the first public high school in the state to secure accreditation from the Southern Association of Secondary Schools and Colleges. In 1938 Simmons encouraged Charles Bailey to apply for admission to the University of South Carolina Law School.[25]

During the summer of 1943 Simmons convinced his cousin Malissa Smith to "take a stand." Orphaned at an early age, Smith had been raised in the same household as Simmons and had enormous respect and admiration for him. "It was Andrew's drive and dedication," she recalled, "that inspired and motivated me." While Hinton and Boulware made it clear that Smith might lose her job, Simmons urged his cousin "not to be afraid." A graduate of Avery and South Carolina State College, Smith was part of the new generation of black teachers whom Grayson brought to Burke in the early 1940s. In her Problems of Democracy courses, Smith worked hard to prepare her students to be "future citizens," but she did not feel that "teaching by concept alone was sufficient." She had to "set an example" by standing up and challenging injustice. In July 1943 Boulware filed a petition on behalf of Smith and all black teachers and principals in Charleston, charging that salary differentials in the city's public schools were based "solely on race or color in violation of the Constitution."[26]

Smith's petition was hardly a surprise to school officials in Charleston, who forestalled legal action by firing Smith. Rhett kept the trustees fully apprised of the NAACP's legal victories in Maryland and Virginia, and on several occasions in the late 1930s and early 1940s the board discussed how it might respond to litigation. After Boulware filed a petition in federal court, the board's attorney, H. L. Erckmann, citing *Mills* and *Alston*, informed the trustees that "whether any particular certificate holder shall be employed is a matter resting in the sound discretion of the school authorities." Acting on Erckmann's advice, the board fired Smith. She was one of the scores of black teachers in the South who lost their jobs during the salary campaign. According to Septima Clark, many teachers "were willing to make great sacrifices in order to obtain, or attempt to obtain, fair dealing for members of their race." Although Walter White and other national NAACP leaders continued to complain about the "pussyfooting of weak-kneed" black teachers, African American educators in South Carolina were engaged in what Clark has called a "radical job," organizing challenges to "the status quo."[27]

Determined to bring the issue to court, Hinton, Boulware, and Simmons found another plaintiff, Viola Duvall. A graduate of Immaculate Conception and Howard University, Duvall held a first-grade certificate and served as chair of Burke's science department. Duvall was young and single, and her parents were financially secure. We all felt that "she would be less vulnerable," recalled Eugene Hunt. After Boulware filed another complaint in November 1943, Marshall told Duvall "not to worry, equalization in South Carolina is long overdue. I don't see any difficulties in the case."[28]

Duvall's case was tried in Judge J. Waties Waring's courtroom in Charleston in February 1944. A descendent of one of the city's oldest families, Waring was born in Charleston in 1880. Educated at the private University School and the College of Charleston, Waring read law with J. P. Kennedy Bryan and was admitted to the bar in 1902. Living in the city's prestigious South of Broad neighborhood, Waring attended St. Michael's Episcopal Church and socialized with the city's patricians in exclusive clubs and societies. Waring used his social prominence and the political connections he developed while working on the campaigns of Burnet R. Maybank and "Cotton Ed" Smith to secure an appointment as an assistant U.S. attorney and a position on the federal bench in 1942. Waring became one of the NAACP's most important allies on the federal bench, but his rulings in teacher-equalization cases in Charleston and Columbia in 1944 and 1945 are notable for the deference they showed to local school officials. As Waring biographer Tinsley E. Yarbrough noted, Waring's teacher-equalization rulings did not "contain the bite of his later pronouncements" and marked a "midway point" between his "acceptance of the old order in southern race relations" and "the aggressive civil rights posture he was soon to assume."[29]

NAACP attorneys had little difficulty convincing Waring that the Charleston school board discriminated against black teachers. Using the school board's 1943–1944 salary schedules, Marshall and Boulware demonstrated that Duvall made $645 while the lowest salary paid to a white teacher with her certificate and experience was $1,100. In an unpublished consent decree Waring enjoined the board from discriminating against African American teachers "solely on the basis of race." However, Waring's ruling, like those in *Mills* and *Alston*, held that school officials were not prohibited from "exercising their judgment as to the respective amounts to be paid to individual teachers based on individual qualifications, capacities, and abilities. This court is not determining what particular amounts of salaries must be paid to either white or Negro teachers." Several months before Waring issued his ruling in Duvall, Rhett wrote Wood and made arrangements for the use of the NTE at "a reduced rate." Apparently, *News and Courier* editor William Watts Ball was aware of the plan to test teachers. In an editorial Ball wrote that litigation "may set up white competition with colored teachers. The Thurgood Marshalls of the colored race may not have a monopoly on shrewdness."[30]

After Waring issued his opinion in the Duvall case, the state board of education announced that it would test a sample group of white and black teachers. African American educators immediately objected, arguing that the NTE would be used to circumvent equalization. Most teachers in Charleston, Hunt recalled, saw the NTE as "a continuation of that same effort to prove that black teachers are inferior and to give advantage to white teachers." Horace Fitchett, dean of Claflin College, did not believe that the test measured "teaching ability or adaptability to teaching situations." Because of wide disparities in public education, Fitchett noted, "if examinations were administered to white and Negro teachers for the purpose of determining salary standards, the Negro would remain relatively in the position at which he is at present." PSTA leaders argued that "because of the questionable or debatable value of such a device, it has not been generally adopted by any other state." Another African American critic asked, "is there not the high probability that schools and teachers will be so preoccupied with the NTE that they will lose sight of [more important] objectives?" These questions led William Bluford, a member of the Charleston County Teachers' Association, to write the NAACP in November 1944 and ask if the "legal staff had made any study of the recertification plan for South Carolina? If you have, would you or would you not, advise teachers in the state to take the test?"[31]

More concerned with contesting the constitutionality of racial classifications than with the complex issue of how to measure competence in the classroom, the NAACP urged black teachers to take the tests. Although Marshall challenged the use of the NTE in Florida "as a sham and a subterfuge behind which to hide a fixed and determined intention to discriminate," the courts upheld the use of tests as objective measures of teaching ability. These rulings and the advice of leading African American educators Horace Mann Bond and Charles S. Thompson, the Howard University dean who edited the *Journal of Negro Education*, convinced Marshall and his colleagues that standardized tests were an advance over both caste constraints and the rating systems that based salaries on attitude, personality, character, and other subjective criteria. Bond had once opposed standardized tests, but as William Thomas has shown, Bond came to accept them as "legitimate measures of mental ability and as mechanisms of class distinction within the black community." By the early 1940s advantaged African American educators and lawyers believed that the use of the NTE would eliminate what one member of the legal staff called "the unfair practice of determining salaries on the basis of race." In a letter to Horace Fitchett, NAACP attorney Leon Ransom wrote that "if examinations were administered fairly, I can see no objection."[32]

The first state-wide administration of the NTE generated results that were analyzed in a four-volume report. The report endorsed the use of the NTE but did not establish a correlation between high NTE scores and superior performance in the classroom. University of South Carolina education professor J. McT. Daniel found that "excellent teachers" made only "respectable scores" on the NTE. He concluded that the exams "to some extent, appear to validate their [academic] preparation." Others were more skeptical and echoed the concerns of both northern critics and southern black educators. In the second volume in the report, H. L. Frick, an education professor at Winthrop College, argued that "there is no assurance that there is any close relationship between what a person can do on this exam and his excellence in teaching." Frick recommended that "differences in rating on the NTE should be comparatively small."[33]

Although these studies offered little evidence of the NTE's validity, racial rather than educational concerns convinced the state legislature to adopt the tests. The results of the state-wide administration confirmed Wood's earlier predictions. On the basis of their scores teachers were divided into four categories: A, B, C, and D. Test results revealed that 90 percent of the white teachers and 27 percent of the black teachers would get A or B certificates while 10 percent of the whites and 73 percent of the blacks would receive C or D certificates. Convinced that this data would persuade the legislature to support the proposed salary plan, J. B. White, director of the state office of teacher certification, told Wood that "we are very anxious to have the results of the first exam ready when the legislature meets in January." When Wood sent the test results to White, he noted that the National Committee on Teacher Examinations "recognizes the unchallenged constitutional authority of state and local authorities in the interpretation and application of test exam results."[34]

Test results went a long way toward allaying the concerns of a state legislature that V. O. Key called "the guardian of the status quo" in South Carolina. With a second NAACP salary-equalization suit looming, the legislature adopted Wood's salary plan in April 1945. The law established a new system of certification and compensation for all teachers. Certificates and salaries would be based on a teacher's experience (from one to fourteen years), educational experience (five categories, from fewer than two years of college to a master's degree), and scores on the NTE: A for the top 25 percent, B for the middle 50 percent, C for the next 15 percent, and D for the bottom 10 percent. State aid to school districts for teachers' salaries increased, but in order to receive state salary supplements, which ranged from $65 to $175, teachers had to take the NTE to be recertified. The new system was considerably more legally defensible than the one it replaced. Many members of the General Assembly supported the recertification plan, one legislator noted, because they believed that "we can get around paying equal salaries to Negro teachers on the basis of our [salary] plan."[35]

A month after the state legislature established the new salary system, Waring upheld its constitutionality in *Thompson v. Gibbes*. NAACP attorneys argued that the new salary plan would delay equalization, but, because they had come to accept the use of standardized tests to determine pay, the legal staff did not vigorously challenge use of the NTE. The absence of such a challenge led Waring to embrace ideas that Wood brought to the South in the early 1940s and to uphold the NTE as a constitutional measure of teaching performance. Like Wood, Waring did not believe that those with "superior qualities and attainments" should be paid the same salaries as those "who are not as well equipped." Waring did not see the injustice of judging whites and blacks against the same test norm in a state that operated a separate and savagely unequal system of public education. No evidence was presented to show that the NTE was a more accurate predictor of competence in the classroom than the degrees teachers held, but Waring found the NTE to be a "proper yardstick by which to measure the stature of a teacher and to pay him accordingly. The question before this court," he concluded, is whether the new salary and certification plan "absolutely removes the question of race or color." The concern of the court was whether it is free of the "tinge of race prejudice, and I find it to be so." Edgar A. Brown, the legislative leader who sponsored the recertification plan, commended Waring for his "masterful understanding of the issue." It is, Brown wrote, "comforting to have your Judicial Conclusion." Columbia school board chairman Heyward Gibbes told Waring that he read the *Thompson* decision "with complete approval."[36]

Rather than eliminating racism, the NTE provided a new vehicle through which it was institutionalized. As new, more rational restrictions replaced those that could no longer be sanctioned by law, the legacies of caste, wide disparities in the state's system of public education, and the class differences that had developed within black communities in the state determined the salaries that African Americans earned. Instead of equalizing salaries, as many historians have claimed, the elimination of separate and unequal pay scales had paradoxical effects. While advantaged black teachers, who graduated from private schools and colleges, earned test scores and salaries that exceeded those of many whites, most black teachers, hampered by family background and a lack of educational opportunity, continued to make less than almost all whites. The NAACP's legal victories in teacher-salary cases were significant, but so too were the new, more rational, legally defensible, and durable educational policies that replaced the caste system.[37]

While not as crude as the caste constraints it replaced, the new salary and certification system was hardly free of discrimination. The new system judged white and black teachers against the same standard in a state that provided white and black teachers with vastly different educational opportunities. Most of South Carolina's six thousand African American teachers, especially those who attended schools in rural areas, were not able to overcome the limitations imposed by disadvantaged family backgrounds and inadequately funded schools and colleges. A majority grew up in households where family income and parental educational attainment were well below those of whites. Although increasing numbers of students graduated from overcrowded and inadequately funded elementary schools, in 1941, nineteen of South Carolina's forty-six counties made no provision for the public schooling of African Americans past the seventh grade. By moving to cities and towns that did operate high schools, growing numbers of African Americans were able to complete secondary school. If they were able to pay for college, prospective teachers enrolled in a system of state-supported higher education that provided whites with access to five institutions and blacks to only one, that appropriated more than ten times as much for postsecondary education of whites as for blacks, and that made no provision for the graduate or professional education of African Americans, even though the new salary schedule offered higher pay for those with master's degrees. Black teachers, PSTA leaders asserted, "are penalized for not being able to show certain reactions which they were never given an opportunity to develop."[38]

Indeed, African American teachers continued to pay a price for the discrimination that financed the educational advancement of their white counterparts. During the 1945–1946 school year, close to 90 percent of the teachers in South Carolina took the NTE and were recertified by the state. As Wood predicted, most African Americans earned lower NTE scores and lower salaries than almost all whites. As table 3 shows, almost three times as many whites as blacks received A or B grades on the NTE, while seven times as many blacks as whites received C or D grades. Educational attainment and teaching experience also determined salaries, but the NTE was the most important determinant of teacher pay because it established which of the four schedules teachers would be paid under. While litigation removed legal barriers to equality, it did not eliminate the legacies of poverty, parental illiteracy, or the lack of educational opportunity. As a result, most black teachers continued to make considerably less than almost all whites. In South Carolina the average annual salary of black teachers in the state rose from 40 percent of what whites earned in 1940 to 67 percent of what whites earned in 1947.[39]

Black teachers in Charleston performed better on the NTE than African Americans in the state as a whole, but most blacks in the city continued to make less than whites. As table 4 shows, five times as many whites as blacks were in the highest pay range, while twice as many blacks as whites were in the bottom two pay categories.[40]

Table 3 *White and Black Teacher Scores on the National Teacher Examinations, South Carolina, 1945–1946*

Grade	Race			
	White Percent	Number	Black Percent	Number
A	39.8	4,113	4.0	250
B	55.4	5,720	40.7	2,513
C	4.2	437	31.4	1,938
D	0.4	42	23.7	1,466

Source: *Annual Report of the State Superintendent of Education of the State of South Carolina, 1946* (Columbia: South Carolina General Assembly, 1946), 174.

Table 4 *White and Black Teacher Salaries, Charleston, 1948*

Salary	Race			
	White Percent	Number	Black Percent	Number
I A $3,636–3,003	51.6	93	10	18
II B $2,988–2,508	14.4	26	23.3	42
III C $2,476–2,023	27.2	49	46.1	83
IV D $1,991–1,606	6.6	12	20.5	37

Source: Charleston Board of School Commissioners Minute Books, 18 March 1948.

Race remained significant, but in Charleston and other southern cities that adopted the NTE, class became an increasingly important determinant of teacher pay. While the average annual salary of African Americans in Charleston remained below that of whites, 10 percent of Charleston's black teachers—a talented tenth, almost all of whom had graduated from Avery and gone on to private black colleges—earned NTE scores and salaries that exceeded those of 48 percent of the city's white teachers. The test scores of William Grayson, Wilmot Fraser, Eugene Hunt, Lois Simms, Viola Duvall, and others confirm the findings of a generation of research that challenged genetic explanations of racial differences and demonstrated that advantaged African Americans outperformed many whites on standardized tests. Thomas E. Davis's study of freshmen at Fisk College, which enrolled many Averyites, showed that Fisk students earned "gross median" scores that were above those of freshmen at the universities of Alabama, South Carolina, and Georgia. The results, Horace Mann Bond argued, are a "measure of the strength of educational and other environmental factors" and demonstrated that advantaged African American families will "continue to furnish the great majority of leaders" because their children are "above their fellows in achievement."[41]

By removing caste barriers litigation and the new salary system heightened class differences that had developed within Charleston's black community. The difference between what the lowest-paid and highest-paid African American teacher earned widened considerably, increasing from $200 under the old salary system to almost $2,000 under the new one. Viola Duvall made $45 more than her lowest-paid black colleague in 1943, but by 1948, she was earning almost $2,000 more. These salary differentials increased as advantaged African Americans used higher salaries to finance graduate study and earn master's degrees at institutions outside the state, something that lower-paid black teachers could not afford. For example, Lois Simms, an Avery graduate who earned an A on the NTE, saw her annual salary rise from $630 in 1943 to $3,013 in 1951. Like others, Simms used her higher salary to finance graduate study at Howard University, and, after she earned a master's degree in 1954, she received another pay increase. In Columbia, Septima Clark used her salary increase to earn a master's degree from Hampton Institute, and her salary rose from $650 in 1929 to $4,000 in 1947. The results of the salary campaign in Charleston offer an early indication of how the end of caste restrictions increased the importance of class within the city's black community in ways that whites used to conceal a continuing pattern of racial inequality and discrimination.[42]

Charleston's white leadership pointed to the performance of the city's talented tenth to legitimize a system of determining salaries that prevented most African Americans from earning pay that equaled that of whites. Although five times as many whites as blacks were in the highest salary range in 1948, when one African American in Charleston became the highest-paid principal in the city, the *News and Courier* published a profile of him to publicize what Wood called "the absence of discrimination." In Charleston and other southern cities that adopted the NTE, the new salary system allowed advantaged African Americans to earn higher pay without altering the subordinate status of most black teachers.[43]

Litigation and local activism forced educational authorities to eliminate separate and unequal salary schedules and increase the pay of black teachers, but the educational outcomes of the campaign in South Carolina signaled the limits of equalization litigation. Federal-court judges held that salaries could no longer be based on race, but as they affirmed the right of school authorities to set salaries on the basis of "individual qualifications," officials adopted merit systems, the most durable of which relied on the NTE to maintain racial salary differentials. Publicly, Marshall continued to claim that salary litigation would "compel complete equalization" and, by increasing the costs of operating separate systems of public education, "inevitably destroy segregation." Inside the association, however, there was a growing recognition that the campaign had not increased the costs of segregation to the point where southern educational authorities would abandon it, as the NAACP expected. Association attorney Robert Carter acknowledged these limits in a speech he drafted for Walter White on the results of the salary campaign. Carter urged White to tell a group of African Americans in Columbia in November 1946 that "the teacher's salary fight is now about over. The entire salary differential is supposed to be wiped out [in the coming school year]." Carter conceded that "there may be a few isolated areas were discrimination still exists, but wherever the situation exists, it is incumbent upon the teachers to avail themselves of their rights under existing laws."[44]

As other southern states adopted the NTE, the problem was no longer one of law but of educational policy. The most significant response to the challenges posed by NAACP salary litigation, South Carolina's adoption of the NTE helped the program survive and become a model that proponents of teacher testing used in their efforts to expand use of the NTE in the South. Wood became "rather frightened at further publicizing our relationship in this matter," but the revenue generated by South Carolina's use of the exams helped sustain the NTE until the Educational Testing Service (ETS) assumed full control of the program in 1950. ETS historians describe South Carolina's adoption of the NTE as "the most significant event during an otherwise discouraging period," one that "laid a firm foundation" for broader teacher testing in the region. Arthur L. Benson, who succeeded Wood as director of teacher testing, waged an aggressive campaign to increase the use of teacher tests in the South in the 1950s. In an address at the annual meeting of the Southern Association of Colleges and Secondary Schools following the *Brown v. Board of Education* decision in 1954, Benson asserted that if other states followed the lead of South Carolina and adopted the NTE, the South could "face its future with confidence." In 1956 the ETS reported that "the number of teachers tested by cities using special tests or services increased by over 65 percent over the preceding year." Much of this growth occurred in the South, where teachers were required to take the NTE to obtain certificates, employment, tenure, and salary supplements. The adoption of the NTE in southern cities foreshadowed broader statewide reliance on the exams. By the early 1960s, when the NTE was required or widely used in Delaware, West Virginia, North Carolina, South Carolina, Georgia, Florida, Mississippi, and Texas, 80 percent of those who registered to take the exams were from south-central or southern states.[45]

Even as the NTE institutionalized durable obstacle to equality, the salary campaign generated resources that encouraged challenges to South Carolina's caste system of higher education. While the new salary system offered higher pay to those with master's degrees, the state provided no opportunities for African Americans at the graduate level. Following Waring's ruling in the *Thompson* case, PSTA leaders announced plans to challenge disparities that prevented "Negro teachers from attain[ing] the highest bracket under the recertification plan." Black teachers, they declared, would seek "immediate admission" to graduate programs at the University of South Carolina unless authorities established similar programs at State College. In September 1945 Hinton told Marshall that "we are ready to act," but African American high school students in Charleston had already initiated a campaign to desegregate higher education in South Carolina.[46]

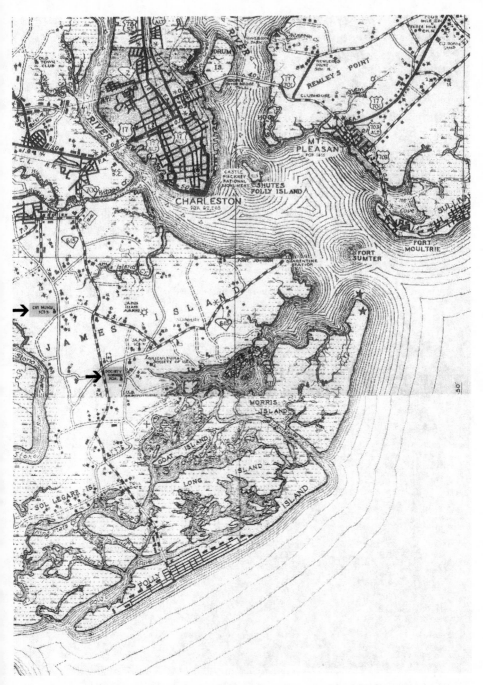

Map of Charleston and James Island, 1940. The locations of Cut Bridge and Society Corner are highlighted. Courtesy of Map Department, Thomas Cooper Library, University of South Carolina

Society Corner students, circa 1938, standing on a basketball court constructed by PTA members. The New Deal funded the health and diet kitchen that stimulated school attendance. Courtesy of the Avery Research Center at the College of Charleston

Mamie Garvin Fields at her desk in Society Corner, circa 1936. The contributions of PTA and Federation of Colored Women's Club members improved Society Corner. Courtesy of Simon and Schuster

Cut Bridge Elementary School students, 1945. Cut Bridge was one of four public elementary schools on James Island. During the 1930s and early 1940s, enrollment at Cut Bridge, Society Corner, and other African American elementary schools in rural South Carolina rose sharply. Courtesy of Avery Research Center at the College of Charleston

Burke Industrial School students, circa 1920. Built on a dumping ground in 1911, Burke Industrial School, like others in the South, was designed to prepare students for "Negro jobs." Courtesy of the Avery Research Center at the College of Charleston

Burke Industrial School principal
William Henry Grayson. Between 1939
and 1945 Grayson and a cadre of committed faculty laid the groundwork for
a generation of institutional development at Burke. Courtesy of the Avery
Research Center at the College of
Charleston

Avery Normal Institute. Like other private and parochial African American schools in
the Jim Crow South, Avery educated the children of advantaged African Americans and
facilitated the intergenerational transmission of class status. Courtesy of the Avery
Research Center at the College of Charleston

J. Andrew Simmons. Leading a generation of African American educators who favored a more activist interpretation of the uplift philosophy, Simmons encouraged Charles Bailey to apply for admission to the University of South Carolina Law School in 1938 and organized salary-equalization suits in Charleston and Columbia in 1944 and 1945. Courtesy of the Avery Research Center at the College of Charleston

Left: Malissa (Smith) Burkehalter, a plaintiff in the Charleston salary-equalization suit of 1944–1945. Burkehalter was one of dozens of black teachers and principals in the South who were fired in the 1930s and 1940s for challenging caste salary schedules for white and black teachers. Courtesy of the Avery Research Center at the College of Charleston

Right: Viola (Duvall) Stewart, a plaintiff in the Charleston salary-equalization suit of 1944–1945. Courtesy of the Avery Research Center at the College of Charleston

Left: Frank A. DeCosta. Like William Henry Grayson, L. Howard Bennett, and Clinton Young, DeCosta was a Deweyite who believed that progressive educational programs should train students in community participation. As principal of Avery Institute, DeCosta instituted educational reforms that inspired John H. Wrighten and other students to challenge the exclusion of black students from the College of Charleston in 1943 and 1944. After earning his doctorate from the University of Pennsylvania, DeCosta served as dean of the graduate school at South Carolina State College. Courtesy of the Avery Research Center at the College of Charleston

Right: John H. Wrighten, 1964. From the 1940s into the 1960s, Wrighten was at the center of efforts to desegregate higher education in South Carolina. A graduate of Avery Institute, Wrighten was one of hundreds of African Americans who applied for admission to southern colleges and universities in the 1940s. After graduating from South Carolina State in 1952 and passing the bar exam in 1953, Wrighten returned to Charleston and served as legal adviser to the Charleston branch of the NAACP. He helped to draft the school-desegregation petition in 1955 and represented African American activists who staged direct-action protests in the 1960s. Courtesy of the Avery Research Center at the College of Charleston

South Carolina State College president Miller F. Whittaker (left) and Benjamin Mays. During his tenure as president (1932–1949), Whittaker found ways of accommodating more and more students, expanding the school's physical plant, and establishing new graduate and professional programs. Courtesy of South Carolina State University

South Carolina State Law School faculty and students, 1948: (seated) Cassandra E. Maxwell, associate professor; Benner C. Turner, professor; Eloise Vaughn, secretary; Leo L. Kerford, associate professor; (standing) first-year law students. Courtesy of South Carolina State University

South Carolina State Law School students, circa 1950. Matthew Perry is the first student on the left. Black lawyers trained at the separate law school at State—like those in North Carolina, Missouri, Florida, Louisiana, and Texas—played an indispensable role in desegregating schools, colleges, and universities in the South during the 1960s. Courtesy of South Carolina State University

Burke Industrial School English teacher Lois Simms in front of the portable classrooms (which students called "doghouses") brought in to accommodate the growing number of students who enrolled in and graduated from Burke. Overcrowding and disparities between white and black schools sparked several student strikes in the South in the late 1940s and pushed the NAACP to challenge segregation directly. Courtesy of the Avery Research Center at the College of Charleston

Thurgood Marshall arriving in Charleston for the *Briggs v. Elliott* trial, 1951. *Briggs* was the first direct attack on state-sanctioned segregation in public education. Courtesy of Cecil J. Williams

James F. Byrnes. A protégé of Ben Tillman, Byrnes served as congressman, senator, adviser to President Franklin D. Roosevelt, Supreme Court justice, and secretary of state, before returning to South Carolina and winning election as governor in 1950. Working with David W. Robinson, William C. McCall, Donald S. Russell, and others, Byrnes developed a sophisticated strategy for excluding African Americans from white schools, colleges, and universities. Courtesy of the University of South Carolina

Burke Industrial School, circa 1954. The additions to Burke's physical plant in the 1950s were part of a frantic rush to make separate facilities equal. Courtesy of the Avery Research Center at the College of Charleston

Burke and former Avery faculty members, 1955. Rising enrollment and NAACP litigation produced a spectacular increase in the number of African American teachers in the South. Eugene Hunt is in the center of the fourth row with many of his colleagues who attended and taught at Avery before it was closed on the eve of the Supreme Court's *Brown* decision. Courtesy of the Avery Research Center at the College of Charleston

Burke extracurricular club, circa 1950. Building on the groundwork laid by William Henry Grayson and his colleagues in the early 1940s, Burke faculty members created extracurricular programs and activities that trained racially and politically conscious student leaders. Courtesy of the Avery Research Center at the College of Charleston

Elloree Training School faculty, 1956. Twenty-one of the school's twenty-four faculty members refused to renounce their support for the NAACP and desegregation and were fired. An estimated thirty thousand black teachers in the United States were dismissed or demoted during the process of desegregation. Courtesy of Cecil J. Williams

State College *Collegian*, October 1954. As the paper heralded the new agricultural building, activist students met in a new student center and worked with Florence Miller on articles that encouraged students to "challenge the traditional way we do things." Courtesy of South Carolina State University

Florence Miller. An English teacher, Miller edited the *Collegian*, which served as a forum and a training ground for the students. Following the boycott in 1956, she was one of several professors who were fired. Courtesy of South Carolina State University

Facing page: President Benner C. Turner, with a notebook under his left arm (*front row, center*) and the nearly two hundred professors who taught at State College in 1953. During the 1940s and early 1950s, Turner oversaw a gigantic building program. Like other African American college presidents, Turner suffered from what historian George R. Woolfolk calls an "amoral survival psychosis that led to intellectual and spiritual sterility." Courtesy of South Carolina State University

South Carolina State College Social Studies Department. According to the 1955 yearbook, the department focused "the attention of students on social, economic, and political problems which affect man directly and indirectly." Members of the department provided important support for the student boycott. Courtesy of South Carolina State University

TAKE YOUR
STAND
FOR FREEDOM

Fred Moore, 1956. A product of Cut Bridge Elementary and Burke High School, Moore organized and led the boycott at State College. The Burke *Parvenue* wrote that Moore "is courteous, diplomatic; knows what he wants, and leaves no stone unturned in getting it." The college's all-white governing board expelled Moore and fourteen other student activists for violating unspecified college regulations. Courtesy of South Carolina State University

South Carolina State students, marching out of Floyd Hall cafeteria in 1956 after refusing to eat dinner in an expression of support for desegregation and the counter boycott organized by leaders of the Orangeburg NAACP. Courtesy of Cecil J. Williams and South Carolina State University

Allen University students applying for admission to the University of South Carolina, 1958. Two weeks after the *Brown* decision, the university began requiring that students submit SAT scores. In the late 1950s and early 1960s, other southern state colleges and universities adopted tests that rationalized restrictions that could no longer rest on race. Courtesy of the University of South Carolina

Burke High School play, circa 1955. African American educational activist Septima Clark wrote that "work in dramatics proved to be good training in later activities not even related to the stage but rather to dealing with audiences and programs of one sort or another." Courtesy of the Avery Research Center at the College of Charleston

Burke High School Senior Council, 1960. The African American students who organized and led the sit-ins in Charleston, and other southern cities, were honor students and leaders of clubs, athletic teams, and student government. The activism that flowed out of black schools and colleges was a necessary condition to the end of segregation in public education. Courtesy of the Avery Research Center at the College of Charleston

Harvey Gantt and reporters on the Clemson College campus, January 1963. An honor student at Burke, Gantt organized sit-ins in Charleston before desegregating Clemson College in January 1963. Courtesy of Cecil J. Williams

Robert Anderson (left), Henrie Monteith, and James Solomon registering for classes at the University of South Carolina, September 1963. Courtesy of the University of South Carolina

African American students demonstrating in Charleston during the summer of 1963. In Charleston, as in other southern cities, African American students played a crucial role in the protests, demonstrations, and boycotts that paved the way for desegregation of the public schools. In the fall of 1963 Charleston was one of more than one hundred fifty districts that desegregated for the first time, more than three times as many as in 1962 and the largest number to desegregate since 1956. Courtesy of the Avery Research Center at the College of Charleston

James Blake, Roy Wilkins, I. DeQuincey Newman, J. Arthur Brown, and others marching in Charleston, summer 1963. The NAACP remained the preeminent civil rights organization in South Carolina during the 1960s and provided important legal and financial support for the Charleston movement. Courtesy of the Avery Research Center at the College of Charleston

Clarence Ford accompanying his daughter Barbara and an unidentified friend as they desegregate James Simons Elementary School, September 3, 1963. On that date eleven African American students crossed the color line and ended the practice of segregation in the Charleston public schools. Courtesy of the Avery Research Center at the College of Charleston

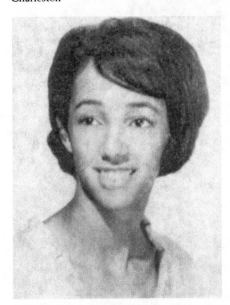

Millicent E. Brown, the daughter of NAACP leader J. Arthur Brown, and ten other African American students desegregated the Charleston public schools in September 1963. Millicent Brown graduated from Rivers High School in 1966 and is shown here in her high school yearbook photo. Courtesy of Millicent F. Brown

Harvey Gantt. After graduating with honors from Clemson in 1965, Gantt earned a master's degree from the Massachusetts Institute of Technology. Following his election as mayor of Charlotte in the 1980s, Gantt ran for the U.S. Senate in North Carolina, but was narrowly defeated by Jesse Helms in 1992 and 1996. Courtesy of the Avery Research Center at the College of Charleston

FOUR

The Veil in Higher Education, 1943–1953

In the spring of 1943 a twenty-two-year-old World War II veteran and Avery graduate applied for admission to the College of Charleston. Officials at the nation's oldest municipally funded college ignored John H. Wrighten's application, but the following spring thirty-two high-school students, acting on what they learned in a Problems of Democracy class at Avery Institute, joined Wrighten's campaign. These applications, like those in other states, brought to the surface contending visions of African American advancement, sparking debates between activists who favored desegregation and accommodationists who wanted to build a parallel system of African American higher education.[1]

Wrighten was one of the hundreds of African American students who revived the NAACP's desegregation campaign in higher education, which had stalled during World War II. Although he was unable to gain access to the College of Charleston, during his senior year at State College, he applied to the University of South Carolina Law School. By the time Wrighten graduated from State in 1947, more than eight thousand black students had completed college, three times as many as in 1940. Encouraged by activist professors, supported by the GI Bill, and emboldened by a new postwar political climate, these students challenged caste constraints and fueled NAACP legal challenges. In South Carolina Wrighten's application to the state's only publicly supported law school renewed debates about access and institutional development that complicated and compromised the desegregation campaign. After educational authorities responded to NAACP-sponsored litigation by creating a separate African American law school at State College, Thurgood Marshall tried to convince black professors and students to boycott what he believed would become "a monument to the perpetuation of segregation." South Carolina's educational and political leadership exploited these divisions, deflecting demands for the desegregation of publicly supported colleges and universities, which remained segregated until 1963.[2]

The outcomes of the campaign to desegregate higher education in South Carolina illuminate the new architecture of southern public higher education that emerged out of conflicts between southern African Americans, the NAACP, and state and local officials during the 1940s. As growing numbers of black students enrolled in the separate law school at State College, political and educational leaders, led by David W. Robinson, drew on their experience in the salary campaign and established new requirements for admission to the legal profession. As much as these new, more rational educational policies limited, unlike the caste constraints they replaced, they could not block black access completely. While hardly equal to the program at the University of South Carolina, the separate law school at State College—like those in Missouri, North Carolina, Louisiana, Texas, and Florida—trained African American attorneys such as Wrighten who played an indispensable role in desegregating schools, colleges, and universities in the 1960s.[3]

John Wrighten was part of a generation of high-school graduates who highlighted the exclusion of African Americans from Charleston's caste system of higher education. Born in 1921, Wrighten grew up on Edisto Island, South Carolina, thirty miles from Charleston. Wrighten recalled that his parents and his eight siblings "lived fairly well," but the 1930 federal manuscript census does not list his father, who was forty-nine when John was born, as part of the Wrighten household. Apparently Wrighten's mother, Rosa, who is listed as widowed, earned "cash wages" outside the home, which her children supplemented by raising cotton and livestock on the family farm. John was "excited" by lessons at Central Elementary School, which he attended between 1929 and 1934. Wrighten's mother and his minister, Reverend W. L. Metz, encouraged him to pursue his schooling past the seventh grade, when public support for African American education ended. Most of the black students in the rural lowcountry who moved to Charleston illicitly enrolled at Burke, but Wrighten managed to secure enough money to pay the fifteen dollar monthly tuition at Avery. The school's 1936 catalog states that "provision has always been made to assist worthy but needy pupils," and it seems likely that Wrighten combined support from his family and church with a scholarship from Avery, and perhaps an National Youth Administration (NYA) grant, to pay his tuition and living expenses. In the fall of 1935 the fourteen-year-old Wrighten moved to Charleston and enrolled at Avery, boarding at 236 Coming Street, several blocks from the school.[4]

Wrighten attended Avery during a time when the American Missionary Association (AMA) was pushing the school in progressive directions. Avery remained firmly committed to the liberal arts, but when Benjamin Cox retired as principal in 1936, the association appointed Frank A. DeCosta and encouraged him to make the school "the leader in progressive movements in the city." A member of the city's "Negro Aristocracy," DeCosta distinguished himself at Avery before earning a B.A. at Lincoln in Pennsylvania and a master's at Columbia University's Teachers College in 1938. Like other African Americans trained during the heyday of the progressive movement, DeCosta was a Deweyite who believed that schooling should train students in "community participation." Progressive reforms continued under L. Howard Bennett, who was appointed principal when DeCosta resigned to pursue a doctorate at the University of Pennsylvania in 1941. Like DeCosta, Bennett was a light-skinned member of the city's elite. An Avery graduate, Bennett attended Fisk, where he studied under Charles S. Johnson. Bennett resisted AMA initiatives that he felt would weaken the school's academic program, but he believed that "the education of the Negro child must equip students with tools and techniques capable of producing united group effort and fuller participation in the full stream of American life." The AMA's director of schools, Ruth Morton, encouraged Bennett "to look beyond the immediate school situation, and make the city of Charleston a social laboratory." Bennett hired and supported teachers who made Avery a "platform or center from which to make social change effective in Charleston."[5]

This progressive agenda flourished while Wrighten was a student at Avery. John Dewey was popular among teachers because they found in his writings support for a more activist interpretation of the African American uplift philosophy. Social-studies teachers William Bluford and Julia Brogdon were progressives who had a strong impact on Wrighten, nurturing his interest in sociology and encouraging his activism. Coming to Charleston from the rural lowcountry, Wrighten was struck by the pervasiveness of segregation in the city. "At home, it was noticeable only on the beaches and in the schools," but in the city, he told journalist William Peters, "it was everywhere." In Bluford's classes Wrighten studied "race relations in the context of American history" and learned that "segregation was a means of exploiting the Negro economically, a way of keeping Negroes blind to the larger part of their surroundings." The more Wrighten learned, "the more every phase of segregation angered me." An active member of the local NAACP, Bluford used the Constitution, the Bill of Rights, and the Thirteenth, Fourteenth, and Fifteenth Amendments to teach students that they were citizens who deserved the same rights and privileges as other Americans. Studying these "articles of our democracy," Wrighten recalled, was "a big experience. These words were alive with meaning." As the young man read them, he felt he had "to do something about it." Avery, Wrighten recalled, "inspired me to become politically motivated."[6]

Wrighten was forced to drop out of Avery for financial reasons, but he was determined to earn his high-school diploma. After his brother-in-law was murdered and authorities failed to investigate, Wrighten became increasingly bitter about "the justice Negroes received in his state." As he worked to support his sister, he married Dorothy Lillian Richardson. Wrighten returned to Avery as a junior in 1941, only to be drafted. Discharged from the military because of a duodenal ulcer, he reenrolled at the school in 1943 and became involved in the NAACP youth chapter that students and teachers organized at Avery in 1942. Designed to attract young people to the NAACP, the youth chapters, Ralph Bunche wrote, "devote themselves to the broad program of the association, with special attention to the problems of youth." National youth secretary Ruby Hurley told the chapter's adviser at Avery, Lois Moses, that youth work was "done inside schools." Advisers were encouraged to acquaint students with "problems" and teach them how to "cope with them." In May 1943, on the eve of his graduation from Avery, Wrighten was elected president of the youth chapter.[7]

Acting on lessons he learned at Avery, Wrighten applied for admission to the College of Charleston in July 1943. In a letter to college officials Wrighten wrote that he "was a graduate of Avery Institute, and a veteran of World War II. I [would] like to make an application for your college this term. I am interested in social science." The acting president of the college, George Grice, acknowledged Wrighten's letter and informed him that the matter had been referred to the board of trustees. By fall Wrighten had not heard from college officials. Reluctantly, he left his two children with Dorothy and her family in Charleston and enrolled at State College in Orangeburg, ninety miles away. Wrighten returned to Charleston on weekends and continued to confer with members of the NAACP youth chapter about desegregating the College of Charleston.[8]

Julia Brogdon's students at Avery joined Wrighten and applied for admission to the college. The daughter of A.M.E. Emmanuel pastor R. E. Brogdon, Julia Brogdon graduated from Allen University in Columbia and earned her master's degree at Atlanta University in 1940, where she studied with Horace Mann Bond and W. E. B. Du Bois. Brogdon was hired by Bennett, and her class engaged students in practical civics lessons. An active member of the NAACP and an avowed Deweyite, Brogdon believed that "a child learns by doing." Schools could build a new social order, she argued, if students were taught how "to cope with economic, political, social, and educational problems intelligently. If the children of today are trained properly through our educative processes," she recalled, "many of our social problems will be solved in the same way that medical research has products for eradicating certain diseases."[9]

In May 1944, thirty-two seniors in Brogdon's Problems of Democracy class acted on these ideas. Their applications to the college grew out of a class discussion about municipal colleges. When students learned that New York's tax-supported City College admitted African Americans, they wondered why the municipally supported College of Charleston barred blacks. Some of the young men in the class faced the draft and resented their exclusion from the college. Students were required to write college officials and inquire about admission. Hazel Stewart brought envelopes and stamps to class, and students were told that "failure" to complete the assignment "would be a mark against their grade." Hortense Scipio's letter is probably typical of those sent to the college. "In June," she wrote, "I am to be graduated from Avery. I am especially interested in the College of Charleston. Please send me one of your catalogs, and any other information concerning entrance requirements." Wrighten also sent a letter and was chosen by the students to represent them. "This time," he recalled, "we were told the board would meet in June and notify us of its decision."[10]

College officials wanted to avoid publicity, but on June 11, 1944, the *News and Courier* reported that "33 negro students, graduates of Avery Institute, have applied to the College of Charleston for admission." Once the matter became public, editorials in the *News and Courier* and the *Evening Post* advocated a return to private control as a way of preventing black students from entering the college. In the late eighteenth and early nineteenth centuries, the college had operated as a private institution, before becoming the first municipal college in the United States in 1837. "If the courts decree that negroes have a right to admission to the College of Charleston because it is, in part, supported by tax revenues," William Watts Ball argued, "the alternative will be for the college to surrender its municipal charter and become again a privately controlled institution." Ball believed that "the application of graduates of Avery Institute is designed to induce the city of Charleston to make annual appropriation from the tax revenue for Avery's support," part of what he called "an aggressive campaign to obtain public money for [African American] schools and colleges." Ball urged educational authorities to resist this demand.[11]

In fact, African Americans were waging more than one campaign, and the publicity surrounding the students' applications brought to the surface contending visions of African American educational advancement and sparked debates about whether blacks should seek access to the College of Charleston or try to obtain public support for a college at Avery. In a letter to the AMA's Ruth Morton, Avery's acting principal, Florence Clyde, wrote that while "some people" supported the desegregation campaign, the "business and professional men who have contact (with the powers that be)" believed it was "the wrong time to get those people against the school." Encouraged by *News and Courier* editorials and endorsements from the mayor, the president of the chamber of commerce, and the superintendent of schools, many wealthy whites made contributions to Avery's most recent fund-raising campaign. The editors of the *News and Courier* made it clear that continued "aid" and "progress" were contingent on African Americans accepting "the separation of the races as a fundamental condition on which white southerners are unalterably determined." Like Clyde and the business and professional men, Morton worried that the desegregation campaign "may rob Avery of some support from public funds which the school had hoped to secure."[12]

Indeed, the city's African American elite was collaborating with whites on a plan to create a college at Avery. By providing an enduring example of what blacks could accomplish in their own institutions, Avery exerted a powerful influence on the educational aspirations of Charleston's black leadership. Convinced that authorities would not admit African Americans to the College of Charleston, black leaders wanted to pursue a strategy of separate development and secure public support for a parallel system of higher education in the city that would serve the growing numbers of black students who sought more advanced training. As teachers, students, and returning World War II veterans demanded more educational opportunity, Charleston's black elite rallied around a plan developed by John A. McFall. McFall wanted Avery to maintain its elementary and secondary programs but also develop a publicly financed teachers' college that offered a B.A.[13]

Born in Charleston in 1878, the light-skinned McFall was one of the African American businessmen who led Avery and the city's black community through the middle decades of the twentieth century. Educated at Avery and the College of Pharmacy in Philadelphia, McFall operated a drugstore, directed the Charleston Mutual Savings Bank, and served on the boards of the Cannon Street Hospital and Avery. As a member of Avery's administrative council, McFall was aware of the AMA's intentions to close the school, but he believed that the school's 1926 charter permitted Avery's "extension into that of a college." Deeply committed to an institution that had schooled most of the city's professionals, McFall hoped that Avery could extend its record of excellence and achievement to the college level. There was considerable support in the city's black community for a separate college. "Many Negroes do not want to attend the College of Charleston," wrote Ethelyn Parker, a leader of the local chapter of the National Council of Negro Women. "But [we] do need a college in Charleston for Negroes." Editorials in the local press reinforced McFall's conviction that collaboration rather than confrontation would persuade whites to publicly fund a college at Avery.[14]

As divided as black Charlestonians were over how to secure access to higher education, the students' applications and the threat of litigation almost certainly increased white support for McFall's plan. Students applied to the College of Charleston three months after Judge J. Waties Waring ordered the Charleston school board to eliminate separate and unequal salary schedules for white and black teachers. Concerns about court intervention grew when officials learned that the college's 1837 charter did not limit admission to whites or explicitly bar blacks. Moreover, if Wrighten took the college to court, under the Supreme Court's *Gaines* ruling, authorities would have three choices: admit black applicants, close the college, or establish a separate college for blacks in Charleston.

McFall's plan offered an opportunity for educational and political leaders to pursue the third alternative.[15]

In October 1945, less than a week before the board was scheduled to discuss the students' applications, Paul Macmillan, a local judge who was chairman of the college's board of trustees, wrote McFall, informing him that "we have been considering the Avery proposition. Many substantial citizens here have agreed that Avery should get the support that is needed." Macmillan told McFall, who was in Nashville at the time, that he would speak to the legislative leaders "at once," and urged McFall to provide state senator O. T. Wallace and state representative Lionel K. Legge with a detailed proposal for a college at Avery. Denying that there was a connection between this support and the applications of black students for admission to the College of Charleston, Macmillan wrote that "it is well to remember that you spoke to me about the needs of Avery before the college received any letters from the Avery students. It would be unfortunate if our present efforts for Avery were defeated by the present situation."[16]

Accustomed to collaborating with whites rather than confronting them, McFall tried to distance the city's white elite from the students' activism. Privately, McFall acknowledged that the students' applications "may perhaps rebound in good for Avery, from [Macmillan's] letter I surmise that some action may be forthcoming." There is no evidence, however, that McFall considered the possibility of using litigation to force whites to fund a college at Avery. In his response to the board chairman McFall made it clear that local black leaders did not support desegregation. After agreeing to provide Macmillan with a statement of the costs involved in supporting Avery, McFall wrote that "no other group of Negroes, other than those affiliated with him, contributed to or backed the movement." Calling the desegregation campaign "a mere youth movement ideal," a product of Wrighten's "exaggerated ego," McFall reported that the adult branch of the Charleston NAACP was "entirely without knowledge of the movement." According to McFall, the applications threatened "to destroy the good relationships between the races in Charleston and may impede the education and advancement of youth there." Worried that students might take some "precipitate action," Avery administrators suspended the NAACP youth chapter's activities at the school. "It is reliably reported," state NAACP president James Hinton told the national office, that Avery's administration "will not permit any further activities of the NAACP in or around the school."[17]

As McFall distanced the city's black elite from the desegregation campaign, Wrighten turned to the NAACP's national office for help. Hoping that he might secure assistance from the NAACP's legal staff, Wrighten informed NAACP youth secretary Ruby Hurley that black students had applied "for admission to the College of Charleston." As news of the desegregation campaign in Charleston reached the national office, Houston and Marshall struggled to keep the NAACP's desegregation campaign in higher education alive. The war complicated the campaign. When the NAACP tried to secure Lucille Black's admission to the University of Missouri's journalism school, officials complied with *Gaines* by closing the program in 1942, citing reduced wartime enrollment. By the end of the war Marshall had become "more than worried" about the campaign in higher education, but Wrighten presented a case that the NAACP was unwilling to pursue. The NAACP did not successfully challenge the exclusion of African Americans from southern municipal colleges until the early 1950s, and African Americans in Charleston, Savannah, Jacksonville, Memphis, Atlanta, and elsewhere were excluded from municipal colleges that helped a generation of whites obtain a college education and advance socially and economically.[18]

Without the support of the city's black elite or the NAACP's legal staff Wrighten was forced to end his campaign to desegregate the college. "I had hoped," Wrighten recalled, "that if we were rejected, the local NAACP would back us up, and file suit against the college. Instead, we were told that we were hurting Avery Institute and race relations in Charleston." Worried that Wrighten's attempts to gain admission to the college threatened McFall's plan, local NAACP leaders Robert Morrison and J. W. Brawley pressured Wrighten to drop the effort. "[They] said the time was not ripe for such a move," Wrighten recalled. "I argued that we should go ahead, that every step of Negro progress had been made in the face of such arguments, but I couldn't convince them." Support for McFall's plan never materialized, but Avery did become part of the public-school system in 1947. Under the terms of an agreement between the AMA and the Charleston school board, the board leased the building from the AMA and provided financial support for Avery, which continued to offer elementary and college-preparatory training.[19]

While Charleston's accommodationist black elite and the NAACP were unwilling to challenge the exclusion of African Americans from the city's institutions of higher education, Avery and Burke students continued to press for access to the College of Charleston. However, educational authorities responded by securing a new charter that insulated the college from legal attack. In 1948, worried that the college would be in a "predicament" if African Americans challenged the trustees in federal court, the college's attorney, H. L. Erckmann, urged the board to privatize the institution. In a letter to Macmillan, Erckmann wrote that "we would certainly be in a very strong position if title to this property were placed again in the Trustees of the College of Charleston." Presaging a privatization strategy that was used to forestall desegregation in the 1960s, the college obtained a new private charter after Avery and Burke students applied for admission to the college in 1949. In March of that year the city council transferred ownership of the college from the city to the college's board of trustees, and the legislature granted the college a new private charter. The following year, Charleston County officials also began funding ten "Negro scholarships" for pupils "who are not able financially to attend college." Advantaged blacks continued to send their children to private colleges and universities, but most African American high-school graduates in Charleston were forced to follow John Wrighten to South Carolina State in Orangeburg, the only public institution in the state that offered African Americans an opportunity for advanced study.[20]

What defined State College while Wrighten was an undergraduate between 1943 and 1947 was overcrowding. Located in the small town of Orangeburg, approximately halfway between Charleston and Columbia, South Carolina Normal, Industrial, Agricultural, and Mechanical College was established by the Tillmanite constitutional convention of 1895 and opened its doors to students in September 1896. Because of meager facilities, the college *Bulletin* noted, "students sat on logs—like the Mark Hopkins ideal college hewn from the campus wilderness." Benjamin Mays, who graduated from State's high-school department in 1911 and went on to become the president of Morehouse College and one of Martin Luther King Jr.'s mentors, wrote that "State College was not designed to prepare Negroes for literary and professional careers. Negroes were to be prepared in agriculture and the trades. Every student had to take a trade whether he liked it or not." As much as State's all-white governing board wanted the college to prepare students in agriculture, the trades, and domestic service, as Kenneth R. Warlick's perceptive history of African American higher education shows, "conformity and conservatism proved difficult to guarantee." During the 1940s rising enrollment, African American activism, and NAACP litigation forced the legislature to increase funding, fueling the development of an institution that—like Society Corner, Avery, and Burke—allowed African Americans to accomplish more than whites intended.[21]

"The progress of Negro education in South Carolina must be measured by the State College," the school's 1942 *Bulletin* asserted. During the early decades of the twentieth century, however, progress was slowed by a lack of facilities and the accumulated disadvantages that students brought from their families and overcrowded schools. Because of a lack of educational opportunity, many of the students who attended State enrolled in the secondary program that existed until 1933. Overshadowed by more prestigious private colleges in South Carolina —Claflin, Allen, Benedict, and Morris—State almost closed in the early 1930s, when the legislature slashed funding. Each fiscal year, wrote Henry H. Lesesne in his history of higher education in South Carolina, "the legislature individually debated and passed the annual budgets for the six publicly-supported institutions." This system benefited "those institutions with well-connected supporters and popular persuasive presidents" and left State with meager annual appropriations. When Wrighten enrolled in 1943, the legislature appropriated $1.1 million for five white colleges and universities, eleven times the $100,000 that was allocated for State.[22]

South Carolina's system of financing higher education required that State's president, Miller F. Whittaker, use circumspection and guile to secure funds that improved State. Reared on the State campus, where his father was a professor, Whittaker attended the college. After earning a master's degree in architecture from Kansas State, he became the only licensed African American architect in South Carolina. Appointed president in 1932, Whittaker found ways of manipulating white interest to black advantage. He secured grants from the General Education Board and the Public Works Administration, and, meeting with the college's governing board in the tailor shop, used these commitments to prod the board and the legislature into appropriating funds that financed the construction of a gym, a cafeteria, a men's dormitory, and a library during the 1930s.[23]

At State—as at Society Corner, Burke, and Avery—NYA grants helped hundreds of students pursue their education. "Desperate for work and eager to learn," wrote William C. Hine, State students "besieged Whittaker with requests for jobs. 'I am one of your College students in the freshman class,' one student wrote in 1934, 'but my father informs me that he is not going to be able to keep me in college unless I can get some work to help him pay my expenses.'" As growing numbers of high-school graduates sought admission, Whittaker eliminated the secondary program in 1933 and upgraded the curriculum. In 1941 State secured a place on the Southern Association of Secondary Schools and Colleges list of Class A Negro Colleges. Even so, students and faculty struggled against powerful obstacles. The 1942 *National Survey of Higher Education of Negroes* reported that State, like other black land-grant institutions, was "below par in practically every area of educational services—in faculty competence, curriculum and instruction, administration, and financial support."[24]

The African American students who flooded State's campus in the 1940s highlighted limitations that were intended to discourage blacks from obtaining a college education. During the 1930s and early 1940s, the number of black students who graduated from high school in the state and the region tripled, and John Wrighten was one of the increasing numbers of high-school graduates who enrolled at State. After educational authorities established a new salary and certification system, teachers flocked to State, mostly during the summer, enrolling in classes to improve their qualifications and raise their salaries. By the middle of the 1940s high-school graduates and teachers were joined by World War II veterans. Wrighten was among the first wave of veterans who used GI Bill benefits to pay for tuition, fees, books, and living expenses. "Nothing in the history of education can compare with the impact of the G.I. Bill of Rights," Whittaker wrote in 1945, when five hundred veterans enrolled at State. "The fall session began with the greatest influx ever experienced." Enrollment at State rose from 906 in 1933 to more than 2,400 in 1945, part of a broader regional trend in which the number of black students enrolled in college rose from 15,000 in 1933 to 44,000 by 1945.[25]

All of South Carolina's colleges were overcrowded after World War II, but this problem was especially acute at State. Total black college enrollment remained well below that of whites, but the rate at which black enrollment in the South grew in the 1940s was three times that of whites. In South Carolina whites had access to five publicly supported institutions of higher education, while State College was supposed to serve all the state's eight hundred thousand African American residents, four hundred thousand of whom were of school age, in facilities that were designed to accommodate eight hundred students. Rising enrollment strained the limits of an institution that State College history professor Lewis K. McMillan called "an excuse for public higher education for South Carolina Negroes." When educational experts from Vanderbilt University surveyed South Carolina's system of public higher education in 1945, they found that State College's physical plant was "totally inadequate to provide all the necessary facilities for the higher education of Negro youth in the state." In 1946 college officials turned away eight hundred applicants, including five hundred veterans, because of a lack of facilities.[26]

Again and again, Whittaker urged greater funding. "The enrollment has outgrown the general plant," he told the legislature. "We need more room, more facilities, more equipment, more classroom space, more office space, more laboratory space, and more dormitory space if the college is to meet the needs of the state." The most acute need was dormitory space. Because of a lack of campus housing, almost one-half of the student body boarded in private residences in the city, and those who did live on campus were crammed three to five to a room, in facilities that McMillan called "slum like." In 1946 Whittaker told the legislature that "many students who desired to attend the college enrolled elsewhere," many in one of South Carolina's four private black colleges.[27]

Whittaker informed the legislature that "the constant increase in enrollment makes mandatory some increase in personnel," but enrollment far outpaced the legislature's willingness to increase funding. At State, as at other African American land-grant colleges, the faculty was overworked and underpaid. Because students were required to complete twenty-four hours in English to graduate, overcrowding was especially acute in the English Department, where classes were so large that they were held in assembly rooms and agricultural buildings. When Wrighten enrolled at State, none of the college's sixty-five faculty members held a Ph.D. and only one-third possessed a master's degree. "While great progress has been made in recent years in improving the education of the [black] faculty members," the National Survey found, "their training, on the whole, is still at a very low level." Because no state-supported institution in the South offered a doctorate, only 128 African Americans held a Ph.D. in the United States in 1943.[28]

Beyond the overcrowded facilities and the overworked faculty, students had limited access to library and reference materials. One State College senior told the Vanderbilt survey staff that she "had no opportunity to know what a library was until her entrance into the college." The governing board and the legislature remained far more receptive to requests for additional funding for State's agricultural and vocational programs than for books and library space. After visiting the college in March 1945, a legislative committee wrote that "we were especially impressed by the fact that the young people [at the college] are being trained in fundamental labor—shoemaking, tailoring, [and] work on motor vehicles." It wasn't until the General Education Board provided a $40,000 grant that the legislature appropriated funds for a modern library. Even then, overcrowding forced administrators to occupy one floor of the building, limiting seating capacity to two hundred. While Whittaker reminded the board that "a good college needs a good library," books remained "scarce." In 1944 State's library held thirty-three hundred volumes, compared to the almost one hundred thousand in the state's five white colleges.[29]

Most of the students who enrolled at State came from a segregated society that the Vanderbilt survey called "feudal." In 1939 African American per capita income in South Carolina was $261, and the median educational attainment of African American adults was 3.9 years. The limitations of the college's physical plant combined with family-background characteristics to restrict the educational advancement of students at the college. Blacks who attended college were, compared to other African Americans, a relatively privileged group, but the *National Survey* reported that the "material home environment of the typical Negro college student has not been as adequate as that of the typical white college student." State's faculty complained that inadequate funding of primary and secondary schools limited what students at the college could accomplish, and most African American land-grant students, the *National Survey* showed, did not "overcome this initial handicap during four years of college work." A 1939 study of 180 first-year students at State found that the average student read at the ninth-grade level.[30]

Still, State College, like Society Corner and Burke, was a vital avenue of advancement. "The children of the Negro masses flooded the colleges," E. Franklin Frazier wrote in 1947, because "a chance for a college education represented for them the chief means of achieving social and economic mobility." The *National Survey* found that "the Negro college acts as a powerful agency in enabling individuals to raise their social and economic status." As much as State's governing board wanted to train students at the college in "fundamental labor," the vast majority of students who graduated from State entered the teaching profession. Even caustic critics such as McMillan believed that State was "a standing possibility, a constant potentiality of what it could become and ought to become. Individual boys and girls who chance to run upon the right teacher or the right upper-classmen or the right activity," he wrote, "flower forth almost overnight into the kind of Negro youth which black and white South Carolina needs so badly." Wrighten recalled that "my years at Orangeburg were among the happiest in my life."[31]

For all its limitations State College encouraged John Wrighten's aspirations. African American colleges, Sarah E. Gardner has noted, "gave students the intellectual space to develop a critique of white supremacy." Christopher Jencks and David Riesman have noted that "the Negro college campus even at its worst provided a freer and more comfortable environment for Negro intellectuals than any other place in the South." Wrighten's schooling at Avery, his age, and his GI benefits placed him at an advantage at State. "I was considered a superb student," he recalled. Pursuing an interest in the social sciences that Bluford and Brogdon had nurtured at Avery, Wrighten majored in sociology. Like all students, even those who earned degrees in agriculture and home economics, he completed liberal-arts courses. As overcrowded as Wrighten's classes were, Adam Fairclough reminds us that professors "exposed students to all manner of ideas in politics, economics, education, sociology, history, and literature." State College history professor Asa Gordon used "Tobias, first class authors, and pictures of Du Bois and others in his classroom," and encouraged students to challenge discrimination.[32]

Wrighten returned to Charleston almost every weekend to be with his family, but during the week he and other veterans participated in the new, more socially conscious organizations—the NAACP youth chapter and the student newspaper, the *Collegian*. McMillan wrote that "among students there is a large degree of democracy in their personal and group relations. Black and mulatto color cleavage of another day has gone; likewise, the cleavage of poverty and well-being." The *Collegian* provided a forum for students to express their dissatisfaction with the status quo, as faculty adviser Florence Miller encouraged students to write critical editorials. "All around you are reminders of democracy as we practice it, not as we preach it," one student wrote in 1943. "We should study hard in our inadequately segregated schools, but we should try even harder to retain the conviction that the basic principles under which we study are wrong." Another editorial declared that "we are not fighting this war just to win. We are trying to win this war, so that we may establish a new economic, social, and political order."[33]

The outlines of this new order began to emerge during Wrighten's junior year at State College. After African American teachers and the NAACP challenged separate and unequal salary schedules in federal court, the legislature authorized college officials "to establish graduate, law, and medical departments" but appropriated no funds for such work. In 1945 the dean of the University of South Carolina graduate school, W. H. Callcott, visited the Orangeburg campus to explore the feasibility of establishing graduate and professional programs at State. Callcott recommended a "limited program of graduate work" that emphasized instruction in agriculture and home economics. Hoping to limit black access to the professions, Callcott urged the legislature to establish an out-of-state scholarship program that would provide black students with subsidies to pursue professional programs in other states, as long as these programs "were available for white students within the state of South Carolina." After Cleveland M. McQueen, a 1935 State College graduate, applied for admission to the graduate program in education at the University of South Carolina, the legislature made a "special appropriation" of $25,000, and by the fall of 1946, six faculty members began offering graduate courses in biology, education, English, and the social sciences at State College. The "special appropriation" included $5,000 for black students to study medicine outside the state. While the *Gaines* decision struck down Missouri's out-of-state scholarship plan, by the middle of the 1940s these scholarships had become what one African American professor called "the current trend in Negro higher education." South Carolina, like other states, provided $400 for tuition and one round-trip railroad coach fare for African Americans, most of whom studied medicine and pharmacy at Howard, Meharry Medical, or Xavier. Callcott recommended that the college establish only programs "in which there is an existing demand," and no funds were earmarked for legal education.[34]

The state's refusal to appropriate funds for a law school at State "angered" Wrighten. In a 1946 article in the *Collegian*, "Yesterday is Dead, Tomorrow is Unborn, Today is Yours," Wrighten wrote that "social, economic, political, and racial discrimination must be fought." During the spring semester of 1946, he worked with K. W. G. Donma, a Liberian-born instructor of German and animal husbandry, on a letter of application to the University of South Carolina Law School. Praised by college officials for his "unsurpassed friendship, guidance, and encouragement of students," Donma read drafts of an application that Wrighten sent to University of South Carolina Law School dean Samuel L. Prince in June 1946, six months before he earned his bachelor's degree. Wrighten's letter was followed by a second application, from Daniel George Sampson. Both applications were rejected on racial grounds. "This time," Wrighten recalled, "I was determined to fight the case in the courts."[35]

Wrighten was one of hundreds of African American students whose applications for admission to southern universities in the late 1940s revived the NAACP's legal campaign in higher education. When Wrighten earned his degree in 1947, more than eight thousand African American students graduated from college, more than twice as many as in 1938, and eight times as many as in 1927. While African American demand for graduate and professional training rose sharply, because of wartime labor and materials shortages, few buildings were constructed on black college campuses in the South in the early 1940s. A month after Wrighten's graduation, Howard University president Mordecai Johnson told the U.S. House Subcommittee on Appropriations that seventeen southern states appropriated $86 million for white higher education and only $5 million for black colleges. A decade after the Supreme Court's *Gaines* decision declared that the constitutionality of segregation laws "rested wholly on the equality of privileges available to separated groups within a state," African Americans had access to only two accredited medical schools, compared to fifteen for whites; two law schools, as opposed to sixteen for whites; one school of pharmacy, in contrast to fourteen for whites; and no school of engineering, even though whites had access to thirty-six. At federally funded Howard University, the only comprehensive public university that admitted African Americans in the South, officials turned away thousands from the university's graduate and professional schools. In 1947, for example, the Howard Medical School admitted only seventy students from a qualified applicant pool of more than one thousand. By the late 1940s African American aspirations collided with caste constraints as hundreds of black college graduates, many of whom were veterans, sought access to southern universities and fueled NAACP legal challenges. "When [blacks] came back [from the war]," wrote Ralph Abernathy, "they were not willing to settle for Jim Crow life, not for long, not when they knew there was something better."[36]

Wrighten's determination to become a lawyer pushed the NAACP to take legal action. In the summer of 1946 Wrighten forwarded his application to state NAACP president James Hinton, but the filing of a complaint was delayed by the inability of the national office to keep pace with demands for legal assistance. Eager to launch a legal campaign against the state's system of higher education, Hinton told Marshall that "we have a returned Negro veteran who is ready to file suit within South Carolina." Although local NAACP counsel Harold Boulware did "everything requested of him," nothing had happened by late November, and Hinton asked Marshall for "some action on our graduate and professional case." Referring to NAACP-sponsored suits in Oklahoma and Texas, Hinton complained that "we notice that other states are getting action, but we are rebuffed each time." Persistent pressure from Hinton led the NAACP to file a complaint on Wrighten's behalf in January 1947. As Wrighten waited for the case to come to trial, he taught Problems of Democracy at Avery Institute. He may have instructed some of the students who applied for admission to the College of Charleston in 1949.[37]

Before the case came to trial, the NAACP attempted to change its legal strategy in the Wrighten case. Wrighten's complaint asserted that the Supreme Court's *Gaines* ruling "did not go far enough." However, the complaint did not directly challenge state constitutional provisions requiring segregation in educational institutions. At a pretrial hearing, Waring recalled, the parties agreed that the issue to be examined was "whether the plaintiff is given law school facilities by the state comparable with those afforded white students." Developments in higher education cases in Oklahoma and Texas, where the NAACP challenged the exclusion of blacks from state-supported law schools, pushed Marshall and his colleagues beyond arguments designed to equalize educational opportunity and toward a direct attack on segregation. Marshall remained uneasy about the prospects of challenging segregation directly, but in April 1947, he told NAACP legal adviser William Hastie that "whether we want it or not, we are now faced with the prospect of going into the question of segregation as such. We should do so because even if we don't take the [Texas] case far, we at least should experiment on the type of evidence we may be able to produce on this question." Having made the decision to present evidence showing that there could be no separate equality in African American law schools in Oklahoma and Texas, the NAACP also wanted to "experiment" in Wrighten's case. In May 1947 NAACP attorney Robert Carter wrote Waring, asking if he could change the terms of the pretrial agreement and "go into the question of the sufficiency of any segregated facility to meet the requirements of the equal protection clause of the 14th Amendment." Waring rejected Carter's request, telling him that the case would be tried "as heretofore stated."[38]

Constrained by the pretrial agreement, the NAACP did not directly challenge segregation at the trial in June 1947. David W. Robinson defended the state of South Carolina. He convinced Waring that Wrighten was not entitled to immediate admission to the University of South Carolina Law School. Like his rulings in the salary-equalization cases, Waring's July 1947 decision in *Wrighten v. Board of Trustees* is notable for the deference it showed to state educational authorities. Citing rulings in Missouri and Tennessee, Waring held that the issue in the case was whether state officials should be given "a reasonable opportunity to provide legal educational facilities substantially equivalent and equal to that of the university at some other institution within the state." In February, before the case came to trial, the legislature appropriated $60,000 for graduate and legal training, instructing college officials to use as much of these funds "as is necessary to maintain and operate a law school during the coming fiscal year." Waring wrote that "due faith and deference must be given to the assurances of responsible state officials that the law school will be in active operation on complete parity with the University Law School." Citing *Gaines*, Waring ruled that the "only restriction is that equal facilities must be given to white and colored." If the state provides a legal education "on substantial parity in all respects with the services furnished at the University Law School," he concluded, "then the demands of the plaintiffs will be adequately satisfied." Waring did warn educational authorities that if they did not "completely and fully" comply with his order, "then the plaintiff will be entitled to entrance at the Law School of the University."[39]

In South Carolina, as elsewhere, the construction of separate law and professional schools for African Americans created dilemmas and sparked debates about whether African American educators should support these institutions and whether black students should enroll in them. In Alabama, Tuskegee Institute president Fred Patterson recalled being "loudly accused of promoting segregation" when he created the only veterinary school that admitted blacks in the South in 1944. Whittaker expressed concerns about graduate work being "imposed on the college," but he believed that the law school would enhance the college's prestige and increase desperately needed funding. Maceo Nance, who was an undergraduate at State in 1947, recalled that "Wrighten's suit was exciting to us." Industrial-education administrator Harold Crawford supported the law school because he believed it would allow the college to train "some capable lawyers." In 1940 there were eleven hundred white and five black lawyers in South Carolina.[40]

Influenced by the national office's opposition to the extension of segregation, NAACP activists in South Carolina called the new law and graduate programs at State "an asinine scheme." State NAACP secretary Modjeska Simkins wrote that "the disrespect and scorn which thousands of Negroes in the Palmetto State hold for most of the legislators can be surpassed only by the utter contempt many of these same persons hold for the administrative officials of the so-called Graduate School at State A and M College at Orangeburg." Simkins suggested that students should not enroll. "The only persons who could become even more objects of derision would be the persons who, knowing the score, deliberately walk into these chump courses." Pressured by the national office, Hinton condemned "the make shift law school in Orangeburg" at the annual NAACP State Conference meeting in 1947.[41]

As State College administrators began recruiting faculty to teach in the new law school, Marshall tried to dissuade them. In July 1947 Frank A. DeCosta, the former Avery principal whom Whittaker hired to be dean of State's graduate school, wrote Marshall asking if he knew of anyone who was qualified to be dean of the new law school. Marshall's reply made it clear that he opposed the establishment of a law school at State College: "I do not know of anyone who is qualified and who would be interested in the job." While Marshall acknowledged that there was a "horrible shortage of qualified Negro law school professors," he wrote that "I don't believe that a Negro lawyer should be interested in being dean of a Jim Crow law school. I, for one, am opposed to the extension of segregation, and the setting up of these small law schools can only be labeled as extensions of segregation." In Marshall's eyes the new law school at State—like those in Missouri, North Carolina, and Texas—would become a "monument to the perpetuation of segregation."[42]

Like other land-grant-college presidents, Whittaker was more interested in creating educational opportunities than in the NAACP's legal agenda. Within weeks of Waring's ruling, Whittaker hired Benner C. Turner as dean of the law school. The son of an affluent Columbus, Georgia, physician, Turner graduated magna cum laude from Phillips Andover and earned his bachelor's and law degrees from Harvard. After practicing law in Philadelphia, he served as a law professor at North Carolina College for Negroes between 1943 and 1947. C. F. Brooks, the vice chairman of the governing board at State College, praised Turner's appointment, telling Whittaker, "I was pleased that an outstanding man has been secured [as dean]. We want nothing less than a man of ability and character and with a correct understanding of the American way of life—especially here in South Carolina." In September 1947 State College began offering classes on property, torts, and criminal law. The program met the requirements of Waring's order in that it was a "going concern," but it was hardly equal to the University of South Carolina Law School. To begin with, the law program at State did not have a separate building or library. It was housed in one classroom in the college's already overcrowded administration building. Books had been ordered, but few had been received. By the fall Leo Kerford and Cassandra Maxwell had been hired to teach, but neither had experience in the classroom. Nonetheless, DeCosta noted that there were more students enrolled in the law school during the 1947–1948 academic year than there were black lawyers in the state of South Carolina.[43]

Unable to persuade Whittaker or DeCosta, the NAACP turned to Wrighten and tried to convince him not to enroll. During the summer of 1947, Wrighten informed Hinton that he was "making plans" to attend the law school. In July Wrighten applied, and he received an acceptance letter from Turner in August. When Marshall and Carter learned of his plans, they pressured him to withdraw his application. The NAACP wanted Wrighten to testify that he had not enrolled at State because it was not equal to the University of South Carolina Law School. (In Texas, Heman Sweatt's refusal to enroll in a separate law school that the legislature funded in response to his application to the University of Texas bolstered the NAACP's contention that there could be no separate equality.) In August 1947 a confused Wrighten wrote Robert Carter: "The case is won, but what should I do? I was told to enter the law school at S.C. State College, and I was told not to enter because it is not equal to that of the University of S.C. Please give me some advice along these lines." After meeting with Marshall, Wrighten withdrew his application, telling Whittaker, "I had intended to enter the law school, but my attorney found some other angles that need to be settled before I enter."[44]

NAACP leaders in Charleston had a different agenda, and in 1947, as in 1944, Wrighten became entangled in it. Charleston's black elite remained optimistic about the possibility that Avery could become a publicly supported college. In June 1947 John McCray, an Avery graduate, told school officials, "we understand that the city of Charleston has assumed operation of Avery Institute and may develop it into a four-year college for negroes." There was certainly a demand for a black college. When educational authorities began funding professional development courses in the city in 1947, hundreds of black teachers enrolled. Citing this demand, black leaders pressed educational authorities to establish a branch of State College in Charleston. In a 1947 article in the *Journal of Negro Education*, Frank DeCosta pointed to the need for a college in the city. Seeing segregation as an advance over exclusion, local NAACP leaders told Wrighten that Marshall was "wrong to advise me to do that [withdraw my application]," and that if he did not enroll "ill feeling might develop among whites." Such sentiments were common among southern black leaders. The NAACP's Herbert Hill recalled that by the late 1940s, "real progress toward equalization was beginning to be made." When he argued that "the new equal facilities ought to be shutdown" because they were segregated, many NAACP branch leaders in the South were skeptical. "You mean that you want us to oppose all this," they wondered. In South Carolina, as elsewhere, many black leaders saw separate professional programs as an advance over exclusion.[45]

Divergent visions of African American advancement doomed Wrighten's appeal. When Wrighten told Marshall that NAACP leaders in Charleston were "indifferent toward his opinion," the NAACP attorney exploded, threatening to bring charges against those who were "speaking in favor of segregation" and "supporting Jim Crow education." Feeling used and mistreated, Wrighten asked Hinton to remove his name from the case. "You see," Wrighten wrote in October 1947, "I stuck my neck out, and it got cut off." Having spent all his savings and "borrowed everything he could from his friends," Wrighten worried about how he was going to support his family. "Every time I go to get a job with a white person, and they find out that I am John H. Wrighten nothing doing." Marshall also wanted to drop the case, and in March 1948 he asked Boulware to withdraw the motion for further relief. "The main reason," he wrote, "is that Wrighten has demonstrated that he is not the type of reliable plaintiff necessary to proceed further in this type of case." Boulware persuaded both to pursue the appeal, but by the time Waring heard the NAACP's motions in June 1948, the legislature had appropriated $200,000 for a law-school building and $30,000 for library acquisitions. "The legislature in South Carolina," Waring recalled, "is very nimble when it comes to racial questions." Waring found it "almost impossible to intellectually compare" State's law school to the program in legal education at the University of South Carolina, but he ruled that the state had met the requirements of his original order and the *Gaines* ruling. "They set up a Jim Crow dump in South Carolina, and called it a law school," a disgusted Marshall wrote, "so I think we are right back in Texas or will be shortly."[46]

A court decision invalidating the constitutionality of separate graduate and professional programs eluded the NAACP in South Carolina, but local activism and litigation did end the exclusion of African Americans from state-supported legal education. For the first time since Reconstruction, the state of South Carolina supported the legal training of African Americans. NAACP-sponsored litigation in Arkansas, Kentucky, and Oklahoma forced university officials to admit black students in 1947 and 1948, but during the 1940s the NAACP won no major victories in higher education. In most southern states there was considerably more separate educational development than desegregation, as educational authorities constructed new buildings and facilities in response to African American demands for graduate and professional training. By 1949 separate law schools existed or were under construction in Missouri, North Carolina, Texas, Louisiana, Florida, and South Carolina. As African Americans continued to apply to the University of South Carolina and as the NAACP continued to litigate, the South Carolina legislature sharply increased funding for State College. In addition to the $200,000 capital appropriation for a new professional-school building, funding for graduate and professional education rose from $30,000 in 1946 to $150,000 in 1949. The legislature increased the college's operating budget from $100,000 in 1943 to almost $600,000 in 1949. As new buildings embedded segregation ever more deeply in a parallel system of state-supported higher education, students, professors, and administrators at State used the law school to prepare a generation of African American attorneys who played key roles in school and university desegregation cases in South Carolina during the 1950s and 1960s.[47]

Created to maintain segregation, South Carolina State Law School trained students who played a central role in dismantling it. One of these students was John Wrighten, who enrolled in State's Law School in 1949. "I entered [the law school]," recalled Wrighten, "because the only way we could break down segregation and discrimination was to have black lawyers." By the time Wrighten entered the program in the fall of 1949, the law and graduate-school building, Moss Hall, the first to be completed on the State campus after World War II, was nearly complete. Designed to accommodate seventy-five students, it included offices on the first floor and classrooms, a practice courtroom, and a library on the second. During Wrighten's first year, many of the sixteen law students were veterans, whom DeCosta described as "mature and serious minded." Enrollment was limited by relatively high tuition, $564 a year, and a demanding schedule of courses that left "little time for outside employment." Matthew J. Perry, who graduated in 1951, recalled that "I had dedicated professors who taught, I think, very well. Some were very good teachers." Ernest A. Finney, who attended the law school in the late 1940s, recalled that "civil rights cases were topics of daily discussion." The Law Club sponsored speeches by noted civil rights lawyers.[48]

Like other African American law schools in the South, State's program was accredited by the American Bar Association (ABA). "The curriculum and methods of instruction," the catalog noted, "accord with practices generally employed by law schools today." Professors used the case method in required courses on contracts, torts, property, and constitutional and labor law. Examinations were given in all courses, and students had to maintain a C average to remain in school. Following a visit to State in November 1949, ABA examiner John G. Hervey told Dean Turner, "I was very favorably impressed on my visit to your campus." After a follow-up visit, the law school was accredited by the ABA in 1950. Political and educational authorities were, of course, relieved. David W. Robinson told Turner, "you and your associates deserve great credit for establishing a fine law school in so short a period of time."[49]

As dedicated as Wrighten's professors were and as adequate as the facilities became, State was simply not comparable to the law school at the University of South Carolina. In 1950, in the NAACP's first victory before the Supreme Court since 1938, the Court ruled that the separate African American law school at Texas Southern University was not equal to the University of Texas. There were limits to how much students could learn "in isolation from individuals and institutions with which the law interacts," Chief Justice Frederick Moore Vinson wrote in *Sweatt v. Painter.* In South Carolina these limits had less to do with faculty and facilities than with the inability of students at State to interact with students, professors, and alumni of the university's law school in the state capital in Columbia. "Few students and no one who has practiced law would choose to study in an academic vacuum, removed from the interplay of ideas and the exchange of views with which the law is concerned," the Court held in *Sweatt.* Attending State deprived African Americans of opportunities to interact with current and future members of South Carolina's political and legal establishment. In 1950 many judges and politicians in the state—including four of six representatives in Congress, one U.S. senator, 44 of 124 state representatives, 20 of 46 state senators, 3 of 5 state supreme-court justices, and 9 of 14 circuit-court judges—had earned law degrees from the law school at the University of South Carolina. These leaders included shrewd politicians and lawyers who understood the limits of the separate law program at State College and exploited them.[50]

Once it became illegal to deny African Americans access to a legal education, the state's legal and political establishment, led by David W. Robinson, turned to other means to restrict black access to the practice of law. When officials in North Carolina and Missouri established separate law schools for African Americans in response to the *Gaines* decision, the South Carolina Bar Association began a campaign to revoke South Carolina's diploma privilege. Established in New York in 1855, the diploma privilege ensured graduates of law schools automatic admission to the bar. Although the American Bar Association waged a long campaign to limit the access of "socially undesirable elements" (mostly Jews and blacks) by replacing the diploma privilege with written examinations, in 1947 the privilege still existed in several southern states including Alabama, Arkansas, Florida, Louisiana, Mississippi, South Carolina, and West Virginia. The number of states permitting students to gain admission through the diploma privilege fell steadily during the twentieth century from nineteen in 1915 to three in 1972, but in South Carolina, Alabama, Georgia, and Florida the elimination of the diploma privilege and the introduction of new admission requirements to state-supported law schools were a clear and direct response to African American demands for access to state-supported legal training and admission to the bar.[51]

In 1948 Robinson convinced the legislature to revoke the state's diploma privilege. A newspaper article on how this privilege operated illustrates the interaction among the law school, the legislature, and the South Carolina courts. In what the *Columbia State* called "a double ceremony" in the Supreme Court Room at the State House, graduates received their diplomas from University president Norman M. Smith, were "presented to the court" by law-school dean Samuel L. Prince, "duly sworn in" as members of the court by the clerk, and addressed by Associate Justice E. Laden Fishburne. Faced with the prospect of twenty-three African American law-school students who were enrolled at State in 1948 joining the "double ceremony" at the State House, the legislature repealed the diploma privilege in April 1948 and began requiring that all law-school graduates pass a written bar examination before they were allowed to practice law in South Carolina. The legislator who introduced the bill that made passing the bar exam compulsory for all prospective lawyers stated that the purpose of the bill was to "bar Negroes and some undesirable whites."[52]

Like black teachers, African Americans who were enrolled in the State College law program resented these new, more rational restrictions, which were intended to limit African American access to the legal profession. Matthew J. Perry, who graduated from State in 1951, recalled that "they changed the rules and announced that hereafter everybody would have to take the exam. It was the first time everyone had to take the bar exam." Wrighten thought the new bar exam requirement was an attempt to "punish" African Americans "for having forced the state to build a law school." After Wrighten graduated in June 1952, he had trouble passing the exam. By then only one of the three State law-school graduates who had taken the exam had passed, and University of South Carolina Law School dean Samuel J. Prince worried that "this will probably mean [law] suits against the university on the ground that the work done at Orangeburg is not equal to that at the University," a concern shared by Turner and South Carolina governor James F. Byrnes. When Wrighten failed his third attempt, he wrote Prince, declaring that the legal education he received at State was not equal to that provided by the University and announcing that he would "seek admission to the University law school to get the education necessary to pass the bar exam." Although state law permitted candidates three opportunities to pass the exam, Wrighten was granted an exemption, probably to avoid litigation. On his fourth attempt he passed, and he was admitted to the bar in November 1953. Between 1950 and 1973 only 15 percent of the African American law candidates passed the bar exam in South Carolina, compared to 90 percent of the whites.[53]

The bar exam limited black access but did not restrict it completely. State's law school, like other African American law programs in the South, trained a generation of African American attorneys who made important contributions to the African American struggle for educational equality and access. NAACP attorney Jack Greenberg, who litigated several cases in the state in the 1950s and 1960s, wrote that "we could have done nothing without lawyers on the front line in the South." Throughout the 1950s and 1960s most African American lawyers in South Carolina, as in other states in the region, received their training at separate law schools. "Had it not been for that law school," Wrighten argued, "blacks would not have been able to get a legal education." As separate and unequal as that education was, State College's law school trained African American lawyers John H. Wrighten, Matthew J. Perry, Ernest A. Finney, Zack E. Townsend, W. Newton Pough, and others who challenged segregation, discrimination, and inequality in public education. South Carolina statutes required that parties to litigation be represented by a member of the state bar, and Greenberg recalled that "black lawyers operating at the local level were essential to civil rights claimants." African American attorneys trained at the State College law school, Perry recalled, "changed the direction of the state."[54]

After he passed the bar exam, Wrighten returned to Charleston, where he began practicing law in January 1954. Serving as legal adviser to the local chapter of the NAACP, he drafted the school-desegregation petition that was submitted to the Charleston school board in July 1955, filed suit to end segregation at beaches on Edisto Island, and arranged for the release of students who staged sit-ins and other direct-action demonstrations in the early 1960s. Matthew J. Perry played a central role in cases that desegregated Clemson College, the

University of South Carolina, and the Charleston public schools. As Greenberg noted, "without southern black lawyers," most of whom were trained at separate law schools, "we could never have accomplished what we did." Much of what these lawyers accomplished depended on the activism of African American students, who staged a wave of school strikes and boycotts that pushed the NAACP to challenge directly the constitutionality of segregation in primary and secondary schools in 1950.[55]

FIVE

Black Schooling and the *Briggs* Decision, 1945–1954

In December 1945 Burke Industrial School students staged a strike to protest severe overcrowding at the school. A year later, high-school students in Lumberton, North Carolina, who felt that it was time for "youth to lead and act," boycotted classes at the "shameful" black high school. In November 1947 students walked out of overcrowded Randolph Colored School in LaGrange, Texas. When educational authorities investigated, student government president James Greene stated "it was a group of high school students, the students held a meeting, the group as a whole started it." In Farmville, Virginia, teachers at R. R. Moton High School taught young people to "think for themselves and criticize," and student council leaders organized a boycott to protest overcrowding. Between 1945 and 1954 African American high-school students organized boycotts and strikes in the Carolinas, Virginia, Kansas, Missouri, Texas, and Washington, D.C. Sharp increases in African American high-school enrollment, severe overcrowding, and glaring disparities between white and black facilities sparked these strikes, but in many cases students were encouraged to act by their teachers and principals.[1]

The wave of student activism that swept through the South in the late 1940s pushed the NAACP to challenge directly state-sanctioned segregation in primary and secondary schools. In the new postwar political climate the disparity between the promise of equality and the practice of discrimination produced protest, as rising African American educational aspirations once again collided with caste constraints. As in earlier campaigns NAACP-sponsored litigation was fueled by a growing demand for schooling, the activism of black students, and the encouragement young people received from teachers and principals. In each of the five cases consolidated under *Brown v. Board of Education* (1954) local—student and teacher—activism preceded legal action. The strikes, boycotts, and protests of the late 1940s—what NAACP attorney Marian Perry called "the courage of the 'little Joes' in the South"—showed cautious NAACP attorneys

that African Americans in the South were ready to challenge the constitutionality of segregation.[2]

The first direct challenge to state-imposed segregation came in South Carolina, where retaliation against students and teachers at Scott's Branch School in
rural Clarendon County united the black community behind a campaign that
began with demands for school-bus transportation but developed into an all-out
attack on state-sponsored segregation in the public schools. The U.S. District
Court's ruling in *Briggs v. Elliott* did not overturn the state's segregation laws, but
it did mandate equalization and led state officials to create a $75 million school-
equalization program. In Charleston, where the *Briggs* case was heard in 1951,
the NAACP's legal challenge and the court's decision emboldened the city's
black elite. After the Charleston school board announced plans to use equalization funds to improve white schools, local NAACP leaders threatened legal
action, forcing the board to construct new facilities to address some of the
inequities that sparked the student-led strike in 1945.[3]

As activism, litigation, and the threat of a Supreme Court decision declaring
state-sanctioned segregation unconstitutional compelled educational authorities
to invest millions in new African American schools, officials retaliated against an
increasingly assertive and insistent black leadership. Foreshadowing the resistance that followed *Brown*, the Charleston school board closed Avery Institute
in 1954. While members of the city's black elite lamented the closing of the
state's oldest black high school, the transfer of students and faculty to a new and
better-equipped facility at Burke accelerated the development of academic and
extracurricular programs. During the late 1950s teachers and administrators at
Burke united students of all classes and colors, and prepared racially and politically conscious student leaders to realize the new educational possibilities created by the *Brown* decision.[4]

The NAACP's campaign against segregation in primary and secondary schools
was fueled by significant increases in African American high-school enrollment.
Poverty remained an important obstacle to black educational advancement, but
by the middle of the 1940s higher incomes allowed more and more black
parents to sustain their children's schooling through the secondary grades. In
Charleston, as elsewhere, a majority of African Americans continued to work in
unskilled jobs, but labor shortages and access to better-paying jobs at military
installations and factories increased black incomes. During the 1940s Charleston's economy grew rapidly, fueled by military spending and population growth.
Between 1940 and 1948 the payroll at the Charleston Naval Shipyard tripled.
Employment in private industry also multiplied. At the West Virginia Pulp and
Paper plant the number of employees grew from four hundred fifty in 1936 to
more than twelve thousand in 1948. The median income of black families in the
city remained one-half that of whites, but the *News and Courier* reported that

"wartime high wages have given Negroes more money than they have ever had." A 1948 survey of the city's public schools reported that "better economic circumstances have permitted more Negro youth to attend school." William Merriweather, who taught math at Burke, recalled that "more kids came to school and more kids stayed in school." The average daily attendance rate of African American students in Charleston rose from 77 percent in 1937 to 83 percent in 1947, approaching the white rate of 85 percent. As parents were able to support more consistent attendance, the number of students who entered high school continued to grow.[5]

For African American adolescents in the South, high school was increasingly the place to realize expectations that soared during the war. Black high schools had long been a key avenue of advancement, the ticket to a better life, and by the late 1940s more and more young people had the resources to realize their aspirations for a secondary education. Educational authorities in Charleston hoped that the incorporation of Avery into the public system in 1948 and the construction of Bonds-Wilson High School in North Charleston and Six-Mile School east of the Cooper River would alleviate overcrowding at Burke. But enrollment at Burke doubled during the 1940s, even as the combined enrollment at new public high schools outside the city approached one thousand students by 1950. Rising enrollment in the Charleston area typified a broader regional trend in which the number of black students enrolled in high school rose by 124 percent in Alabama, 123 percent in Mississippi, 113 percent in Georgia, 69 percent in South Carolina, and 58 percent in Virginia between 1940 and 1952. Led by the most educated, millions of African Americans left the South in the 1940s, but African American secondary enrollment in thirteen southern states rose by 54 percent at the same time that white secondary enrollment fell by 2 percent.[6]

As African American enrollment rose sharply during the 1940s, conditions in black high schools deteriorated. Wartime labor and material shortages put a freeze on construction, and by the end of World War II African American high-school students were crammed into portables, tar-paper shacks, and discarded army barracks. During the war African American leaders in Charleston repeatedly urged the board to enlarge facilities at Burke, but school officials used portable classrooms to house growing enrollment. After visiting Burke in the summer of 1945, one observer wrote that "the simple management, accommodation, and direction of this overwhelming student body [is] beyond the comprehension of those who have not personally observed [it]." In June 1945 Rhett urged the board to consider acquiring "two large buildings which the Army has used as a mess hall." Rhett believed that they "would make fairly good classrooms and a principal's office." While the board decided not to purchase the buildings, officials in Hearne, Texas, obtained a former POW barracks to accommodate black students at Blackshear High School. A local newspaper reported that the discarded buildings were "sawed in half, dragged to the school location and joined together with no apparent regard for beauty or concealing their prison-camp appearance." Students boycotted the structure, remaining out of school for a month in protest.[7]

When building materials and funds became available after 1945, educational authorities in Charleston used them to expand facilities for whites, widening disparities between the white and black high schools. After Charleston voters approved a $1 million school bond in 1948, the board spent almost $700,000 on improvements at the white high schools. However, because whites with school-age children were moving to the suburbs, enrollment at the city's white high schools declined during the 1940s and classroom space was unused, while at Burke, hundreds attended classes in portable buildings that students and teachers derided as "doghouses." The board did construct a $246,000 classroom addition at Burke, but within a year, school superintendent George Rogers, who replaced Rhett in 1946, told the trustees that "all the [new] classroom space [was] occupied."[8]

School officials in Charleston quelled the strike at Burke by suspending strike leaders for several months and launching an investigation of teachers whom they believed encouraged activism, but in other African American schools students and teachers remained out of school for weeks, staging protests that pushed the NAACP to challenge state-sponsored segregation in the South. African American student activism made high schools a key battleground in the struggle for educational equality in the South during the late 1940s, the site of struggles between whites who sought to maintain their supremacy and blacks who challenged it. In Farmville, Virginia, and Clarendon County, South Carolina, African American protests attracted the attention of the NAACP's legal staff and led to litigation challenging state segregation laws. Increasing enrollment and overcrowding sparked protests at R. R. Moton High and Scott's Branch School, but there, as elsewhere, African American educators encouraged student activism.[9]

The student-led strike that we know the most about occurred in Farmville, Virginia, where R. R. Moton High School principal M. Boyd Jones created a progressive educational environment that inspired students to act. A Hampton College graduate who earned his M.A. from Cornell, Jones was influenced by John Dewey's contention that schools could be instruments for the democratization of society. Barbara Johns, the Moton junior who organized the boycott, recalled that "Jones' teaching made it all seem inevitable." Boyd Jones "had the idea," wrote Bob Smith in his history of the boycott, "that the high school had to serve as a training ground for democracy." The president of the local chapter of the NAACP, Reverend L. Francis Griffin, recalled that "Jones's school was the most democratic thing that ever happened around here. He taught them [students] to think for themselves and criticize, and ask questions."[10]

At Moton, as at other black high schools in the South, enrollment rose steadily in the 1940s. By 1950, 477 students were crammed into a building that was designed to accommodate 180. While PTA leaders repeatedly urged the school board to improve Moton, officials claimed that neither money nor materials were available and accommodated students by constructing shacks and covering them with tar paper. By midcentury resentment about conditions at Moton were running deep in Farmville's black community.[11]

The boycott at Moton, like those at other black high schools, was organized by student government leaders. Barbara Johns was deeply involved in Moton's academic and extracurricular programs, as were other strike leaders. She not only excelled in her classes but also participated in the chorus, the drama group, and the student council. One day in the fall of 1950, Johns told her English and music teacher, Inez Davenport, "how sick and tired I was of the inadequate buildings and facilities." When Davenport, who was engaged to Principal Jones, suggested that Johns "do something about it," Johns "decided to use the student council." Like the students in Lumberton, who felt it was time for youth "to lead and act," the student council planned, organized, and carried out a boycott. At an assembly in the spring of 1951 Johns told students "not to accept" conditions at the school and led four hundred students out of the auditorium. As students picketed the school with placards that stated "We're Tired of Tar Paper Shacks; We Want a New School," strike leaders used the Moton High School office phone to call NAACP lawyers Oliver Hill and Spottswood Robinson. When the attorneys met with the students and warned them that they were violating the state's compulsory school-attendance laws, the young people shouted, "the jail is not big enough for all of us." NAACP lawyers remained reluctant to take up the students' cause, but Hill recalled later that "these kids turned out to be so well organized and their morale was so high, we just didn't have the heart to tell 'em to break it up." In May 1951, a month after the boycott began, Jones helped to convince the students to return to school. After they did, Jones told Barbara Johns, "keep up the good work. I am behind you 100 percent, but I must not publicly acknowledge this." After the NAACP filed suit in federal court in May 1951, the school board fired Boyd Jones, one of several teachers and principals who lost their jobs during this wave of student activism.[12]

More than three hundred miles away in rural Clarendon County, South Carolina, reprisals against black activists who pressed for improvements at Scott's Branch School led to the NAACP's first direct attack on state-sanctioned segregation in public education. Located in the heart of the black belt, Clarendon County was one of the poorest counties in South Carolina. Well into the

twentieth century, schooling there followed the rhythms of the county's agricultural economy. "We need the following children of Charlie Weathers to pick cotton," one planter wrote to a school official in 1951. They wanted "us to keep the
schools closed until we can get the cotton picked and sometimes that runs a little late," school superintendent H. B. Betchman recalled. As Richard Kluger
wrote in his riveting account of the Clarendon County case, African Americans
were caught in an "unbreakable cycle of poverty and ignorance breeding more
poverty and a bit less ignorance, generation upon generation." By midcentury
one-third of the county's African American adults remained illiterate. "The black
man in the county had had nothing to look forward to," recalled Billie Fleming,
an NAACP member who operated a funeral home. "Without the schools, there
was no way to break out."[13]

In 1947, encouraged by state NAACP leaders, J. A. De Laine, a local elementary-school principal, organized a campaign to improve Scott's Branch School,
where his son was a high-school sophomore. Like most black teachers in South
Carolina, De Laine attended summer school in the 1940s, enrolling in George
Singleton's Race and Culture course at Allen University in Columbia. In June state
NAACP conference president James Hinton addressed the class, challenging
teachers to find a plaintiff who had the courage to challenge bus-transportation
practices in the state. In rural Clarendon County school officials supported
thirty buses for white pupils but none for blacks. African American parents in
the county raised money to purchase a used bus, and improved transportation
contributed to rising enrollment at Scott's Branch, where the number of students in the secondary program grew from 85 in 1939 to 190 in 1947. In addition to transportation problems "we needed more rooms," one parent recalled.
"One class had to meet in the hall with the teacher sitting in the principal's
office." De Laine convinced Levi Pearson, whose three children—Daisy, James,
and Eloise—attended Scott's Branch, to serve as plaintiff, and in March 1948
Harold Boulware filed suit on their behalf, asking that "transportation be fur-
nished, maintained, and operated out of public funds." Three months later, Pearson's challenge was dismissed because he paid property taxes in one of the
county's districts while his children attended school in another.[14]

Hoping to quell the campaign, local authorities retaliated against teachers
and students. The principal of Scott's Branch, A. M. Anderson, was fired for
encouraging the suit and replaced by an administrator who started what one
parent called a "fire that no water was going to put out." The new principal,
B. F. Benson, absconded with $800 the PTA raised to supplement Scott's Branch's
meager budget and inserted "uncomplimentary remarks" in the transcripts of
seniors. Led by the president of the senior class, Reverdy Wells, eighteen students filed formal charges against Benson, and in June 1949 three hundred black
parents assembled to hear students present their complaints against Benson.

"This was the psychological meeting which conditioned the minds of the mass of parents. Before the class of 1949 started something," De Laine recalled; few black parents in the county were willing to support what Thurgood Marshall called "a major test case." At a meeting in Columbia Marshall told De Laine that the association would sponsor litigation seeking complete equalization of school facilities if twenty parents would sign a complaint. Encouraged by teachers, who were among the most active supporters of litigation, more than one hundred students, parents, and teachers did so. "We figured anything to better the children's condition was worthwhile," recalled Harry Briggs, a World War II veteran whose name was at the top of the petition. Like many teachers and principals in the county, including De Laine, Briggs was immediately dismissed from his job at a local gas station.[15]

The activism of Barbara Johns, the encouragement of Boyd Jones, the leadership of J. A. De Laine, and the courage of parents in Clarendon County played an important role in pushing the NAACP to challenge directly southern segregation laws. In 1948 the NAACP board of directors endorsed a resolution declaring that the association would not participate "in any case which has as its direct purpose the establishment of segregated public facilities." Members of the legal staff, however, wondered if southern African Americans would support the new policy. Spottswood Robinson, for example, did not think that the association could "get many parents willing to make a test of the segregation laws of their community." Robinson was mistaken. Marshall learned that African American students, teachers, and parents were not only ready to challenge segregation but "hell-bent on getting these cases started." In Virginia, Hill initially thought the strike was "an angry and momentary reaction" and that older, "long-suffering" black leaders would settle for any relief. "It was when the younger group came along that this all changed."[16]

This wave of activism prepared Marshall for further prodding by Judge J. Waties Waring, who met with Marshall in a pretrial conference on the Clarendon County case in Charleston in November 1950. By then Waring had moved beyond the gradualist approach to racial reform that had shaped his rulings in teacher-equalization and higher-education cases and had become the most outspoken critic of segregation on the federal bench. Waring did not think Marshall was militant enough. "The NAACP legal staff apparently was quite hesitant about bringing a formal attack on legal segregation in the schools," he recalled in a series of interviews in the 1950s. At the pretrial hearing Waring urged Marshall to amend his complaint and challenge the constitutionality of South Carolina's school-segregation statutes. In December 1951 the NAACP filed *Briggs v. Elliott*, a class-action suit on behalf of all black students in South Carolina. The amended brief asked the court to invalidate "the practice of separate schools for Negro children because of race and color."[17]

As the NAACP prepared for the trial, South Carolina governor James F. Byrnes developed a sophisticated strategy for maintaining racially separate schooling. Born in Charleston in 1882, Byrnes was elected to Congress in 1910 and became the state's most influential politician in Washington since John C. Calhoun. "This is a white man's country and will always remain a white man's country," the one-time protégé of Ben Tillman told his colleagues in Congress during the summer of 1919. During his thirty-five years in Washington, as a senator, adviser to President Franklin D. Roosevelt, Supreme Court justice, and secretary of state, Byrnes refined his racial views. Returning to South Carolina in 1946, Byrnes saw himself, wrote Walter B. Edgar, "as a twentieth century Calhoun unifying the South to defy the North." In 1950 Byrnes ran for governor and was overwhelmingly elected.[18]

Preserving racial separation in education became the central objective of his administration. Before the Clarendon County case came to trial, Byrnes proposed several "preparedness measures." In his inaugural address in January 1951 Byrnes declared that "if we demand respect for state's rights, we must discharge state responsibilities. It is our duty to provide for the races substantial equality in school facilities. We must have a state school building program." Byrnes used his prestige to secure passage of a controversial $75 million school-equalization program, financed by a three-cent sales tax and administered by the Educational Finance Commission (EFC). The construction of new African American schools was only part of the state's strategy. In April 1951, a month before the Clarendon County case was scheduled to begin, the legislature established a fifteen-member "Segregation Committee," chaired by State Senator L. Marion Gressette. The first of many such committees that were created by southern legislatures in the 1950s, Gressette's committee was charged with coordinating state policy and recommending lawful ways of preserving school segregation. State legislatures in South Carolina, Georgia, Mississippi, Virginia, and Alabama, journalist Ralph McGill wrote, are "considering not how to retain legal segregation, but how to effect it without legal compulsion." As in teacher-equalization and higher-education cases, state officials in South Carolina were one step ahead of the NAACP.[19]

The showdown over segregation in South Carolina forced reluctant state officials to begin the process of equalizing school facilities. As significant as local activism was in pushing the NAACP to challenge state-sanctioned segregation, litigation produced educational changes that strikes and boycotts could not. "The political bosses of this state have never acted decently until and unless they had the club of a policeman over their head," wrote African American newspaper editor and Avery graduate John McCray in the *Lighthouse and Informer*, "and the only policeman they fear is the federal courts."[20]

"Charleston will be the scene beginning tomorrow of the nation's first frontal assault on the policy of separating white and Negro races at the public school level," the *News and Courier* reported on May 27, 1951. As the sun rose over a federal courthouse constructed in 1896, hundreds of African Americans from throughout eastern South Carolina, including many from Clarendon County, streamed into the city. The city's black elite, which had begun to socialize with Judge Waring and his wife, were among the 250 spectators who secured seats in the courtroom. "We were right in the midst of a revolution," recalled Ruby Cornwall, a teacher at Avery, who got up early so she could get a seat. "I wanted it to happen now while I could participate." So did leaders of the Palmetto State Teachers Association (PSTA) and the state conference of the NAACP, which financed the legal challenge. For the blacks who sat in the courtroom, stood in the halls, or lined the streets around the federal building, the trial was an opportunity to see America's most renowned black attorney, Thurgood Marshall, publicly excoriate state educational officials. "The burning question," John McCray wrote on the eve of the trial, is "whether or not segregation of the races in education shall be continued."[21]

Before they heard Marshall's stunning summation, the predominantly African American audience witnessed a shrewd defense of school segregation. Robert Bell McCormick Figg Jr., a College of Charleston and University of South Carolina Law School graduate who served as Charleston County district solicitor for more than a decade, defended the state. When Figg visited the schools in Clarendon County in preparation for the trial, he found that facilities in the black schools were "embarrassingly unequal." The value of white schools in the county was four times that of the black schools. After conferring with Byrnes, Figg decided that rather than being drenched with testimony demonstrating unmistakable educational inequities, he should concede them. When the court came to order, Figg told presiding judge John Parker and his colleagues, George Bell Timmerman and J. Waties Waring, that "inequalities in the facilities, opportunities, and curricula in the schools of this district do exist." Pointing to the school-equalization program, the EFC, that opened its doors two weeks before the trial, Figg asked the court to give the school trustees "a reasonable time" to bring about "equality of buildings, equipment, facilities and other physical aspects of the district." Having undercut an important part of the NAACP's case, Figg argued that the courts had long recognized school segregation as a constitutional and valid exercise of legislative power and authority. Challenging the NAACP's contention that school segregation caused psychological damage in black students, Figg declared that the courts could not compel local school authorities to gear their educational program to the "personality development" of students.[22]

Exhausted by a recent trip to Korea to investigate allegations of discrimination against black soldiers, Marshall was caught off guard by Figg's concession. Challenging state constitutional provisions requiring that "separate schools be provided for children of the white and colored races," the NAACP's case against the state had two parts: first, that the white and black schools in Clarendon County were unequal; and second, that the separation of white and black students was "in and of itself" a form of inequality that was unconstitutional. Because Figg had already admitted that the schools were unequal, Marshall had to persuade a reluctant court to allow him to present educational experts from Howard and Columbia, who testified on the educational disparities in Clarendon County. When Marshall asked Matthew Whitehead, a professor of education at Howard University, if white and black students were receiving "equal classroom instructional opportunities and advantages," Whitehead had little trouble saying, "no, not at all."[23]

At the heart of the NAACP's case in *Briggs* was the contention that state-sanctioned segregation caused irreparable damage to African American students. It was a contention that rested on the writings of John Dewey, who wrote that schools were designed to provide "an opportunity to escape from the limitations of the social group in which [a child] was born and to come into contact with a broader environment." Segregation, the NAACP argued, deprived African Americans of this opportunity. Building on the sociological arguments developed in *Sweatt v. Painter* (1950), the NAACP presented experts who documented the detrimental effects of segregation. No expert proved more persuasive than social psychologist Kenneth Clark. Like others, Clark had "some doubts about the effectiveness of the legal approach in curing basic problems," and he warned Marshall and Carter that it was not possible "to isolate the harmful effects of school segregation from the collective damage done by prejudice and segregation outside it." Still, NAACP attorneys believed that his tests of black children showed more clearly than any other available evidence the effects of state-imposed segregation. Clark tested sixteen students in Clarendon County and testified that "the Negro children of Clarendon County have been subjected to an obviously inferior status and have been definitely harmed."[24]

In what Richard Kluger has called "one of the better efforts of his career," Marshall's summation emphasized these detrimental effects. In South Carolina, Marshall declared, "all your state officials are white. All your school officials are white. That's not just segregation, its exclusion from the group that runs everything." Marshall argued that "segregation sets up a roadblock that prevents black children from achieving a full absorption of the educational process." You can teach a black child "the Constitution and citizenship, but he knows it is not true." Turning to the state equalization program, Marshall noted that it was little more than a promise to "build some schools later." Drawing on *Sweatt*, Marshall concluded that "there is no relief for the Negro children of Clarendon County except to be permitted to attend existing and superior white schools." The court must "end this injustice now." Marshall's closing, John Popham wrote in the *New York Times*, moved "a score of people to leave their seats and shake his hands in admiration." They wanted to "touch him," his secretary Alice Stoval recalled, "just touch him."[25]

The trial had a profound impact on the African American audience, illustrating Charles H. Houston's belief that litigation provided an opportunity to lead and teach. Matthew Whitehead vividly recalled the effect of his testimony. "It was all down there on the record. And you could see it on the faces in the courtroom—a sort of sigh of relief that it had finally all come out." In some cases cross-examination was aimed as much at the spectators as the judges. Marshall's cross-examination of EFC director E. R. Crow, Clark remembered, was "merciless, simply merciless." To the delight of spectators, who joked that "Marshall sure loves to eat Crow," the NAACP attorney forced Crow to admit that it was possible "for the Negro schools not to get a nickel of funds" from the school-equalization program. Many of the black spectators had probably never seen an African American so forcefully rebuke a white. MaeDe Brown, the wife of local NAACP activist J. Arthur Brown, recalled, "Thurgood was a brain, and he really proved it that day. Everyone there [was] excited by seeing the 'old Charleston types' exposed."[26]

As moving as this testimony was for the African American audience, it failed to convince Judges Parker and Timmerman. In an opinion issued in June 1951, Parker held that the *Sweatt* decision did not "disturb" the doctrine of separate but equal. Finding university education fundamentally different from primary and secondary schooling, Parker warned that "if public education is to have the support of the people it must not go contrary to what they deem for the best interests of their children." In *Sweatt*, Parker wrote, "all the Court said" is that "the opportunities afforded the Negro student must be equal to that afforded the white student." How this was done, Parker ruled, was a matter for "school authorities," not the courts. "In no field is [the] right of the several states more clearly recognized than in that of public education," the *New York Times* reported. Parker concluded that "if equal facilities are offered, segregation as prescribed by the Constitution and the laws of South Carolina is not of itself violate of the 14th Amendment." The court ordered school officials to file a report in six months on the steps they had taken to equalize educational facilities at Scott's Branch and other schools in Clarendon County.[27]

Waring was not impressed by the NAACP's case, and to compensate for it he filed a spirited dissent. Waring believed that Marshall's brief was "lackluster" and "colorless." In a letter to Herbert Delany, a New York judge who was on the NAACP board of directors, Waring wondered if "the present legal staff [was] sufficiently equipped" to pursue the case. "Between you and me," Waring told Delany, *Briggs* "was not very well presented in the court here." Waring urged the NAACP to retain "special counsel" so that the *Briggs* appeal would "be handled in a militant manner and not in routine pedestrian fashion." Waring's dissent held that segregation "is per se inequality. The system of segregation in education adopted and practiced in the state of South Carolina must go and must go now." Marshall appealed Parker's ruling, and the NAACP turned its attention to school-segregation cases in Kansas, Delaware, Virginia, and Washington, D.C. In July 1951 J. Arthur Clement, the president of the Charleston branch of the NAACP, sent Waring a letter applauding the judge's final blast from the federal bench.[28]

As much as the trial encouraged black leaders in Charleston, educational and political authorities in the state saw Parker's ruling as something of a victory. While the school-equalization program was central to the state's defense in the *Briggs* trial, when the sales tax that funded the program took effect in July 1951, opposition mounted. Several legislators who opposed the plan challenged its constitutionality in court, and editorials in the *News and Courier* urged the South Carolina Supreme Court to declare the program unconstitutional. In the face of this opposition Byrnes asserted that the school-equalization program could be used to benefit whites as well as blacks. Arguing that the program should "go ahead," he suggested that new schoolhouses for whites would be used as private schools if the Supreme Court declared segregation unconstitutional. In an address to the Association of School Trustees in November 1951, Byrnes announced that "state funds could be used to improve the white schools." As Marshall showed in the *Briggs* trial, the legislation that established the EFC did not require that school-construction funds be used to improve black schools.[29]

Like court rulings in salary-equalization and higher-education cases, Parker's decision left compliance with the constitutional command of educational equality to local school officials, and outside Clarendon County there was no rush to equalize facilities. In Charleston, as elsewhere in the state, educational authorities resented the "outside interference" of the NAACP. "Numerous white citizens, an appreciable number of school officials among them," wrote W. D. Workman in the *News and Courier,* "are bitterly resentful of the federal mandate to equalize the schools and are frankly inclined to begrudge, impair, or resist an effort to improve the lot of Negro schools or students." On several occasions in the early 1950s, Superintendent George Rogers urged the trustees to not let NAACP litigation "deter us" and to "take some steps [toward equalization] before we are forced to do so by the courts." Most of the trustees, however, saw in a redefined equalization program a source of funds for the improvement of the city's white schools. Following Byrnes's lead, the board proposed allocating EFC funds evenly between the city's white and black institutions. After Rogers told the trustees that Charleston would receive $2.5 million from the EFC, the board announced a building program that allocated $1.2 million for white schools and $1.2 million for black schools. It was a construction program of defiance rather than compliance. "The old pattern is reasserting itself," McCray wrote in the *Lighthouse and Informer*.[30]

The *Briggs* trial and the district court's ruling created a new political and legal climate that emboldened Charleston's black elite. The board underestimated the impact the proposed school-building program would have on the city's black leadership in this new climate. The NAACP's challenge to South Carolina's segregation laws in education and the court's ruling pushed Charleston's black leadership past the politics of polite protest. Inspired by Marshall's passionate attack and Waring's dissent, local NAACP leaders blasted the board's proposed building program and vowed to take legal action to force the board to comply with Parker's decision. Pressure from a more assertive black leadership and the threat of a Supreme Court decision striking down segregation forced the school board to alter its building plans and fund the construction of a "modern" facility at Burke.[31]

In late January 1952 local NAACP leaders presented a petition to the Charleston school board, and—for the first time in the city's history—threatened legal action. A businessman who had served on Avery's administrative council, NAACP president A. J. Clement told the board: "we read, we study, we analyze, we understand a lot more than we did even 10 years ago. We know how to be vocal under the laws of our state and nation." Arguing that the intent of the EFC was to "equalize school facilities," the petition stated that by dividing equalization funds evenly between white and black schools, the board's proposed building plan would "perpetuate existing inequalities." The petition used data from the county superintendent's reports to show even if the board spent "every cent you have listed in your priorities for Negro students and not a cent more on any other local schools, the per capita valuation of school property for the two races would be $392 for white pupils against $345 for Negro pupils." Under the "meaning" of Parker's decision in the *Briggs* case, Clement demanded that the board equalize the city's white and black schools by constructing new elementary and secondary schools and adding cafeterias, gyms, and other facilities that existed in the white but not the black system. "You established the separate but equal theory, it has protected you for these many years, and now you are faced with the problem of paying for it," the petition charged. John McCray did not believe that the city or the state had "the money to operate a first-class system for whites, let alone another for Negroes."[32]

Clement's appearance impressed Waring, who praised the local NAACP's "protest against [the school board's] announced program, and in a fine, deliberate, and well calculated speech laid down the law and told [the school board]

that the colored people intend to press for their rights in every particular." Waring told Delany that African Americans in Charleston were beginning to "pick
up courage" and "insist that they [be] treated as citizens."[33]

While Clement's petition marked a tactical turning point, the city's black
elite continued to focus on the future of Avery. After the school became part of
the public system in 1948, the board did little to maintain the school's deteriorating ninety-year-old building. Like other black leaders, Clement remained
deeply concerned about the school's survival and worried that the board would
close it. During the late 1940s and early 1950s Averyites urged the board to
build "a new high school" to replace Avery. Hoping that Avery would be able to
continue its tradition of academic excellence, Clement's petition urged the board
to provide Avery students "with a complete pre-planned modern high school
building" and to limit "physical additions at Burke" to expansion of the school's
"vocational training facilities." Even as the city's black elite became more assertive
and insistent, its educational aspirations and goals continued to be shaped by
Avery.[34]

As Charleston's black elite continued to press the board, the NAACP pursued its appeal in the *Briggs* case. The progress report filed by Clarendon County
school officials in December 1951 showed that construction had begun on a
new $216,000 Scott's Branch High School and that building contracts for three
new African American elementary schools were being negotiated. By the time
the Supreme Court considered the NAACP's appeal of *Briggs* in the fall of 1951,
school officials in Clarendon County had appropriated $500,000 for the equali-
zation of educational facilities, and a majority of justices wanted the district
court to "consider the implications of equalization" before the Supreme Court
granted review. Assistant Solicitor General Philip Elman recalled that "the Justices (except for Black and Douglas) were deliberately pursuing a strategy of
procrastination."[35]

At the hearing in March 1952, Figg convinced the court that Clarendon
County officials had done everything "humanly possible" to equalize the schools.
Marshall conceded that authorities were acting in good faith, but he argued that
because the county's schools were not yet equal, the plaintiffs had a right to
attend "superior" white schools. When a skeptical Armstead Dobie, who joined
the court following Waring's retirement in February, asked Marshall how he
would determine where the county's twenty-five hundred black and three hundred white students would attend school, Marshall replied "it would be a problem of shifting some of the white children by district lines, and mixing them, or
sharing the school equally. They wouldn't all go to the white school." Marshall's
colleague Robert Carter recalled that "it wasn't our concern to figure out how
integration would work." Nor was it the court's, in Parker's view. Affirming his
earlier ruling, Parker held that "as a result of the program in which the defendants

are engaged, the educational facilities and opportunities afforded Negroes within the district will, by September 1952, be made equal to those afforded white persons." A disappointed Marshall immediately appealed. On June 9, 1952, the Supreme Court noted probable jurisdiction and scheduled oral arguments for *Briggs* and a school segregation case from Kansas, *Brown v. Board of Education*, for October 1952.[36]

Hoping to capitalize on the uncertainties created by the Court's consideration of *Briggs*, NAACP leaders made several appearances before the board in 1952, urging compliance with the demands Clement made in January. While the EFC approved several construction projects in Charleston, by September 1952 the *News and Courier* was reporting that "not a penny has been requested." In a letter to Waring in late September, Clement wrote that the "local school building campaign maintains its status quo." Clement believed that the board was waiting to see what happened at the Supreme Court before it acted.[37]

Pressure from the local NAACP and the threat of a Supreme Court ruling striking down segregation forced the board to revise its proposed building program and allocate 70 percent of its equalization funds for construction projects in the African American system. The board was clearly concerned about the possibility of a local equalization suit, but the timing of its actions shows that it was even more concerned, as Clement suggested, about a Supreme Court decision striking down segregation. In the fall of 1952, the board requested $1.8 million from the EFC. On December 8, 1952, the day before oral arguments in the *Briggs* case were presented to the Court, Rogers announced that the board would tear down Burke's antiquated main building, replace it with a series of four "campus style" academic structures, and construct a new auditorium and gymnasium adjacent to the school. Plans for Burke were part of a revised program that included the construction or renovation of six African American elementary schools in the city. While the board took steps toward equalization, it continued to begrudge the improvement of black schools. When the first EFC-sponsored project, the renovation of Buist Elementary School, was completed in February 1954, the school "opened suddenly, without ceremony, and without furniture" according to the *News and Courier*.[38]

As the board began to comply with the separate but equal doctrine, it closed the state's oldest African American high school on the eve of the Court's May 17, 1954 ruling. Officials claimed that the school was shut down because "the building is very rapidly deteriorating," but Edmund L. Drago has argued that "Averyites viewed the closure as a conspiracy. It was no coincidence that the school's termination coincided with the historic ruling of the U.S. Supreme Court in 1954." The decision to close Avery foreshadowed a broader pattern of resistance that began before and intensified after *Brown*. Like his counterparts in other southern states, Governor Byrnes urged voters to repeal the state constitutional provision requiring "free and liberal support" for public schools. Following the referendum in November 1952, the editor of the *News and Courier*, Thomas R. Waring, campaigned to privatize schooling in the city, asking readers if it was "Christian, to load the white man's burden on the frail shoulders of a grade school child—on your child." Waring's editorials helped push enrollment in private white schools from 2,257 in 1950 to 7,322 in 1954. As Byrnes and other state officials warned that court-ordered desegregation would bring about the wholesale dismissal of the state's seven thousand black teachers, school-board members reminded Charleston's black teachers that their combined earnings exceeded $500,000 a year. In an address to the Charleston Civic Club, *News and Courier* reporter W. D. Workman told white leaders that Gressette's Segregation Committee was considering how the "tightening of academic requirements" might be used to preserve segregation. African American leaders saw the board's decision in this context and believed that the board's closing Avery was an act of retaliation against an increasingly assertive black leadership. During one of his appearances before the school board, Clement called desegregation not only economically, educationally, and morally "wise" but also "inevitable." For Averyites the board's decision was an effort to eliminate the possibility that white students might ever be compelled by the courts to attend the school.[39]

While the Supreme Court concluded its deliberations in the school-segregation cases, Charleston's black elite rallied to save Avery. On April 15, 1954, two hundred Averyites gathered at the school and signed a petition protesting "the abandonment of Avery on the grounds of overcrowding, a lack of recreational facilities, and inequality of opportunity." The school's closing, the petition stated, "would aggravate present educational inequalities between the races" by concentrating four thousand black students—twenty-two hundred from Burke and eighteen hundred from Rhett Elementary—on one city block. On May 6, 1954, NAACP leader J. Arthur Brown, who was a graduate of the school, urged the board not to close Avery "without first having built a pre-planned modern high school building complete with auditorium, gymnasium, and cafeteria." With the additions to Burke scheduled to be completed in the fall, on May 12, 1954, less than a week before the Supreme Court declared school segregation unconstitutional, the board announced that it would close Avery and transfer the school's students and teachers to Burke. NAACP president J. Arthur Clement called the closing of the school "a tragedy."[40]

As tragic as the closing of Avery was for the city's black elite, State College historian Lewis K. McMillan saw "a new day" in black schooling "slowly, dimly, dawning in the city" because Burke "served every element of Negro life in Charleston." Avery made significant contributions to the educational advancement of the city's black community, but it also perpetuated class and color divisions. After the board closed Avery, Burke became the focus of African American educational advancement in Charleston. The merging of the two schools united a class- and color-conscious black community behind the development and improvement of Burke.[41]

The merger of the two high schools was relatively smooth because a decade of activism, litigation, and initiative made Burke a much stronger institution. Even as educational authorities institutionalized new barriers to black equality, teachers seized on resources and incentives created by the new salary system to finance more advanced training. The National Teacher Examinations (NTE) prevented most blacks from earning salaries that equaled those of whites, but the average annual salary of black teachers in Charleston rose from $722 in 1936 to $2,300 in 1948. "By their improved economic status," Eugene Hunt has argued, "many teachers were able to further their own education." Higher salaries, financial incentives, and broader, if still unequal, educational opportunities accelerated the advancement of black teachers in Charleston and South Carolina. In 1948, for example, eight of the ten new teachers who were appointed to the school's faculty held master's degrees. During the 1950s the percentage of African Americans who held bachelor's and master's degrees continued to rise. By 1957 the average educational attainment of African American educators in South Carolina exceeded that of whites even though the average salary of blacks remained below that of whites because of the NTE. More broadly, the threat of litigation and the specter of desegregation led educational authorities in Charleston gradually to increase expenditures for transportation, library books, science equipment, and athletic supplies, and to secure accreditation from the Southern Association of Secondary Schools and Colleges on the eve of the *Brown* decision.[42]

Even as litigation and educational initiative improved Burke, school officials continued to resist equalization, and at Burke, as at other black schools, change occurred within a continuing pattern of inequality and discrimination. In September 1954, twenty-two hundred African Americans, including four hundred former Avery students, enrolled in what the *News and Courier* called "one of the most modern school units in the nation." The school was completed just in time for the start of school, and hasty construction produced problems. When it rained, the walkways that connected the school's campus-style buildings were inundated with several inches of water. "It was like a lake," recalled math teacher William Merriweather. While the $511,000 building provided African American students with access to a large library, science labs, and a one-thousand-seat auditorium, the school remained overcrowded, even after more classrooms were added in September 1954. Teachers and students remember that the facility was filled to capacity, and the board had difficulty complying with the Southern Association requirement that teachers instruct no more than one hundred fifty students a day. School officials asserted that Burke's physical plant was "second to none in the city," but black parents, especially those whose children had attended Avery, resented problems that the merging of the two schools was supposed to correct. "Burke's size," one former Avery student wrote in the *Parvenue,* "places a premium on order, decorum, and discipline."[43]

Tangible disparities between the city's white and black high schools persisted, but the transfer of former Avery students and teachers to Burke accelerated the development of academic and extracurricular programs. More than students and teachers moved to the new facility. With them came the intellectual capital that Avery's liberal-arts curriculum transmitted to the children of the city's most advantaged African American families. The twenty former Avery teachers who joined Burke's faculty included some of the best teachers in the city. Some Burke faculty members believed that Avery teachers had a "sense of superiority," but Eugene Hunt and Sarah Oglesby, who were themselves graduates of Avery, helped eased these tensions. Most of the former Avery students enrolled in college-preparatory courses that Oglesby, Viola Duvall, and others established in the 1940s, as increasing numbers of Burke students sought access to higher education. Conservative members of the city's black elite complained that "intellectual and cultural standards" at Burke were not as high as they had been at Avery, but many former Avery students joined extracurricular programs—the Hi-Y Club, the Quill and Scroll Society, and the National Honor Society—that Burke faculty members created in the early 1950s to recognize and reward exemplary academic achievement. In April 1955 forty-nine students who had academic averages of 90 or above were eligible for membership in the Burke chapter of the National Honor Society.[44]

Drawing on the increased resources made available by better jobs and higher incomes, a broad-based network of civic and voluntary organizations offered prizes, scholarships, and other incentives for student leadership and achievement. Increased public funding did not eclipse the tradition of self-help that continued to supplement per-pupil expenditures that remained well below those at the city's three white high schools. African American parent-teacher associations remained key educational advocates, raising money for black institutions at the same time that they pressed educational authorities to increase expenditures for Burke. After the two high schools were joined, the Burke PTA became the largest African American parent-teacher organization in the state. Burke PTA president Lucille Poinsette recalled that by the 1950s, more and more parents were financially able to pay PTA dues and purchase tickets to plays and athletic events, which made the school a center of community attention. Athletic events, plays, skits, and operettas played to packed houses and raised substantial sums. In 1954 the PTA set an $8,000 annual fund-raising goal. Fraternities, sororities, and alumni associations—Omega Psi Phi, Alpha Kappa Alpha, the Talladega College Association, and the Avery Class of 1926, among others—funded scholarships that by 1961 totaled more than $38,000. "Today with better incomes and more scholarship aid available," one student wrote in the *Parvenue*, "more parents can afford to send their children to college." Fred Moore, Rudolph Pyatt, and other top students at Burke won $1,200 scholarships to State College that local officials began funding after black students applied to the College of Charleston in 1949.[45]

Building on the groundwork laid by Grayson and his colleagues in the early 1940s, teachers, administrators, and community activists nurtured these student leaders in extracurricular activities. Clinton Young, who was appointed principal of Burke in 1955, followed in the footsteps of his progressive predecessors, William Henry Grayson, Frank DeCosta, and L. Howard Bennett. Like them, Young completed his high-school education at Avery. After graduating from Talladega, he earned his master's degree from Teachers College at Columbia University. Young made the training of student leaders the goal of the school's extracurricular program. "We are constantly emphasizing the quality of leadership," he wrote in 1956. "We are constantly searching out in our student body those who have the possibilities of leadership."[46]

Although an evasive culture had long existed at Burke, by the 1950s that culture had become increasingly oppositional, as African American assertions of dignity and equality became more insistent and as national support for racist assertions of African American inferiority weakened. Teachers became more assertive and insistent about the teaching of black history, injecting racial perspectives into their courses in spite of the board's refusal to support formal courses in African American history and literature. Student leaders were selected to participate in special programs such as Freedom Train, where they read the Declaration of Independence and the Constitution and discussed how "all races have fought and struggled for the precious prize of liberty and equality." The *Parvenue* reported that the program ended with Emmanuel A.M.E. minister Frank Roland leading students in the freedom pledge: "in order to have freedom, fight for it. In order to maintain freedom, struggle for it." Some of these students were members of the NAACP youth chapter that was led by history teacher and youth adviser Henry Hutchinson. Others sang in the school choir, directed by music teacher H. H. Fleming, which by the 1950s regularly performed at state and local NAACP meetings, traveling to these events in a bus the PTA purchased in 1952. Charlayne Hunter-Gault, who attended Turner High school in Atlanta during the late 1950s, recalled that her teachers "supplied a sense of pride in who we were and where we came from and where we were going." At Burke, Young wrote, students were taught that solutions to social problems required "thought as well as action."[47]

Encouraged by political and educational currents, teachers used the student council, United Burke, and the school newspaper, the *Parvenue*, to prepare student leaders who, the 1958 yearbook noted, "organized the school and trained future citizens for our democratic way of life." Teachers drew on the democratic language of progressive education to teach citizenship. They found support for these efforts in the progressive educational philosophy of George Rogers, who made "learning the ways of democracy" an important objective for all Charleston schools during his tenure as superintendent between 1946 and 1954. After Waring struck down the state's white primary in *Elmore v. Rice* (1947) and forced the state of South Carolina to "rejoin the Union and adopt the American way of conducting elections," more attention was devoted to teaching students the mechanics of registration and voting. Social-science teacher Leroy Anderson had students study Waring's *Elmore* decision in his Problems of Democracy course. Students were required to write Waring as a homework assignment. In 1953 student council leaders brought a voting machine to the school and, working with social-studies teacher Frederick Cook, used it to "familiarize students with voting, how it is done, and accustom them to [registration] procedures." A picture of the machine appeared in the *Parvenue*. Hutchinson and NAACP youth-chapter members conducted door-to-door campaigns to make "elders mindful of using the ballot." These activities helped push the number of African Americans who were registered to vote to more than seventy-five hundred in 1952, almost twice what it had been in 1948.[48]

The leaders of the student council, United Burke, were appointed to editorial positions on the *Parvenue* staff. Student journalists and faculty adviser Marjorie Howard used the paper to educate students about their rights and responsibilities as citizens. The "free press" is a "mighty weapon in the hands of the American people," one student wrote, that could "light the way to freedom by printing the truth." But if the *Parvenue* was to do this, editor Fred Moore declared, students had to be bolder and more assertive and not "be afraid of expressing ourselves." In April 1955 the *Parvenue* reported on a campaign by students at Morgan State College in Baltimore to end the "policy of not serving Negroes at its fountain counters."[49]

The merger of Burke and Avery, Eugene Hunt recalled, united the "children of favored and not so favored families" at a time when stiffening white resistance heightened black solidarity. Constantly emphasizing the importance of leadership, teachers and administrators culled from classes and clubs a cadre of student leaders who were prepared, the 1958 yearbook noted, to "carry the torch of leadership and serve the school and community." More so than other activities at Burke, dramatic events honed the leadership skills of a generation of Burke students who organized and led direct action protests and demonstrations in the 1950s and 1960s. Acting on lessons that were taught in classes and clubs, plays and skits provided opportunities for students to demonstrate their leadership. As white resistance to African American demands for equality and access stiffened in the 1950s and the content of dramatic events became increasingly oppositional, the process of standing up and asserting African American rights became increasingly significant. Septima Clark, who taught seventh grade at Charleston's Archer Elementary School in the 1950s, recalled that "this work in dramatics proved to be good training in later activities not even related to the stage but rather dealing with audiences and programs of one sort or another."[50]

African American activism, NAACP litigation, and the Supreme Court's rulings in *Briggs* and other school-segregation cases forced educational authorities to launch a multimillion-dollar school construction campaign in the South. The new $800,000 Moton High School in Farmville, the $216,000 secondary structure at Scott's Branch in Clarendon County, and the $511,000 facility at Burke are only three of the hundreds of new black high schools that were constructed in the 1950s and 1960s. The frantic rush to make separate equal did not eliminate educational problems that were generations in the making, but it did address some of the disparities that sparked student-led strikes and boycotts and provide facilities that accommodated the increasing numbers of black students who sought a secondary education. Like other black high schools, Burke remained overcrowded and underfunded, but new facilities and the transfer of former Avery students and teachers accelerated the development of an institution where teachers prepared students to lead the struggle for equality and access. In the years after 1954 Burke students acted on lessons taught at the school to realize educational possibilities created by the Supreme Court's *Brown* decision.[51]

SIX

Contesting *Brown*, 1954–1960

The product of a generation of African American activism and NAACP litigation, the Supreme Court's 1954 *Brown* decision opened what Ralph Ellison called "a wonderful world of possibilities" for black students. Defining what those possibilities were became the central educational issue in the South after 1954. Michael J. Klarman has argued that "*Brown* was not necessary as an impetus to challenge the racial status quo," but in South Carolina, as elsewhere in the region, the Court's ruling emboldened African Americans. Part of a wave of black activism that swept through the South in the years after 1954, hundreds of African Americans in South Carolina petitioned school boards to desegregate the public schools. Across the state black teachers publicly proclaimed their support for desegregation as students organized a week-long boycott of classes to demonstrate their backing of integration in 1956. Student leaders at the state's private black colleges raised money to support the boycott and applied for admission to the University of South Carolina. In the first demonstration of African American power at the polls since Reconstruction, African American voters in Charleston blocked passage of a school bond that was intended to prolong segregation in the schools. While Klarman and others discount *Brown's* effects on African Americans, the educational activism that accelerated after 1954 demonstrates just how much the Court's repudiation of state-sanctioned segregation inspired black students, teachers, and professors in South Carolina.[1]

This activism unleashed a savage wave of repression that prevented local activists and the NAACP from creating desegregated educational institutions where blacks and whites could share power and resources on equal terms. Prominent whites organized Citizens' Councils and unleashed a campaign of coercion that forced vulnerable African Americans to withdraw their names from desegregation petitions. Still, African Americans stood up to the Citizens' Councils. The inability of the councils to quell demands for desegregation led the South Carolina General Assembly to pass a series of statutes in 1956 that school and college officials used to dismiss teachers, professors, and students who supported desegregation and the NAACP. Retaliation and repression deprived local activists and the NAACP of the resources and momentum needed to mount an effective campaign for desegregation in the late 1950s.[2]

When it was announced on May 17, 1954, the *Brown* decision seemed to offer African Americans the opportunity to enter the mainstream of American education. The Court's decision expressed in unmistakably progressive terms the faith Americans placed in public schools. By 1954, the Court found, education had become "the most important function of state and local governments." A generation of progressive educational reforms made schools increasingly inclusive, enrolling a majority of young southerners in an institution that the Court called "the very foundation of good citizenship." Only by considering public education "in the light of its full development and its present place in American life," Chief Justice Earl Warren wrote, could the Court determine "if segregation in the public schools deprives these plaintiffs of the equal protection of the laws." Public schools prepared students to perform "basic public responsibilities" and equipped them for "later training," and the Court held that state-sanctioned segregation prevented African Americans from realizing these "educational benefits." Drawing on precedents established in higher-education cases, the justices found that intangible considerations, "the ability to study with [others], engage in discussion, and exchange views, apply with added force to children in grade and high schools." Even where separate schools were tangibly equal, segregation deprived African Americans of equal educational opportunity. "Separate educational facilities," the Court concluded, "are inherently unequal."[3]

In the summer of 1954 public education in South Carolina was at a crossroads. The Court's ruling set the stage for change, and the direction that public education took depended on how assertive African Americans were at pressing for their rights and how successful local educational and political authorities were at limiting those rights. Political leaders in South Carolina continued to assert that African Americans did not support desegregation, but *News and Courier* reporter W. D. Workman warned that this was a "dangerous delusion." Workman's 1955 survey of black opinion found that "a large percentage [of blacks] and an even greater percentage of their leaders very definitely do want integration of the races and as soon as possible." Educators and NAACP officials urged acceptance and immediate compliance with *Brown*. State NAACP president James Hinton declared that African American parents wanted their children to attend schools where both races "can learn to study and live as citizens." The African American teachers' association, renamed the Palmetto Educators' Association (PEA) in 1953, praised *Brown* as "consistent with the Association's belief" in democracy and pledged one thousand dollars to help local school officials in implementing plans for "universal public education within the framework of the recent ruling of the United States Supreme Court." Charleston NAACP leader A. J. Clement urged the state to accept the *Brown* decision and immediately implement desegregation. "Integration is practical and possible," one black principal in Charleston told John McCray. "We're ready."[4]

The Court's repudiation of state-enforced segregation invigorated African American leaders in South Carolina. Following a meeting of southern NAACP state leaders in Atlanta in June 1955, branches were "authorized" to file school-desegregation petitions, and African Americans submitted hundreds of desegregation petitions after 1954, citing *Brown* to support demands for access. Unlike earlier legal victories in teacher-equalization and higher-education cases, *Brown* touched all black parents who had children in the public schools. As Aldon Morris argues, by appealing to "blacks' widespread desire to enroll their children in better equipped white schools [*Brown*] reached into black homes and had meaning for people's personal lives." During the summer of 1955 NAACP chapters throughout South Carolina demanded that school officials "initiate the process of desegregation." Drawing on language from a sample petition published in the *Crisis*, State College Law School graduates Lincoln Jenkins, Matthew J. Perry, Newton Pough, and John Wrighten drafted petitions that stated: "the maintenance of racially segregated schools is a violation of the Constitution of the United States. You are duty bound to take immediate steps to reorganize the public schools under your jurisdiction on a nondiscriminatory basis."[5]

African American demands for access in Clarendon County confronted bitter white opposition. "It's a new day," declared Reverend R. E. Ritchburg, a teacher who led the desegregation drive after whites drove J. A. De Laine out of the state in the summer of 1955. Ritchburg was dismissed from his teaching job, and his daughter, his son, and their spouses, who were also educators, were blacklisted. White leaders warned that they would close the schools if African Americans pressed for desegregation. At a meeting with Thurgood Marshall and local NAACP leaders in July 1955, Charles N. Plowden, a local planter and former legislator, declared that you "can't make us mix. I told them they've got more to lose than we have. We've got twelve white teachers; they've got sixty. They'd all be out of work. You can go ahead and push us if you want to, and we'll close our schools." By the summer of 1955 Plowden and others had secured pledges of $34,000 to operate private schools. Influential whites endorsed privatization. Thomas Waring argued that "many thoughtful citizens in South Carolina have long been dissatisfied with the educational performance of our public schools." Progressive educational reforms, he argued, "have lowered educational standards in the public schools." Waring believed that South Carolinians should be encouraged to send their children to private schools and that the state should subsidize "private school tuition" payments. Such a system would create competition, and the private institutions "which offered a good education, would thrive and multiply." In Georgia one segregationist declared that private academies would "contribute to the advancement of education" and "get John Dewey out of the schools." Facing bitter opposition, the NAACP shifted its attention to other areas in the state.[6]

In Charleston newly elected NAACP branch president J. Arthur Brown and activist teachers pressed the school board to desegregate the schools. The Court's ruling and Brown's election as president energized the local branch. Local teachers Henry Hutchinson and Septima Clark played important roles in the desegregation campaign. A history teacher at Burke, Hutchinson was adviser of the city's NAACP youth chapter and was a "close ally" of J. Arthur Brown. An Avery graduate, Clark was a longtime member of the NAACP, who had organized the salary campaign in Columbia in 1945. Returning to Charleston in 1947, Clark taught at Archer Elementary and led an astonishing array of civic and education organizations, including the local NAACP chapter, the City Federation of Colored Women's Club, the Metropolitan Council of Negro Women, the sorority Alpha Kappa Alpha Xi Omega, and the local YWCA. After Brown and local counsel John Wrighten submitted a desegregation petition signed by forty-seven parents in July 1955, Clark and Hutchinson organized a series of forums to build community support for desegregation. At one workshop in the summer of 1955 Clark distributed *A Guide to Community Action Public School Integration*, which she had written at Highlander Folk School. In late July Brown submitted petitions to school-district officials in Mt. Pleasant and North Charleston.[7]

African American demands for school desegregation unleashed a ferocious wave of white opposition. In Charleston and other parts of the state, desegregation petitions led to the formation of Citizens' Councils, whose announced aim was to exert "economic pressure on all persons connected to the NAACP." After blacks in the Charleston area petitioned local school boards, Thomas Waring published a series of articles on the council movement in Mississippi, which were designed to encourage "the creation of similar groups in the state." The Citizens' Councils, Waring wrote, were led by "pillars of the community" who were accustomed to performing "civic chores" and whose leadership was needed "in uncertain times." In South Carolina, as elsewhere in the South, the councils were led by political, economic, and civic leaders. Following a meeting in September 1955, a "Committee of 52" prominent South Carolinians publicly "reassure[d] the people of South Carolina that many substantial citizens are standing steadfast against usurpation of the constitutional right of the state to maintain its public schools." A month later Citizens' Council leaders met in Columbia and formed a statewide organization, selecting Clarendon County attorney S. Emory Rogers as executive secretary. Under Rogers's leadership council membership in the state rose to forty thousand by 1958.[8]

Council leaders used their control of newspapers, school boards, and businesses to intimidate African Americans who supported school desegregation. Intimidation began with the publication in local newspapers of the names of

African Americans who signed desegregation petitions. After African Americans in Charleston demanded desegregation, James Hayes of the State's Rights League, a forerunner of the eight Citizens' Councils that were organized in Charleston County by October 1955, asked school superintendent Robert Gaines "to release to the public press" the names of the petitioners. "I appreciate your interest in our perplexing school problem, and I hope it will continue," the superintendent told Hayes, the day before the names were printed on the front page of the *News and Courier* in August 1955. In an editorial Waring wrote, "surely white people are entitled to bring counter pressure to protect the interests of their children." Waring urged white employers to study the names of those who had signed. "There is no need for violence," Waring counseled. "Many other means are in the hands of the dominant people who in large measure own the South. Among these means, the most useful may be economic." Employers, bankers, landowners, and insurance agents were encouraged to fire blacks who were not willing to observe what Waring called "community customs." "We intend to make it difficult, if not impossible, for a Negro who advocates desegregation to find and hold a job, get credit, or renew a mortgage," one Citizens' Council leader in Alabama declared.[9]

Economic reprisals and retaliation forced many African Americans to withdraw their names from school-desegregation petitions, but in South Carolina, as elsewhere, blacks continued to press for desegregation. Economic coercion was most successful in the state's rural Black Belt, where African Americans were more dependent on whites and where violence was used. In Elloree, South Carolina, a small town in the heart of the state, fourteen of seventeen African Americans were coerced into removing their names from the desegregation petition. Newspapers heralded the withdrawals in front-page headlines. But many African Americans refused to be intimidated. Although a majority of petitioners in Orangeburg were forced to withdraw their names, the twenty-six who remained organized a counterboycott. In Charleston almost all of the forty-eight African Americans who signed the petition worked in black-owned businesses or in federal jobs that were beyond white control, and only one name was withdrawn. In North Charleston, where many African American signers were employed at federal military installations, little effort was made to intimidate the two hundred fifty African Americans who signed the desegregation petition.[10]

Because the Citizens' Councils were unable to quell demands for desegregation, the power and resources of the state of South Carolina were used to retaliate against African Americans who pressed for educational access. What historian Howard Quint has called "the sound and the fury of the Citizens' Councils" received substantial support from the state legislature. State policy was directed by State Senator L. Marion Gressette's Segregation Committee, which was created before the *Briggs* trial to coordinate the state's defense of segregated schools. The fifteen-member committee was advised by Chief Counsel David W. Robinson and a legal staff of the state's ablest attorneys. As I. A. Newby noted, "no policy of any significance was implemented without its approval, and nothing it endorsed was ever rejected by the legislature." Committee chairman Gressette pledged to use "every legal means to preserve segregation." In 1956 the committee secured passage of fourteen laws designed to maintain segregation, repealing the state's compulsory-education law and giving school boards the right to sell or lease school property. Other statutes strengthened the "preparedness measures" that had been enacted between 1951 and 1955.[11]

The most significant legislation passed during the Segregation Session of 1956 was a series of anti-NAACP statutes that became part of what Septima Clark called "a systematic campaign to wipe out the NAACP." Activist students and teachers provided significant support for the NAACP's campaign against segregation, and in 1956 the legislature used state power to strike back. Having already repealed the state's tenure law, the Gressette Committee legal staff drafted and the legislature approved Act 741, which made it unlawful for any member of the NAACP to be employed by the "state or a school district, county, or municipality." Following passage of the measure in May 1956, school officials were authorized to require that teachers "submit written oaths regarding NAACP membership." Teachers who failed to complete the questionnaires could be "summarily discharged."[12]

Throughout the state, school officials used the measure to dismiss dozens of black teachers who refused to renounce their membership in the association or their support for desegregation. The Charleston school board knew who was "spreading the NAACP line," Waring wrote in the *News and Courier.* "Such teachers should be discharged as firmly but with as little fuss as possible." In the spring of 1956 Hutchinson and Clark received letters from the superintendent stating that "your contract with this board will not be renewed." Both protested, sending letters to Gaines asking him to explain the board's action and enlisting the support of the PEA, the National Education Association, and the NAACP. PEA executive secretary Walker E. Solomon urged the NAACP to challenge the anti-NAACP measure in court "using Mrs. S. P. Clark, Henry P. Hutchinson, or others similarly affected as subjects for legal action."[13]

The NAACP worried about the dismissal of hundreds of African American teachers in the South, but as association attorney Jack Greenberg noted, litigation did not deter school officials from firing activist teachers. In 1954 the NAACP established a "teacher security fund" to protect the region's seventy-six thousand black teachers and, after *Brown,* pledged that "the fullest resources of the association including the legal staff will be utilized to insure that there will be no discrimination against teachers." Clark and Hutchinson continued to press for action on their case, but NAACP lawyers thought the dismissal of twenty-one teachers in Elloree provided a better opportunity to challenge the anti-NAACP statute. In May 1956 Elloree school superintendent M. G. Austin distributed employment applications and questionnaires that asked: "Do you feel that an integrated school system would better fit the colored race for their life's work? Do you favor integration of the races in the schools? Do you support the aims of the NAACP?" After twenty-one of twenty-four teachers at Elloree County Training School refused to complete the questionnaire, they were fired.[14]

In October 1956 Greenberg and Lincoln Jenkins, a State College Law School graduate, challenged the anti-NAACP oath in federal court in Charleston, arguing that it denied teachers the right of freedom of speech and association. A three-judge panel upheld the law, ruling that state courts should be given an opportunity to interpret it. The same day the NAACP filed an appeal with the Supreme Court, the legislature repealed the statute and replaced it with a new one requiring that teachers list memberships in associations and organizations. The new measure was more legally defensible. During the McCarthy era, the courts upheld educational authorities' right to require that teachers disclose memberships in organizations in which membership "might bear on job performance." South Carolina's amended law and the Court's consistent defense of the right of school boards to exercise their discretion about whom to employ left African Americans vulnerable to reprisals. The more than five hundred African American teachers who were fired in the South during the late 1950s were among the estimated thirty thousand black educators who were dismissed or demoted in the decades after 1954.[15]

In South Carolina, as elsewhere in the South, attacks on African American educators sharply curtailed membership in the NAACP. The dismissal of black teachers, Hutchinson recalled, "created an atmosphere in which people were afraid." Eugene Hunt recalled the chilling effect that the action had on his colleagues at Burke. "Everyone knew that to be too aggressive was to endanger one's job." Concerned about the impact of the anti-NAACP measure on membership, Roy Wilkins, who was appointed executive secretary of the NAACP following Walter White's death in 1955, appealed to black teachers in the state, encouraging them to continue to pay dues or at least make "contributions." Some teachers did so, but in South Carolina, as elsewhere, most resigned from the association. "Since our teachers have been forbidden to join the NAACP here in South Carolina, we have lost membership," state conference treasurer Levi Byrd told the national office. By 1958 statewide membership had fallen to 1,418, less than one-quarter of what it had been in 1954, part of a broader regional trend where southern membership in the association fell precipitously. "It is not an easy job during these trying times," J. Arthur Brown wrote. "These people are doing all in their power to get rid of us."[16]

The NAACP never regained the initiative it lost in 1955, but as Aldon Morris has argued, repression of the NAACP created an organizational vacuum in southern black communities and opened the way for the use of new tactics. The possibilities created by the Supreme Court's initial *Brown* decision and attacks on the NAACP produced what August Meier and Elliott Rudwick have called "a surge of non-violent direct action in the deep South beginning in 1955." Unlike other southern states, where the Southern Christian Leadership Conference (SCLC) and the Congress of Racial Equality (CORE) replaced the NAACP as the leading civil rights organizations, new protest organizations did not emerge in South Carolina, and African American schools and colleges filled the void left by repression of the NAACP by serving as a base from which blacks challenged the status quo.[17]

The most significant challenge to segregation in South Carolina during the late 1950s occurred in Orangeburg, where NAACP leaders and students and professors at State and Claflin colleges used new forms of protest to press for desegregation. In Orangeburg, as elsewhere, school desegregation petitions led to the formation of Citizens' Councils, reprisals, and the use of state power to repress black demands for access. As Citizens' Councils in Orangeburg retaliated, local NAACP leaders organized a counterboycott that was supported by students and professors at State and Claflin colleges. In March 1956 student-council leaders organized a series of demonstrations that culminated in a week-long boycott of classes in the spring of 1956. Standing up to the college's all-white governing board and the legislature, State College faculty members supported the students, publicly voicing their support for the NAACP and desegregation. In the Carolinas, Alabama, Florida, Texas, and elsewhere, activism grew out of institutions that African American students, teachers, and lawyers had done so much to improve. The protests at State College produced no cracks in the color line, but the boycott and student-led strike illustrate how *Brown* inspired African American students and teachers, who employed direct-action tactics to realize new educational possibilities.[18]

As Clark, Hutchinson, Brown, and Wrighten urged school officials in Charleston to reorganize the schools on a "nondiscriminatory basis," the Orangeburg chapter of the NAACP petitioned the school board "to take immediate and concrete steps leading to the elimination of segregation in the public schools." Drafted by State College Law School graduate Newton Pough, the petition was signed by fifty-seven individuals. While the petitioners came from a cross section of the town's black community, a significant number were teachers in the public schools or employees at State or Claflin. Local whites were stunned. Echoing arguments that southern attorneys made during oral arguments before the Supreme Court, the *Orangeburg Times and Democrat* declared that "the people

in this state and this community are not ready for integration." The desegregation of schools, the newspaper warned, would lead to the "worsening of relations between the races, friction, and much ill-will." Determined to protect the
separation of the races, whites organized twenty Citizens' Councils in Orangeburg and surrounding Black Belt counties during the late summer and fall of
1955.[19]

The Orangeburg Citizens' Council was led by W. T. C. Bates, a local insurance agent, and supported by the sheriff, the mayor, and State Representative
Jerry Hughes. In late August the council staged a rally that attracted more than
three thousand people, almost one-half the town's white population, who listened to local political leaders denounce the *Brown* decision. Following the rally,
Mayor Robert H. Jennings, who owned the Palmetto Bakery and Parades Ice
Cream and operated the local Coca-Cola franchise, and other council leaders
launched a campaign of economic intimidation to force African Americans who
signed the school-desegregation petition to withdraw their names. "The strategy
of the [Orangeburg] Citizens' Councils," the *Pittsburgh Courier* reported, "is to
apply economic pressure on businesses, fire those who are employed by whites,
run sharecroppers and tenants off farms, and terrorize Negroes who can't be
reached otherwise." Local suppliers stopped delivering to African American
businesses, revoked the franchise of a service-station owner, fired workers, refused to renew insurance policies, and demanded immediate repayment of loans
and mortgages. The council offered a $10,000 reward for the membership list
of the local NAACP chapter. By October 1955 more than thirty African Americans had lost their jobs, and a dozen African American–owned businesses had
been driven to the brink of bankruptcy. Unable to support themselves, thirty-
one grocers, teachers, and heads of large households were forced by economic
necessity to withdraw their names from the petition. Each withdrawal was heralded as a headline in the *Orangeburg Times and Democrat*.[20]

Local NAACP leaders responded by organizing a boycott of their own in
the fall of 1955. Matthew McCollum and James Sulton targeted the owners of
twenty-three firms that supported reprisals against African Americans. The firms
were listed on a flyer, "Don't Patronize These Firms," which was distributed at
black churches. African Americans stopped buying the bread, Coca-Cola, and
ice cream that Mayor Jennings's companies no longer supplied to black grocers.
After Coble Dairy ended milk deliveries to signers of the desegregation petition,
African Americans boycotted that dairy's products. Because much of the town's
economy was tied to Claflin and State colleges, Sulton saw the support of two
thousand black students and almost five hundred faculty and staff members
—nearly one-quarter of the town's black population—as crucial to the boycott's
success. State College faculty and staff members Robert Hubbard, Alba Lewis,
and Samuel Pinckney's names remained on the petition, and in the fall Sulton

asked State College student-government president Fred Moore to organize support for the campaign among students.[21]

Rising African American enrollment, NAACP legal victories, and African American applications for admission to the University of South Carolina and Clemson fueled institutional development at State. In the decade following John Wrighten's application to the University of South Carolina Law School, the legislature funded a massive building campaign at State and sharply increased appropriations for the college's operations. Governor James F. Byrnes used his prestige in the legislature and his influence in philanthropic circles to fund a $4 million construction campaign on the campus. "The endless digging continued," one student wrote in the 1955 State College yearbook. "A new agricultural building and a new student center opened. A new men's dormitory, faculty houses, and a new athletic facility were started." Somehow, "the long awaited academic building managed to remain in the blue-print stage." Even though fourteen new buildings were constructed on the campus between 1949 and 1956, administrators continued to turn hundreds of students away, as African American demand for more advanced training outpaced the willingness of the legislature to expand facilities at State.[22]

The college's governing board gave priority to construction projects in the college's agricultural program, but State's new president, the former law-school dean, Benner C. Turner, steered funds toward the training of black professionals. After Whittaker died of a heart attack in 1949, Turner was appointed president. Cautious and compliant, Turner worked well with Byrnes and the all-white governing board, even as he used the prospect of desegregation to secure additional funding, manipulating white interest to black advantage. Many former students and professors remember Turner as a tyrant and a "plantation overseer," but even critics concede that he was an efficient administrator who strengthened the college's academic and extracurricular programs. Turner's papers and interviews with students and faculty suggest that he was less of a President Bledsoe than a leader who possessed what George R. Woolfolk has called an "amoral survival psychosis that led to intellectual and spiritual sterility."[23]

"Emphatically suggesting" that blacks receive the same training offered in South Carolina's white colleges, Turner used Southern Association of Secondary Schools and Colleges accreditation standards to recruit professors with doctorates, reduce heavy teaching loads, and raise faculty salaries. Between 1950 and 1954 the faculty and staff grew from 153 to 183. While the salaries of professors at State remained well below those at white colleges, the aggregate pay of teachers and administrators almost doubled during this period, increasing to more than $700,000 in 1954. State's operating budget rose from $195,000 in 1946 to more than $1.3 million a decade later. The specter of desegregation and what Turner called "the expanded building program, increasing faculty personnel, and emphasis on student leadership" led the legislature to change the institution's name from South Carolina Normal, Industrial, Agricultural, and Mechanical College to South Carolina State College in 1954.[24]

As State College moved into the mainstream of American higher education, the expansion of the physical plant, better-trained faculty, and extracurricular programs encouraged student activism. Trained at northern universities, new faculty members with doctorates—W. N. Smith, R. C. Henderson, and Ashriel Mose—exposed students to new ideas, as did older students in the law school and teachers in the graduate program. Students talked about these ideas in the newly opened student center, which provided a place to "congregate for social and recreational purposes." Inside and outside class, faculty members taught students that leadership was the main challenge facing "Negro youth in college today." A greater emphasis on scholarship and leadership helped the student government, the National Honor Society, ROTC, the NAACP youth chapter, and the campus newspaper compete with frivolous rituals that remained fixtures of college life. At State, as at Burke, top students aspired to leadership positions in student government and spots on the *Collegian* staff. In 1950 a new student-government organization offered "training in leadership" and "opportunities in self-government." While Byrnes believed that better facilities would "allay unrest among the colored people," five months after the *Brown* decision, student-government president Benjamin Payton wrote in the *Collegian* that "if the physical facilities of the college are expanded, then we, the students, must expand, politically, socially, and spiritually. I do mean to challenge the traditional way we do things. I do mean to provoke well-planned activities."[25]

The desegregation petition, retaliation against African American activists, the counterboycott, and institutional development at State fueled challenges to the status quo at the college and in the community. During the fall of 1955 Moore tried to persuade Turner to support the boycott, but Turner told him that he had "no intention of becoming involved." Concerned with the college's survival, Turner told Moore that "I've got the welfare and well being of students and faculty members to protect." In Turner's view "students' first priority should be educational not political activities." Like other African American land-grant presidents, Turner worried that the college "cannot expect to survive if it is allowed to become a political, social, or economic battleground."[26]

In spite of Turner's opposition State became a battleground in the spring of 1956. "We supported the boycott to show support and sympathy for those blacks who petitioned for [school] desegregation," Moore recalled. Students learned to live without Coca-Cola, certain brands of potato chips, peanuts, and ice cream, one reporter noted. Turner refused to cancel a $17,000 laundry contract, but students stopped sending their laundry to a firm owned by a Citizens' Council supporter. Women who taught at the college and in the public schools stopped patronizing Becker's, a clothing store owned by a member of the Citizens' Council, driving the firm out of business. At private Claflin College students persuaded administrators to cancel a bread contract with Mayor Hughes's bakery. "The selective buying campaign was very effective," James Sulton recalled. White merchants felt the pinch. The loss of African American patronage led to a sharp decline in sales. Roy Wilkins had reservations about the campaign, but state NAACP president James Hinton was an enthusiastic supporter. "Negroes in the South can do great harm to businesses operated by those who would try economic reprisals against Negroes," Hinton wrote. "Orangeburg teaches a lesson, one that it will do well for other communities to follow."[27]

In Orangeburg, as in Charleston, the inability of the Citizens' Councils to quell African American demands for desegregation brought legislative action. In March 1956 council member and Orangeburg County state representative Jerry Hughes sponsored a resolution to investigate NAACP activities on the campus. Like other anti-NAACP measures enacted in 1956, Act 920 declared that the NAACP was "intent on fomenting and nurturing resentment among members of the Negro race with their status in the social and economic structure of the South." The investigation was designed to determine which students and faculty were "misleading Negroes."[28]

The legislature's action "only served to bring us closer together," Fred Moore recalled. While the chairman of the college's governing board, W. C. Bethea, asserted "there is definitely leadership, somewhere outside the college," the students who organized demonstrations on the State campus in March 1956 were products of a generation of institutional development in African American schools and colleges. Student leaders Fred Moore and Rudolph Pyatt personified the qualities of scholarship and leadership that African American educators had worked hard to develop, and they acted on lessons that were woven through academic classes and extracurricular activities. Fred Moore was born on James Island and attended Three Trees Elementary School, where Elizabeth DeCosta, a colleague of Mamie Fields, encouraged him to pursue his schooling at Burke. Part of the first generation of black students on James Island who were transported at public expense to Burke, Moore excelled at the school. A member of the Burke chapter of the National Honor Society, Moore was elected president of United Burke and appointed to the *Parvenue* staff. "He is courteous, diplomatic, knows what he wants, and leaves no stone unturned in getting it," a profile in the paper noted. Graduating with honors in 1952, Moore earned one of the ten scholarships that local educational officials funded after Avery and Burke students applied to the College of Charleston in 1944 and 1949. Moore flourished at State, where he majored in chemistry. An honor student, he won election to the student council and became president of the student body during his senior year. Rudolph Pyatt worked with Moore in the student government and on the *Collegian* staff. Like Moore, Pyatt was a Burke graduate who was elected to United Burke and wrote for the *Parvenue*. Because of our work in high school and college organizations, Pyatt recalled, "we had the capability and logistics to do what we needed to do."[29]

Encouraged by activist faculty members Alfred Issacs, Edward Ferguson, Willard Smith, and Ashriel Mose, students staged protests to persuade Turner to cancel food contracts with Citizens' Council merchants. On March 23, less than a week after the legislature authorized the investigation of the NAACP, students chalked statements on sidewalks at the college opposing the use of Sunbeam bread, Coble milk, and other products used in the dining hall. Two days later, students poured water on the bread, refused to drink milk, and marched en masse out of the dining hall without eating Sunday dinner. That night, local supporters delivered food to the students in their dorms, and students began boycotting the dining hall and purchasing food off-campus. When Turner met with students and urged moderation, they scraped their feet and marched to the president's campus residence, writing "Be a Man" on the front of his house. The following morning, in a quiet, carefully organized demonstration, the students hanged in effigy Turner, Governor George Bell Timmerman, and State Representative Jerry Hughes, an event that attracted reporters from throughout the nation. The governor dispatched the State Law Enforcement Division (SLED) to campus to "arrest any law violators."[30]

In a show of solidarity faculty members criticized the state's political leadership and declared its support for the boycott, the NAACP, and school desegregation. Following a "free and lively discussion" led by sociologist Dr. R. C. Henderson, 99 percent of State's faculty signed a resolution declaring that "effective teaching cannot be accomplished if pressure and attempts at intimidation are leveled against us." The resolution chastised the legislature and governor for their attempts to "censure" students and faculty "on the basis of irresponsible accusations [and] suspicions." Affirming their support for the Constitution "as interpreted by the United States Supreme Court," faculty members urged "compliance with the Court's *Brown* decision" and expressed support for the NAACP, calling it "an organization which gives vitality to constitutional principles." On April 4, 1956, Henderson sent copies of the resolution to the wire services and asked Turner to forward copies to the college's governing board and Governor Timmerman.[31]

When students returned to campus following spring break, Moore, Pyatt, and other student leaders called a meeting in White Hall. "This is not a mental institution, nor a penal institution," Moore declared, "but an institution of higher learning attended by free people in a free land." As long as SLED officers remained on the campus, Moore announced, students would remain out of class. Using skills developed in student government and on the *Collegian* staff, Moore,

Pyatt, and others organized regular meetings and published a bulletin that told students what to do. Students exhibited many of the characteristics that distinguished the sit-in movement. Reporters who covered the strike commented on the students' discipline and organization. The *Columbia State* reported that students could be seen reading and studying while professors staffed empty classrooms. The students were careful not to engage in activities that might discredit faculty members, and Moore and Pyatt recall that faculty members supported "what we were doing," telling them, "you are doing what a whole lot of us would like to see done."[32]

Turner's attempts to resolve the crisis drew attention to his leadership and demands for reform of the college's authoritarian atmosphere. In a letter to Moore on the second day of the strike, Turner wrote that he would be "pleased" to negotiate with the student council after students returned to classes. Publicly, Turner made it clear that he was in "no position to tell the governor what to do" and that negotiations would be confined to issues "within the scope of college resources and regulations." At the end of the fourth day of the strike, he issued an ultimatum, warning that "continued absence could result in dismissal" and suggesting that the college might be closed if the boycott persisted. The suggestion fed demands for the desegregation of colleges and universities. "If you close down our school," Murray Kempton reported the students' shouting, "you'll have 900 Autherine Lucys knocking down the doors of the University of South Carolina." (Autherine Lucy attempted to desegregate the University of Alabama in 1956.) Claflin College dean Lemuel Hayes told Kempton that he hoped Timmerman would close State and that students "as a body will apply to the University of South Carolina, Clemson, and The Citadel."[33]

The threat of students' applications to white colleges led the governing board to increase pressure on Turner. Student-led meetings focused attention on the need for change at State. According to Rudolph Pyatt, "the strike represented both a challenge to the racial status quo, and opposition to Turner's autocratic regime. The issues fed into each other." In meetings with college administrators Moore and other leaders continued to press for the removal of food products from the campus dining hall. Initially reluctant to speak with reporters, Moore began talking to African American journalists, telling them that "this is merely a peaceful effort to unite all of mankind. It is tied to integration efforts. It is one phase." Activist faculty members urged students to draw up a list of grievances. "You must respond," Moore recalled Alfred Issacs telling him, "but it must be your response." In a statement issued to the United Press, the student council declared that they would remain out of class "until Timmerman issues a statement that he will withdraw [SLED] officers." Working with Issacs, Moore, Pyatt, and other leaders drew up a list of grievances and sought assurances that there would be "no reprisals against students for the part played in these recent protests."

They sent the grievances to Turner, declaring that "our growth and development as students in a democratic institution [has been] seriously hindered and stifled."[34]

The hope that they might reform State, pressure from Turner's allies in the administration, and the threat of expulsion led students to return to classes after six days. Throughout the boycott Turner assured student-council leaders that he would negotiate with them once students returned to classes. Echoing the arguments that African American leaders in Charleston made during Wrighten's campaign to desegregate the College of Charleston in 1944, accommodationist administrators told Moore that the boycott threatened progress at State. Several student leaders were from Charleston and attended college on full scholarships that were funded by educational authorities in the city and the county. "If you stay out of class," dean of industrial education Howard Jordan told Moore, "you'll jeopardize that. Think about the investment your parents, teachers, and professors have made in your education." These arguments led strike leaders to question their resolve. After Turner warned that seniors who failed classes because of unexcused absences would not be able to graduate, students returned to classes.[35]

Once classes resumed and students began preparing for final exams, the college's all-white governing board retaliated against student and faculty activists. Moore was called before the board and, after he refused to implicate faculty members, was immediately expelled for violating unspecified college regulations. The board launched a thorough investigation of faculty support for the boycott, which led to the dismissal of five faculty members, including *Collegian* faculty adviser Florence Miller, who was discharged for not "exercising control" over the paper. During the summer and the following academic year, several faculty members with doctorates resigned, including Edward Ferguson and Willard Smith, delaying the college's attempts to secure accreditation from the Southern Association of Secondary Schools and Colleges.[36]

The board's investigation also led to the expulsion of fourteen other students, six of whom were graduates of Burke. After classes ended, Turner sent letters to these students informing them that they would not be able to return to the college because their influence "is not deemed in the college's welfare." Most of these students, including Moore, were honor students and deeply involved in the college's extracurricular program. Vivian Lennon, for example, was a member of the National Honor Society, president of the Dramatic Club, editor of the yearbook, and a member of the *Collegian* staff. After Moore and others received letters from Turner in June, Septima Clark wrote Roy Wilkins, telling him that "these students have fought long and hard and now need legal assistance and financial security to enter another college. They have really had no trial and are being thrown out [without] a hearing." Wilkins responded, but in a time when the courts did not recognize student rights to due process, there was little the

NAACP could do about the board's right to decide who taught and studied at State College.[37]

Still, black students continued to press for desegregation. In January and February 1958, fifteen African American students applied for admission to the University of South Carolina. These applications were motivated in part by South Carolina governor George Bell Timmerman's campaign to silence those who spoke out for desegregation and illustrate what might have occurred if authorities had closed State. During the summer of 1956 Timmerman pressed Allen University president the Reverend Frank Veal to fire professors John G. Rideout, Erwin Hoffman, and Forest Wiggins. The professors, all of whom held doctorates, had urged Allen students to challenge segregation on buses in Columbia. When Allen's board refused to dismiss them, Timmerman had the South Carolina State Board of Education revoke the accreditation of Allen's teacher-training program, leaving seniors, most of whom were education majors, ineligible for teaching positions in the public schools.[38]

In January 1958 eleven African American students from Allen struck back, applying for admission to the University of South Carolina (USC). Alarmed by the students' action, USC president Robert L. Sumwalt convened a series of meetings with David W. Robinson, who provided William C. McCall with explicit instructions on the "exact wording" McCall should use to address black applicants. When four black students from Benedict, another private black college in Columbia, appeared in McCall's office on January 22, he told them, "I have nothing to say to you." Robinson drafted letters telling the students that the university would not "accept their applications."[39]

The students contacted John Wrighten but were unable to secure the support of the NAACP legal staff. State NAACP president James Hinton did not believe the students were suitable plaintiffs and resented the fact that they had "acted on their own." By March 1958 no action had been taken, and in a letter to NAACP executive secretary Roy Wilkins, James Jones, Thelma McClam, Cornell F. Mitchell, and Mary Alston complained that "we are being discouraged by the very person [Hinton] who should be welcoming and promoting our efforts." While the students asked Wilkins to intervene, the cautious NAACP leader missed what local activist Modjeska Simkins called "a long-awaited, God-sent opportunity to make a driving wedge toward entry into the state-supported higher institutions." J. Arthur Brown, I. DeQuincey Newman, and other NAACP leaders in the state urged the national office to take action, but Wilkins resisted, writing that "it is our duty to calculate as much as possible and to forgo action merely for action's sake."[40]

Like the outcomes of teacher-equalization and higher-education campaigns, attempts to desegregate schools in South Carolina after *Brown* illustrate the limits of local activism and NAACP litigation in a state where educational and political authorities exercised complete control over public education. The threats of school closings in Clarendon County, the firing of black teachers and professors in Charleston, Elloree, and Orangeburg, and the expulsion of student activists at State College paralyzed the NAACP, depriving it of the resources it needed to desegregate schools, colleges, and universities during the 1950s. Forced to devote dwindling resources to defend its right to exist, the NAACP was unable to defend teachers and students who kept the possibility of desegregation alive during the late 1950s. By then Thurgood Marshall's faith in justice had been "shattered," and he conceded that "this problem is not going to be solved in the courts alone." More than legal action would be required to crack the color line in educational institutions in South Carolina and other states in the Deep South.[41]

As Marshall, Carter, and other NAACP lawyers defended the association against antibarratry laws, J. Arthur Brown organized an electoral campaign to prevent school officials from constructing new black schools in Charleston. While David W. Robinson and other members of the Educational Finance Commission (EFC) believed "newer more modern buildings will tend to keep the Negro in the Negro schools," in Charleston, as in other southern cities, the frantic rush to make separate equal could not keep pace with rising African American demand for education or black migration to cities. African Americans did not have the power to desegregate schools, but the bond-election campaign in Charleston in 1957 illustrates how local activists in Charleston sustained the struggle for equality and access after *Brown*.[42]

Increased funding for new black schools could not compensate for generations of neglect or keep pace with rising African American enrollment, and activists in Charleston seized on continuing overcrowding to build support for desegregation. Fueled by migration and rising attendance and school-persistence rates, Charleston's African American school population skyrocketed in the 1950s, growing by more than 20 percent to 8,646 students in 1960. Between 1953 and 1956 the board appropriated $2 million for construction and renovation projects in the black system, but African American schools remained overcrowded. At Burke, where enrollment was 158 percent of the school's capacity, students attended classes in the antiquated annex, where the ceilings were "loose and falling, and the floors were badly worn and splintered." African American parents, especially those of former Avery students, were bitter about conditions at the school. PTA leaders repeatedly complained about "overcrowded, unhealthy, and dilapidated conditions" at Burke, heightening the board's concerns about how it was going to maintain segregation. After PTA leaders warned Gaines that they might "start something the board couldn't handle," the superintendent told the trustees that unless it corrected the problems at Burke, they would face an "integration suit." Echoing the advice of Crow and Robinson, Gaines argued that until facilities were improved, the board had "no room to argue with [black] extremists."[43]

As concerned as local officials were, by 1956 the board had already spent all the funds it was slated to receive from the EFC until 1960, and Gaines urged the board to consider holding a bond election to raise $1.1 million. "If we show evidence of moving ahead rapidly on these projects," Gaines told the trustees in December 1956, "the Negro population will be satisfied. If we do not, we will quite probably be faced with an integration suit." Endorsing Gaines's proposal, board chairman C. A. Brown felt that a program of improvements would "place the board in a very good position with the Negroes." Board members recognized that improvements in the black schools were needed to avoid "racial strife," but Gaines believed that "a bond issue involving only the Negro schools would have little chance of success. The only way a bond issue could be successful would be to take in as many of our white schools as possible." By 1957 increasing numbers of white parents with school-age children had either moved to the suburbs or enrolled their children in private schools, and board attorney Hugh Sinkler wondered if there was a "driving force" of white voters who would support the bond. Hoping to increase the interest of white voters, the board promoted the measure as one that would "put every school in good condition" and proposed spending $300,000 for work on the High School of Charleston, Rivers, and James Simons Elementary, as well as $800,000 for improvements at Burke and Archer and Simonton Elementary Schools. As Gaines cultivated the support of moderate African American ministers and educators, some of whom "took an active part" in urging African American voters to vote for the bond, the trustees lobbied business leaders, the editors of the newspapers, white teachers, and PTA officers in the weeks leading up to the election. In May 1957 Gaines predicted that "the election will be carried."[44]

In the first demonstration of black political power in Charleston since Reconstruction, local NAACP leaders campaigned against the bond and defeated it. Arguing that it was "high time" for the board to comply with the Supreme Court's decision, J. Arthur Brown urged black voters to oppose the measure because it was designed to "prolong segregation." Using tactics that Marshall and Wilkins believed would hasten the desegregation of schools, local NAACP members distributed handbills at the polls that urged the city's black voters to "wake up and vote no. Respect your birthright; hold your head up with dignity. Support for the bond issue will allow segregation to live on."[45]

The election revived divisions in the black community between moderates who favored improvements in the segregated system and militants who supported desegregation. The principal of Archer Elementary, William Merriweather, whose school was slated to receive $119,000 for a cafeteria, supported the measure, arguing that additional facilities were needed "regardless of how the schools are operated." While some blacks voted for the bond, most African Americans opposed it. The measure was defeated in all the predominately black wards in the city, with the most significant opposition coming in wards where the largest numbers of advantaged blacks lived. By increasing the number of African American voters who opposed the measure in an election where the board needed strong black support, the NAACP contributed to the bond's defeat. African American activism and white apathy defeated the bond by a vote of 930 to 714.[46]

Local NAACP activists blocked the board's efforts to improve the black schools, and increased support among African Americans for desegregation. J. Arthur Brown was elated, calling the results a "moral victory" for the NAACP. Roy Wilkins, who had little to cheer about in the late 1950s, praised the local NAACP's campaign and its demands for "compliance with Supreme Court rulings." School officials did not want to admit it, but the trustees were frightened by the NAACP's show of political power and Brown's demands for desegregation. The board considered putting another bond up for a vote, but the trustees rejected the idea, worrying that the NAACP might defeat it and increase the association's "prestige among the colored people." As black enrollment continued to grow and white enrollment continued to fall, the board feared that empty classrooms in the white schools and increasing overcrowding in the black system were an "invitation to integration." In 1958 the board reassigned white students who attended Courtenay Elementary School and transferred the building to the black system, a move that J. Arthur Brown denounced as an "appeasement measure." As school officials began exploring other sources of funding, J. Arthur Brown announced that "we have been contacted by several parents disgusted with the inequities in our local schools."[47]

The defeat of the bond election—like the desegregation petitions, the direct-action protests at State, and the black applications for admission to USC—pushed the black struggle for educational equality and access forward during a time when the NAACP struggled to survive. Looking back, Marshall argued that the NAACP should have done more to capitalize on the momentum it had in May 1954. "The major blame was on us, in not pushing, in not planning." After *Brown*, "we should have sat down and planned. The other side did. And so they took the initiative. During the late 1950s, [we] lost all of our initiative." The inability of the NAACP to push harder and the Court's refusal to become involved in desegregating southern schools, allowed South Carolina's political and educational leadership to seize the initiative and institutionalize new, more rational barriers to the admission of black students to schools, colleges, and universities in the 1950s.[48]

SEVEN

Evading *Brown*, 1954–1960

The most significant achievement of massive resistance was delaying desegregation and providing educational and political authorities with time to institutionalize new, more legally defensible barriers to African American access to schools, colleges, and universities. In South Carolina and other southern states massive resistance was only part of a broader, more sophisticated effort to preserve segregation. As educational and political authorities retaliated against African Americans who pressed for access and equality, David W. Robinson and Senator L. Marion Gressette's Segregation Committee insulated white educational institutions by providing legal assistance to school and university officials who adopted new college-admission requirements and expanded testing and tracking in the public schools. State and local authorities retained control over educational policy because the Supreme Court's implementation decree, *Brown II*, gave local political and educational leaders primary responsibility for solving the problems posed by the elimination of state-sanctioned segregation. In South Carolina and other southern states the most durable resistance to African American demands for desegregation came from moderates not extremists. Unlike extremists, who defied the courts, moderates recognized the legitimacy of *Brown* and used state and local control of educational policy to evade desegregation.

While the Supreme Court's May 17, 1954, decision defined one set of possibilities, southern attorneys convinced the justices to limit those possibilities in 1955. When the Court announced *Brown*, it asked parties to the case to submit briefs and participate in oral arguments, which were held in April 1955. The Court's implementation decree was shaped by the arguments of southern lawyers, who urged the Court to let state and local officials "work the matter out on a local level." Clarendon County attorney S. Emory Rogers declared that compliance in South Carolina would depend on "the decree handed down." Robert Figg Jr. told the Court that immediate desegregation "would destroy the public school system of South Carolina." Citing racial differences in "the general level of educational capacity," attorneys representing Farmville, Virginia, urged "a now indeterminate period to elapse before requiring integration of the races" in the state's public schools. There were, southern lawyers suggested, more "subtle ways" of preserving segregation.[1]

The NAACP opposed a gradual remedy, but it did not question the rights or prerogatives of southern school officials to define the problems posed by the end of state-sanctioned segregation. "That the Negro is so disadvantaged educationally and culturally in the states where segregation is required," the NAACP's brief declared, "is the strongest argument against its continuation. Yet those who use this argument as a basis for interminable delay in the elimination of segregation in reality are seeking to utilize the product of their own wrongdoing as a justification for continued malfeasance." Thurgood Marshall and his colleagues failed to question the good faith of southern school officials, referring to them as the "finest people in the community," and as Mark V. Tushnet has noted, Marshall "seemed to be more confident in the good faith of southern whites than the southern lawyers were." When Justice Felix Frankfurter expressed concerns about the Court becoming a "super-school board," Marshall replied: "the problems can be worked out locally." Responding to Frankfurter's concerns that desegregation would "lower educational standards," Marshall conceded that school officials could devise "whatever other plan they want to work out. The question is made about the educational level of children. They give tests to grade children, so what do we think is the solution? Simple. Put the dumb colored children in with the dumb white children, and put the smart colored children with the smart white children—that is no problem." In an attempt to eliminate what Marshall called the racial test, the NAACP provided southern school officials with the opportunity to use "the product of their own wrongdoing as a justification for continued malfeasance."[2]

Like earlier rulings in teacher-salary and higher-education cases, the implementation decree left compliance to southern educational authorities, sanctioning resistance and leaving the door open to evasions that institutionalized more rational forms of segregation. Emphasizing "local problems," the Court gave "school authorities primary responsibility for elucidating, assessing, and solving these problems." In sending the *Brown* cases back to the district courts, the Court let southern judges and school officials decide just what possibilities it had created.[3]

The most significant ruling to emerge from the district courts' reconsideration of the school-segregation cases was Judge John Parker's 1955 ruling in *Briggs v. Elliott*. After declaring that the U.S. District Court had a duty "to accept the law as declared by the Supreme Court," Parker ruled that the Supreme Court "has not decided that the federal courts are to take over or regulate the public schools of the states." In what became known as the *Briggs* dictum, Parker held that the "Constitution does not require integration; it merely forbids discrimination." All the Supreme Court had decided, he wrote, "is that a state may not deny to any person on account of race the right to attend any school that it maintains." The district court declared South Carolina's school-segregation laws "null and void" but emphasized that nothing in the Court's *Brown* decision "takes away from the people freedom to choose the schools they attend." The 1955 *Briggs* ruling set no deadline for desegregation, and school officials were not "restrained from refusing" to admit students "on account of race" until after school officials made "the necessary arrangements."[4]

In South Carolina the architect of these arrangements was David W. Robinson. During the 1940s Robinson had chaired a special committee that convinced the legislature to adopt the National Teacher Examinations (NTE), defended the state in *Wrighten v. Board of Trustees*, and convinced the legislature to replace the diploma privilege with new requirements for admission to the state bar. In 1951 Robinson was appointed to the Educational Finance Commission (EFC), and after *Brown*, he became chief counsel to Gressette's Segregation Committee, supervising a legal staff that conducted research, conferred with lawyers in other southern states, and advised local school and university officials on how to meet "educational problems" within the law. Drawing on and refining educational policies and practices the state had adopted in response to NAACP-sponsored challenges in teacher-equalization, higher-education, and school-desegregation cases, Robinson designed legally defensible and durable solutions to the challenges posed by *Brown*.[5]

Calling for "calm and considered thinking," Robinson outlined a strategy for limiting and controlling the process of desegregation. The strategy rested on a shrewd analysis of precedents established in the NAACP's legal campaign against segregation, where the courts struck down racial classifications but vested in local educational authorities the responsibility for complying with the constitutional command of equality. *Brown II* and Parker's 1955 decision in *Briggs* reaffirmed the right of state and local educational authorities to define the problems posed by desegregation. Robinson believed that the Gressette Committee's legal staff could "limit the federal court's responsibility to racial matters" and protect the prerogatives of local authorities in educational matters. Working with university presidents and school officials, Robinson encouraged authorities to exploit racial differences in educational achievement that generations of exclusion and discrimination had produced. Robinson knew that standardized tests could be used to "legitimately disqualify" most African American applicants "for educational reasons" and prevent the "mixing" of large numbers of white and black students. He recognized that some African Americans would qualify for admission, but he wrote that "a few Negroes" would not "create severe problems." As Robinson worked to institutionalize new, more legally defensible restrictions, he used his position on the EFC to press local officials to equalize facilities, arguing that "newer, more modern buildings will tend to keep Negroes in Negro schools."[6]

As counsel at the University of South Carolina, Robinson helped university officials adopt new admission requirements that limited black access. Race may not have been the only reason for changes in university admissions policies, but the timing of the decision, ten days after *Brown*, and the comments of University of South Carolina (USC) President Donald Russell and other administrators reveal an unmistakable intention to discriminate. During the late 1950s other colleges and universities in the state and region followed Russell's "pioneering" policy, adopting standardized tests that institutionalized restrictions that could no longer be based on race.

Educational authorities in South Carolina considered new admission requirements in the early 1950s, but they did not adopt them until after *Brown*. The Court's 1950 ruling in *Sweatt v. Painter* and African American applications for admission to the University of South Carolina led Governor Byrnes to encourage public college and university presidents to prepare for the possibility of desegregation. In the early 1950s USC, like other public universities in the region, had what was essentially an open-admissions policy. Students who graduated from high schools that were accredited by the state were ensured admission. Since the state also accredited African American high schools, Byrnes was concerned that the state's four white public colleges—the Citadel, Clemson, the University of South Carolina, and Winthrop—would be compelled to admit African American applicants. Hoping to insulate the university, Robinson approved a statement that appeared for the first time in the 1952 catalog: "In order to safeguard its ideals, the university reserves the right to decline admission, when for any reason, it is deemed in the interest of the university." Like other southern universities, USC also began requiring that applicants submit a photograph.[7]

Still, Byrnes and Robinson knew the university was vulnerable, and the governor continued lobbying. In 1952 a committee consisting of members of the South Carolina College Association, an organization of white institutions of higher education, endorsed the use of standardized exams, noting that they would be "a valuable safeguard should the Supreme Court fail to uphold segregation in the state's schools." However, most college and university presidents in South Carolina did not support the use of tests. At the time fewer than 5 percent of the nation's college applicants took the Scholastic Aptitude Test (SAT). In the South only a handful of private colleges, including Agnes Scott, Duke, Emory, and Sophie Newcomb of Tulane, required applicants to submit SAT scores. University of South Carolina president Norman O. Smith worried that requiring tests in a region where "almost no one took them" would hurt recruitment and enrollment, which had fallen to postwar lows. Powerful members of the university's board, Solomon Blatt Jr., son of the former speaker of the South Carolina House of Representatives, and A. C. Todd worried that the exams might "eliminate some football talent." Winthrop College president Henry R. Simms argued

that "too many human qualities are, as of now, unmeasurable by present methods
—character, motivation, determination, ambition, leadership, social cooperation, among others."[8]

Brynes's protégé, Donald S. Russell, who was appointed president of USC in
1952, continued the campaign for the adoption of new admission requirements.
A USC graduate, Russell served under Byrnes at the Office of War Mobilization
and in the U.S. State Department before returning to South Carolina to become
a partner in Byrnes's law firm in Spartanburg. Appointed to the university's board
in 1947, Russell quickly won the respect of college administrators and faculty,
who applauded his appointment to the presidency. Bringing vigor to a campus
that had languished after the war, Russell recruited new faculty members and
secured funds for expansion of the physical plant. Enrollment rose, fueled in
part by a series of football victories over Clemson and the increasing number of
women who chose USC over Winthrop, the state-supported women's college.
Russell had political ambitions and knew that he would have to preserve segregation at USC to realize them. Like Byrnes and Robinson, Russell saw that
standardized tests could be used to exclude legally most African American
applicants.[9]

As the Supreme Court concluded its deliberations in the *Brown* cases, Russell appointed a faculty committee that enlisted the prestige of the Educational
Testing Service (ETS) in the effort to restrict the admission of African Americans.
Chaired by mathematics professor W. L. Williams, the committee also included
W. C. McCall, the director of the university's counseling bureau, who—along
with Robinson and Ben Wood—had convinced the General Assembly to adopt
the NTE in 1945. In November, Russell sent Williams to Princeton to confer
with ETS and College Board officials about the "possibility and feasibility" of
using the SAT "as a requirement for new students entering the university." Following the meeting, Williams sent a memo to Russell that outlined the reasons
why the university and other public colleges in the state should adopt ETS tests
as a requirement for admission. Williams told Russell that ETS was eager to
"help us with our problem." Williams argued that the tests would provide an
objective basis for selecting the best students and protect the university from
being "overrun with poorly prepared students." Some members of the committee wanted the university to administer its own admissions tests, but Williams
counseled against this, writing that "if the time should ever come when colored
people are admitted to the university, the NAACP would undoubtedly attack
any plan which the university may have for limiting students. However, if the
limiting were done on the basis of tests given by an outside agency with national
prestige," he argued, "the NAACP would be less likely to try to intervene."[10]

While the ETS offered "prestige" and "expertise," the University of South
Carolina provided the testing service with an opportunity to expand use of the

SAT in the South at a time when no state system of higher education in the region required college applicants to take the SAT. The ETS had been established with a small grant from the Carnegie Foundation in 1948, but the income generated by the Carnegie endowment was never sufficient to support the organization. As Nicholas Lemann has shown, ETS was "set up in a way that guaranteed its first priority would be to work aggressively to expand testing. The push was to continually look for ways of expanding its offerings." In the 1950s the most promising opportunity for expansion was the testing of college applicants. Fueled by rising persistence rates, the baby boom, and economic prosperity, studies predicted "an impending tidal wave" of college students, with the sharpest increases occurring after 1960. The university's proposal presented the ETS with the opportunity to reach beyond the handful of private institutions that required the SAT in the South and administer standardized college entrance exams to students who sought admission to southern colleges and universities. In correspondence with university officials ETS leaders wrote that they were very interested in helping South Carolina "become the very first state" in the South "to require the full program of the College Board." In the 1950s, as in the 1940s, NAACP legal victories provided opportunities for the expansion of standardized testing in the South.[11]

On May 27, 1954, fewer than two weeks after the Court issued the *Brown* decision, Russell secured faculty and board approval of a new admissions policy that required all applicants to submit standardized-test scores. When Russell presented the proposal to the USC faculty on May 27, 1954, one professor, echoing the sentiments of colleagues on other southern campuses, asked Russell, "let's face it, Mr. President. Is it not true that these entrance examinations are, in reality, being introduced as a means of keeping out Negro applicants?" Russell acknowledged that the new admissions policy would allow the university to "legally exclude students" by establishing "a system of entrance examinations that are not based on racial standards." After assuring the faculty that "qualified" Negroes who passed "these proposed entrance examinations" would be "admitted," the proposal was adopted. The next day, the board approved the new policy. On June 1, 1954, the University of South Carolina became the first state college or university in the South to require that the "admission of all new students would be by examination." The new policy was widely publicized in South Carolina newspapers. Thomas Waring conceded that "there will be some intelligent well-prepared Negroes who would pass the tests," but the new policy, he wrote, will be "an immediate guarantee that tens of thousands of diploma-bearing Negro high school graduates would not show up next autumn at the gates of our white colleges."[12]

Concerned that the timing of the decision would attract unwanted attention, university administrators discussed how the new policy should be announced and implemented. After conferring with Robinson, Russell circulated a draft, but one university official called it "timid. Only a lawyer would extract the meaning, and that is precisely what we don't want." In May, Dean Orin F. Crow announced that "applicants for admission on or after June 1, 1954" would be required to take entrance examinations. Statements by Crow and Russell emphasized that a faculty committee had been "working on such a program for a year" and that the new requirements were "conducive to the promotion of sound academic standards." The new requirement was adopted so suddenly, however, that the ETS could not provide the tests, and McCall had to use "acceptable and safe materials I possess" to test students who applied to the university in the summer and fall of 1954. In July 1954 the Committee on Entrance Examinations established minimum-score requirements that excluded 5 percent of the freshman applicants and 7 percent of the transfer applicants. As the ETS prepared tests for the coming academic year, McCall wrote R. H. Plumlee at the testing service, telling him to "cut the number of items. We need to curtail our entrance exam until the financial problems become modified through participation by other state-supported colleges." McCall encouraged Russell to secure funds to support the new testing program. "South Carolina led the nation in instituting and administering the NTE," McCall wrote. "Let us insist on the money necessary to enable a 'South Carolina Entrance Examination Program' of which we can be equally proud."[13]

To reduce costs Russell continued to campaign for statewide adoption of standardized entrance examinations, and by 1958 all South Carolina public colleges had adopted the new admission requirements. In the summer of 1954 Russell sent members of the South Carolina College Association copies of the university's new requirements, informing them that "this imminent situation demanded a new look at entrance tests. We have been concerned for some time," he wrote, "with the abnormal expansion in student load to be reasonably anticipated in the next fifteen years." At USC, as at other state-supported institutions, desegregation was far more imminent than "abnormal expansion" of student enrollment. In the fall of 1954 enrollment at USC was 2,980, almost 1,000 students below what it had been in the fall of 1949. At Winthrop College enrollment fell from 1,600 to 1,000 between 1946 and 1956. Reversing a position he had taken in 1951, Winthrop president Henry R. Simms convinced the college's board to adopt the new requirements to "protect our academic standards." After an African American applied to Clemson in 1955, it too signed on. In spite of objections from Turner, the board at South Carolina State also adopted the new requirement, providing another institution to share the costs of the program.[14]

Having secured the support of Winthrop, South Carolina State, and Clemson, Russell and McCall signed a contract with the ETS to supply "a series of aptitude tests for college admission." In August 1956 ETS vice president William

Turnball told university officials, "the South Carolina program represents a significant undertaking especially in the extended form now proposed for it, and one in which it is entirely appropriate for us to work directly with you on." ETS officials were especially interested in South Carolina because it offered an opportunity to "extend services particularly appropriate to state-wide testing programs." As many expected, Russell resigned as USC president in 1958 to run for governor. During his unsuccessful campaign against Ernest Hollings, Russell asserted that because of his leadership, the state's system of higher education had "pioneered in protecting our southern way of life and in taking a necessary precautionary step."[15]

During the late 1950s other southern states followed South Carolina's "pioneering" policy and began requiring that applicants to state-supported colleges and universities submit SAT scores. When University of North Carolina sociologist Guy B. Johnson interviewed university administrators in several southern states in the fall of 1953, he found that "in practically all the schools surveyed, the administration has an interest in holding down the number of Negro enrollees." Standardized tests provided a legally defensible way of restricting black access after *Brown*. University officials told Johnson that "the majority of Negro students are handicapped by an inferior educational background, as well as by other social and economic factors, and are not ready to compete with white students on equal terms." Several southern universities changed admission policies in 1956, at the height of massive resistance. In Florida and Georgia educational authorities institutionalized new entrance policies that required applicants to submit scores on specially designed ETS tests in 1956. State officials in Virginia wrote McCall that year, informing him that "state-supported colleges are considering a proposal to test all high school seniors who wish to apply for admission to one of the colleges." North Carolina adopted new entrance requirements in 1958 that required applicants to the Women's College in Greensboro, North Carolina State, and the University of North Carolina to submit test scores.[16]

Southern university administrators justified the new policies on educational grounds, arguing that rising demand for higher education required greater selectivity. The number of students attending college in the South did increase, from 565,000 students in 1950 to 954,000 in 1960, and some southern colleges and universities were overcrowded. However, in the years leading up to the changes in college and university requirements, African American college enrollment rose much more sharply than white enrollment.[17]

The statements of educational and political leaders in Florida, Tennessee, and Mississippi, like those in South Carolina, show that race rather than rising white enrollment was the main motivation for the adoption of new admission requirements. In 1956 the chair of the State Board of Higher Education in Florida, Fred Kent, acknowledged that requirements for admission to the state's undergraduate colleges were "tightened with the segregation issue in mind." J. Lewis Hall, an attorney who served on the state's segregation committee, stated that when test scores were combined with other factors, the number of African Americans who would be eligible for admission to white universities would be reduced "to a comparatively small percent." According to Kent, "if there is any great influx of applicants to our overcrowded institutions, we can take only the best qualified ones. Maybe some will be Negroes." In Tennessee university officials claimed that they could not admit black students because Memphis State University was overcrowded. Enrollment at that municipally funded institution was at an all-time high, but the court found that it included more than one thousand nonresident white students. After the court ordered university officials to admit black students in 1955, the university officials "announced that a special entrance examination would be established for applicants to the graduate school." Members of the board of trustees acknowledged that the examinations were "intended to limit the enrollment of Negro students." In 1958 the Tennessee State Board of Education authorized each public institution of higher education in the state "to establish whatever scholastic entrance requirements it deemed necessary." Three days after James Meredith applied for admission to the University of Mississippi in 1961, the registrar informed him that "pending applications had been discontinued due to alleged 'overcrowded conditions.'" Soon after he was admitted in 1962, standardized-test scores became the sole criterion for admission to the University of Mississippi. This requirement was adopted, the courts found, "because it deterred black enrollment" and could be used to minimize desegregation.[18]

In the years after *Brown*, Robinson and the Gressette Committee legal staff also played a key role in encouraging school officials in South Carolina to erect new barriers to black access at the same time that they improved black schools as a way of enticing African Americans to remain in their own institutions. Charleston educational authorities were far more successful at rationalizing restrictions that could no longer rest on race than equalizing white and black schools, because, as we saw in chapter 6, NAACP opposition to a $1.1 million school bond prevented the trustees from raising the funds needed to improve Burke and other black schools.

Acting on Robinson's advice, school officials in Charleston expanded testing and tracking in public schools. After Parker's 1955 ruling in *Briggs* declared the state's school-segregation statutes unconstitutional, "one of the first things the staff recommended," Robinson recalled, "was passage of legislation that gave local school boards the discretion and power to assign pupils in the best interests of education." Passed by the legislature in 1955, South Carolina's pupil-placement law, like those enacted in nine other southern states, strengthened the power and authority of local officials over student assignment.[19]

A week after African Americans petitioned the Charleston school board for desegregation in July 1955, Superintendent Robert Gaines attended "an interesting and encouraging" meeting with members of the Gressette Committee. Acting on the committee's advice, school officials wrote J. Arthur Brown in September 1955, telling him that "the application of each pupil must be taken up on its merits. There are many considerations other than color that must be taken into account by the board in assigning pupils in this district." The NAACP challenged pupil-placement laws in several southern states, arguing that they were part of a package of policies designed to evade desegregation, but the courts consistently affirmed the right of school officials to determine student assignments. In North Carolina the court upheld the state's placement-law ruling that "we can think of no one better qualified to undertake the task" of enrolling pupils in the schools "than officials of the schools and school boards." The most significant challenge came in Alabama, where the court held that the state's placement law provided for "the admission of qualified pupils upon a basis of individual merit without regard to their race or color." *New York Times* reporter Arthur Krock found that the ruling, which was upheld by the Supreme Court in 1958, indicated how desegregation "could legally be held to a very small percentage for a long time, as measured in decades, if the purpose and result of Negro exclusion were to preserve the moral and adequate standards of a public school."[20]

Robinson paid close attention to the court's desegregation rulings and argued that "there are few Negroes educationally qualified to go to schools with similarly aged white children." While the use of standardized tests in the United States grew during the 1950s, the wave of testing that swept through the South after *Brown* was clearly designed to rationalize restrictions that had been based on race. In 1955 and 1956 white and black students in Alexandria, Atlanta, Baltimore, Charleston, Charlotte, Louisville, Memphis, Miami, New Orleans, St. Louis, Washington, Wilmington, and other southern cities were tested. School officials used test results to expand tracking, the separation of students on the basis of presumed ability. One survey of southern school districts in 1959 found that "a growing number of districts in the South are establishing 'track' systems. Numerous public schools also have developed 'honors' courses in science, mathematics, English, foreign languages, and sometimes other fields."[21]

Robinson encouraged school officials to use standardized-test scores to restrict African American admission to elementary and secondary schools. Educational authorities in Charleston, like those other southern cities, administered standardized tests and used the results to expand tracking in the public schools, institutionalizing new, more legally defensible barriers to black access. In the spring of 1956 twenty-five hundred white and black high-school students in Charleston took the California Test of Mental Maturity. As table 5 shows, 79 percent of the white students scored above 90, while 77 percent of the black students scored below 90. In 1957 the school board established a three-tiered track system at the High School of Charleston, Rivers, and Burke that assigned those with scores above 90 to an honors track, those with scores between 70 and 90 to a general track, and those with scores below 70 to a remedial track. School superintendent Robert Gaines described the honors program as a "very selective" program that was "very demanding of a student's effort" and would only be open to the "more able students." The *Evening Post* described the "classical curriculum" as "a rigid course of study" that included "four years of Latin or French, three years of science, three years of solid math, and little room for electives." After Gaines reported that the program was "going well," tracking was extended to the elementary schools.[22]

The track system that was established in Charleston, like those that were created or expanded in other southern school districts after *Brown*, exploited differences in academic achievement that were generations in the making. While the social, economic, and educational determinants of African American achievement improved in the 1940s and early 1950s, the legacies of poverty, low parental educational attainment, and overcrowded schools exerted a profound intergenerational drag on what students learned. Postwar educational research showed how menial jobs, meager incomes, low parental educational attainment, and crowded living conditions continued to limit the achievement of most African Americans. Summarizing these findings, Richard Kluger has written that all too often, black children grew up in overcrowded households that had "high noise levels." During the 1950s researchers found that black children learned to tune out sounds, which reduced "their hearing acuity and their ability to distinguish subtle differences in sounds essential in learning how to read." Many children lived in households, studies found, where parents did not use "standard English." In Charleston, as in other southern cities, more than 40 percent of African American adults worked as laborers or domestic servants and came home exhausted by the demands of their jobs. In 1949 the median income of black families was 49 percent that of white families. By 1960 two of every three

Table 5 *White and Black Student Scores on California Test of Mental Maturity, Charleston, 1956*

	White		Black	
	Number	Percent	Number	Percent
90+	883	79.7	328	23.0
70–90	217	19.6	921	64.8
>70	7	0.7	172	12.1

Source: Charleston Board of School Commissioners Minute Books, 27 November 1956; 27 January 1957.

African American adults in the city had completed fewer than six years of schooling, several years fewer than whites. As a result, many were unable to help their children with high-school-level homework assignments. Hampered by exclusionist employment policies, low family incomes, overcrowded living conditions, and limited parental educational attainment, most African American students entered school at a disadvantage. Robinson saw these disadvantages as a rational basis for continued segregation.[23]

The policies of the Charleston school board magnified the differences black and white students brought to school. For generations Burke students were confined to an overcrowded and inadequately funded institution where even the most determined efforts of black students were constrained by a lack of resources. After 1954 school officials continued to argue that Burke students should be excluded from a curriculum that prepared students for college and the professions. During the extended discussions about the establishment of a track system in the city's high schools, several school board members objected to the introduction of an honors course at Burke, arguing that "more emphasis should be placed on courses that would be most useful to the Negroes." While some board members did not believe "Negroes" were capable of doing honors work, pressure from Gaines convinced the trustees that blacks "deserved" an honors course because, as Gaines put it, there was "a very wide range of ability among [black] pupils."[24]

As much as Robinson hoped that test results would limit access to a "few Negroes," 23 percent of the students at Burke qualified for the honors track. Many of the students who enrolled in the honors course at Burke were heirs of the city's black elite. In 1954, 25 percent of the students enrolled at Burke had transferred from Avery. These students' class background and access to a liberal-arts education prepared them to compete with whites. Generations of inadequate funding and overcrowding "disqualified" most Burke students, but Avery created another legacy—one that prepared the sons and daughters of Charleston's professional and commercial classes to compete with whites. In a letter to NAACP executive secretary Roy Wilkins, Thomas Waring wrote that "the racial problem is thus also a class problem. Perhaps as the Negro middle-class grows, adjustments will be easier on both sides."[25]

Well before student activists, the NAACP, and the federal government forced the state of South Carolina to desegregate schools, colleges, and universities, educational and political leaders constructed a new, more rational educational order that limited the possibilities of the Supreme Court's May 17, 1954, *Brown* decision.

EIGHT

Disorder and Desegregation, 1960–1963

"The protests hit at the right time," Thurgood Marshall recalled. "[We regained] the initiative once the protests and demonstrations achieved their momentum. Yes, I think [the protests] saved it. I think it might have died on the vine." During the early 1960s African Americans turned to new forms of protest to realize the educational possibilities of the *Brown* decision. Part of what C. Vann Woodward called "one of the great uprisings of oppressed people in the twentieth century," the sit-ins in Charleston and Orangeburg, like those in more than one hundred other southern cities and towns, were organized by African American high-school and college students. Like earlier generations of student activists, the young people who led direct-action demonstrations in the early 1960s acted on lessons of equality and used skills developed in extracurricular programs that were taught in black high schools and colleges. Direct-action demonstrations expressed deepening African American resentment at the lack of desegregation in a way that could not be ignored.[1]

In Charleston, as elsewhere, student activism stirred the NAACP, which renewed its campaign to desegregate schools, colleges, and universities. As students sought redress in the streets and raised the political and economic costs of continued segregation, the violent resistance to the desegregation of the University of Georgia and the University of Mississippi pushed political leaders in South Carolina to desegregate Clemson College and the University of South Carolina in 1963. Although black students crossed the color line in higher education, officials continued to resist desegregation of the public schools, and during the summer of 1963 students staged direct-action demonstrations that made continued segregation of the public schools incompatible with order and paved the way for the court-ordered desegregation of the Charleston public schools in the fall of 1963. What was required, Marshall recalled, was the "conglomeration" of "legal movements in the courts, protest movements in the streets, and pressure in legislative halls."[2]

As the 1950s drew to a close, the public schools in South Carolina, Alabama, Georgia, Louisiana, and Mississippi remained completely segregated. Elsewhere in the region, violence, pupil-placement laws, and educational evasions kept desegregation at token levels. The Supreme Court did intervene when the authority of the Court was directly challenged, as in Little Rock, but the Court's ruling in *Cooper v. Aaron* (1958) provided little encouragement for a renewed assault against school segregation. In 1960 fewer than 1 percent of African American students in the South were attending school with whites. A similar pattern prevailed in higher education, where legal, educational, and violent resistance kept colleges and universities in Alabama, Georgia, Mississippi, and South Carolina completely segregated and limited access to token numbers of black students in other southern states. Increasing numbers of advantaged African Americans attended desegregated institutions in Arkansas, Delaware, Maryland, and Missouri, but in North Carolina, Louisiana, Tennessee, and Virginia, progress toward desegregation was slow. Here too, the Court failed to clarify the meaning of *Brown* beyond telling lower courts to consider African American applications "under conditions that now prevail." By the end of the 1950s the imprecise estimates at hand suggest that perhaps three thousand of the region's almost one hundred thousand black college students attended desegregated institutions of higher education in the South.[3]

African Americans continued to press for access, but securing admission to schools, colleges, and universities, remained a long and arduous process as vicious white opposition to desegregation persisted. Facing a labyrinth of legal, administrative, and educational obstacles that the NAACP could not navigate, African Americans were by the end of the 1950s increasingly resentful about the lack of change in educational institutions. Clearly, more than legal action was needed.[4]

In the spring of 1960, impatient with the glacial pace of change in the schools, young people launched a new phase of the African American struggle for equality and access. When *New York Times* reporter Claude Sitton visited Charlotte, North Carolina, in February 1960, he found that "the [sit-in] movement reflected growing dissatisfaction over the slow pace of desegregation in schools and other public facilities." The sit-ins that swept through the South in the spring of 1960 were a product of a generation of institutional development in southern black communities. Much has been made of the students' youth and spontaneity, but as Aldon D. Morris, William H. Chafe, and others have shown, the sit-in movement drew much of its inspiration and strength from a network of existing African American institutions. "The inspiration, the energy, the power, the recruits, and the leaders of the mighty movement against segregation came out of the tightly segregated communities of the South," Woodward wrote. "The whole thing is inconceivable without these all-black churches, colleges, and schools." African Americans were educated through a tightly knit network of families, churches, and voluntary associations, but African American schools played a central role in fueling the direct action demonstrations that began in 1960 and continued through 1963. Much of the literature on the sit-ins examines black colleges, but as Morris and Chafe have shown, the seeds of the sit-ins were planted in black high schools.[5]

The four North Carolina Agricultural and Technical freshmen who initiated the sit-ins in Greensboro in February 1960 were inspired by high-school teachers. Chafe's history of the sit-ins in Greensboro, where the movement began, shows that "black high schools generated the pride and aspiration that motivated the sit-in demonstrators." Three of the four students who walked into the Woolworth's store in Greensboro on February 1, 1960, graduated from the city's Dudley High School, where Vance Chavis and Nell Coley inspired a generation of African American students. Both were members of the local NAACP. Chavis taught physics, but he constantly reminded his students "not to go in the back way at the movie theater and climb all those steps in order to pay for segregation." In her English classes Coley proffered similar lessons. "We were always talking about issues," she recalled. "We might read [a poem or a novel] as a kind of pivot," but the texts were always related to "the inalienable rights of all human beings." Like Chavis, she taught students that "the way you find things need not happen. You must not accept." Looking back on her years at Dudley, she recalled that "we were leading the children to be the best persons that they could be. And if the spin-off leads the kids who are going to be leaders in [protests] so be it. We were just trying to inspire folks, trying to make them realize their potential." Not every African American educator was as inspiring as Chavis or Coley, but teachers and professors provided crucial encouragement.[6]

In February 1960 the sit-ins spread through what Morris has called "well-forged" educational networks as student-government leaders used leadership and organizational skills developed in extracurricular programs to mobilize students, who were "linked by fraternities and sororities and cultural and athletic events." Following nonviolent training workshops, Claflin and State College students in Orangeburg staged sit-ins in late February. Two weeks later, as one thousand students from Claflin, State, and Wilkerson High School marched toward downtown, they were confronted by police. After they refused to retreat, police turned fire hoses on the marchers and arrested 388. State College education professor Charles Thomas persuaded homeowners to post bond, and many students were bailed out that evening on the assets of teachers and professors. The Orangeburg County Teachers' Association published a resolution commending the students for their "orderly demonstration for first-class citizenship." That night, State College Law School graduates Matthew J. Perry, Lincoln Jenkins, Zack E. Townsend, and Newton Pough conferred with the law-school faculty preparing for a court appearance the following day.[7]

In Charleston, as in other southern cities that did not have African American colleges, high-school students spearheaded the movement. While Burke students emulated the example of other young people, they acted on the lessons of dignity and equality that were woven through courses and clubs. Families, youth groups, and churches educated students who staged sit-ins in Charleston, but Burke High School played a particularly important role in launching sit-ins in the city. "Teachers gave us high ideals and ambition," recalled James Blake, who led the movement in Charleston. "They taught us we were first-class citizens and not to let the color of our skin or our background to keep us from achieving." Most of the Burkites who participated in the sit-ins were honor students who were deeply involved in extracurricular activities that faculty and administrators used to develop leadership skills. In clubs, the *Parvenue* noted, students learned "how to cooperate with each other, make adjustments, to express one's opinion intelligently, and to realize the true meaning of living in a democracy." The young people who organized the sit-ins were leaders of clubs, athletic teams, and student government. Mamie Lou White was valedictorian and president of the senior council; Harvey Gantt, salutatorian and captain of the football team; Cornelius Fludd, president of the student council; James Blake, editor of the *Parvenue*. The leadership and organizational skills these students learned at Burke were a key ingredient in the Charleston sit-ins.[8]

The sit-ins in Charleston were a product of a generation of institutional development at Burke. In March 1960 *Parvenue* editor James Blake attended a meeting of the Palmetto Scholastic Press Association at State College, where he learned firsthand about the sit-ins by college students. When he returned to Burke, he urged his peers to "Stand Up and Be Counted" in an editorial in the school newspaper. "Throughout the history of America man has been asking for his inalienable rights to live and be respected as a human being," Blake wrote. But some Americans have "been denied those rights and privileges due him. Is it wrong to try to obtain one's rights? Is it wrong to want what is rightfully ours?" Harvey Gantt remembers feeling that "if the kids in Greensboro and [State] College can sit at lunch counters, then maybe we can do it too." The example set by other young blacks in the South led Burke students to turn to two of the school's most respected teachers for advice and guidance.[9]

Like Vance Chavis and Nell Coley, Eugene Hunt and J. Michael Graves encouraged the students to act. "There was nothing we couldn't talk to them about," recalled Blake. "What should we do? What would you do? Would you stage a sit-in at Woolworth's?" Graves remembered them asking. "I told them that I would probably go and sit down and be served. We encouraged them to do the kind of thing they did." After discussing the idea with Hunt and Graves, the students held a series of evening meetings at Burke, the Reid Christian Center, and in Minerva Brown's house, where they developed plans and reviewed the techniques of nonviolence. Although they did not tell their parents, the students kept Hunt and Graves apprised of their intentions.[10]

As Burke teachers attended a Palmetto Educators' Association meeting in Columbia on April 1, 1960, twenty-four Burke students walked into the local S. H. Kress store and asked to be served at the lunch counter. Although they were allowed to shop in the store, state law prohibited blacks from eating at the lunch counter. Shocked by the students' action, the waitress tried to dissuade them by pouring ammonia on the counter. They sat patiently for more than five hours, reciting the Twenty-third Psalm and the Lord's Prayer. At 4:45 the store received a bomb threat, and Police Chief William Kelly asked the students to leave. When they refused, Kelly arrested them. In the weeks that followed, more than seventy-five students from Burke, Immaculate Conception, Gresham Meggett, and other black high schools in the area staged eight separate sit-ins. The students were charged with trespassing. John Wrighten helped arrange for their release, using funds raised by local NAACP leaders. Graduating from Burke that spring, sit-in leaders Gantt, Blake, White, Fludd, and others were showered with awards and scholarships by parents, teachers, and alumni in a graduation ceremony that celebrated their activism. "We were heroes," Blake recalled.[11]

In Charleston, as in other cities in the Deep South, the sit-ins did not lead to the desegregation of lunch counters, but student activism united African Americans in a way they had not been before 1960. "They didn't necessarily say so," noted Blake, but "parents were behind us." Harvey Gantt recalled that the sit-ins caused quite a stir, but they "gave me a sense of responsibility. A lot of other people felt the same way: We ought to do something to change the system." J. Arthur Brown, whose daughter Minerva participated in the sit-ins, announced that "direct action protests and demonstrations would continue. We are no longer content to remain complacent while gross injustices are thrust upon us." Initially, the NAACP legal staff was reluctant to support student activism, but after a three-day lawyers' conference convened the weekend after the arrests of almost four hundred students in Orangeburg, Marshall announced that "every young person arrested as a result of participation in peaceful protest against racial segregation will have adequate legal defense." NAACP attorney Constance Baker Motley recalled that "we certainly wouldn't have counseled people to march down the street and defy the city officials. But they did it. And once they did, we had to represent them. That's why I felt this was a real revolution: because now the people themselves were involved." The students who staged the sit-in at Kress left Charleston for college in the fall of 1960, but they left behind new ways to express resentment about the unwillingness of whites to meet black demands for change in the schools.[12]

The sit-ins in Charleston pushed PTA leaders toward a confrontation with the school board. In Charleston, as in other cities in the South, PTA leaders resented school boards' unwillingness to construct enough classrooms to accommodate black students. Although the Charleston school board added two new elementary schools to the black system in the late 1950s, Columbus Street and Courtenay, black enrollment continued to outpace the number of classrooms. Overcrowding remained a serious problem, and all the black schools were filled well beyond capacity. More than 1,900 black students crowded into Burke, but the city's three white high schools had a combined enrollment of 1,503. While African Americans from the rural lowcountry continued to move into the city, white parents, encouraged by Waring's editorials in the *News and Courier*, enrolled their children in private schools or moved to the suburbs. Accelerating a process that began in the late 1930s, white enrollment continued to decline, and by 1960 only 25 percent of the students in the Charleston public schools were white. White flight left increasing numbers of classrooms in the white system underutilized, widening the differences in per-pupil expenditures and student-teacher ratios between the white and black schools and complicating the school board's attempts to maintain segregation.[13]

Influenced by the activism of students, the citywide PTA council and the local African American Teachers' Association planned a boycott to dramatize overcrowding in the black schools. In order to accommodate all the black students in the elementary schools, classes in Charleston's elementary schools operated morning and afternoon sessions with one group of students going to school between 7:30 and 12:00 and a second group attending school between 12:30 and 5:00. Parents and teachers instructed all elementary students who attended school in the afternoon to go to Courtenay Elementary School at 8:30 on the morning of October 11. Organizers published an open letter in the *News and Courier*, outlining their plans and threatening legal action. In an unprecedented show of unity, almost all black parents and students supported the boycott. On October 11, hundreds of elementary students arrived at Courtenay Elementary, the most overcrowded of the African American schools, at 8:30 A.M. Henry Hutchinson remembered standing in front of the school on the corner of Meeting and Mary Streets. "There was no way to describe the feeling; I saw so many children coming to school even the ones that played truant were coming. They [all] came to school." The next day, 95 percent of the city's eight thousand African American students boycotted classes in all the public schools. "The PTAs were powerful back then," recalled George Stanyard, who taught at Burke, "and the board was feeling their power."[14]

The following night, four thousand African American parents packed Emanuel A.M.E. Church and approved motions to end the boycott and to seek assignment to schools closest to their homes. Newly elected NAACP chapter president B. J. Glover explained that "the request should be made for assignment to a school nearest [your] home or the one that bests suits the child's needs." Like the sit-ins, the boycott dramatized black dissatisfaction in a way that school officials could not ignore and forced the board to find funds to construct more classrooms. Publicly, the board claimed that "these problems can not be corrected overnight," but privately, Governor Ernest Hollings and State Educational Finance Commission (EFC) director E. R. Crow helped the board secure a $1 million "grant" from the state to build a new black high school and finance a twelve-classroom addition to Courtenay Elementary. "The chief desire of the board," chairman C. A. Brown noted, "is to furnish separate but equal facilities for both races." African American parents who had children enrolled in the schools welcomed the improvements. "It was a matter of getting the most we could while our kids were still in school," recalled George Stanyard, who had three children at Courtenay.[15]

Stirred by the discipline and determination of students, teachers, and parents, NAACP leaders renewed the legal campaign to desegregate the schools. On October 15, three days after the boycott, fifteen African American students applied for admission to white schools, initiating an application process that lasted almost three years. The Charleston school board immediately rejected the applications, announcing that it "may use standards including intelligence and cultural tests" to assign students. Before the students could submit to these tests, however, applicants were required to ask for permission to desegregate a school. If the application was denied, parents could appeal the decision to a subcommittee of the board, then to the county board of education, and finally to a county appeals board. In May 1961 the board subcommittee staged hearings to determine if the transfers were in "the best interest of the child to be transferred." In the eyes of the trustees, no black student was qualified to attend a white school. J. Arthur Brown's youngest daughter, Millicent, was a "popular" honor student, but the board held that she "is progressing satisfactorily and is geographically attending the school closest to her home." In other cases, where students did not have records as strong as Millicent's, the board denied the application because "the child would not do well in a strange environment." In rejecting all the applications for transfer, the trustees decided that in each case "the child's interest would be seriously harmed if the petition was granted." The parents continued to appeal, and, after completing hearings before the county board of education and the county appeals board, Perry filed a school desegregation suit in federal court in May 1962.[16]

As African Americans inched toward a showdown with the school board in federal court, they continued to raise the costs of continued segregation through direct-action demonstrations. In 1961 black high-school and college students from throughout the state descended on the state capital in Columbia, staging protests against segregation and discrimination in employment that led to the "mass arrest" of 187 African Americans. Employing tactics that African Americans had used in

Orangeburg in 1955 and 1956, J. Arthur Brown launched a selective-buying campaign in Charleston against white merchants who refused to hire African Americans as clerks, salespersons, and office staff. During the spring of 1962 members of the local NAACP Youth Council picketed Woolworth's, Kress, and W. T. Grant for refusing to serve African Americans at lunch counters. In May NAACP leaders reported a breakthrough, as four African Americans were employed in "jobs with dignity" as cashiers and sales clerks. The national office was eager to demonstrate its support. Wilkins and other members of the national office visited the city, pledging "the fullest resources of the association to the state and local NAACP."[17]

NAACP attorneys turned their attention to sit-in leader Harvey Gantt's application for admission to Clemson College in upcountry South Carolina. Born in Charleston County in 1943, Gantt grew up in a close-knit neighborhood that included domestics and laborers as well as African American professionals. His father, Christopher, held a secure and relatively well-paying job as a skilled mechanic at the Charleston Naval Shipyard and was a longtime member of the NAACP. "For a kid like me," Gantt recalled, "that [May] seventeenth was a very significant day. I don't forget it." As Harvey and his siblings made their way through the city's overcrowded public schools, civil rights became a "preoccupation." After the sit-ins, he remembered, "what lived in my own mind was this glimmer of light that said there was some hope. There were those of us who believed that it could change." Gantt's professional aspirations also fueled his application to Clemson. As a student at Burke, Gantt had become interested in architecture, and teachers and counselors had encouraged him to attend a desegregated college because architecture "is one of those professions in which most practitioners were white. It made sense for me to go to a school where they were going."[18]

Gantt was certainly qualified for admission to Clemson. Eugene Hunt, who taught Gantt, remembered him as a brilliant student, salutatorian of the senior class, and a recipient of a Negro National Achievement Scholarship. College officials at Clemson rejected his application; because State College did not offer a program in architecture, the state provided him with an out-of-state scholarship to pursue his studies at Iowa State. Gantt gained experience in "dealing with a mostly white college environment," but he found Iowa State "cold and lonely. Why should I be out here in Iowa going to school, when I could be in South Carolina?" In January 1962, Gantt applied to Clemson again, but officials rejected his application, claiming that he had not submitted enough samples of his work in architecture. Seeing Gantt as an ideal plaintiff and Clemson as a good place to initiate desegregation, NAACP attorneys filed suit in federal court in July 1962.[19]

By the fall of 1962 African American protests and demonstrations in Charleston and other cities and towns in South Carolina were only one of the threats to social stability and continued control of public education. Violent opposition to the desegregation of higher education persisted into the 1960s. The post-*Brown* pattern was established at the University of Alabama in 1956. After Autherine Lucy enrolled at Tuscaloosa in February 1956, a crowd of more than one thousand students assembled around a burning cross, singing "Dixie" and shouting "keep 'Bama white." The next day, Lucy and the deans who accompanied her were pelted with eggs. The NAACP charged that administrators were conspiring with the crowd, and university authorities used this allegation, which the NAACP could not substantiate, to expel Lucy for making statements that violated university rules. Violence also occurred at the University of Georgia. Shortly after Hamilton Holmes and Charlayne Hunter were admitted to the university in 1961, a crowd of one thousand students descended on Hunter's room, throwing bricks through the window, setting fire to the woods around the dorm, and chanting "one, two, three, four, we don't want no nigger whore." Holmes and Hunter were forced to withdraw briefly from the university. The most significant and sobering violence occurred at the University of Mississippi a year later. Anxious to avoid the appearance of federal enforcement, the Kennedy administration sent four hundred lightly armed federal marshals to "Ole Miss" to ensure air-force veteran James Meredith's admission in October 1962. As President John F. Kennedy went on national television and called on students to uphold "the honor and traditions of the university," a crowd of two thousand began pelting marshals with bricks, chunks of concrete, and metal spikes. During the night, the crowd began firing on marshals with shotguns and rifles. When university chaplain Wofford Smith asked the crowd to desist, it shouted, "give us the nigger and we'll quit." By morning 2 marshals were dead and 375 had been injured.[20]

These confrontations convinced South Carolina's leadership that desegregation had become the only alternative to violence and disorder. Gantt still harbors doubts about what the state would have done "if Mississippi had not occurred," but he recalls the "message" that the confrontation over Meredith's admission sent through the state's leadership. "It was, Jesus Christ, you know we don't want that kind of thing to happen." Before the violent confrontation in Oxford, Thomas Waring urged white Mississippians to resist Meredith's admission "with the blood of patriots," but after the riot he acknowledged that "Oxford supplies a lesson that every southern state must study carefully in gauging its future actions." By then, Waring had acknowledged that accommodations would have to be made. The state's leaders were shrewd enough and unified enough to recognize that the best way to avoid federal interference was to show that the state could manage its own educational affairs.[21]

As Elizabeth Jacoway, David R. Colburn, and John G. Sproat have argued, businessmen played an important role in pushing political and educational leaders to desegregate. In a series of speeches in the early 1960s Greenville businessman Charles E. Daniel told audiences throughout South Carolina that "the issue of segregation cannot satisfactorily be settled at the lunch counter or the bus station." Working with John K. Cauthen, a lobbyist for the South Carolina Textile Manufacturers Association, Daniel argued that "we must handle it ourselves or it will be forced on us in the harshest way. Either we act on our own terms, or we forfeit the right to act." As NAACP attorneys prepared to litigate Gantt's case in federal court, Daniel and Cauthen persuaded political leaders in Columbia that desegregation was inevitable and the issue was who would control and direct the process.[22]

By the end of 1963 educational and political leaders recognized that the best way to avoid federal interference was to assure that South Carolina did not become another Alabama, Georgia, or Mississippi. After the Fourth Circuit Court of Appeals ordered Gantt's admission to Clemson, political and public-opinion leaders laid the groundwork for the peaceful desegregation of Clemson. In his farewell address as governor in January, Hollings conceded that the state was "running out of courts." Calling desegregation "a hurdle that brings little progress to either side," Hollings warned that failure to clear the hurdle would cause the state "irreparable harm." On January 16, L. Marion Gressette, chair of the state Segregation Committee, declared that "we have lost this battle, but we are engaged in a war. But this war cannot be won by violence or inflammatory speeches." The best way for the state to retain control of its educational system, Gressette stated, was by maintaining "good order on and off the campus." These public statements and careful planning by the State Law Enforcement Division (SLED) convinced an anxious Kennedy administration that federal intervention was not required, a point driven home by Hollings and his successor, Donald S. Russell, in repeated conversations with both the attorney general and the president. Clemson officials made it clear that any student who caused a disturbance would be "given his or her walking papers." When Gantt enrolled at Clemson in late January 1963 and became the first African American to attend class with whites in South Carolina since 1877, there was no violence or disorder. Coming between the crisis at Oxford and Alabama governor George Wallace's stand at the schoolhouse door in Tuscaloosa in June 1963, the peaceful and "dignified" desegregation of Clemson won praise from Kennedy administration officials and burnished the state's reputation for moderation.[23]

As significant as violence at the University of Mississippi was in shaping the state's decision to admit Gantt, the new entrance examinations that Clemson adopted in 1956 certainly made desegregation more palatable to whites. Constance Baker Motley, the NAACP attorney who argued Gantt's case, recalled that compliance was based on the belief that "if Harvey was in, he'd probably be the only one." David W. Robinson's colleague, Columbia attorney R. Beverly Herbert, suggested that "lowering racial barriers at colleges was acceptable because few Negroes could meet entrance requirements." Herbert voiced strong opposition to the desegregation of the public schools, but he told W. D. Workman that "admitting token numbers of African Americans would give whites the opportunity to train Negro leaders and relieve racial tensions." When Clemson admitted a second African American, Lucinda Brawley, in the fall of 1963, Dean James L. Williams told reporters that "Clemson would accept anyone who could meet entrance requirements." However, the number of blacks enrolled at the college remained small. By 1970 only 58 of Clemson's 6,068 students were African American.[24]

Gantt and Brawley did not suffer the indignities that Lucy, Hunter, Holmes, and Meredith endured, but they remained isolated, tolerated but not accepted. Former governor James F. Byrnes encouraged students to treat Gantt "like any other man who forces himself where he is not wanted." A group of concerned alumni sent letters to students urging them to "ignore [Gantt], offer him no assistance, and ostracize him and those who associate with him. He should be treated with cold silent contempt which he has earned." Clemson University president Robert C. Edwards praised Gantt's academic performance, but he was pleased that Gantt "did not inject himself in any social activities."[25]

In September 1963 Henrie Monteith, Robert Anderson, and James Solomon Jr. were peacefully admitted to the University of South Carolina. While Solomon received a "warm welcome" as a graduate student in the math department, undergraduates Monteith and Anderson had a more difficult time. Both ate their meals alone and were regularly harassed. Anderson sought solace in his room in Macey College, but students took turns bouncing a basketball outside his room late into the night. "I was in a very closed environment," he recalled. "I didn't do anything but study, go to class, go to the library, and go home." Anderson has "bitter memories" of his experience, scars left by the "raw racism" he encountered. Monteith's experience was better, but she too recalled that the campus climate was "not ideal." The slow growth of undergraduate and graduate enrollment and the absence of black faculty members, who were not appointed until 1968, left black students at USC isolated in what many found to be an inhospitable environment. Carla Smalls George, who enrolled at USC in 1966, recalled feelings of "alienation, invisibility, and a sense of exclusion" from the majority of white students and faculty. By 1970, 280 of the 10,699 students at the University of South Carolina were African American. For most of the African Americans who crossed the color line in higher education in the South in the 1960s, isolation was the price of access.[26]

As the state political leaders complied with court-ordered desegregation at Clemson, they vowed to use every legal means to oppose the admission of black students to elementary and secondary schools. The day after Gantt was admitted to Clemson, newly elected governor Donald S. Russell told the legislature that "we have not altered our convictions. We have sought and shall continue to seek to maintain those convictions in all similar situations by every legal means." Russell recommended, and the legislature approved, state funding for students who wanted to attend private schools. Thomas Waring, who had long favored privatization as a solution to the problems posed by desegregation, called Gantt's admission a "strategic retreat, a decision to live and fight another day."[27]

As local black leaders waited for the Charleston school-desegregation case to come to trial, they planned a direct-action campaign that was designed to create the kind of disorder and instability that would force educational and political authorities to desegregate the city's public schools. The events of the early 1960s—the sit-ins, the school boycott, the desegregation of Clemson, and the demonstrations in Birmingham in the spring of 1963—convinced local NAACP leaders J. Arthur Brown and James Blake that whites had come to fear social instability and disorder even more than token desegregation and that organized disruptive demonstrations could be used to force change. In education—as in voting, employment, and public accommodations—disruptive protests were required because, as David R. Goldfield has argued, during the early 1960s southern whites tended to make concessions "only when the economic balance sheet could not withstand further disruption." If the city's black leadership could not convince whites that desegregation was the right thing to do, they could, by staging street demonstrations, convince them that it was the expedient thing to do.[28]

In Charleston, as in other cities in the Deep South where the public schools were still segregated, school-desegregation suits were part of a broader assault on segregation and white supremacy. While the new civil rights groups—the Southern Christian Leadership Conference (SCLC), the Congress of Racial Equality (CORE), and the Student Nonviolent Coordinating Committee (SNCC)—led struggles in Mississippi and Alabama, the movement in Charleston was organized and led by local NAACP leaders, leadership that highlights the connection between desegregation efforts in the schools and those in other areas. CORE and SNCC activists worked to establish an organizational presence in the state in the early 1960s, but neither group was able to loosen allegiances to the NAACP, which remained the preeminent civil rights organization in South Carolina. Local NAACP leaders James Blake and J. Arthur Brown had strong ties to the national office. In 1963 Blake was appointed to the NAACP board of directors. As president of the local chapter and state conference of the NAACP in the late 1950s and early 1960s, J. Arthur Brown developed a strong relationship with Roy Wilkins. Eager to keep the state in the NAACP's column, Wilkins provided significant legal and financial assistance for the demonstrations, marches, and protests that laid the groundwork for peaceful desegregation of the schools in the fall of 1963.[29]

From Baltimore to Birmingham, school desegregation was one of the goals of those who demonstrated in the streets in the summer of 1963. Following the SCLC-led demonstrations in Birmingham, African Americans in hundreds of cities and towns staged protests and demonstrations to desegregate the southern social order. In Birmingham Martin Luther King Jr. and his colleagues mobilized African Americans through what he called "the package deal," staging demonstrations that were designed to desegregate schools, public accommodations, stores, parks, and other facilities. In early June 1963 NAACP leaders in Charleston launched a direct-action campaign to "eliminate all state imposed and state upheld racial segregation and discrimination." J. Arthur Brown announced that black Charlestonians would stage massive demonstrations unless negotiations began on nine black demands, including the "banning of racial segregation in the schools," the desegregation of public accommodations and parks, the employment of African Americans in clerical and managerial positions, and the establishment of a biracial committee to resolve racial differences. Brown indicated that blacks would use an array of direct action and legal tactics to "dramatize and resolve" the problems of racial segregation and discrimination. After Charleston mayor J. Palmer Gaillard refused to negotiate with movement leaders, Blake announced that "street demonstrations" were the only "alternative for resolving the problem."[30]

The Charleston movement was launched on June 7, 1963. Led by Blake, thousands of students from area high schools marched, picketed, and demonstrated in the streets during the next three months. Disrupting traffic, commerce, and recreational activities, the protests threatened the area's $25-million-a-year-tourist trade and created the kind of disorder that made whites wince. "The Charleston movement was led by the young people of this community," Blake recalled. Day in, day out, hundreds of black youths demonstrated in the streets and assembled at night for mass meetings at one of the area's churches. The great-great-grandchildren of slaves "are marching through the streets in a bold protest," the *Charleston Inquirer,* a local black newspaper, reported, "singing songs that end in freedom now, freedom now." One element of freedom was school desegregation, and the black protesters also sang: "If you miss me at Burke School and cannot find me anywhere, come on over to Charleston High, I'll be sitting up there, I'll be sitting up there." While young people formed the backbone of the movement, adults also played an important role. "The kids said we're tired of doing this," J. Arthur Brown recalled, "you go." Many state and local NAACP leaders, including Brown and state conference president I. DeQuincey Newman, were arrested during the summer. Adults who did not participate in the demonstration supported the movement by putting their houses up for collateral to raise the more than $1.4 million needed to bail out protestors from jail or by contributing to the $10,000 cash account that the movement amassed.[31]

While the Charleston movement, like direct-action campaigns in other southern cities, was not without its detractors in the black community, Blake has argued that "for the first time in the history of this community we came together. We came together in 1963." The *Charlotte Observer* reported that "the city's caste system has been broken and the city's many-hued Negroes are united to a larger degree than ever before."[32]

Picking up where he left off in 1960, Blake organized a series of sit-ins that desegregated lunch counters. Progress in other areas was slower. As picketing and selective buying in the downtown retail district continued in late June and early July, hundreds of students snarled traffic at busy intersections throughout the city, creating what a local police officer called "a tense and electric situation." Unlike the police in Birmingham, Chief William Kelly's force was, Blake recalled, generally "restrained." After the city obtained a restraining order in early July prohibiting further street demonstrations, Blake organized a series of swim-ins, pray-ins, and play-ins at pools, theaters, churches, parks, and playgrounds. After dozens of African Americans were arrested, Mayor Gaillard ordered parks and playgrounds closed. In early July local political leaders tried to quell the protests by obtaining a restraining order that raised the costs of bail bonds to as much as $15,000, but support from the NAACP's national office and contributions from African Americans in the city and state sustained the Charleston movement. As local business leaders launched a statewide fund-raising effort, Blake contacted Roy Wilkins, who agreed to provide Blake with "whatever support I needed." After sending $40,000 to Charleston, Wilkins visited the city, telling a crowd of two thousand at Emanuel A.M.E. Church to continue to "make whites feel uncomfortable."[33]

While almost all of the protests in Charleston were peaceful, violence did occur. On July 16, 1963, a demonstration organized to protest the *News and Courier's* white-supremacist editorial policies, developed into a violent clash between police and protestors in front of the newspaper's offices. The newspaper claimed that a crowd of seven hundred fifty "jeering Negroes" threw rocks at police and firemen. The incident led to the arrest of sixty-five blacks and left six police and firemen injured, heightening tensions in the city. Mayor Gaillard announced that he would "meet lawless force with overwhelming lawful force," and South Carolina governor Donald S. Russell sent 125 SLED officers to Charleston. After Gaillard convened meetings with white and black citizens, local NAACP leaders agreed to a forty-eight-hour cooling-off period.[34]

Movement leaders blamed the violence at the *News and Courier* on the refusal of the mayor or the merchants to negotiate with them and vowed to continue protesting. "The mayor is the cause of this business being in the streets,"

Reverend B. J. Glover declared, "because of his refusal to accept suggestions by responsible citizens, Negro and white." Blake declared that "a state of war now exists." At a mass meeting state NAACP president Newman declared that the cooling-off period did not mean that blacks would compromise. "There will be no compromise as long as our skin bears the stigma of second-class citizenship." Blacks would continue to protest and demonstrate, Blake told an enthusiastic crowd at the Jerusalem Baptist Church in July 1963, in order to "remove all barriers of racial segregation and discrimination in public institutions, restaurants and hotels, and [to] lower the color bar in employment." By late July the Charleston movement had staged daily demonstrations for almost eight weeks, held twenty-six consecutive nightly meetings, and involved fifteen thousand black Charlestonians in protests that led to more than eight hundred arrests. Merchants reported sharp declines in sales in the commercial district around King Street.[35]

Faced with the prospect of continuing demonstration and disorder, Gaillard convened a series of meetings with civic and business leaders. On July 25, a fourteen-member biracial committee was formed that included black leaders Herbert Fielding, local NAACP president F. O. Pharr, and Christopher Gantt. Although white businessmen rejected an initial proposal, after demonstrations resumed in early August, more than ninety local merchants agreed to many of the movement's economic demands, including equality in pay and job opportunities for black employees, restrooms and dressing rooms, use of courtesy titles, the privilege of trying on clothing, and waiting on customers on a first-come, first-serve basis. Movement leaders ended picketing and selective buying at stores that "opened their facilities to all irrespective of race or color" but continued to picket those that did not. Many hotels and restaurants continued to discriminate against African Americans, and Blake vowed to continue demonstrating until "everything is open to us or completely closed."[36]

In Charleston, as in many other southern cities, the business community was considerably more responsive to black demands than city government or the school board. By picketing stores, disrupting commerce, and engaging in selective buying, the Charleston movement won concessions from the city's mercantile establishment. But the movement's demands on the city remained unmet. At nightly mass meetings Blake argued that the protests should continue until "all the doors are open." While "business had undertaken desegregation steps and had adopted non-discriminatory employment policies," Blake declared, "the city has failed to take any action to improve conditions." He urged the resumption of mass demonstrations to force the city and the school board to meet the demands of the movement. Gaillard agreed to hire and promote more black municipal workers but resisted demands for the desegregation of parks and playgrounds. The schools remained totally segregated, and local educational authorities vowed to defend vigorously segregation in the schools.[37]

It was in this context of continuing protests, demonstrations, and disorder that the NAACP-sponsored school-desegregation suit came to trial. By the time the case reached Judge Robert J. Martin's courtroom in Columbia on August 5, 1963, the courts and the Kennedy administration had become increasingly impatient with the slow pace of school desegregation and had begun to sweep away what Lawrence A. Cremin has called "the paraphernalia of massive resistance." In *McNeese v. Board of Education* (1963), the court struck down pupil-placement laws, ruling that black plaintiffs did not have to exhaust "unpromising" administrative remedies before seeking relief in the federal courts. A rising tide of black protest pushed the court to accelerate implementation of a decision that for the most part remained unenforced. By late summer of 1963, protests and demonstrations in more than 750 cities led to the arrest of more than twenty thousand African American activists. "We cannot continue a city by city battle without intolerable risks," wrote Assistant Attorney General Ramsey Clark. Responding to events in Birmingham and other cities, President Kennedy proposed a sweeping civil rights bill that authorized the U.S. Justice Department to initiate school-desegregation suits. The NAACP welcomed the administration's initiative and pressed for desegregation orders in three states where the public schools remained completely segregated: Alabama, Mississippi, and South Carolina.[38]

At issue in *Millicent Brown v. School District Number 20* was whether the schools were segregated on the basis of race. The school board claimed that the schools remained segregated because of "voluntary adherence to custom and tradition," but NAACP attorneys Constance Baker Motley and Matthew J. Perry had little difficulty demonstrating that the schools were segregated because of the policies and practices of the school board. Perry's cross-examination of the new school superintendent, Thomas Carrere, established that while many blacks lived closer to white schools and many whites closer to black schools, all students attended segregated institutions. When Motley asked board chairman Laurence Stoney if the board had a plan to desegregate the schools, he said no. The board's rejection of black applications for admission to white schools in 1955, 1960, and 1961, and its refusal to come up with a desegregation plan, Motley concluded, required that the court issue an order that established a "unitary nonracial system which shall include a plan for the assignment of children and other school personnel on a nonracial basis."[39]

Using arguments developed by Gressette Committee lawyers, the Charleston school board argued that "intellectual differences represented a rational basis for racial separation in public education." Having systematically underfinanced black schooling for generations, whites now attempted to use differences in scores on intelligence and achievement tests to justify continued segregation. As in teacher-equalization and higher-education cases, standardized-test scores were central to the state's strategy for limiting black access and equality. Although school-board attorneys acknowledged that *Brown* prohibited the assignment of students "solely on the basis of race," they argued that the decision did not preclude the assignment of students on the basis of test scores. The school board's chief attorney, George Leonard, presented the results of achievement tests in reading and math, arguing that "Negro students consistently lagged behind white students on tests of educability." These differences, Leonard claimed, were "inherent, not caused by the home or school environment of the students." According to Leonard, black students were responsive to different "types of teaching" and different "subject matters."[40]

School-board lawyers argued that "the innate differences between members of the two races were such as to require a different curriculum [for blacks]," but the tests also showed an enormous range of ability within racial groups. Almost one-quarter of the city's black students qualified for the "honors" track that school officials created in 1956, undercutting the board's contention that there were inherent racial differences between whites and blacks. To get around this problem Dr. Ernest Van den Haag testified that desegregation would cause "psychological confusion about one's racial identity" and deprive the masses of black students of their "leaders." If the schools were desegregated, Van den Haag argued, blacks would become "frustrated" and "demoralized." The school board would be forced to "lower academic standards," and "chaos" would result. Both whites and blacks would be better off, Leonard concluded, if whites and blacks attended segregated schools that offered different courses of study.[41]

Motley responded by arguing that racial differences in achievement-test scores were the result of unequal educational opportunity. Despite pressure from local black activists, the educational opportunities available to white and black students in Charleston remained unequal. Although the black schools were not as crowded as they once were, class sizes were considerably larger and per-pupil expenditures considerably lower in the black system. These inequities tended to be in what James S. Coleman called the most "academically oriented activities," that is, educational opportunities that were most closely correlated to academic achievement. Motley argued that black students earned lower scores on achievement tests because they were taught by teachers who received lower scores on the National Teacher Examinations (NTE). In 1957, the board adopted a policy of employing black teachers who earned 425 or better on the NTE, while it continued to require white teachers to score at least 500. The board claimed that it was forced to do this because it could not find enough teachers who "measured up to white standards." To Motley this "proved that Negro children received an inferior education." She argued that for black students to receive an equal education, they must be taught by white teachers, and she urged Martin to order the complete integration of school personnel.[42]

As the NAACP and the Charleston school board waited for Martin's opinion, sporadic protests and demonstrations continued. In mid August, Blake went to New York for a strategy session at the NAACP's national office. He argued that "demonstrations by day and prayers by night should continue" to focus attention on the "evils of the [segregation]" and the failure of local officials "to meet the demands of the Negro." By 1963 the NAACP had become an enthusiastic supporter of what it called "boycotts, picketing, and other forms of protest demonstrations" in support of more widespread school desegregation. In Charleston Bishop D. Ward Nichols told a mass meeting at St. Luke's A.M.E. Church that "many of our people were calling for more direct action" and that "the NAACP had a six-figure sum to finance the campaign." While Motley anticipated a favorable ruling from Martin, Blake wanted to continue demonstrating to ensure compliance with a desegregation order.[43]

The Kennedy administration wanted to avoid more demonstrations, and in August federal officials pressured the board to comply with a likely desegregation order. Assistant Attorney General Ramsey Clark was concerned that the school board might close the schools or defy a desegregation order. Clark told board member and attorney Hugh Sinkler that "if we did not voluntarily obey such a court order, force to the extent necessary to insure compliance would be used." With Alabama and Mississippi school districts facing school-desegregation orders, administration officials hoped that the Charleston school board would follow the example set at Clemson. U.S. Attorney Terrell Glen met with Sinkler and asked him how the board planned to respond if Martin ordered an end to segregation in the schools. "He asked again and again if we would comply," Sinkler noted. "He made it very clear that the attorney general would require absolute obedience to any order of integration." Sinkler told school-board chairman Laurence Stoney that Glen's visit provided "evidence of the determination and might of the Washington government, and an undisguised warning that we must be obedient children or we would be punished."[44]

On August 23, 1963, Judge Robert Martin ordered the Charleston school board to admit the twelve black plaintiffs to the city's white schools. Refusing to rule on the board's contention that intellectual differences formed "a rational basis for continued segregation," Martin found the Charleston public schools to be "completely segregated" and the board's attendance policies "inadequate" since they failed to establish the right of school choice. Martin enjoined the board from "refusing admission to the minor plaintiffs herein on the basis of race or color." Because his opinion was issued fewer than two weeks before the schools were scheduled to open, Martin limited desegregation to the eleven black plaintiffs. (The twelfth plaintiff had already graduated.) He ordered the board to inform all black parents of their children's right to attend schools of their choice and to come up for a plan for system-wide desegregation of the schools. J. Arthur Brown, whose youngest daughter, Millicent, was one of the plaintiffs in the desegregation suit, urged the board to comply "and not bring shame and disgrace to South Carolina by non-compliance or violence."[45]

In the face of pressure from local black demonstrators, the NAACP, the court, and the Justice Department, the Charleston school board had little choice but to comply with Martin's ruling. James Blake has argued that the demonstrations of the summer of 1963 "helped with the desegregation of schools." By making continued segregation incompatible with order, "whites were forced to accept school desegregation." Thomas Waring acknowledged the power of these protests when he wrote that the trustees had decided to accept the ruling "in order to avoid chaos. The events of the past summer demonstrated the practical necessity of the decision." In announcing that the public schools would remain open and that the board would admit eleven black students, board chairman Stoney hoped that the public would recognize that the board was operating "the public schools on the only terms available to it." In the fall of 1963 Charleston was one of more than one hundred fifty districts that desegregated for the first time, more than three times as many as in 1962 and the largest number to desegregate since 1956.[46]

As the board took steps to comply with Martin's ruling, it set out, as it had in the past, to limit the scope and impact of change. To avoid federal intervention the trustees made sure that desegregation would be peaceful. Stoney urged students and teachers "to respect the board's decision and to observe and maintain proper discipline." The *News and Courier* issued similar pleas for calm. Stoney and Mayor Gaillard made it clear that they would not tolerate violence or disorder from anyone. Local police chief Kelly announced that crowds would be prohibited from gathering around schools and informed the press that it would not be allowed inside classrooms or in corridors. A bomb threat disrupted classes at Rivers High School on the first day of classes, but on September 3, 1963, eleven African American students crossed the color line and desegregated the Charleston public schools.[47]

NINE

A New Educational Order, 1963–1972

Persistent legal and political pressure made desegregation an enduring reality, but the new, more rational restrictions that were institutionalized in schools, colleges, and universities in the years after 1945 created durable barriers to educational equality and access for most African American students. Drawing on educational policies and practices developed in the 1940s and 1950s—privatization, standardized testing, and the improvement of separate educational facilities— political and educational authorities refined a new racial order in education. Unable to segregate students by race, the Charleston school board turned to testing and tracking to limit black access to desegregated schools and encouraged parents to abandon desegregated public schools. As white flight from the city and the public schools accelerated, the NAACP pressed for metropolitan desegregation, but political leaders created a consolidated school district that made class, not caste, and residence, not race, the new arbiters of educational opportunity. The NAACP attempted to restructure public higher education, but here too legal remedies were undercut by political, economic, and educational realities.

This new educational order divided African Americans along class lines, shaping paradoxical patterns of inclusion and isolation. By promoting the advancement of some African Americans, desegregation heightened the isolation of others. While increasing numbers of advantaged blacks crossed the color line, most African Americans, constrained by the legacies of exclusion and discrimination, were sequestered in historically black schools and colleges that lost vitality as they became segregated by class as well as race. In South Carolina, as elsewhere in the region, desegregation was both a triumph and a tragedy, expanding opportunities for advantaged blacks in ways that heightened the isolation of most African Americans.

During the 1960s Charleston's white leadership did everything it could to undermine desegregation. Having argued for more than two decades that desegregation would not work, white leaders used their power, influence, and prestige to make sure that it did not. Acting on the advice of lawyers for Senator L. Marion Gressette's Segregation Committee, the board limited the scope and effects of Judge Robert Martin's 1963 desegregation order. This resistance and steady white flight from the public schools, which white political and educational leaders did much to encourage, deprived the schools of the students and community support needed to make desegregation succeed. By encouraging whites with school-age children to abandon the city and its public schools and by discouraging blacks from seeking access to white schools, Charleston's power structure doomed desegregation. As J. Arthur Brown noted, "the local power structure can and does set the stage for whatever happens."[1]

The Charleston school board's acceptance of token desegregation was based largely on its desire to maintain control of the public schools. While the demonstrations in the summer of 1963 convinced whites that rigid segregation was no longer compatible with order, the trustees were hardly committed to creating a system of public education that was free of segregation and discrimination. The board responded to Martin's desegregation order by instructing its attorneys "to take all steps possible to reverse the District Court's decision." The board also announced that it would participate in a statewide program that provided tuition payments for parents who wanted to enroll their children in private schools to avoid desegregation. The board's staunch opposition to desegregation and its decision to participate in the private tuition program, encouraged white parents to withdraw their children from the public schools. When the schools opened in September 1963, white enrollment was 20 percent below what it had been in 1962.[2]

By sanctioning and supporting the formation of private schools, the board and other influential whites undermined confidence in desegregation and accelerated white flight. The establishment of segregated private educational institutions had been used to insulate whites before the 1960s. In 1949, educational authorities forestalled desegregation of the College of Charleston by securing a new charter that allowed it to continue to operate as a segregated, private institution. College president George Grice and state representative Nathan Cabell both supported that effort, and both established private segregated schools in Charleston during the 1960s. Thomas Waring praised officials in Prince Edward County, Virginia, who closed the public schools and created segregated academies, arguing that they provided an example of how "victory" could be "snatched from the mouths of defeat."[3]

After the school board announced that it would participate in the state's private-school tuition-grant program, Grice, Cabell, Waring, and others encouraged whites to enroll in segregated private schools that offered a haven for growing numbers of white students in Charleston. Cabell withdrew his daughter from Memminger Elementary School when it was desegregated, offered political advice to those who wanted to establish segregated academies, and arranged a meeting between private-school leaders and South Carolina governor Donald S. Russell. Grice served as the movement's "education advisor" and made arrangements for the college to offer "refresher courses" for those who wanted to teach in the new segregated academies.[4]

Waring used the *News and Courier* to rally public support for segregated private schools. The newspaper's coverage of school desegregation was limited, but Waring wrote inflammatory editorials warning that "mass integration" would destroy public education. Waring offered what amounted to free advertising to the supporters of private schools. When Grice organized a meeting at the college, a front-page article informed readers about the time, date, and place of the gathering. Waring equated support for segregated private education with civic virtue. "Solid citizens who want their children to be educated both in mind and manners had better start thinking about a new budget in which private schooling has a place." Although he repeatedly criticized the NAACP for destroying public education, Waring is responsible for undermining confidence in the public schools.[5]

Grice lent the resources and the prestige of the college to the movement. He helped found College of Charleston Prep, a secondary program for students in the eighth through twelfth grades, and announced that "certain facilities of the college may be used—gym, library, science laboratories." Grice tried to legitimize the venture, arguing that "colleges and universities in many areas today operate secondary and grammar schools." Waring praised the college's support for Prep, asserting that it was "extending another important educational service to this city. Charleston is fortunate in having an institution with so keen a sense of community responsibility." In September 1964 College Prep and four other segregated private schools opened their doors in the Charleston area. Between 1960 and 1970 the percentage of school-age whites in the city who attended private school in the city rose from 34 to 68 percent. After the courts ordered all districts in South Carolina to eliminate dual school systems in 1970, enrollment in private schools in the state rose by 34 percent.[6]

So much energy, effort, and publicity were devoted to the formation of private schools during the fall of 1963 that many parents began to wonder if the public schools would remain open. During a meeting at Rivers High School in October 1963, four hundred parents voiced concerns about the future of public education in the city. While Grice, Waring, and Cabell were ready to abandon the public schools, others were not. Several parents and teachers voiced support for desegregation. Emily Jackson, a teacher at the High School of Charleston, argued that "the system of public schools can be continued only if parents face all the facts realistically and become willing to make moderate accommodation to changing times." Others urged the community to support public schools for all "instead of running away from the problem and leaving its solution only to those who must depend on the public schools for an education." These voices were drowned out by the shrill cries of segregationists, who undermined confidence in the public schools. Rather than using its power and influence to make desegregation succeed, Charleston's white leadership encouraged whites to form segregated private academies and flee the public system.[7]

Whites had been leaving the city and its public schools since the 1930s, but the rate of white flight accelerated during the 1960s. While private schools became a temporary haven for an increasing percentage of white students, most parents could not afford the five hundred dollars that local private schools charged. The NAACP obtained an injunction that prevented the state from providing tuition assistance for private, segregated schools, but it could not keep growing numbers of whites from moving to the predominately white school districts that surrounded Charleston.[8]

Between 1960 and 1970 the number of whites enrolled in the public schools fell by more than three thousand, almost three times the decline of the previous decade. Falling white enrollment was not simply the result of white migration from the city. The number of whites who lived in Charleston fell by 42 percent during the 1960s, but the percentage decline in white school enrollment was twice as great. Nor were these declines the result of a falling birth rate among whites, since enrollment in predominately white suburban school districts around Charleston increased. Declines in enrollment were strongly correlated to the court's desegregation orders. The years when the schools experienced the greatest loss of white students were those when Judge Martin ordered desegregation in 1963 and when he established geographic attendance zones in 1970. As white enrollment dwindled with each passing year, so too did the prospects for sharing power and resources within desegregated institutions. When the public schools opened in the fall of 1964, black students outnumbered whites almost four to one.[9]

As Charleston's leadership encouraged whites to leave the public schools, the Gressette Committee legal staff urged the board to use standardized achievement tests to limit African American access to once all-white schools. Here too, the board drew on past policies and practices to limit change in education. In teacher-equalization, higher-education, and school-desegregation cases, officials learned how to concede just enough to meet constitutional requirements without endangering their control of educational policy and practice. Although the court rejected the board's contention that genetic differences "were a rational basis for segregation of races in schools," David W. Robinson argued that "our fight since 1954 has not been to defeat the principle [desegregation], but to limit the federal court's responsibility to racial matters." As an adviser to the Gressette Committee, Robinson "tried to obtain decrees that recognize [the] board's responsibility to assign pupils to further the best educational interests of the pupil." In December 1963 he wrote that "we need to press for a state-wide I.Q. and achievement test administered in all of our schools." Robinson believed that test results could be used to limit desegregation, especially in the high schools. "This difference in achievement between the two races," he told Senator Gressette, "may be our last line of defense."[10]

The day after Martin issued his ruling in the (Millicent) *Brown* case, Gressette Committee lawyer Augustus T. Graydon sent school officials "A Plan in Regard to the Integration Push in the Public Schools of South Carolina." Graydon argued that test results "suggest the desirability of certain educational criteria in public education as necessary to meeting the problems of an integrated school system." Graydon acknowledged that his plan would not result in "absolute segregation," but like Robinson, he believed that the state should establish a state-wide testing program. Graydon met with Dr. W. B. Royster, coordinator of Testing and Guidance Services for the South Carolina State Department of Education, "to determine possible uses of achievement tests in classifying pupils to obtain some measure of de facto segregation." In secondary schools, Graydon argued, "the imposition of strict academic standards would cause the higher grades to be almost entirely white."[11]

In spite of the objections of the NAACP, in April 1964 Judge Robert Martin approved a desegregation plan that assigned elementary students to schools that they attended the preceding year. The only students who were eligible for transfer were those who were promoted to high school. By limiting transfers to black students who were scheduled to enter high school, the board reduced the number of students who were eligible. Although assignments were ostensibly made without regard to race, the plan was based on Robinson's argument that the "educational needs" of students could be used to maintain segregation.[12]

The board used students' scores on the Iowa Tests of Educational Development to deny transfers, arguing that their "educational needs" could be best met in the segregated schools. Hampered by generations of educational exclusion, segregation, and discrimination, most blacks were not prepared to compete academically with whites, and during the 1960s, as before, educational authorities used standardized tests to limit African American access. "Negro education was strong enough to produce leaders who successfully directed the course of desegregation," wrote historian Henry Allen Bullock, "but was too weak to produce students who, when placed within the mainstream of American life and education, would show no effect of having grown up outside of it." By 1964, the tenth anniversary of the Supreme Court's *Brown* decision, only seventy-nine African American students, less than 1 percent of the almost ten thousand black students in Charleston, attended desegregated schools.[13]

This isolation exacted an enormous toll on the black students who desegregated the Charleston public schools. Like the outcomes of the teacher-equalization and higher-education campaigns, the results of the school-desegregation campaign in Charleston were problematic. Many black students were not prepared for the demands of desegregation. Those who were lost the recognition and leadership awards that awaited them in the black schools. All were ostracized. Segregation was no longer sanctioned by law, but educational authorities in Charleston and other southern cities did everything they could to improve African American schools in an effort to "keep the Negro in the Negro schools," as David W. Robinson put it. Standardized testing and the improvement of black schools created what Martin Luther King Jr. called "planned and institutionalized tokenism. Many areas of the South are retreating to a position where they will permit a handful of Negroes to attend all-white schools," King wrote in 1962. "We have advanced in some places from all-out, unrestrained resistance to a sophisticated form of delaying tactics, embodied in tokenism. In a sense, this is one of the most difficult problems that the integration movement confronts."[14]

Millicent Brown and the ten other black students who desegregated the Charleston public schools confronted these problems. A sensitive adolescent, Brown was academically prepared to meet the challenges that awaited her as a sophomore at Rivers High School in 1963 and 1964. "Growing up in J. Arthur Brown's household," she recalled, "with all the very rich experiences, Highlander [Folk School], MLK, that was such a very rich background to have had, that made a big difference." At Burke, Millicent flourished. In April 1963 she was inducted into the National Honor Society, and her grade average of 92 qualified her for the school's honor roll. Based on her record at Burke, Brown could have expected to assume leadership positions on the student council, the yearbook staff, and on the school's newspaper, the *Parvenue*. "I was very happy at Burke. I was going to start dating pretty soon. I had friends," she recalled. "To go from that to absolute zero was devastating. Because from the day I entered Rivers High School, none of that popularity or my plans for being a teenager was ever realized." This sense of loss taints Millicent Brown's memory of school desegregation in Charleston, and her experience personifies its dilemmas.[15]

Many of Millicent's peers and teachers, influenced by the wide publicity given to the school board's contention that African Americans were "genetically inferior," were surprised by her academic ability. Like other heirs of the city's African American elite, Brown's class background and schooling prepared her to compete with and outperform white students. She did very well at Rivers, finishing the year with a B+ average. Her English teacher described her as "enchanted with literature. She is the bright light in the class." Solomon Briebart, who taught

Millicent history, remembered her as "a very good student, critical, and informed about what was going on." In fact, other students in the class resented her "fine" work. This resentment helps explain the isolation she had to endure and the slights that Millicent received inside and outside of class.[16]

These taunts scared Millicent, who was caught between white and black worlds. When she appeared in the corridor, other students would clear the hall and cling to the wall, forcing her to walk down the hall alone. When she entered the bathroom, students chanted "2-4-6-8 we don't want to integrate" and "go back to your own school, jigaboo." Another African American student, Jacqueline Ford, who joined Millicent at Rivers in 1964, recalled feeling "like I didn't belong." Some teachers made Millicent feel responsible for the frequent bomb scares that disrupted classes during the fall of 1963, telling her "we sure would like to get on with our teaching." Some whites, such as Robert Rosen, who attended Rivers at the time, reached out to Millicent. Although she had some friends who sat with her in the cafeteria, "most students," Solomon Briebart recalled, "wouldn't associate with her." These incidents took a toll on Millicent, in part because of the pressure she felt from her parents. "When I was at Rivers," Millicent remembered, my mother was always in the background, "saying be bigger, be bigger, you can't give in, be bigger than they are, and I was about to go crazy, trying to be bigger than these folks." It was a heavy burden for an adolescent to shoulder. Constantly trying to show that she was bigger, Brown internalized the slights, and during her junior year she was hospitalized.[17]

Feeling that she was a token, a nonentity, and that some whites accepted her because she was light-skinned and a good student, Brown sought solace in the black community. She found little support. When she returned to Burke for a basketball game, black students "rejected me. I don't think anything hurt more than this experience." She begged her "iron-willed" father to allow her to return to Burke, telling him that she couldn't take the slights and taunts anymore. "He understood my unhappiness," she remembered. "But he never considered the possibility." Still, Millicent lived for the day that "I could go back to Burke." In a comment that captures the bitterness, pain, and anger she still feels, Brown said, "I hated those years. They left marks on my psyche." The scars stayed with her after she and four other black students became the first African Americans to graduate from Rivers in the spring of 1966.[18]

The autobiographies of Josephine Bradley and Melba Pattillo Beals underscore how Millicent Brown's experience is by no means unique. Desegregation involved losses as well as gains. "Had I gone to Burke I would have come out with a sense of worth, of self-confidence. I would have been in the National Honor Society, probably on the *Parvenue*, yearbook, and student council," she recalled. "No doubt I would have received scholarships and other leadership awards. This was denied me. Black kids who went to white schools were harmed."

NAACP activists like her father, who was forced to travel to Orangeburg to obtain a higher education that whites could receive at the Citadel or the College of Charleston, saw desegregation as a crucial step for black Charlestonians. But his daughter experienced it differently. Millicent was denied access to the National Honor Society at Rivers, and her high-school counselor unsuccessfully tried to discourage her from attending college. After graduating, she languished, drifting from college to college, still confused and hurt by her experience at Rivers. "The flaw that came from early integration is that physical integration was superficial. Black bodies being under the same roof as white bodies is not integration," Millicent argued. "And harm has been done to our psyche, and to our feeling of self-worth, because we somehow thought if we could just be with white children that was going to alleviate our ills. Somebody had to do what we did, but it posed new questions and new dilemmas."[19]

The difficulties and dilemmas that Millicent Brown faced hardly encouraged others to attend desegregated schools. By the time she graduated in 1966, only 185 blacks, 1.8 percent of Charleston's black enrollment, attended school with whites. No white had chosen to enroll in a black school. Because black students remained isolated in unfamiliar and unfriendly white schools, many black parents did not want to sacrifice their children at the altar of integration. In this sense the school board's policy of tokenism worked because it reinforced African American reservations about attending desegregated schools that Millicent Brown and others found to be lonely, hostile, and harmful educational environments.[20]

The growing involvement of the federal government in the process of school desegregation sought to end this isolation. Passed in response to the disorder and demonstrations of the summer of 1963 and steered through Congress by President Lyndon B. Johnson, the Civil Rights Act of 1964 authorized the Justice Department to initiate desegregation suits, and granted the Department of Health, Education, and Welfare (HEW) the power to enforce a ban on racial discrimination in any educational institution that received federal funds. In 1965 Congress passed and the president signed the Elementary and Secondary Education Act (ESEA), which made millions of dollars of federal aid available to school districts for compensatory educational programs for disadvantaged students. To receive funds a school district had to increase the number of black students who attended school with whites and desegregate its faculties and extracurricular activities. By threatening to withhold funds from school districts that were not making progress in school desegregation, the Civil Rights Act and ESEA forced the South to increase the number of black students who attended school with whites from 7 percent in 1965 to more than 12 percent in 1968. HEW pushed the Supreme Court to resume responsibility for ensuring compliance with *Brown*. In 1968 the Court rejected freedom-of-choice plans and the *Briggs* dictum on which they rested in *Green v. School Board of New Kent County* (1968) and ordered school boards to dismantle dual systems "root and branch," and create not white schools or black schools, but just schools.[21]

These new conceptions of school desegregation steadily increased the number of black students who attended desegregated schools in Charleston and other southern cities. In April 1967 Judge Martin ruled that the school board had failed to "comply with the court's directives" and that its desegregation plan did not meet "minimum constitutional requirements." The new desegregation plan required every student or parent to choose the school they wanted to attend during the 1967–1968 school year. Once blacks had a genuine opportunity to choose, growing numbers selected desegregated schools. During the freedom-of-choice period in the spring of 1967, more than one thousand black students, five times as many as in 1966, asked for assignments in formerly all-white schools. Many students made this choice because they knew that they would not be isolated.[22]

In 1968, as in 1963, desegregation led to white flight from the city and its public schools. The end of one kind of isolation heightened another. Once blacks became a significant presence in desegregated schools, whites fled. While some white parents tolerated token numbers of black students in desegregated schools, most would not send their children to schools with significant numbers of black students. At James Simons, for example, the percentage of black students increased from 27 percent to 62 percent between 1966 and 1967; at Rivers it rose from 20 percent to 50 percent.[23]

Desegregation remained elusive in Charleston because once black enrollment approached what was a comfortable point for African Americans, whites left. The percentage decline in white enrollment was twice as high in 1967 as it had been in 1966. Whites were simply unwilling to share schools with blacks on anything approaching equal terms, reinforcing the ambivalence blacks felt about desegregation. While new definitions of desegregation ended the isolation of black students within the city's desegregated schools, it accelerated white flight from the public schools, increasing interdistrict segregation. With each African American advance, came a white retreat. By 1967 blacks composed more than 86 percent of the students enrolled in the city's public schools. It was increasingly clear that meaningful desegregation would have to involve not simply the city schools but also the predominately white suburban schools in Charleston County.[24]

If desegregation in the city was short-lived, other forces brought improvements in Charleston's historically black schools. Although the board continued to resist desegregation, it was receptive to Martin's order requiring that all schools have "equal facilities, equipment, instructional material, and courses of instruction" and to continuing PTA demands for improvements in the city's African American schools. Instead of dismantling the dual system, as HEW, the Justice Department, and the NAACP hoped, the school board responded to

Martin's order and pressure from PTA leaders by using ESEA and stat
heighten the racial identification of African American schools and fur
tutionalize the separation of the races. The elimination of most of the
inequalities between white and African American institutions highlig
family-background factors that James S. Coleman's 1966 report *Equality of Educational Opportunity* found to be the most important determinant of academic
achievement.[25]

Here too, the board drew on policies and practices developed before *Brown*
to limit educational change after 1954. Since 1950, when South Carolina governor James F. Byrnes convinced voters to fund a $75 million school-equalization
program, the improvement of black schools was a central tenet in the Charleston school board's strategy for maintaining segregation. During the 1950s the
board used state equalization funds to eliminate many longstanding problems in
the city's black schools. It made additional improvements in the early 1960s in
response to PTA petitions for better schools, the NAACP's demands for desegregation, and Judge Martin's rulings.[26]

Educational authorities were motivated by a desire to minimize desegregation, but they were also responding to demands from PTA leaders, who continued to press for better educational facilities. Desegregation did not eclipse this
tradition of PTA activism. "There was no rush to get into the white schools,"
recalled Lois Simms, who taught at Burke and the High School of Charleston.
"We had our own institutions." A generation of NAACP litigation and local
black activism had done much to improve the city's black schools, heightening
the attachment of parents, students, and teachers to schools that had long been
important community institutions. During the 1960s local African American
activism and NAACP litigation led the school board to construct a new high
school, C. A. Brown, and renovate Burke, Courtenay, Henry P. Archer, and A. B.
Rhett elementary schools. While disparities shaped by decades of inadequate
financing remained, for the first time in its history, the board provided black students with something approaching an adequate system of public education.
Both the school board's desire to improve the black schools as a way of mini-
mizing desegregation and the PTA's attempts to strengthen black institutions
brought improvements in the schools, heightening African American ambivalence about desegregation. In Charleston, as elsewhere, meaningful desegregation remained elusive not simply because of white resistance but also because
of black reluctance.[27]

Much attention has been paid to the ways in which HEW and the courts
used ESEA funds to increase the number of black students who attended school
with whites, but in Charleston and other parts of the South, programs and
opportunities established by the ESEA perpetuated racial separation in education. Designed to combat poverty and improve the academic performance of

black students through compensatory education, the ESEA funded school lunch and remedial programs. In Charleston 40 percent of African American students lived in households with incomes below the poverty line, and as a result the school system was eligible for more than $360,000 from the ESEA. Educational leaders in Charleston used these funds to upgrade libraries in black elementary schools and to establish foreign-language labs at Burke and C. A. Brown high schools. Like other school boards in the state, Charleston officials made free lunch and remedial education programs, funded under Title I of the ESEA, available only in the city's black schools. Hays Mizell, of the local branch of the American Friends Service Committee, has argued that ESEA-funded programs played "a major role in retarding school desegregation."[28]

ESEA funds, as well as continuing pressure from the PTAs and the courts, improved the city's public schools. As the numbers of black students enrolled in desegregated schools grew, as black migration into the city slowed, and as African American birth rates fell, most of the black schools were no longer over-crowded. Student-teacher ratios and class sizes in the black schools were generally no larger than those in desegregated schools. By the late 1960s the academic courses offered in the black schools were essentially the same as those offered in the city's desegregated schools, although Murray Vocational School, which was desegregated, offered courses in air-conditioning repair and metal working that were not available at Burke or C. A. Brown. Still, hasty construction and the location of new schools on the impoverished eastern side of the city institutionalized patterns of segregation based on class as well as race. C. A. Brown was built in the heart of Charleston's poorest neighborhood, and many of the students who attended the school came from families that had recently moved to Charleston from the rural lowcountry. While no white student ever attended C. A. Brown, students at school were also isolated from the children of advantaged African Americans who lived on the western side of the city or in the suburbs.[29]

The improvement of facilities in Charleston reinforced the tendency of black students to attend segregated rather than desegregated schools as it shaped enrollment patterns that were based on class as well as race. More black students were choosing to attend desegregated schools, but most continued to choose schools with African American identities. During the enrollment period in 1968, almost eighteen hundred students chose Burke: more than the school could accommodate. Students chose Burke because it had more prestige than C. A. Brown. The reluctance to seek access to once all-white schools and the preference for Burke reflected the ambivalence many black Charlestonians felt about desegregation and the class consciousness that persisted in Charleston's black community.[30]

Although the NAACP attributed this ambivalence to the "deep and long term effects of segregation," far more was involved. African Americans had built powerful educational institutions that played an indispensable role in dismantling the practice of segregation in education. The large number of black students who remained in African American schools and PTA demands for additional facilities attest to the continuing faith many African Americans had in these institutions. As whites continued to leave the city and its public schools and as the disparities between desegregated and black schools continued to narrow, most black parents believed that their children would be better off in schools that were rooted in the black community, that reflected its culture and traditions, that were staffed by black teachers, and that were tied to African American institutions. The growing influence of Black Power in Charleston also reinforced African American support for these institutions. "There emerged a notable continuity between older, more conservative African American voices which had given the building of strong black schools priority over desegregation," wrote David S. Cecelski, "and the newer 'militant' expressions of black separatism and community control." The *Charleston Chronicle* noted that "many black citizens feel they have gained little from desegregation. At least in remaining in black schools, their children are free to participate in school activities to the maximum degree and thereby take advantage of opportunities to develop leadership potential." These traditions were more than a response to white racism. They were shaped by the achievements of African Americans within the segregated system and the class divisions that developed within the black community. These divisions widened in the late 1960s as the heirs of the black elite moved out of the city and as political and educational authorities created a new consolidated school district that shaped paradoxical educational outcomes.[31]

Many African Americans in the city had grown increasingly skeptical about desegregation, but in 1969 the NAACP sought to join the predominately white school districts that surrounded the city in a desegregation suit. Just as Charleston's political and educational leadership had limited the educational impact of previous legal challenges, in the late 1960s it created a new school district that stymied the NAACP's attempts to achieve interdistrict desegregation. Drawing on an equalization strategy that had been a cornerstone of city and state attempts to maintain segregation in the schools, white leaders created a consolidated school district that equalized educational expenditures between districts and preserved constituent district boundaries that remained the chief obstacle to desegregation across district lines. Consolidation allowed whites to satisfy a central requirement of *Brown*, that educational opportunity "be made available to all on equal terms," in a way that preserved and perpetuated high levels of interdistrict segregation.[32]

By the mid-1960s the racial topography of schooling in Charleston County resembled a series of concentric circles. The predominately black city schools were surrounded by a ring of largely white suburban districts that were in turn encircled by mostly black rural districts. These districts had been created in 1951, after the NAACP challenged the constitutionality of South Carolina's segregation laws. The twenty school districts in Charleston County were consolidated into eight constituent districts, each of which received funds from the Educational Finance Commission (EFC) to "equalize" its separate school systems. At the time of consolidation South Carolina governor James F. Byrnes urged local educational officials to gerrymander boundaries in order to create white and black school districts.[33]

In Charleston County school-district lines were drawn to maximize racial segregation. By creating racially identifiable districts, consolidation encouraged whites to move into certain districts and not others, heightening the extent of segregation between the districts. By 1967 all the districts in the county had become predominately white or black, as table 6 shows.

In 1967 Charleston state senator Charles Gibson proposed legislation that was designed to consolidate the county's eight school districts into a single district that would be one hundred miles long, enroll sixty thousand students, and employ two thousand teachers. A generation of litigation brought parity in the city schools, but dramatic disparities existed between the tax bases, educational facilities, and per-capita expenditures in the county. The assessed value of property per child was three to four times greater in the urban and suburban districts than in the predominately black rural districts. A study by the South Carolina State Department of Education in the mid 1960s found that per-pupil expenditures ranged from a high of $298 to a low of $212. Another survey reported serious inequities in the "levels of services." Under Gibson's bill the eight districts would be consolidated into one, and tax revenue would be collected on a countywide basis and distributed according to the fiscal needs of each district.

Table 6 *Racial Composition of Public School Enrollments, Charleston County School Districts, 1967*

District	Percent White	Percent Black
1	13	87
2	58	42
3	69	31
4	72	28
9	35	65
10	84	16
20	14	86
23	21	79

Source: *United States and Ganaway v. Charleston County School District*, Plaintiff's exhibit, number 1403, National Archives and Records Center, Atlanta, Georgia.

The intent of the bill, Gibson noted, was "not to move kids but to take the money and move the money." Facing the prospect of countywide desegregation, white leaders once again turned to equalization as a way of maintaining segregation between the predominately black urban and rural districts and the largely white suburban districts.[34]

There was considerable support for Gibson's bill among both white and black leaders in Charleston. Charleston school superintendent Thomas Carrere argued that it was the "only solution to the problem of unequal education." The *Evening Post* endorsed the bill because it provided "a means by which the schools can be improved." Some of the strongest support came from local African American leaders who believed the bill would improve educational opportunities for African Americans throughout the county.[35]

Many whites opposed Gibson's bill because they believed it would bring about "the loss of local control of schools and damage the educational structure in the individual districts." In some cases local control was a code word for opposition to desegregation. Many whites argued that the bill would promote busing, mass integration, and "mongrelization." At one meeting an opponent of the bill bluntly stated, "I don't want my kids going to school with Niggers. I don't want my kids riding school buses with Niggers. I don't want Niggers teaching my children."[36]

Stiff opposition to the original bill led Gibson to amend it. Under the new version the county's eight constituent districts would still be consolidated into a single district for financial purposes, but the district lines and the constituent boards' power to assign students and faculty would be preserved. It was a shrewd political compromise that maintained local control (that is, interdistrict segregation) at the same time that it secured the economic benefits of a consolidated tax base for the entire county. When black students from Charleston tried to transfer out of the city, their requests were consistently denied. By providing a way to equalize expenditures across the district, preserve local control, and inhibit interdistrict desegregation, Gibson's amended bill had broad appeal and was passed by the South Carolina General Assembly in July 1967.[37]

The Act of Consolidation was a fitting conclusion to a quarter century of sophisticated white resistance, another example of how educational and political leaders rationalized restrictions that had once rested on race. By equalizing expenditures and maintaining constituent-district boundaries, consolidation stymied African American attempts to create a school system where whites and blacks merged educational institutions and traditions. Like earlier responses to African American demands for equality and access, the act withstood judicial scrutiny in the federal courts, which held that consolidation was "passed to equalize funding throughout the county and to remedy the economic disparities which existed between districts." Such a narrow reading of this legislation, however, ignores the central role equalization played in constructing a new educational order. Equalization was always a means to a larger end: the creation of a more sophisticated system of white supremacy in education. That is why the state adopted the National Teacher Examinations (NTE), why it established a separate law school at South Carolina State College in the 1940s, why educational authorities invested millions of dollars in Charleston's black schools in the 1950s and 1960s, and why per-pupil and capital expenditures were higher in the predominantly black districts than in the majority white districts during the 1970s and 1980s. Throughout the campaign for equality and access, educational authorities in Charleston and South Carolina as a whole were considerably more race conscious than cost conscious. By blocking desegregation across district lines, consolidation embedded schools in racially segregated and economically unequal social environments.[38]

While consolidation confined most black students in the city and county to segregated schools, it did not prevent growing numbers of middle-class blacks from moving to predominately white districts and enrolling their children there. Advantaged African Americans, many of whom spearheaded the campaign for equality and access, led this movement. In the mid 1960s J. Arthur Brown moved to James Island. Brown sponsored a number of open houses on James Island, including one in the Westchester subdivision on Folly Beach Road, not far from the school at Society Corner. Teachers from Immaculate Conception High School helped Brown market the houses. Lucille Whipper, who taught at Burke at the time, recalled, "black people with high incomes started to move to the suburbs." Another teacher, Alma Wigfall, was one of those who did. Wanting to own a home, Wigfall and her husband moved to Washington Park, a black neighborhood in St. Andrews. Her son became one of the first black students to attend predominately white schools in the suburbs. Like the black elite that had enrolled its children at Avery Institute, the middle-class blacks of the early 1970s sought educational opportunities in the suburbs that whites refused to support in the city. During the 1970s heirs of this elite pressed for access to suburban schools. Long the chief supporters of the NAACP, advantaged African Americans became the chief beneficiaries of the association's legal victories.[39]

For Charleston's growing black middle class, the elimination of caste constraints expanded opportunities. Many of the sons and daughters of black teachers, businessmen, ministers, and lawyers attended Middleton High School in St. Andrews, where 15 percent of the student body was black by 1975. Although a *News and Courier* report on the school found little interaction between whites and blacks, African American students enjoyed the benefits of the school's "sprawling 20 acre campus," which was surrounded by a solidly middle-class residential neighborhood, palm trees, and well-tended lawns and fields. The affluence of students at the school, the newspaper noted, was "evident from the crammed parking lot. Finding a [parking] space is not easy." In many ways Middleton High School reflected this affluence. The school's curriculum was geared to those who planned to attend college. "Middleton students," the newspaper reported, "arrive there essentially prepared for high school work." A majority of the school's graduates went to college.[40]

Like Millicent Brown, many of the African American students who desegregated Middleton High School faced problems and bore burdens that limited their ability to realize fully the benefits of desegregation. At Middleton, as at other desegregated high schools in the South, racial discrimination and differential treatment were widespread. African American students were tracked into lower-level classes, subjected to differential disciplinary policies, and excluded from extracurricular activities. Alma Wigfall enrolled her son at Middleton High because she believed the school offered opportunities for advancement, but, like others, she found that her son "just wasn't involved. He just wasn't encouraged."[41]

One of the reasons discrimination remained so prevalent was that the very process that brought significant numbers of black and white students into the same schools also led to increased reliance on the NTE. The state had adopted the NTE in 1945 to maintain racial salary differentials, and during the 1960s and 1970s the exam was used to limit the presence of African American teachers in desegregated schools. In South Carolina, as elsewhere, educational and political authorities responded to the specter of desegregation by establishing or raising minimum cut-off scores that teachers had to earn to be certified, hired, or rehired. In 1956 the South Carolina State Board of Education established minimum NTE score requirements for certification. As the NAACP and the courts pressed for more widespread desegregation, in 1969 the state board raised the minimum NTE score that teachers had to attain to earn certificates, a decision that eliminated more than 40 percent of the prospective black teachers but fewer than 1 percent of the whites. Minimum-score requirements were established arbitrarily without studies to determine if cut-off scores actually distinguished those who were competent from those who were not. According to Gressette Committee lawyer Augustus Graydon, the new teacher licensure policies were adopted because the state "cannot defend a situation where lower standards are set for the hiring of Negro teachers. As a matter of practice, only the higher level white teachers need be accepted, but the standards cannot be different." The NTE provided a rational and legally defensible way of limiting the presence of African American teachers. The paucity of African American teachers and principals in predominately white schools left black students without adult advocates, without African American teachers who could help students understand the hostility and harassment that drove many African Americans back into historically black schools.[42]

The price of access remained high, but as Numan V. Bartley has argued, African Americans who were "sufficiently educated, ambitious, and psychologically prepared" realized durable benefits. A generation of sociological studies has shown how desegregation provided African Americans with access to "high-status" educational institutions and the social networks inside them. As problematic as the desegregation of Middleton High School was, those who persisted were more likely to enter and graduate from desegregated colleges and universities.[43]

By fueling the advancement of some African Americans, desegregation heightened the isolation of others. While the elimination of racial restrictions broadened opportunities for Charleston's black middle class, most African American students in both the city and county remained in schools that were segregated not simply by race but also increasingly by class. The differences between Middleton High School and C. A. Brown High School in Charleston illustrate how, in spite of a trend toward tangible equality, educational institutions remained unequal. Although C. A. Brown and Middleton were about the same age and size and received comparable levels of funding, the student populations they served and the educational outcomes they produced were as separate as they were unequal.

Constructed in 1962 to alleviate overcrowding at Burke, C. A. Brown was located in the heart of one of Charleston's poorest neighborhoods. The school's five-acre campus was surrounded by an abandoned factory and deteriorating houses. A *News and Courier* reporter described the school as "dingy. Its not-so-hallowed halls reflect deterioration. So does the crumbling neighborhood it serves." C. A. Brown was totally segregated; every student, teacher, and administrator was African American. Most students at Brown were poor, and school officials referred to Brown as a "Title I School." The average family income of Brown's students was less than three thousand dollars, one-half of the median white family income in the city. Almost two of every three students lived in female-headed households, more than twice as many as at Middleton. The school offered courses that were comparable to those at Middleton, but one-half of Brown's ninth graders read below the fifth-grade level, more than a quarter below the fourth-grade level. Many of the courses offered at the school were "watered down" versions of those taught in schools with more affluent students. Almost one-third of Brown's students went to college, but a larger percentage, more than one-half of its graduates, left the school only to join the growing numbers of black teenagers in the area who were unemployed. By the early 1970s African American teenage unemployment in urban America approached 50 percent, and many students at Brown did not believe that hard work and good grades would lead to college or well-paying jobs. Anthropologists John Ogbu and Signithia Fordham have argued that African American students equated academic achievement with "acting white."[44]

By 1975 more than 95 percent of the students enrolled in the Charleston public schools were African American, and for those who remained in the city there is evidence that the schools they attended were not as good as they had once been. Burke High School, for example, lost many of the middle-class black students and teachers who had made Burke an important educational and community institution. "Something happened to the atmosphere of the school," recalled Eugene Hunt, a veteran teacher who resigned in 1972. Other teachers followed. Lois Simms transferred to the High School of Charleston because she felt that Burke no longer placed enough emphasis on academics. In 1971 Burke principal William Merriweather complained in the school's yearbook that "a large number of students [saw] excellence in academic achievement [as] a sign of weakness or a sign of being square." Lucille Whipper, a teacher who left the school in the early 1970s, recalled that the loss of the most affluent, involved, and engaged black students magnified the family background characteristics that students brought to the school. Racked by discipline problems and vandalism, Burke lost the support of many faculty members, students, and parents. Burke's PTA, which had long been a catalyst for improvements at the school, was not as active as it had once been. Articles in the student newspaper, the *Parvenue*, reflected this sense of loss. One student noted that the school lacked many "of the things that the good old days had." Another argued that Burke was in "gradual decline."[45]

In higher education, as in primary and secondary schools, desegregation divided African Americans along class lines. African American enrollment in four-year colleges in the South rose sharply during the 1960s, but at flagship state universities in the state and the region, more rational restrictions—the most durable of which relied on standardized tests—limited access to advantaged African Americans. There is no denying the continuing significance of race in southern higher education, but as William Julius Wilson has argued, the removal of racial restrictions created the greatest opportunities for the better educated segments of the black population. Increasingly, class rather than race defined where students went to college. As the "old-style southern segregation" gave way to a "new-style" class segregation, Christopher Jencks and David Riesman found that the "abler children of college educated Negroes," who were "often well enough schooled and well enough heeled to compete on equal terms with white college applicants," gained admission to the best state universities in the southeast. Like the NTE, the bar exam, and tracking in the public schools, the SAT created patterns of access based on class as well as race, shaping what Wilson calls "vastly different mobility opportunities for different groups in the black population."[46]

As inhospitable as USC, Clemson, and other predominately white colleges and universities were, many of the students who graduated from these institutions realized significant benefits. Harvey Gantt personifies this process. After graduating from Clemson with honors, Gantt earned his masters in urban planning from the Massachusetts Institute of Technology. Moving to Charlotte, he established an architectural firm, Gantt Huberman Associates. Using skills he had developed during the sit-ins, at Iowa State, Clemson, and MIT, Gantt built bridges between conservative business leaders and the black community. With significant white support Gantt was elected mayor of Charlotte in 1981 and 1983, and secured the North Carolina Democratic Party nomination for the U.S. Senate seat in 1992 and 1996, only to be narrowly defeated by Jesse Helms in racially charged campaigns. Like other African Americans who desegregated southern schools, colleges, and universities, Gantt gained access to personal contacts and networks that long-term studies of desegregation have shown to be a key to black mobility. In the South these contacts and networks were particularly important because, as David R. Goldfield has noted, "a good deal of the southern economy is honeycombed with a good-ole-boy network that extends back to college days and beyond." As private companies and public agencies began to recruit African Americans in the late 1960s, these networks helped African American graduates of flagship universities secure jobs in corporations, law firms, banks, and other institutions and organizations. In Charleston the desegregation of educational institutions, access to new employment networks, and enforcement of antidiscrimination and affirmative-action laws increased the percentage of African Americans who held professional, managerial, and technical jobs. Better jobs brought higher incomes, and during the 1970s increasing numbers of middle-class African Americans moved to suburban neighborhoods and enrolled their children in desegregated schools such as Middleton, which prepared students for admission to prestigious colleges.[47]

While desegregated educational institutions created avenues of access for advantaged African Americans, students at State became increasingly isolated. Desegregation aggravated longstanding problems at State College. Dwindling enrollment in the antiquated agricultural program led to its closing and the transfer of the farm extension program to Clemson in 1965. By then, enrollment in the law school had dropped to four students, and, after State College students Jasper M. Cuton and John Lake were admitted to the program at USC, the State College Law School was closed in 1967. By the 1970s increasing numbers of African American students whose parents were well-educated, affluent, and held professional jobs were lured to predominately white public institutions. State College president Maceo Nance worried about "a brain drain," as State was unable to attract "top black students," who won scholarships to larger and more affluent white institutions. At State College, as at C. A. Brown and Burke high schools, the loss of the most able pupils occurred at a time when it became increasingly difficult to hire the most promising black professors, who were recruited by white institutions even more aggressively than top black students.

"Society has opened up for those who can afford it," noted State College librarian Barbara Jenkins. "For those who can't, there has been no change."[48]

As the "best and brightest" black students enrolled in predominately white colleges and universities and as educational authorities refused to enhance State's program, the college lost vitality, even as public funds expanded its physical plant and facilities. The NAACP's decade-long legal challenge in *Adams v. Richardson* (1973) sought fundamentally to restructure southern systems of public higher education in the 1970s, but officials in South Carolina pursued an equalization strategy launched in the 1950s that heightened the isolation of State College. Part of the broader conception of school desegregation that was defined by the Civil Rights Act of 1964, *Adams* suggested that southern educational authorities should enhance the role of once marginal black colleges by locating prestigious programs in medicine, law, and engineering at institutions such as State College, making it a full partner in public higher education in the state. South Carolina responded to *Adams* by increasing State's operating budget and capital appropriations rather than enhancing its curriculum, embedding racial and class segregation ever more deeply in the state's public colleges and universities. Enriched by federal funds, State's operating budget rose from $4.5 million in 1968 to more than $15 million a decade later. The state initiated a $20 million building campaign that exceeded that of the 1950s, constructing new residence halls, a library, an auditorium, and new classrooms that allowed administrators for the first time since the 1920s to admit all the black students who sought access. Throughout the 1970s State granted more B.A.'s than all other four-year colleges in South Carolina combined, but the refusal of educational authorities to enhance State's program and locate prestigious professional programs in Orangeburg left ambitious blacks and whites with little choice but to pursue advanced study at other institutions.[49]

A half-century of African American activism and NAACP litigation changed public education in South Carolina, and created the possibility that whites and blacks might merge separate educational cultures, traditions, and institutions. That possibility, the possibility of whites and blacks sharing power and resources in desegregated educational institutions was foreclosed by educational and political leaders who used their control of education to institutionalize a new, more rational and legally defensible educational order. By dividing African Americans and insulating whites, educational authorities deferred the day when whites and blacks might create educational institutions that served all students on equal terms.

Epilogue

African Americans eliminated significant legal barriers, but in South Carolina and other southern states educational authorities responded by institutionalizing new, more rational barriers to equality and access. During the 1970s the federal government challenged these policies, but the state of South Carolina defended its use of the National Teacher Examinations (NTE), the adoption of new requirements to admission to the state bar, and the structure of public higher education. These federal-court decisions affirmed a system of access and opportunity that was increasingly based on class, and sanctioned broader use of policies and practices that have come to govern educational arrangements in the region and the nation.

This trend was initially evident in teacher testing. First adopted on a statewide basis by South Carolina in 1945, the use of the NTE spread rapidly through the urban South following *Brown*, and was institutionalized in most southern states after the courts required widespread desegregation in the late 1960s and early 1970s. In 1975 the United States challenged South Carolina in court, charging that the state adopted and used the NTE to discriminate against black teachers. Although the Educational Testing Service (ETS) and the state were unable to validate the NTE against other available measures, such as the ratings of principals or supervisors, the testing service convened a panel of 450 white and black professors who validated the exams against the content of teacher-training programs in the state. The ETS hired prestigious Washington lawyers who, along with some of South Carolina's ablest attorneys, convinced the court that the NTE was institutionalized to improve "the quality of public school teaching."[1]

After a divided Supreme Court refused to review a U.S. District Court's 1977 ruling in *United States v. South Carolina*, southern states staged what critics called "partially rigged plebiscites," to establish the content validity of teacher exams. By 1982 sixteen of the seventeen southern states that sanctioned segregation before 1954 had provisions or plans for teacher testing. (With two exceptions, states that required these exams were in the southern tier of the nation.) While teacher testing in the late 1970s contributed to a sharp decline in the number of African Americans who were licensed to teach, studies show that African Americans who performed well on the exam came from advantaged backgrounds where parental educational attainment and income were well above those of most blacks. Teacher tests have been used in South Carolina for almost sixty years, longer than any other state in the nation. The test scores of teachers in the state and region have risen, but the NTE has done more to perpetuate patterns of racial and class discrimination than raise the caliber of the state's teaching force.[2]

The state of South Carolina also successfully defended the adoption of new requirements for admission to the state bar. This policy went into effect in 1950, the year the first class of students graduated from South Carolina State Law School. Between 1950 and 1973 only 15 percent of the African Americans who took the bar exam in South Carolina passed, compared to 90 percent of the whites. The plaintiffs in *Richardson v. McFadden* (1976) charged that the bar-exam requirement was a more sophisticated form of exclusion from the legal profession. The testimony of bar examiners did not, the court held, provide clear evidence that the exam bore a "fair and substantial relationship" to the determination of minimal competency. The court ruled that two African American plaintiffs were denied admission to the bar because of the "arbitrary and capricious" actions of the bar examiners. Nonetheless, the court did not find that the results of the exam were "so unrelated to state objectives as to violate the Equal Protection Clause."[3]

South Carolina was the first southern state to require that all applicants for admission to public colleges and universities submit Scholastic Aptitude Test (SAT) scores, but the state's adoption of this policy on May 27, 1954, eluded scrutiny in the most significant challenge to continuing segregation in higher education that began in the 1970s in *Adams v. Richardson* (1973) and continued in the 1980s in *Adams v. Bell* (1983). Several southern states, notably North Carolina, Louisiana, and Mississippi, resisted the NAACP's attempts to restructure public higher education in the region, but South Carolina, well-schooled in the ways of avoiding federal interference, submitted a desegregation plan that was accepted by the courts and the Department of Health, Education, and Welfare (HEW). During the 1970s, the patterns of class segregation in higher education that emerged with the adoption of standardized-test requirements became more pronounced as a growing number and percentage of advantaged African Americans enrolled in southern flagship universities. Increasingly, class rather than race determined where students went to college. As with the NTE, however, there is little evidence that the policy requiring undergraduate applicants to submit SAT scores has improved the caliber of students at the University of South Carolina (USC). By 1982 the average SAT scores of entering first-year students at USC trailed those of every state university in the southeast except Alabama.[4]

In the public schools as well, increased reliance on standardized tests has done more to limit opportunity for most African Americans than expand it. For more than fifty years educational authorities in South Carolina and other southern states have argued that testing and tracking would improve student performance and promote movement into the higher tracks, but the evidence supporting these claims is thin. When Judge Skelley Wright examined the track system in Washington in the 1960s, he found that there was "a minimal amount of fluidity [movement into the higher tracks]." Advantaged African Americans gained access to gifted, honors, and advanced placement courses, but most African Americans remained in lower-level courses. In South Carolina 13 percent of the students enrolled in advanced trigonometry and algebra classes in 1960 were black. Forty years later, a survey by the U.S. Commission on Civil Rights found that white students in South Carolina were still seven times more likely to perform at the advanced level in math than blacks.[5]

During the 1970s and 1980s New South governors established minimum-competency testing programs that were designed in part to raise the achievement of African Americans by requiring that all students pass a high-school graduation test. By 1996 eighteen states, thirteen of which sanctioned segregation before 1954, required students to pass a standardized test to earn a diploma. "There is a curious pattern to the geographical location of the states," that require these exams, Linda A. Bond and Diane King have written. "They are primarily located along the southern and eastern coasts of the United States." Throughout the region, minimum-competency testing has done as much to limit high-school completion as raise achievement. In South Carolina, only 50.7 percent of the students who entered ninth grade in 1997 earned a high school diploma by 2001—the lowest graduation rate in the nation.[6]

Although it has become fashionable to suggest that standardized testing will narrow achievement gaps, more than fifty years of standardized testing in South Carolina has produced educational outcomes that are considerably more problematic and paradoxical. Advantaged African Americans gained access to the most prestigious educational institutions and the most valuable programs within them, but for a majority of blacks in the state, region, and nation, standardized tests remain durable barriers to access and equality. Institutionalized in response to black demands for equality, the test-driven systems of schooling that have come to govern public education are leaving too many children behind.

Introduction

1. Coles, *Farewell to the South*, 83–84. On the dismissal of African American teachers who stood up for the equalization of teachers salaries in the 1930s and 1940s see Lewis, *In Their Own Interests*; Tushnet, *The NAACP's Legal Strategy against Segregated Education*; Bolton, "Mississippi's School Equalization Program, 1945–1954." On the fierce struggles over the desegregation of southern universities see Clark, *The Schoolhouse Door*; Shabazz, *Advancing Democracy*; Pratt, *We Shall Not Be Moved*; Doyle, *An American Insurrection*; Cohodas, *The Band Played Dixie*; Carter, *The Politics of Rage*. On the bitter battles over school desegregation in the South see especially Fairclough, *Race and Democracy*; Douglas, *Reading, Writing, and Race*; Beals, *Warriors Don't Cry*; Colburn, *Racial Change and Community Crisis*; Norrell, *Reaping the Whirlwind*; Wolters, *The Burden of Brown*; Lassiter and Lewis, eds., *The Moderates' Dilemma*.

2. On the history of African American education in the South, see Anderson, *The Education of Blacks*; Cecelski, *Along Freedom Road*; Walker, *Their Highest Potential*; Fairclough, *Teaching Equality*; Jones, *A Traditional Model*.

3. Eskew, *But for Birmingham*.

4. Klarman, *From Jim Crow to Civil Rights*; Klarman, "How *Brown* Changed Race Relations"; Bell, *Silent Covenants*; Harold Cruse, *Plural But Equal*.

5. Synnott, "Desegregation in South Carolina."

6. Foucault, *Discipline and Punish*, 184–85.

7. Myrdal, *An American Dilemma*, 205; Jaynes and Williams, eds., *A Common Destiny*, 271; Lewis, "The Origins and Causes of the Civil Rights Movement," 11.

8. Charleston Board of School Commissioners Minute Books (CBSCMB), December 6, 1939, Office of Archives and Records (OAR), Charleston County School District (CCSD), Charleston, South Carolina; Houston, "Cracking Closed University Doors," 370.

9. Thurgood Marshall to Carter Wesley, October 16, 1947, box II-B-204, NAACP Papers, Library of Congress, Manuscript Division, Washington, D.C.

10. Fairclough, *Race and Democracy*, ix; *Briggs v. Elliott*, 98 F. Supp. 529 (1951).

11. Russell, quoted in Black, *Southern Governors and Civil Rights*, 82; David W. Robinson to L. Marion Gressette, December 10, 1963, *United States and Ganaway v. Charleston County School District*, plaintiff's exhibit 927, National Archives and Records Center (NARC), Atlanta, Georgia.

1. Mamie Fields and the School at Society Corner, 1926–1938

1. Fields with Fields, 204, 205, 208; Mamie Garvin Fields, School Planners, box 7, folder 2, Mamie Garvin Fields Collection, Avery Research Center (ARC), College of Charleston, Charleston, South Carolina.

2. Tushnet, *The NAACP's Legal Strategy against Segregated Education*; Greenberg, *Crusaders in the Courts*; Kluger, *Simple Justice*.

3. Powdermaker, *After Freedom*; Johnson, *Shadow of the Plantation*; Johnson, *Growing Up in the Black Belt*; Johnson, "The Negro Public Schools"; Dollard, *Caste and Class*; Raper, *Preface to the Peasantry*.

4. Fields with Fields, 2, 47; Brownlee, *A New Day*, 135. For a discussion of color consciousness in African American educational institutions see McPherson, *The Abolitionist Legacy*, 292; Frazier, *Negro Youth at the Crossways*, 51–53; Davis and Dollard, *Children of Bondage*, 253; Drago, *Initiative, Paternalism, and Race Relations*, 128–38.

5. Leloudis, *Schooling the New South*, 228; Fields with Fields, 1, 83, 99, 104.

6. Gilmore, *Gender and Jim Crow*, 148.

7. Fields with Fields, 189–90, 235–36; Shaw, *What a Woman Ought to Do*.

8. Tindall, *South Carolina Negroes, 1877–1900*, 214; Perman, *Struggle for Mastery*, 5–6, 91; Kousser, *The Shaping of Southern Politics*, 228–29; Gordon, "South Carolina Negro Common Schools," 330; Margold Report, box I-C-200, NAACP Papers, 3; Harlan, *Separate and Unequal*; Powdermaker, *After Freedom*, 304.

9. Harlan, *Separate and Unequal*, 261; Charles H. Houston, "Proposed Legal Attacks on Educational Discrimination," August 1, 1935, box I-C-429, NAACP Papers; Charles H. Houston, Memo for the Secretary, Joint Committee of the American Fund on Public Service and the NAACP, October 1937, box I-C-197, NAACP Papers; McMillen, *Dark Journey*, 73; Dollard, *Caste and Class*, 194–95.

10. McMillen, *Dark Journey*, 308; Gilmore, *Gender and Jim Crow*, 147–75; Powdermaker, *After Freedom*, 313.

11. Fields with Fields, 205; Charles Joyner, foreword to *When Roots Die*, xi; Bureau of the Census, "1930 Federal Population Schedules, James Island Township," South Carolina State Department of Archives and History (SCDAH) Columbia, South Carolina; Sterner, *The Negro's Share*, 63, 68. Jaynes and Williams estimate that in 1940, 48 percent of the white families and 87 percent of the black families had incomes "below federal poverty thresholds," see Jaynes and Williams, eds., *A Common Destiny*, 271; Edgar, *South Carolina: The W.P.A. Guide*, 279.

12. Federal Population Schedule, James Island, 1930; Johnson, *Shadow of the Plantation*, 129–30.

13. Fields with Fields, 205, 211, 219; Joyner, foreword to *When Roots Die*, xi; Herskovits, *Myth of the Negro Past*, 296.

14. Johnson, "The Negro Public Schools," 116; Powdermaker, *After Freedom*, 304; Dollard, *Caste and Class*, 201, 203; Johnson, *Shadow of the Plantation*, 149; Johnson, *Growing Up in the Black Belt*, 118; Levine, *Black Culture and Consciousness*, 189.

15. Fields with Fields, 206–10, 218–19, 225; Johnson, *Growing Up in the Black Belt*, 118.

16. Fields with Fields, 227, 230; Clark, *Echo in My Soul*, 40, 49; Du Bois, *Dusk of Dawn*, 182.

17. Fields with Fields, 206–10, 225; Robinson, *Bell Rings at Four*, 33; Myrdal, *An American Dilemma*, 880.

18. Anderson, *The Education of Blacks*; Walker, *Their Highest Potential*; Powdermaker, *After Freedom*, 299–300, 310; Myrdal, *An American Dilemma*, 895; State Superintendent of Education, *Annual Report*, 1926, 37; State Superintendent of Education, *Annual Report*, 1943, 119; Raper, *Preface to the Peasantry*, 328.

19. Mamie Garvin Fields Papers, box 7, ARC; Fields with Fields, 226–27; Anderson, *The Education of Blacks*, 179.

20. Fields with Fields, 225; Tyack, Hansot, and Lowe, *Public Schools in Hard Times*, 189.

21. Fields with Fields, 232–33; South Carolina General Assembly, *Acts and Joint Resolutions*, Act 344, 1937, South Carolina State Library, Columbia, South Carolina; State Superintendent of Education, *Annual Report, 1938*, 56–57; State Superintendent of Education, *Annual Report, 1941*, 18.

22. Fields with Fields, 234; Sitkoff, *A New Deal for Blacks*, 71; Sterner, *The Negro's Share*, 218–53; Tindall, *The Emergence of the New South*.

23. Fields with Fields, 218, 226; Powdermaker, *After Freedom*, 315.

24. Fields with Fields, 231; Margo, *Race and Schooling in the South, 1880–1950*, 12; Myrdal, *An American Dilemma*, 343.

25. Fass, *Outside In*, 131; Johnson and Harvey, *The National Youth Administration*, 7; Weiss, *Farewell to the Party of Lincoln*, 144; Cook, *Eleanor Roosevelt*; Badger, *The New Deal*, 207–8; Bethune, "A Tribute to Franklin Delano Roosevelt," 8, 23, National Council of Negro Women Papers, series 13, box 1, folder 1, Washington, D.C.; Bethune, "My Secret Talks with FDR," 57.

26. Fields with Fields, 231–32, 237–39, 224.

27. Fields with Fields, 231, 232, 239, 224; "Proceedings, The Second National Conference on the Problems of the Negro and Negro Youth," January 12–14, 1939, Records of the National Youth Administration, series 75, 31, National Archives, Washington, D.C.; Final Report of South Carolina, National Youth Administration Records, Record Group 119, Final Report Series, National Archives; NYA, "File of Statistics and Other Information Concerning High School Aid," State of South Carolina, May 1936, box 1, Record Group 119, National Archives; Lindley, *A New Deal for Youth*, 299.

28. Fields with Fields, 212, 224; statistics on the number of black teachers are drawn from Johnson, *The Negro in American Civilization*, 240; Pierce and others, *White and Negro Schools in the South*, 184; Fields, School Planners.

29. Myrdal, *An American Dilemma*, 74, 343, 465–66, 1000–1001; State Superintendent of Education, *Annual Report, 1943*, 113.

30. Fields, School Planners; Fields with Fields, 209, 214; Shokes, "Presentation," in "Complete Transcription of Conference, South Carolina, Voices of the Civil Rights Movement," November 5–6, 1982, ARC.

31. Wilkerson, *Special Problems of Negro Education*, 15, 17, 19, 36, 49, 99; Fields with Fields, 209, 214; U.S. Office of Education, *Biennial Survey of Education, 1932–4*, 56–57, 96; Fields, School Planners.

32. Fields, School Planners.

33. Fields, School Planners; Estill, *The Beginner's History of Our Country*; Johnson, *The Negro in American Civilization*, 140; Powdermaker, *After Freedom*, 309–10.

34. Fields with Fields, 208; Johnson, *Shadow of the Plantation*, 130; Fields, School Planners; Estill, *The Beginner's History of Our Country*; Couch, "Rural Education in Mississippi," 226–28; Mays, *Born to Rebel*, 40; Powdermaker, *After Freedom*, 320.

35. Fields, School Planners; Turner acknowledged Fields's assistance in *Africans in the Gullah Dialect*, vii; Alma Shokes, "Presentation," in complete transcription of the conference South Carolina Voices of the Civil Rights Movement, November 5–6, 1982.

36. Cell, *The Highest Stage of White Supremacy*, 230–75; Shokes, interview by author, Charleston, July 12, 1990; Nell Coley, interview by William H. Chafe, 5; Fields with Fields, 214, 220; Raper, *Preface to the Peasantry*, 334–35, 340; Johnson, "The Negro Public Schools," 124; Walker, *Their Highest Potential*, 151.

37. Fields with Fields, 127; Jackson, "Charleston Memorandum" and "Report on Three Sea Islands," Special Collections, 2051, box 82, Ralph F. Bunche Papers, Special Collections Department, University of California Los Angles, Los Angles, California; Bunche, *The Political Status of the Negro in the Age of FDR*, 246.

38. Fields with Fields, 226, 213, 236; Myrdal, *An American Dilemma*, 367; Raper, *Preface to the Peasantry*, 345; Johnson, *Growing Up in the Black Belt*, 132; Lewis with D'Orso, *Walking with the Wind*, 46; Bond, *The Education of the Negro in the American Social Order*, 13, 293; Margo, *Race and Schooling in the South*, 4.

39. Fields, School Attendance Register, 1937–1938; Fields, School Planners; Fields with Fields, 207, 212, 233, 234; Raper reported African American average daily attendance rates of 51.8 percent in Macon County and 55.9 percent in Greene County, Georgia, during the 1927–1928 school year, see *Preface to the Peasantry*, 339; Johnson, *Shadow of the Plantation*, 134, 135; Caliver, *Availability of Education*, 63; Twining and Baird, *Sea Island Roots*, 13; Johnson, "The Negro Public Schools," 132.

40. Fields, School Planners; Fields with Fields, 212; Johnson, *Shadow of the Plantation*, 134; Wilkerson, *Special Problems of Negro Education*, 17–18.

41. Blose and Caliver, *Statistics on the Education of Negroes*, 4–5; Caliver, *Availability of Education*, 63; Sterner, *The Negro's Share*, 33; Smith, "Race and Human Capital," 1227; State Superintendent of Education, *Annual Report, 1943*, 113.

42. Kaestle and others, *Literacy in the United States*, 26.

43. Powdermaker, *After Freedom*, 309–10; Raper, *Preface to the Peasantry*, 334; Myrdal, *An American Dilemma*, 903.

44. Johnson, "The Negro Public Schools," 164–65; "The Mineral Springs School," Mrs. E. M. Riddle's Report [1934], box 335, folder 1, Julius Rosenwald Papers, Fisk University. For background information on Riddle's work see Shaw, *What a Woman Ought to Do*, 135–63.

45. Fields, School Planners; Walker, *Their Highest Potential*, 126; Fields with Fields, 233; Johnson, "The Negro Public Schools," 140; Myrdal, *An American Dilemma*, 902; Margo, *Race and Schooling in the South*, 131–32.

46. Fields with Fields, 212; Anderson, *The Education of Blacks*, 186–87, 197; Wilkerson, *Special Problems of Negro Education*, 36, 46; Myrdal, *An American Dilemma*, 950; Caliver, *Availability of Education*; Caliver, *Secondary Education for Negroes*, 24–30; Shokes, "Presentation," in complete transcription of the conference South Carolina Voices of the Civil Rights Movement, November 5–6, 1982; Alma Shokes, interview by author, Charleston, July 12, 1990; Marjorie Howard, interview by author, Charleston, January 15, 1991; Fields with Fields, 137. On the migration of African Americans to southern cities in the 1930s, see Vance, *All These People*, 33, 35; Sterner, *The Negro's Share*, 20, 98; Tindall, *The Emergence of the New South*, 570; Johnson and Campbell, *Black Migration in America*, 90–101; Caliver, *A Background Study of Negro College Students*, 76; Dollard, *Caste and Class*, 200; Johnson, "The Negro Public Schools," 133; Johnson, *Shadow of the Plantation*, 143; Powdermaker, *After Freedom*, 211.

2. "The First Signs of a Mass Movement," 1938–1945

1. [Charleston] City Board of School Commissioners, Minute Books (CBSCMB), August 20, 1940; February 4, 1942; April 6, 1944; April 4, 1945; A. B. Rhett to William Grayson, December 13, 1945, Improvement of Negro Schools, box 896, Office of Archives and Records (OAR), Charleston County School District (CCSD), Charleston, South Carolina; CBSCMB, September 21, 1938; December 6, 1939; Fraser, *Charleston*, 380.

2. Houston, "Cracking Closed University Doors," 370.

3. Naipaul, *A Turn in the South*, 77; Ball, "Improvement in Race Relations," 389; Cell, *The Highest Stage of White Supremacy*, 131–91; Woodward, *The Strange Career of Jim Crow*, 67; Bureau of the Census, *Sixteenth Census of the United States, 1940, Volume II*, 425 and *Population, Volume III*, 429; Kantrowitz, *Ben Tillman*, 156–97.

4. Ball, "Improvement in Race Relations," 389; Fredrickson, *White Supremacy*, 271–72; Bureau of Census, *Sixteenth Census of the United States, 1940, Population, Volume III*, 425, 429; Edgar, *South Carolina: The W.P.A. Guide*, 187; Myrdal, *An American Dilemma*, 282, 1001; McMillen, *Dark Journey*, 307; Fraser, *Charleston*, 382; Brownlee, *A New Day Ascending*, 134; Chafe, *Civilities and Civil Rights*, 18.

5. Greer, "The High School of Charleston," 3–4; CBSCMB, January 10, 1940; January 8, 1941; *Charleston News and Courier*, November 11, 1932; April 19, 1939; Eckelberry, *The History of Municipal Universities in the United States*, 22; Manegold, *In Glory's Shadow*; Lynch, *Medical Schooling in South Carolina*; Bureau of the Census, *Sixteenth Census of the United States, 1940, Population, Volume III*, 89, 395; Sterner, *The Negro's Share*, 60, 366; Myrdal, *An American Dilemma*, 341, 343.

6. Gibson, *Industrial Education Survey*; Strohecker, *Present Day Public Education*; Avery Research Center (ARC), "The History of African-American Education in Charleston County, South Carolina," Research Conference, February 16, 17, 18, 1989, ARC; Moore, "A History of the Negro Public Schools," 25–40; CBSCMB, March 4, 1925; June 11, 1937; December 6, 1939; April 3, 1940; September 3, 1941; August 7, 1946; September 14, 1946.

7. CBSCMB, May 6, 1936; February 3, June 11, 1937; January 10, 1940; July 8, 1946; *School Directory of South Carolina, 1940*, 100; Moore, "A History of the Negro Public Schools," 46; *Charleston News and Courier*, July 15, 1945; Improvement of Negro Schools, 1943, box 896, OAR, CCSD.

8. Gordon, *Sketches of Negro Life*, 331; Drago, *Initiative, Paternalism, and Race Relations*; Lewis, "The Origins and Causes of the Civil Rights Movement," 11; Wadelington and Knapp, *Charlotte Hawkins Brown*; Davis and Dollard, *Children of Bondage*; Brown, "African American Education."

9. Brownlee, *A New Day Ascending*, 135, 136; Sherwood, *The Oblates*, 253–56; Irvine and Foster, eds., *Growing Up African American*; Drago, *Initiative, Paternalism, and Race Relations*, 60, 62; Meffert, Pyatt, and the Avery Research Center, *Charleston, South Carolina*, 49.

10. Davis and Dollard, *Children of Bondage*, 256; Brownlee, *A New Day Ascending*, 134; Drago, *Initiative, Paternalism, and Race Relations*, 154; "South Carolina's Oldest Negro High School," *National Negro Digest* [circa 1940], 42–43, Manuscript Department, Caroliniana Library (MDCL), University of South Carolina, Columbia, South Carolina; Myrdal, *An American Dilemma*, 694.

11. Brownlee, *A New Day Ascending*, 136; Beam, *He Called Them*, 89, 150–54; McPherson, *The Abolitionist Legacy*, 292; Drago, *Initiative, Paternalism, and Race Relations*, 154, 187; McMillan, *Negro Higher Education*, 4, 5; Gordon, *Sketches of Negro Life*, 69.

12. American Missionary Association, *Annual Report, 1938*; Brownlee, *A New Day Ascending*, 134, 137; Fields with Fields, 24; Paddock, "Avery Institute," 64–65; Davis and Dollard, *Children of Bondage*, 253; Frazier, *Negro Youth at the Crossways*, 96. In New Orleans, Adam Fairclough wrote, "the difference between the public schools and the private schools helped to perpetuate long-standing class/color divisions. Some Louisiana school boards adopted a semi-official policy of supporting separate public schools for Creoles of color"; see Fairclough "Black Teachers in the Jim Crow South," 72.

13. American Missionary Association, *A Continuing Service*, 33–34; Drago, *Initiative, Paternalism, and Race Relations*, 198, 166–67; Brownlee, *A New Day Ascending*, 281.

14. J. Michael Graves, interview by author, Charleston, July 16, 1990; Brownlee, *A New Day Ascending*, 136–37; Drago, *Initiative, Paternalism, and Race Relations*, 142, 165, 167–68, 200; McMillan, *Negro Higher Education*, 6.

15. L. Howard Bennett, interview with Edmund Drago and Eugene Hunt, ARC; Brownlee, *A New Day Ascending*, 137, McMillan, *Negro Higher Education*, 6; Robert Bagnell to Dr. E. B. Burroughs, December 3, December 17, 1930; January 2, 1931; Dr. E. B. Burroughs to Robert Bagnell, January 1, 1931, box I-G-196, NAACP Papers; Bagnell, "Lights and Shadows in the South," 124.

16. Johnson, "Present Trends," 146–48; Myrdal, *An American Dilemma*, 279, 281, 301, 302, 1001; Cann, "Burnett Rhett Maybank," 75, 46–136; Bond, *The Education of the Negro in the American Social Order*, 215–16; Oliver Hasell, interview by author, Charleston, July 18, 1990; Margo, *Race and Schooling in the South*, 104.

17. Final Report of South Carolina, National Youth Administration Records, Record Group 119, box 1, Final State Report Series, National Archives; File of Statistics and Other Information Concerning High School Aid, State of South Carolina, May 1936, Record Group 119, box 1, National Archives; Report of State Director of Negro Affairs, 1936–1939, Record Group 119, box 5, National Archives; Lindley, *A New Deal for Youth*, 299; Fass, *Outside In*, 132; *Burke Spotlight*, 1937, Burke High School Library (BHSL), Charleston, South Carolina.

18. Newbold, "The Public Education of Negroes and the Current Depression," 5–15; Thompson, "Current Events of Importance in Negro Education: The Effect of the Depression," 117–18; CBSCMB, December 7, 1938; May 3, July 7, 1939; January 30, October 9, 1940; Moore, "A History of the Negro Public Schools," 46, 50; Du Bois, "A Negro Nation Within the Nation," 79; McMillen, *Dark Journey*, 85, 94; Wolters, *The Burden of Brown*, 10; Duke, *The School That Refused to Die*, 22; Rousseve, *The Negro in Louisiana*, 144.

19. Powdermaker, *After Freedom*, 322; Dollard, *Caste and Class*, 202; Houston, "Educational Inequalities," 300; Hoffman, "The Genesis of the Modern Movement," 207; Sterner, *The Negro's Share*, 252; Rousseve, *The Negro in Louisiana*, 136.

20. Caliver, "Certain Significant Developments," 111–19; Houston, "Enrollment," 141; Houston, Travel Voucher number 40, September 9, 1935, box I-C-196, NAACP Papers; McNeil, *Groundwork*; Houston, "Cracking Closed University Doors," 365.

21. Charles H. Houston to Walter White, November 2, November 4, November 7, 1934; February 9, February 19, April 10, July 31, 1935, box II-L-14, reel 63–65, NAACP Papers; Charles Thompson, "Editorial Note," 290; Kluger, *Simple Justice*, 186, 202; *University of Maryland v. Donald G. Murray*, 169 Md. 478 (1936) at 488; Shabazz, *Advancing Democracy*, 27–33.

22. Charles Bailey to Walter White, April 9, 1938, box I-C-202, NAACP Papers; CBSCMB, June 1, 1938; January 24, 1939; J. C. Prioleau Jr. to Walter White, May 22, 1939, box I-C-202; J. C. Prioleau Jr. to Thurgood Marshall, June 1, 1939, box I-C-202, NAACP Papers; Houston, "Cracking Closed University Doors," 370.

23. Charles B. Bailey to J. N. Frierson, April 24, 1938, box I-C-202, NAACP Papers; Charles H. Houston to K. Norman Diamond, no date, box II-C-198, NAACP Papers; Memo for the Joint Committee from Charles H. Houston, July 24, 1936, box 29, Spingarn Papers, Library of Congress, Manuscript Division, Washington, D.C.; Charles H. Houston to Charles Bailey, April 11, 1938, box I-C-202, NAACP Papers; Houston, "Cracking Closed University Doors," 364.

24. *Missouri ex. rel. Gaines v. Canada*, 305 U.S. 337 (1938) at 349; Thurgood Marshall to S. Morgan, July 6, 1939, box I-C-202, NAACP Papers.

25. M. F. Whittaker to Walter White, March 6, 1939, box I-C-202, NAACP Papers; *Columbia State*, January 19, 1939; Memo to Mr. White from Mr. Marshall, March 10, 1939, box I-C-202, NAACP Papers.

26. *Charleston News and Courier*, January 21, February 4, 1939; *Louisiana Weekly*, September 10, 1938; *New York Times*, December 18, 1938.

27. Walter White to Charles H. Houston, August 11, 1939, box I-D-95, NAACP Papers; Johnson, "A Letter from Guy Johnson," 271; Marshall, quoted in Fairclough, "The Costs of *Brown*," 51.

28. Thurgood Marshall to Charles Bailey, July 6, 1939, box II-C-202, NAACP Papers; Charles Bailey to Thurgood Marshall, June 17, 1940, box II-C-202, NAACP Papers; Thurgood Marshall to Charles Bailey, June 25, 1940, box II-C-202, NAACP Papers; Rowan, *Dream Makers*, 83; Burke and Hine, "The South Carolina State Law School," 26.

29. Kenneth Hughes to Charles H. Houston, January 24, 1939, box I-C-202, NAACP Papers; Kenneth Hughes to Walter White, February 7, 1939, box I-C-202, NAACP Papers.

30. Charles H. Houston to Kenneth Hughes, January 27, 1939, box I-C-202, NAACP Papers.

31. Stein, *The World of Marcus Garvey*, 131–32, 161–62; Charles H. Houston to Roy Wilkins, May 22, 1935, box I-C-63–5, reel 2, NAACP Papers; Ralph J. Bunche, quoted in Fairclough, *A Better Day Coming*, 182–83; E. B. Burroughs to Robert Bagnell, January 19, 1931, box I-G-196, NAACP Papers; William Miller to William Pickens, April 3, 1940, box II-C-176, NAACP Papers; Wilhelmina Jackson, "Charleston Memorandum," 4, Bunche Papers; Memo to White, Wilkins, and Morrow from Thurgood Marshall, June 17, 1942, box II-C-181, NAACP Papers; NAACP Membership Reports, Charleston, South Carolina, May 25, 1938, box II-C-196; November 18, 1940; October 26, 1942, box II-C-196, NAACP Papers.

32. Diggs, *It All Started on Winters Lane*, 133–34; *Williams v. Zimmerman*, 172 Md. 563; 192 A. 353 (1937); Walter White to Charles H. Houston, August 11, 1939, box I-D-95, NAACP Papers; Tushnet, *The NAACP's Legal Strategy against Segregated Education*, 68; Tushnet, *Making Civil Rights Law*, 3; Klarman, "How *Brown* Changed Race Relations," 82.

33. Moore, "A History of the Negro Public Schools," 46; *Parvenue*, April 1945, BHSL; Bennett interview.

34. Fraser, *Charleston*, 387; Lewis, "The Origins and Causes of the Civil Rights Movement," 175; Charleston Community Council Petition, March 14, 1941, box II-B-180, NAACP Papers; CBSCMB, December 6, 1939; July 23, November 6, 1940; September 3, 1941; May 25, June 3, 1942; January 5, June 19, 1944; February 5, May 7, November 5, March 25, 1941; June 2, 1943; *Charleston Evening Post*, March 1, 1934; January 6, October 26, February 2, 1937; November 11, 1940; July 4, 1941; *Charleston News and Courier*, July 19, July 27, 1942; Hamer, "A Southern City," 57.

35. Daniel, "Going among Strangers," 906; Lewis, "The Origins and Causes of the Civil Rights Movement," 175; Goldfield, *Black, White, and Southern*, 35; National Defense, box 863, OAR, CCSD; Reed, *Seedtime*; Hamer, "A Southern City," 63; Fairclough, *A Better Day Coming*, 186; Myrdal, *An American Dilemma*, 410, 415; Margo, *Race and Schooling in the South*, 92; Newby, *Black Carolinians*, 297; Bureau of the Census, *Seventeenth Census of the United States, Population: 1950, Volume 2*, 52, 53; Division of Surveys, *Public Schools of Charleston, South Carolina*, 134–35.

36. Brown, "An Evaluation of the Accredited Secondary Schools," 4; CBSCMB, March 1, 1939; *Burke Spotlight*, May 1937, BHSL; *Parvenue*, May 1945, BHSL.

37. CBSCMB, June 1, 1938; March 8, June 26, November 2, December 6, 1939; August 6, 1943; Moore, "A History of the Negro Public Schools," 50.

38. Dollard, *Caste and Class*, 194; Johnson, *The Negro College Graduate*, 94; Frazier, *Black Bourgeoisie*, 81; Myrdal, *An American Dilemma*, 945, 895.

39. *Charleston News and Courier*, June 26, June 3, June 7, July 15, 1945; Walter G. Daniel, "The Availability of Education for Negroes, 455; CBSCMB, October 3, 1945; High School Application, 1945–1946, Burke Industrial School, High School Accreditation Reports, Record Group S 152116, SCDAH; Lonnie Hamilton, interview by author, Charleston, July 12, 1990.

40. CBSCMB, February 2, 1938; July 17, 1939.

41. Kelley, "We are Not What We Seem: Rethinking Black Working-Class Opposition in the Jim Crow South," 76, 78, 79; Fairclough, *Teaching Equality*, 67.

42. Genovese, *Roll Jordan Roll*; Myrdal, *An American Dilemma*, 880; Nevada Heyward, interview by author, Charleston, July 9, 1990; Viola Duvall (Stewart), interview by author, Philadelphia, Pennsylvania, September 4, 1990; Eugene Hunt, interview by author, Charleston, July 11, 1990; Dorothy Holmes, interview by author, Charleston, July 31, 1990; Lois Simms, interviews by author, Charleston, January 6, 10, 1991; Newby, *Black Carolinians*, 86–87; Tyack, Hansot, and Lowe, *Public Schools in Hard Times*, 183. Looking back on her long career as a teacher in East Texas, Dorothy Robinson remembered that "I was a rather free agent and did just about what I wanted to do, as long as I did not ask for anything that would entail the expenditure of money," Robinson, *Bell Rings at Four*, 33.

43. "Recognition Day," no date, Miscellaneous Documents, BHSL; Simonton PTA to A. B. Rhett, November 1, 1938, Improvement of Negro Schools, box 896, OAR, CCSD; Chafe, *Civilities and Civil Rights*, 18–19.

44. Hunt interview; Drago, *Initiative, Paternalism, and Race Relations*, 218–19; *Charleston News and Courier*, February 8, 1989; Howard interview.

45. CBSCMB, November 2, 1939; September 3, 1941; June 2, April 7, 1943; July 12, 1944.

46. Caliver, *Education of Negro Teachers*, 33; Moore, "A History of the Negro Public Schools," 49; Hunt interview; *Parvenue*, May 1941; *Charleston News and Courier*, February 8, 1989; Malissa Smith (Burkehalter), interview by author, Atlanta, Georgia, July 28, 1990; CBSCMB, June 4, 1941; October 9, 1940; Burke High School Student Records, OAR, CCSD; Anderson, *The Education of Blacks*, 223–24; Jones, *A Traditional Model*, 25–26, 124–25; Cecelski, *Along Freedom Road*, 65; Myrdal, *An American Dilemma*, 899.

47. Duvall interview; George Stanyard, interview by author, Charleston, July 9, 1990; Hunt interview; Holmes interview; *Parvenue*, 1942; Frederick Cook, interview by author, Charleston, January 10, 1991; Drago, *Initiative, Paternalism, and Race Relations*, 218; Brownlee, *A New Day Ascending*, 137.

48. Burke yearbook, 1942, BHSL; Fass, *Outside In*, 73–111; Tyack, Hansot, and Lowe, *Public Schools in Hard Times*, 183; Ravitch, *Left Back*, 377.

49. Duvall interview; Hunt interview; Merriweather interview; *Parvenue*, May 1945; CBSCMB, December 6, 1939; February 2, 1944; Moore, "A History of the Negro Public Schools," 49–50.

50. Howard interview; Ruth Cook, 1945 Burke graduation memorabilia; *Parvenue*, 1942; *Parvenue*, May 1946; Hermine Stanyard, interview by author, Charleston, July 9, 1990.

51. CBSCMB, December 7, 1938; *Parvenue*, May 1945; Heyward interview; Hamilton interview; Hermine Stanyard interview; Caliver, "Certain Significant Developments," 116.

52. Baker, "Testing Equality."

3. Testing Equality, 1936–1946

1. Margold Report, 95, box I-C-200, NAACP Papers; Murray, *The Negro Handbook*.

2. The salary-equalization campaign has been examined by Kluger, *Simple Justice*; Lewis, *In Their Own Interests*; Bolton, "Mississippi's School Equalization Program"; Tushnet, *The NAACP's Legal Strategy against Segregated Education*; Margo, *Race and Schooling in the South*, 52–68; Fairclough, *Teaching Equality*, 57–60; Greenberg, *Crusaders in the Courts*, 67, 85–86; Nieman, *Promises to Keep*, 130–39; Beezer, "Black Teacher's Salaries," 200–213; Bullock, *A History of Negro Education in the South*, 213–20.

3. Myrdal, *An American Dilemma*, 824; Wilkerson, *Special Problems of Negro Education*, 24; Margo, *Race and Schooling in the South*, 53, 62; Thurgood Marshall, Memorandum to Branch Presidents, September 13, 1937, box I-C-290, NAACP Papers; Thurgood Marshall, "An Evaluation of Recent Efforts to Achieve Racial Integration in Education Through Resort to the Courts," 318; Teachers' Salaries in Black and White, box II-B-176, NAACP Papers; A. B. Rhett, Deposition in *Duvall v. Seignious*, box 110–27, J. Waties Waring Papers, Moorland Spingarn Library, Howard University, Washington, D.C.; [Charleston] City Board of School Commissioners, Minute Books (CBSCMB), June 30, 1938; January 24, July 17, November 6, 1939; June 6, 1940; November 5, December 3, 1941; April 1, June 2, June 3, 1942; Salaries Comparative, 1938–1943, box 896, Office of Archives and Records (OAR), Charleston County School District (CCSD); Hunt interview; Jay Deiss to C. H. Scott, August 4, 1941, box II-B-174, NAACP Papers.

4. Charles H. Houston to Roy Wilkins, May 22, 1935, NAACP Papers, I-C-63–65, reel 2; Charles H. Houston Report to Joint Committee, November 14, 1935; Walter White, Report to Joint Committee, July 29, 1935, Spingarn Papers, box 29; Charles H. Houston to Secretary of Joint Committee, September 25, 1937, NAACP Papers, box II-L-14; Kluger, *Simple Justice*, 195–97; Clark, *Echo in My Soul*, 81.

5. Kluger, *Simple Justice*, 173–86; Williams, *Thurgood Marshall*, 15–92; Tushnet, *Making Civil Rights Law*, 17.

6. Thurgood Marshall, interview by Ed Erwin, February 15, 1977, Butler Library, Columbia University, New York, New York, 98; Johnson, *The Negro*, 240; Pierce and others, *White and Negro Schools in the South*, 184.

7. *Mills v. Board of Trustees of Anne Arundel County*, 30 F. Supp. 245 (1939) at 248–49, 251; *Alston v. School Board of the City of Norfolk*, 112 F. 2d. 992 (1940) at 995; Tushnet, *The NAACP's Legal Strategy against Segregated Education*.

8. *Mills* at 249, 251; Tushnet, *The NAACP's Legal Strategy against Segregated Education*, 161.

9. Teachers' Salaries, box II-B-176, NAACP Papers; Marshall interview, 88; Williams, *Thurgood Marshall*, 91; Myrdal, *An American Dilemma*, 320; Memorandum from Thurgood Marshall, Latest Developments in Teacher Salary Cases, July 28, 1941, box II-B-176, NAACP Papers; Thurgood Marshall to Walter White, September 23, 1943, box II-B-176, NAACP Papers; NAACP Brief, *Reynolds et. al. v. Board of Public Instruction for Dade County, Fla. et al.*, box II-B-175, NAACP Papers; *McDaniel v. Bd. of Public Instruction for Escambia Co., Florida*, 39 F. Supp. 638 (1941).

10. Downey, *Ben D. Wood*; Lagemann, *Private Power*, 104; Wilson, "Knowledge for Teachers"; Wood, "Making Use," 278.

11. Wood, "Making Use," 280; Wood, *An Announcement*; Wood and Beers, "Knowledge Versus Thinking?" 487–99.

12. In 1940 the exam fee was five dollars per candidate. Downey, *Ben D. Wood*, 60; Wilson, "Knowledge for Teachers," 163–65; Pilley, "The National Teacher Examination Service,"

180; Wood, "Dr. Wood's Statement," 155–56. For an excellent review of the literature on the NTE see Haney, Madaus, and Kreitzer, "Charms Talismanic."

13. Ben Wood to F. S. Beers, February 18, 1941, file 147, reel 18, Ben D. Wood Papers, Educational Testing Service Archives, Princeton, New Jersey; Wilson, "Knowledge for Teachers," 165; Downey, *Ben D. Wood*, 61.

14. Ben Wood to A. J. Stoddard, March 29, 1941, file 143, reel 18, Wood Papers; Ben Wood to A. J. Stoddard, April 15, 1941, file 143, reel 18, Wood Papers.

15. Ben Wood to M. E. Thompson, April 6, 1941, file 147, reel 18, Wood Papers; Ben Wood to Dean Lyman, April 16, 1941, file 147, reel 18, Wood Papers.

16. Ben Wood, Adaptation of Certification-Salary Classification Plan for Use by Local Educational Authorities, April 11, 1941, file 149, reel 18, Wood Papers; Ben Wood to A. J. Stoddard, January 5, 1942, file 143, reel 18, Wood Papers; Ben Wood to A. J. Stoddard, April 15, 1941, file 143, reel 18, Wood Papers; Ben Wood to David W. Robinson, March 18, 1941, file 149, reel 18, Wood Papers; Ben Wood to M. E. Thompson, April 6, 1941, file 148, reel 18, Wood Papers.

17. Ben Wood to F. S. Beers, April 14, 1941, file 147, reel 18, Wood Papers; Ben Wood, Memo to the National Committee, January 22, 1942, file 143, reel 18, Wood Papers; F. S. Beers to Ben Wood, January 25, 1941, file 147, reel 18, Wood Papers; F. S. Beers to Ben Wood, March 5, 1940, file 147, reel 18, Wood Papers; Ben Wood to D. Copeland, June 5, 1941, file 148, reel 18, Wood Papers; Ben Wood to J. A. True, March 13, 1941, file 145, reel 18, Wood Papers; Boehm, ed., Papers of the NAACP, Part 3, The Campaign for Educational Equality: Legal Department and Central Office Records, 1913–1950, series B, Legal Department and Central Office Records, 1940–1950, Teacher's Salaries, Virginia, reel 6; NAACP press release, Dade County Teachers' Salary Case, no date, box II-B-174, NAACP Papers; Memo from the Legal Department for Press Release, June 11, 1942, box II-B-175, NAACP Papers; Edwin Clark to Walter White, April 23, 1942, box II-B-175, NAACP Papers; *Turner v. Keefe*, 50 F. Supp. 647 (1943) at 652; Teachers' Salary Cases Pending as of May 1, 1943, box II-B-175, NAACP Papers; NAACP press release, April 6, 1943, box II-B-175, NAACP Papers; Ransom, "Education and the Law," 569; Marshall, "The Legal Battle."

18. Bolton, "Mississippi's School Equalization Program," 799–804; Fairclough, *Teaching Equality*, 58–61.

19. Ben Wood interview by Gary Saretsky, November 7, 1977, volume 2, 35, Wood Papers; W. C. McCall to Ben Wood, November 15, 1940, file 149, reel 18, Wood Papers; Ben Wood to David W. Robinson, March 24, 1941, file 149, reel 18, Wood Papers.

20. Dubose, *South Carolina Lives*; Report of Special Committee.

21. Report of Special Committee.

22. Caliver, "Certain Significant Developments," 119; W. C. McCall to Ben Wood, November 15, 1940, file 149, reel 18, Wood Papers.

23. W. C. McCall to Ben Wood, November 15, 1940, file 149, reel 18, Wood Papers; Ben Wood to David W. Robinson, March 24, 1941, file 149, reel 18, Wood Papers.

24. Joseph Murray to Thurgood Marshall, July 30, 1941, box II-B-180, NAACP Papers; L. Raymond Bailey to Thurgood Marshall, November 28, 1940, box II-B-180, NAACP Papers; Thurgood Marshall to L. Raymond Bailey, November 11, 1940, box II-B-180, NAACP Papers; *Columbia State*, July 10, 1941; Aba-Mecha, "Black Woman Activist," 176–90.

25. Charles Bailey to Walter White, April 9, 1938, box II-C-202, NAACP Papers; Simmons, "Professional and Cultural Background," 2, 23, 38; Aba-Mecha, "Black Woman Activist," 8; J. Arthur Brown interview; Smith interview; Hunt interview; Bagnell, "Lights and Shadows in the South," 124.

26. Smith interview; Duvall interview; Hunt interview; Malissa Smith Burkehalter, letter to author, August 22, 1990; James Hinton to Thurgood Marshall, July 15, 1943, box II-B-180, NAACP Papers; NAACP Complaint, *Duvall v. Seignious, et. al.*, box II-B-180, NAACP Papers; CBSCMB, July 7, 1943; Prentice Thomas to Harold Boulware, April 30, 1943, box II-B-180, NAACP Papers; Prentice Thomas to Harold Boulware, August 18, 1943, box II-B-180, NAACP Papers; Milton Konvitz to Harold Boulware, July 15, 1943, box II-B-180, NAACP Papers; Harold Boulware to Thurgood Marshall, August 3, 1943, box II-B-180, NAACP Papers.

27. CBSCMB, July 17, 1939; July 3, 1940; February 4, May 25, January 7, May 6, August 6, September 1, October 6, 1942; March 9, July 7, May 5, 1943; Hunt interview; Smith interview; Janken, *White*, 263–64; Clark, *Echo in My Soul*, 82.

28. Hunt interview; Hasell interview; Duvall interview.

29. J. Waties Waring, interviews by Harlan B. Phillips and Louis M. Star, 1955–1957, Butler Library, Columbia University, New York, New York; Yarbrough, *A Passion for Justice*, 46; John Egerton raises questions about Yarbrough's interpretation in *Speak Now against the Day*, 593; see also Kluger, *Simple Justice*, 295–305.

30. *Duvall v. Seignious*, unpublished consent decree, box 110–27, J. Waties Waring Papers, Moorland-Spingarn Research Center, Howard University, Washington, D.C. In March 1944 Marshall wrote Hinton and asked for $113.37, "resulting from my trip to Charleston for preparation and trial of teacher's salary case." See Thurgood Marshall to James Hinton, March 14, 1944, box II-B-180, NAACP Papers; *Charleston News and Courier*, undated clipping, box II-B-180, NAACP Papers.

31. Hunt interview; Howard interview; Fitchett, "The New Program," 708–9; William Bluford to Leon Ransom, November 7, 1944, box II-B-180, NAACP Papers.

32. *Reynolds*, NAACP brief, box II-B-175, NAACP Papers; Thurgood Marshall to Walter White, July 28, 1941, box II-B-176, NAACP Papers; Thomas, "Black Intellectuals," 496; Leon Ransom to Acting Dean Fitchett, April 1, 1942, box II-B-180, NAACP Papers; CBSCMB, December 6, 1944.

33. Daniel, *Excellent Teachers*, 236, 275, 280; Frick, *A Proposed Plan*, 55; Hunter, *Education of Teachers*; Brewton, *Excellent Schools*.

34. *United States v. South Carolina*, 445 F. Supp. 1094 (1977) at 1101; J. B. White to Ben Wood, July 18, 1944, file 149, reel 18, Wood Papers; Ben Wood to J. B. White, January 14, 1945, file 149, reel 18, Wood Papers.

35. Key, *Southern Politics*, 154; NAACP press release, March 23, 1944, box-II-B-180, NAACP Papers; Harold Boulware to Thurgood Marshall, February 15, 1944, box II-B-180, NAACP Papers; Fitchett, "The New Program," 710; Deficiency Appropriation Act, 1945–1946, section 76, 86, box 110–34, Waring Papers.

36. *Thompson v. Gibbes*, 60 F. Supp. 872 (1945) at 875, 876; Yarbrough, *A Passion for Justice*, 46. In an interview in the late 1950s Waring stated that the new salary plan was "a pretty fair scheme of adjusting the whole thing." He conceded that "some [black] teachers were going to have a bad time under it because they were so inadequately prepared," Waring interview, 230–31. Ben Wood also acknowledged that the tests favored whites. When asked why, he replied: "You go into the average home of a black teacher anywhere and you may find a local newspaper, but you will not find *National Geographic*, or *Harpers*, or *Colliers*. You may not even find a dictionary. It was certainly true down there. Negro teachers in the South had not even seen the *New York Times*," Wood interview, 36; Bell, *Faces at the Bottom of the Well*, 104.

37. Nieman, *Promises to Keep*, 88–104; Beezer, "Black Teacher's Salaries," 200–213; Bullock, *A History of Negro Education in the South*, 213–20; Greenberg, *Crusaders in the Courts*, 67, 85–86.

38. Fitchett, "The New Program," 709; DeCosta, "The Education of Negroes," 410; DeCosta, "Negro Higher and Professional Education," 350–60. Margo, *Race and Schooling in the South*, 73, 76, 85.

39. Teachers' Salaries, box II-B-176, NAACP Papers; Federal Security Agency, *Biennial Survey of Education, 1948–1950*, 49. Peter F. Orazem and Robert A. Margo estimate that inequities in southern segregated systems of education accounted for one-third of the variation between white and black scores on standardized tests during this period; see Orazem, "Black-White Differences," 714–23; Margo, *Race and Schooling in the South*, 56, 73, 76, 85.

40. CBSCMB, March 18, 1948; South Carolina State Board of Education, *Requirements for Teacher Education and Certification*, 49; CBSCMB, September 18, 1935; May 6, 1936; March 18, 1948. These comparisons are based on weighted averages.

41. CBSCMB, March 18, 1948; Simms interview; Howard interview; Hunt interview; Henry Hutchinson, interview by author, Charleston, July 18, 1990; George Stanyard interview; Davis, "A Study of Fisk University Freshman," 477–83.

42. Viola Duvall to John McCray, September 30, 1944, McCray Papers, Manuscript Department, Caroliniana Library (MDCL), University of South Carolina, Columbia, South Carolina; Simms, *A Chalk and Chalkboard Career*, 26–31; Clark, *Echo in My Soul*, 82–83.

43. *Charleston News and Courier*, undated clipping, box 929, OAR, CCSD; *Charleston News and Courier*, September 24, 1950; Ben Wood to David W. Robinson, March 24, 1941, reel 18, file 149, Wood Papers.

44. Teachers' Salaries, box II-B-176, NAACP Papers; U.S. Office of Education, *Biennial Survey of Education, 1948–1950*, 49; U.S. Office of Education, *Biennial Survey of Education, 1946–1948*, 41; U.S. Office of Education, *Biennial Survey of Education, 1944–1946*, 29; Robert Carter to Walter White, November 4, 1946, box II-B-180, NAACP Papers.

45. Ben Wood to David Ryans, February 22, 1946, file 134, reel 17, Wood Papers; Wilson, "Knowledge for Teachers," 221–71; Benson, "Problems of Evaluating Test Scores," 176; Educational Testing Service, *Annual Report, 1953–1954*, 53, 63; Educational Testing Service, *Annual Report, 1954–1955*, 70; Educational Testing Service, *Annual Report, 1955–1956*, 91–92; Educational Testing Service, *Annual Report, 1959–1960*, 36, 58–59; Educational Testing Service, School Systems Using Tests Prepared By Educational Testing Service, September 1959, NTE History File, Educational Testing Service Archives, Princeton, New Jersey, 47.

46. "Negroes to Sue for Graduate Opportunities," undated clipping, box II-B-176, NAACP Papers; James Hinton to Thurgood Marshall, September 16, 1945, box II-B-146, NAACP Papers; McMillan, *Negro Higher Education*, 211.

4. The Veil in Higher Education, 1943–1953

1. Eckelberry, *The History of Municipal Universities in the United States*, 9.

2. Thurgood Marshall to Carter Wesley, October 16, 1947, box II-B-204, NAACP Papers.

3. Washington, "Comment: History and Role of Black Law Schools," 385–421.

4. In reconstructing John Wrighten's campaign to desegregate higher education, this chapter relies on William Peters's 1960 interviews with Wrighten, which were published in "A Southern Success Story"; Wrighten's presentation at the 1982 conference at Avery, Voices of the Civil Rights Movement; Edmund L. Drago's correspondence with Wrighten in 1986;

William C. Hine's 1989 telephone interview with Wrighten, as well as documentary sources. Bureau of the Census, *Fifteenth Census of the United States, Federal Population Schedules, 1930 Edisto Island, South Carolina*, South Carolina State Department of Archives and History (SCDAH); Peters, "A Southern Success Story," 99; Avery Memorabilia Collection, box 3, folder 3, Avery Research Center (ARC).

5. Frank A. DeCosta Papers, box 7, ARC; Bennett interview; J. Arthur Brown interview; Drago, *Initiative, Paternalism, and Race Relations*, 202, 205, 228; "South Carolina Fights Illiteracy," *National Negro Digest* (circa 1940), 12–54.

6. Peters, "A Southern Success Story," 100; John Wrighten to Edmund L. Drago, August 26, 1986, unprocessed documents, ARC.

7. Peters,"A Southern Success Story," 100, 102; Bunche, quoted in Myrdal, *An American Dilemma*, 1402; Lois Moses to Madison Jones, January 18, 1943, box II-E-94, NAACP Papers; J. Simmons to Ruby Hurley, April 9, 1945, box II-C-177, NAACP Papers; Julia Alston to Ruby Hurley, May 14, 1943, box II-E-94, NAACP Papers; Julia Alston to Ruby Hurley, August 1, 1943, box II-E-94, NAACP Papers; "Charleston's Snobbish Aristocracy 'Passing' Out of Existence," 17; J. W. Alston to Ruby Hurley, October 17, 1943, box II-E-94, NAACP Papers; Moses White, interview by author, Charleston, January 10, 1991; David Mack to NAACP, no date, box II-C-177, NAACP Papers; Hunt interview.

8. John Wrighten to College of Charleston, July 17, 1943, Correspondence Relating to the Applications by Negroes for Entrance into the College, Special Collections, Robert Smalls Library, College of Charleston (SCCOC), Charleston, South Carolina; George Grice to Judge P. M. Macmillan, May 19, 1944, Correspondence, SCCOC.

9. Julia Brogdon (Purnell), interview by Edmund L. Drago, November 13, 1987, ARC.

10. Brogdon interview; Hortense Scipio to Registrar, May 15, 1944, Correspondence, SCCOC; Peters, "A Southern Success Story," 102.

11. *Charleston News and Courier*, June 11, 1944; *Charleston Evening Post*, June 12, 1944.

12. Drago, *Initiative, Paternalism, and Race Relations*, 233; *Charleston News and Courier*, June 12, 1944; *Charleston Evening Post*, June 12, 1944.

13. *Parvenue*, May 1945, Burke High School Library (BHSL); Avery Graduation Program, 1944, Avery School Memorabilia, box 3, ARC.

14. Drago, *Initiative, Paternalism, and Race Relations*, 101, 234; *Charleston News and Courier*, February 8, 1949.

15. *Missouri ex. rel. Gaines v. Canada* (1938).

16. Paul Macmillan to John McFall, October 11, 1944, Correspondence, SCCOC.

17. John McFall to Paul Macmillan, October 19, 1944, Correspondence, SCCOC; James Hinton to Ruby Hurley, July 24, 1944, box II-C-177, NAACP Papers.

18. John Wrighten to Ruby Hurley, September 4, 1944, box II-C-177, NAACP Papers; Peters, "A Southern Success Story," 102; Tushnet, *Making Civil Rights Law*, 122–23.

19. Voices of the Civil Rights Movement, 87; Peters, "A Southern Success Story," 102; [Charleston] City Board of School Commissioners, Minute Books (CBSCMB), February 5, May 5, 1947; *Charleston News and Courier*, August 13, 1947.

20. Ruth Bryan to Registrar, March 15, 1949, Correspondence, SCCOC; *Charleston News and Courier*, February 8, January 30, February 1, February 22, February 23, March 2, March 18, March 24, 1949; August 30, 1950; H. L. Erckmann to Paul Macmillan, January 23, 1948, Correspondence, SCCOC; Levine, *The American College*; *Wilson v. City of Paducah*, 100 F. Supp. 116 (1951); *Battle v. Wichita Falls Junior College District*, 101 F. Supp. 82 (1951); *Constantine v. Southwestern Louisiana Institute*, 120 F. Supp. 417 (1954).

21. Klein, *Survey of Negro Colleges and Universities*, 665–80; Potts, *A History of South Carolina State College*; Nix, "Tentative History of South Carolina State College," Nelson Nix Papers, 5.13, Miller F. Whittaker Library (SCSUA); *State Agricultural and Mechanical College, Annual Report, 1943* (hereafter *Annual Report*), 15; Mays, *Born to Rebel*, 42; Warlick, "Practical Education and the Negro College," 409.

22. *Annual Report, 1943*, 5; Newby, *Black Carolinians*, 264; Lesesne, *A History of the University of South Carolina*, 53; Enrollment and Appropriations for the Past Six Years, General Files, 2.10, 1947–1948, SCSUA.

23. T. J. Crawford, interview by William C. Hine, March 9, 1989, SCSUA; Martin and others, *South Carolina State University*, 30, 51–52.

24. Hine, "South Carolina State College," 158; Job Applications, 1937–1943, 2:10.20; National Youth Administration Forms, 2.20.2, SCSUA; Potts, *A History of South Carolina State College*, 73; U.S. Office of Education, *National Survey of Higher Education among Negroes*; Newby, *Black Carolinians*, 259.

25. Miller F. Whittaker, Notebook, Office of the President, 2.3, SCSUA; Caliver, "Certain Significant Developments," 117–18; Newby, *Black Carolinians*, 259; *Annual Report, 1945*; Olsen, *The G.I. Bill*, 74–75; Atkins, "Negro Educational Institutions and the Veterans' Educational Facilities Program," 151; Potts, *A History of South Carolina State College*, 78.

26. McAdam, *Political Process*, 102; Bullock, *A History of Negro Education in the South*, 175; McMillan, *Negro Higher Education*, 199; Division of Surveys, *Public Higher Education in South Carolina*, 332–33, 339; Report of the President to the Board of Trustees, June 1, 1947, to October 1, 1947, President's Reports, 2.3, folder 70, SCSUA; *Annual Report 1945–1946*, 29; McMillan, *Negro Higher Education*, 199.

27. *Annual Report, 1945*, 20; *Annual Report, 1946*, 10, 30, 31; McMillan, *Negro Higher Education*, 173; Division of Surveys, *Public Higher Education*, 339, 360.

28. *Annual Report, 1945*, 8; *Annual Report, 1946*, 9; *Annual Report, 1947*, 8; *Annual Report, 1948*, 9; Division of Surveys, *Public Higher Education*, 343; U.S. Office of Education, *National Survey*, 26; Greene, *Holders of Doctorates among American Negroes*, 216.

29. Division of Surveys, *Public Higher Education*, 347; Report of Committee to Study Present and Postwar Needs of State Agricultural College, in *Annual Report, 1946*, 20; McMillan, *Negro Higher Education*, 186; DeCosta, "The Education of Negroes," 410.

30. Division of Surveys, *Public Higher Education*, 332, 343; U.S. Office of Education, *National Survey*, 47, 52, 61; Davenport, "A Background Study," 189.

31. Frazier, *Black Bourgeoisie*, 81; U.S. Office of Education, *National Survey*, 45; McMillan, *Negro Higher Education*, 199; Peters, "A Southern Success Story," 102.

32. Sarah E. Gardner, foreword to *Teaching Equality*, viii; Fairclough, *Teaching Equality*, 36, 38; Jencks and Riesman, *The Academic Revolution*, 421; "General Discussion," in *Quarterly Review of Higher Education among Negroes*, 254.

33. Wrighten Powell, "John Wrighten: Overlooked Black Hero," John Wrighten, General Files, 2.10, SCSUA; Peters, "A Southern Success Story," 102; McMillan, *Negro Higher Education*, 187; *Collegian*, January 1943; December 1949, 11.2, SCSUA; Lewis C. Roache, interview by William C. Hine, August 16, 1990, SCSUA; College Files, box IV-E-7, NAACP Papers.

34. *Annual Report, 1946*, 41–42; Cleveland M. McQueen to W. H. Callcott, Norman O. Smith Papers, Negro File, University of South Carolina Archives (USCA), Columbia, South Carolina; *Annual Report, 1945*, 28; *Charleston News and Courier*, September 7, 1947; *Annual Report, 1946*, 14; Jackson, "Financial Aid," 37.

35. *Collegian*, January 1946, 11.2, SCSUA; Voices of the Civil Rights Movement, 88; *Annual Report, 1950*, 14; John Wrighten to Dean of Law School, June 30, 1946, box II-B-204, NAACP Papers; Peters, "A Southern Success Story," 102; *Annual Report, 1948*, 18; Daniel George Sampson to Registrar, July 29, 1946, Negro File, Smith Papers.

36. Thompson, "Editorial Note," 221–22; Caliver, "Certain Significant Developments," 119; DeCosta, "Negro Higher and Professional Education in South Carolina," 357; Kluger, *Simple Justice*, 257; Greenberg, *Crusaders in the Courts*, 79; Jenkins, "The Availability of Higher Education," 459–73; Abernathy, *And the Walls Came Tumbling Down*, 112.

37. James Hinton to Thurgood Marshall, November 29, 1946, box II-B-204, NAACP Papers; James Hinton to Thurgood Marshall, no date, box II-C-204, NAACP Papers; Robert Carter to Harold Boulware, October 25, 1946, box II-B-204, NAACP Papers; Peters, "A Southern Success Story," 102; *Charleston News and Courier*, January 3, 1950.

38. Robert Carter to J. Waties Waring, May 22, 1947, box II-B-294, NAACP Papers; Thurgood Marshall to William Hastie, April 3, 1947, box II-B-Universities-Texas File, NAACP Papers.

39. *Wrighten v. Board of Trustees*, 72 F. Supp. 948 (1947), at 949–53; *Gaines; State ex. rel. Michael v. Witham*, 165 S.W. 2d 378 (1942).

40. Goodson, ed., *Chronicles of Faith*, 94–95; Maceo Nance, interview by William C. Hine, March 14, 1989, SCSUA; Crawford interview.

41. *Norfolk Journal and Guide*, May 24, 1947; Minutes of the Seventh Annual Meeting of the State Conference of the NAACP, 1947, box III-C-181, NAACP Papers; James Hinton to Gloster Current, October 21, 1947, box III-C-181, NAACP Papers.

42. Thurgood Marshall to Frank DeCosta, July 1, 1947, box II-B-204, NAACP Papers; Frank DeCosta to Franklin Williams, May 29, 1947, box II-B-204, NAACP Papers; Thurgood Marshall to Carter Wesley, October 16, 1947, box II-B-204, NAACP Papers.

43. Potts, *A History of South Carolina State College*, 92; Martin and others, *South Carolina State University*, 69; C. F. Brooks to Miller F. Whittaker, July 28, 1947, University Board of Trustees, 1.0, SCSUA; Harold Boulware, Memo on S.C. Law School Facilities, October 1, 1947, box II-B-204, NAACP Papers; NAACP press release, November 20, 1947, box II-B-204, NAACP Papers; DeCosta, "Negro Higher and Professional Education in South Carolina," 353.

44. John Wrighten to James Hinton, no date, box II-B-204, NAACP Papers; John Wrighten to Thurgood Marshall, October 6, 1947, box II-B-204, NAACP Papers; John Wrighten to Robert Carter, August 6, 1947, box II-B-204, NAACP Papers; John Wrighten to NAACP, August 21, 1947, box II-B-204, NAACP Papers.

45. John McCray to G. C. Rogers, June 9, 1947, Avery Institute, box 891, Office of Archives and Records (OAR), Charleston County School District (CCSD); DeCosta, "Negro Higher and Professional Education in South Carolina," 350–358; John Wrighten to Thurgood Marshall, October 3, 1947, box II-B-204, NAACP Papers; John Wrighten to Thurgood Marshall, September 27, 1947, box II-B-204, NAACP Papers; Thurgood Marshall to John Wrighten, September 29, 1947, box II-B-204, NAACP Papers; *Charleston News and Courier*, September 23, 1947; Herbert Hill, interview by Richard Kluger, March 2, 1971, Sterling Library, Yale University, New Haven, Connecticut.

46. John Wrighten to Thurgood Marshall, October 3, 1947, box II-B-204, NAACP Papers; Thurgood Marshall to John Wrighten, September 29, 1947, box II-B-204, NAACP Papers; Thurgood Marshall to Hinton, Boulware and Rev. Beard, September 30, 1947, box II-B-204, NAACP Papers.

47. Washington, "Comment: History and Role of Black Law Schools," 385–421; Finance General, 1947–1948, General Files, 2.10, SCSUA; Acts and Joint Resolutions, 1949, 668–70.

48. Voices of the Civil Rights Movement, 87–88; John Wrighten, interview by William C. Hine, June 6, 1989, SCSUA; Law School and Law School Alumni, Law School, 19.0, SCSUA; State A and M College, *Announcements*, South Carolina State School of Law, 1952–1953, 7–11; Matthew Perry, interview by William C. Hine, June 19, 1995, SCSUA, *Collegian*, May 1950, SCSUA; *Columbia State*, November 10, 1950; *Annual Report, 1950*; Ernest A. Finney Papers, 5.8, SCSU.

49. *Announcements*, 1952–1953, 8; *Collegian*, March 1950; *Annual Report, 1951*, 25; Dewitt, *School of Law: South Carolina State College*.

50. *Sweatt v. Painter*, 339 U.S. 629 (1950) at 634–635; Rogers, *Generations of Lawyers*, 203.

51. Auerbach, *Unequal Justice*, 293–94; Stevens, *Law School*, 182; Rogers, *Generations of Lawyers*, 205; *Richardson v. McFadden*, case number 73–2512, trial transcript, National Archives and Records Center (NARC), Philadelphia, Pennsylvania. On the use of tests to restrict black access to the legal profession in Alabama see *Ex. Parte Banks*, 48 So. 2d 35 (1950); Washington, "Comment: History and Role of Black Law Schools," 419; in Georgia see *Tyler v. Vickery*, 517 F. 2d 1089 (1975); in Mississippi see McMillen, *Dark Journey*, 166; in Florida see *New York Times*, May 17, 1958; U.S. Commission on Civil Rights, *Equal Protection of Laws in Public Higher Education*, 50–96; *Race Relations Law Reporter* 4 (1959): 82; *Race Relations Law Reporter* 2 (1957): 372; *Hunt v. Arnold*, 172 F. Supp. 847 (1959).

52. Transactions of the Fifty-Third Annual Meeting of the South Carolina Bar Association, 1947, 24, University of South Carolina Law School Archives, University of South Carolina, Columbia, South Carolina; Transactions of the Fifty-Fourth Annual Meeting of the South Carolina Bar Association, *Law Quarterly*, 1 (September 1948): 15, University of South Carolina Law School Archives, University of South Carolina, Columbia, South Carolina; *Journal of the Senate, 1948*, 1472; *Richardson v. McFadden*, 540 F. 2d 744 (1976); "Law Graduates Get Diplomas; Admissions," *Columbia State*, undated clipping, University of South Carolina Law School Archives, University of South Carolina, Columbia, South Carolina; Samuel Prince to Norman Smith, January 8, 1952, Negro File, Smith Papers, USCA.

53. *Richardson v. McFadden*, trial transcript, II: 543, NARC, Philadelphia, Pennsylvania; Peters, "A Southern Success Story," 104; Voices of the Civil Rights Movement, 87–88; South Carolina Law School, Graduates, Law School, 19.0, SCSUA; Matthew J. Perry, interview by Grace J. McFadden, August 18, 1980, in "The Quest for Civil Rights," University of South Carolina Film Library; Bender, "One Week That Changed the State," 37; *Richardson v. McFadden*, trial transcript, volume 1, 10, NARC, Philadelphia, Pennsylvania.

54. Greenberg, *Crusaders in the Courts*, 38; *Richardson v. McFadden*, trial transcript, volume 2, 543, National Archives and Records Center (NARC), Philadelphia, Pennsylvania; Peters, "A Southern Success Story," 104; Voices of the Civil Rights Movement, 87–88; South Carolina Law School, Graduates, Law School, 19.0, SCSUA.

55. Voices of the Civil Rights Movement, 87; Peters, "A Southern Success Story," 104; *Richardson v. McFadden*, trial transcript, volume 2, 521–43; NARC, Philadelphia, Pennsylvania; Greenberg, *Crusaders in the Courts*, 41.

5. Black Schooling and the *Briggs* Decision, 1945–1954

1. [Charleston] City Board of School Commissioners, Minute Books (CBSCMB), November 7, December 12, 1945; Memo to Mr. Current from Mrs. Hurley, February 5, 1947, box II-B-146, NAACP Papers; *Pittsburgh Courier*, July 12, 1947; NAACP press release, March 25,

1948, box II-B-147, NAACP Papers; "Negro School Children's Walk-out," *Fayette County Record*, no date, box II-B-147, NAACP Papers; Smith, *They Closed Their Schools*, 60; McNeil, "Community Initiative," 25–41; Meier and Rudwick, *Along the Color Line*, 360.

2. Rowan, *Dream Makers*, 6.

3. *Briggs v. Elliott*, 98 F. Supp. 529 (1951); *New York Times*, May 27, 1951.

4. McCauley and Ball, eds., *Southern Schools*, 49–54.

5. Sass, *Charleston Grows*, 44; Bureau of the Census, *Seventeenth Decennial Census of the United States, Census of Population, Volume 2*, 40, 168–70; *Charleston News and Courier*, June 21, 1947; "The Economic Growth of Charleston County, 1946–1954," Charleston County Public Library (CCPL), Vertical File; Thomas R. Waring Papers, 23/2, 32/2, South Carolina Historical Association, Charleston; Division of Surveys, *Public Schools of Charleston, South Carolina*, 2, 3, 4; *Annual Report of the Superintendent, 1947*, 8, Office of Archives and Records (OAR), Charleston County School District (CCSD); Merriweather interview.

6. *School Directory of South Carolina, 1948*, 72; *School Directory of South Carolina, 1949*, 77; Directory of Charleston County Black Schools, Avery Research Center (ARC); Pierce and others, *White and Negro Schools in the South*, 104–5.

7. CBSCMB, June 14, May 5, 1943; June 6, 1945; *Charleston News and Courier*, July 15, 1945; Division of Surveys, *Public Schools of Charleston*, 142; *Lighthouse and Informer*, September 27, 1947, box II-B-147, NAACP Papers.

8. CBSCMB, September 3, 1947; *Charleston News and Courier*, October 20, 1947; CBSCMB, March 18, July 6, October 5, October 6, 1948; *Charleston News and Courier*, April 3, 1949; CBSCMB, October 5, 1949.

9. CBSCMB, December 12, 1945; White interview.

10. Smith, *They Closed Their Schools*, 60, 31.

11. Ibid., 15, 36, 13.

12. Ibid., 31–33, 38, 40, 61–62.

13. C. A. Harvin to L. B. McCord, October 27, 1951, Clarendon County Board of Education, 1949–1950, 14166, South Carolina State Department of Archives and History (SCDAH); Testimony at Trial, *Briggs v. Elliott*, May 28, 29, 1951, volume 1, 132, J. Waties Waring Papers, box 110–25, Kluger, *Simple Justice*, 7; Billie Flemming, interview by Richard Kluger, October 22, 1971, Sterling Library, Yale University.

14. De Laine's Opposition, Joseph A. De Laine Papers, Manuscript Department, Caroliniana Library (MDCL), University of South Carolina, Columbia, South Carolina; *School Directory of South Carolina, 1940*, 107; *School Directory of South Carolina, 1948*, 78; Martin, *The Deep South Says "Never,"* 46; Lochbaum, "The World Made Flesh"; Harold Boulware to Edward Dudley, March 17, 1948, box II-B-146, NAACP Papers.

15. J. A. De Laine, A Summary of Incidents in the Summerton School Affair, January 1950, De Laine Papers; The Parents of the Action Committee to County Board of Education of Clarendon County, July 9, 1949; Committee on Action to Trustees of District 22, June 9, 1949; Parent Committee on Action to Superintendent and Trustees, April 13, 1950, 14166, SCDAH; Lochbaum, "The World Made Flesh," 99, 107, 128; Williams, *Freedom and Justice*, 59; Kluger, *Simple Justice*, 23, 339; Mr. and Mrs. Harry Briggs, interview by Richard Kluger, November 29, 1971, Sterling Library, Yale University.

16. Resolution, box II-A-40, NAACP Papers; Spottswood Robinson to Thurgood Marshall, October 1, 1950, box II-B-171, NAACP Papers; Thurgood Marshall to Gloster Current, January 20, 1947, box II-B-145, NAACP Papers; Marian Perry to A. Maceo Nance, August 19, 1947, box II-B-147, NAACP Papers; Smith, *They Closed Their Schools*, 44–45, 48.

17. J. Waties Waring to Hubert T. Delany, June 28, 1951, Waring Papers; Yarbrough, *A Passion for Justice*, 174; Waring interviews, quoted in Williams, *Thurgood Marshall*, 200.

18. Kantrowitz, *Ben Tillman*, 306; Edgar, *South Carolina: A History*, 522.

19. James F. Brynes, "Inaugural Address," in *South Carolina's Educational Revolution*, CCPL, vertical file; *New York Times*, May 28, 1951; Ashmore, *The Negro and the Schools*, 133.

20. *Lighthouse and Informer*, no date, box 110–43, Waring Papers; Egerton, *Speak Now against the Day*, 597.

21. *Charleston News and Courier*, May 27, 1951; Kluger, *Simple Justice*, 435; Yarbrough, *A Passion for Justice*, 179; Egerton, *Speak Now against the Day*, 597.

22. Robert McCormick Figg Jr., interview by Richard Kluger, October 17, 1971, Sterling Library, Yale University; Testimony at Trial, *Briggs v. Elliott*, May 28, May 29, 1951, 31, 2, 6–9, 128, Waring Papers; *New York Times*, June 3, 1951.

23. Kluger, *Simple Justice*, 321–22; 350; *Briggs*, trial transcript, 1951, 10–11, 63–68, 91–92, Waring Papers.

24. Kluger, *Simple Justice*, 363; John Dewey, quoted in Kluger, *Simple Justice*, 319; Testimony at Trial, *Briggs v. Elliott*, 1951, Waring Papers; *New York Times*, June 3, 1951; Kenneth Clark, interview by Richard Kluger, November 4, 1971, Sterling Library; *Briggs*, trial transcript, 1951, 81–92.

25. Kluger, *Simple Justice*, 363; *New York Times*, June 3, 1951.

26. Matthew Whitehead, interview by Richard Kluger, March 18, 1971, Sterling Library, Yale University; *Lighthouse and Informer*, June 2, 1951; *New York Post*, May 29, 1951; Brown, "Civil Rights Activism," 68.

27. *Briggs v. Elliott*, 98 F. Supp. 529 (1951) at 531, 535, 538; *New York Times*, June 24, 1951.

28. J. Waties Waring to Hubert Delany, June 28, 1951, Waring Papers; *Briggs v. Elliott*, 98 F. Supp 529 at 548; A. J. Clement to J. Waties Waring, July 29, 1951, box 110–10, Waring Papers.

29. *Charleston News and Courier*, September 21, October 10, October 11, 1951.

30. CBSCMB, November 7, 1951; *Charleston News and Courier*, November 15, 1951; testimony at trial, *Briggs v. Elliott*, 1951, 121, Waring Papers; CBSCMB, April 12, June 6, October 4, 1950; January 3, September 14, 1951; January 2, January 3, 1952; *Lighthouse and Informer*, October 13, 1951.

31. Lucille and Peter Poinsette, interview by author, Charleston, July 19, 1990; *Lighthouse and Informer*, October 13, 1951.

32. *Charleston News and Courier*, August 24, December 14, 1950; Poinsette interview; Peter Poinsette, President of Negro PTA Council, to County Board of Education, Peter Poinsette Collection, ARC, Charleston; A. J. Clement to Charleston School Board, January 23, 1952, Henry Hutchinson Collection, ARC, Charleston.

33. J. Waties Waring to H. T. Delaney, January 28, 1952, Waring Papers.

34. A. J. Clement to Charleston School Board, January 23, 1952, Henry Hutchinson Collection, ARC.

35. Testimony at Trial, *Briggs v. Elliott*, March 3, 1952, 6, 12, 13, case number 2657, National Archives and Records Center (NARC), Atlanta, Georgia; *Briggs v. Elliott*, 342 U.S. 350 (1950); Philip Elman, interview by Richard Kluger, August 19, 1971, Sterling Library, Yale University.

36. *Briggs* transcript, 1952, 21, 43, 13, 34–36, 26–28, NARC, Atlanta, Georgia; *Briggs v. Elliott*, civil action number 2657, in Friedman, ed., *Oral Argument*, 559–60; Robert Carter,

interviews by Richard Kluger, January 23 through May 14, 1971, Sterling Library, Yale University.

37. CBSCMB, February 6, April 16, June 4,1952; *Charleston News and Courier*, August 17, May 12, 1952; August 17, 1952; A. J. Clement to J. Waties Waring, September 24, 1952, box 110–10, Waring Papers.

38. CBSCMB, December 8, December 21, December 24, 1952; January 7, January 8, March 4, December 3, 1953; Annual Report of County Superintendent, Charleston County, 1953–1954, table 12, SCDAH; *Charleston News and Courier*, March 3, 1954.

39. *Charleston News and Courier*, July 3, September 7, 1951; October 31, November 20, December 7, December 8, December 14, December 21, 1953; September 9, 1954; CBSCMB, October 27, 1952; *Charleston News and Courier*, June 12, September 7, December 3, 1953; Drago, *Initiative, Paternalism, and Race Relations*, 248; A. J. Clement to Charleston School Board, January 23, 1952, Hutchinson Collection, ARC; Yarbrough, *A Passion for Justice*, 204.

40. CBSCMB, March 3, March 15, March 24, 1954; *Charleston News and Courier*, March 15, May 6, 1954; CBSCMB, April 21, May 12, June 28, 1954.

41. McMillan, *Negro Higher Education*, 5.

42. Hunt interview; CBSCMB, March 18, 1948; Comparative Salaries, 1938–1943, OAR, CCSD, box 896; Division of Surveys, *The Public Schools of Charleston, South Carolina*, 36; Clark, *Echo in My Soul*, 86; McCauley and Ball, eds., *Southern Schools*, 44, 132, 152; *Parvenue*, December 1948, Burke High School Library (BHSL); *Charleston News and Courier*, September 24, 1954; CBSCMB, September 22, October 7, 1954.

43. *Charleston Evening Post*, September 29, 1954; *Charleston News and Courier*, November 1, 1954; Robert Gaines to Robert Morrison, box 900, OAR, CCSD; CBSCMB, October 7, October 13, 1954; May 29, 1957; Merriweather interview; *Parvenue*, December 1954, BHSL; *Charleston News and Courier*, February 22, 1954.

44. J. Michael Graves, interview by author, Charleston, July 16, 1990; Drago, *Initiative, Paternalism, and Race Relations*, 265; *Parvenue*, March 1947, March 1948, November 1948, December 1948, March 1949, March 1950, December 1951, June 1952, October 1952, December 1952, February 1955, April 1955, April 1956, May 1956, BHSL.

45. Poinsette interview; PTA Founder's Day, Poinsette Collection, ARC; Thelma Hargrave to George Rogers, June 12, 1953, box 900, OAR, CCSD; CBSCMB, December 12, 1950; May 7, 1952; June 9, 1953; *Parvenue*, March 1947, December 1947, March 1948, May 1948, October 1952, April 1953, February 1954, May 1954, February 1955, December 1955, BHSL; Hunt interview; Jeanette W. Brown to Mrs. V. F. Fraser, October 12, 1950, Charleston Junior Council, series 17, box 9, National Council of Negro Women Papers, National Council of Negro Women Archives; Book Lovers Club, Minutes, May 8, 1945; December 30, 1947; June 23, 1953, ARC; *Parvenue*, June 1952; April 1953, June 1953, December 1953, April 1955, April 1956, May 1957, BHSL; Class Night Program, 1961, Hunt Papers, box 1, ARC; Clark, *Echo in My Soul*, 109–12; Daniel, *Excellent Teachers*, 246; Jones, *A Traditional Model*, 5, 71; Newby, *Black Carolinians*, 210; Ginzberg, *The Negro Potential*, 141.

46. Frederick Cook interview; Brockington interview; *Burke Bulldog*, 1958, BHSL; *Parvenue*, December 1956, May-June 1956, BHSL.

47. *Parvenue*, November 1946, January 1948, March 1949, December 1951, December 1956, February 1956, BHSL; Hunter-Gault, foreword to *Maggie's American Dream*, xv.

48. CBSCMB, July 30, 1951; June 9, 1953; *Elmore v. Rice*, 72 F. Supp. 516 (1947) at 528; *Parvenue*, June 1953, October-November 1954, April 1957, BHSL; Cook interview.

49. *Parvenue*, November 1949, November 1950, October 1951, March 1952, October 1952, April 1955, BHSL.

50. Hunt interview; *Burke Bulldog*, 1958, BHSL; *Parvenue*, February 1954, December 1954, February 1956, May 1956, May 1957, December 1958, March 1959, December 1959, June 1960, BHSL; Clark, *Echo in My Soul*, 78.

51. Smith, *They Closed Their Schools*, 103; Friedman, ed., *Oral Argument*, 559; *Charleston Evening Post*, September 29, 1954.

6. Contesting *Brown*, 1954–1960

1. Callahan, "American Culture Is of a Whole," 38; Klarman, "How *Brown* Changed Race Relations," 89; Klarman, *From Jim Crow to Civil Rights*; Bell, *Silent Covenants*; Kevin Gaines, "Whose Integration Was It"; Rosenberg, *The Hollow Hope*.

2. Bartley, *The Rise of Massive Resistance*; Quint, *Profile in Black and White*.

3. *Brown v. Board of Education*, 347 U.S. 483 (1954), in Friedman, ed., *Oral Argument*, 329–30.

4. *Charleston News and Courier*, August 26, December 7, 1955; March 1, March 15, 1956; *Columbia Record*, January 14, 1956; "Teachers Ready for Integration," McCray Papers, Manuscript Department, Caroliniana Library (MDCL).

5. *Crisis* (June-July 1954): 358; ibid. (June-July 1955): 340.

6. *Southern School News*, August 1955, September 1955, November 1955; Martin, *The Deep South Says "Never,"* 62; *Columbia Record*, August 30, 1955; Marshall interview, 1954; Bartley, *The New South*, 197; *Charleston News and Courier*, May 26, 1955.

7. *Charleston News and Courier*, December 7, 1955; January 29, 1954; October 9, 1955; Drago, *Initiative, Paternalism, and Race Relations*, 269, 274; Clark, *Echo in My Soul*, 89, 91, 109, 111, 120, 132–34; *Charleston News and Courier*, July 15, 1955; January 21, 1956; Memo to Mr. Wilkins from Lucille Black, August 3, 1956, box II-C-174, NAACP Papers.

8. *Southern School News*, August 1955, September 1955; Martin, *The Deep South Says "Never,"* 1–41; *Charleston News and Courier*, May 26, 1955; October 4, 1956; September 15, September 16, September 17, 1955.

9. Robert Gaines to C. A. Brown, August 25, 1955, box 863, Office of Archives and Records (OAR), Charleston County School District (CCSD); James Hayes to Robert Gaines, July 29, 1955, box 863, OAR, CCSD; *Charleston News and Courier*, August 5, 1955; J. Wilbur Jones to Robert Gaines, August 24, 1955, box 929, OAR, CCSD; *Charleston News and Courier*, August 25, 1955; *Southern School News*, January 1955, Bartley, *The New South*, 204–5.

10. Quint, *Profile in Black and White*, 51; Williams, *Thurgood Marshall*, 81; J. Arthur Brown to Simeon Booker, August 10, 1955, J. Arthur Brown, unprocessed documents, Avery Research Center (ARC); Brown, "Civil Rights Activism," 76–77.

11. Quint, *Profile in Black and White*, 92; Newby, *Black Carolinians*, 344; *Southern School News*, August 1956.

12. Brown, *Ready from Within*, 36; *Southern School News*, August 1956; Shoemaker, ed., *With All Deliberate Speed*, 140; *Race Relations Law Reporter* 1 (October 1956): 751–53.

13. *Charleston News and Courier*, July 15, 1955; January 21, 1956; Dismissals, 1956, box 863, OAR, CCSD; [Charleston] City Board of School Commissioners, Minute Books (CBSCMB), May 9, November 19, December 12, January 9, 1956; Clark, *Echo in My Soul*, 110–17; W. E. Solomon to Septima Clark, box III-95A, Septima Clark Collection, Robert Smalls Library, College of Charleston, Charleston; Hutchinson interview; Simms interview; Hunt interview; Graves interview; Cook interview.

14. Greenberg, *Crusaders in the Courts*, 391; *Crisis* (June-July 1954): 359; NAACP to Mrs. Marion Blutt, no date, Bracey and Meier, eds., *Papers of the NAACP, Part 3: The Campaign for Educational Equality. Series D: Central Office Records, 1956–1965. Group III, Series A, General Office File, Desegregation—Schools, South Carolina*, reel 8; Roy Wilkins to Robert Klein, August 1, 1956, Teachers Reprisals, box II-A-508, NAACP Papers; *New York Herald*, September 6, 1959; NAACP press release, May 17, 1956, Teacher Reprisals, box II-A-508, NAACP Papers; Williams, *Thurgood Marshall*, 123–24; Voices of the Civil Rights Movement, 81–82; *Southern School News*, May 1956, June 1956.

15. *Bryan v. Austin*, 354 U.S. 933 (1957); Tushnet, *Making Civil Rights Law*, 294; Fultz, "The Displacement of Black Educators," 11–45.

16. Hutchinson interview; Hunt interview; Memo to Mr. Wilkins from Lucille Black, August 3, 1956, Teacher Reprisals, box II-A-508, NAACP Papers; Roy Wilkins to the Teachers of South Carolina, no date, Teacher Reprisals, box II-A-508, NAACP Papers; Levi Byrd to Gloster Current, July 18, 1956, box II-C-143, NAACP Papers; J. Arthur Brown to Gloster Current, September 21, 1956, box II-C-176, NAACP Papers; J. Arthur Brown to Gloster Current, no date, box II-C-176, NAACP Papers; Morris, *The Origins of The Civil Rights Movement*, 33.

17. Morris, *The Origins of The Civil Rights Movement*, 38; Meier and Rudwick, *Along the Color Line*, 364.

18. Norrell, *Reaping the Whirlwind*; Robinson, *The Montgomery Bus Boycott*; Morris, *The Origins of The Civil Rights Movement*, 63–64; Shabazz, *Advancing Democracy*, 138–206.

19. Williams, *Thurgood Marshall*, 77–122; *Orangeburg Times and Democrat*, August 24, July 31, 1955.

20. Hine, "Civil Rights and Campus Wrongs," 314–16; *Pittsburgh Courier*, September 17, 1955; Teacher Reprisals, box II-A-508, NAACP Papers.

21. Gamarekian, "The Ugly Battle of Orangeburg," 32; Bracey and Meier, eds., *Papers of the NAACP, Part 3: The Campaign for Educational Equality. Series D: Central Office Records, 1956–1965. Group III, Series A, General Office File, Desegregation—Schools, South Carolina*, reel 8; *Papers of the NAACP, Part 22: Legal Department Administrative Files, 1956–1965. Group V, Series B, Administrative Files. General Office File-Schools South Carolina, Part 20*, reel 10; reel 26; Fred Moore, interview by author, Orangeburg, South Carolina, April 15, 2003.

22. Adam Moss to Governor James F. Byrnes, January 28, 1952; James F. Byrnes to Robert D. Calkins, February 18, 1952; Robert D. Calkins to Governor James F. Byrnes, February 13, 1952; John D. Rockefeller to Governor Byrnes, February 21, 1952; James F. Byrnes to Foster Dulles, March 12, 1952; Robert D. Calkins to Governor Byrnes, April 14, 1952, General Education Board, series 1, subseries 3, box 479, Rockefeller Archive Center, Tarrytown, New York; Hine, "South Carolina's Challenge," 44; *South Carolina State Bulldog*, 1955; *State Agricultural and Mechanical College, Annual Report, 1953* (hereafter *Annual Report*), 9–11, 52; *Annual Report, 1954*, 27–28; *Annual Report, 1955*, 61; *Collegian*, October 1955, January 1956; Benner Turner to W. C. Bethea, February 1, 1956, Office of the President, 2.0, Miller F. Whittaker Library (SCSUA); Rudolph Pyatt, interview by William C. Hine, August 25, 1994, SCSUA.

23. Lewie C. Roache, interview by William C. Hine, August 16, 1990, SCSUA; Moore interview; Woolfolk, *Prairie View*, 40.

24. *Annual Report, 1950*; *Annual Report, 1951*, 29; *Acts and Joint Resolutions, 1954*, 1590, 1674, 1722; McAdam, *Political Process*, 103.

25. Moore interview; Pyatt interview; Office of the President, 2.0, Student Council, 1955–1956; *South Carolina State Bulldog*, 1954; *Annual Report, 1951*, 11; Governor James

F. Byrnes to John D. Rockefeller, III, February 14, 1952, General Education Board, subseries 1.3, box 479, folder 5098, Rockefeller Archive, Tarrytown, New York; *Collegian*, April 1950, October 1950, October 1951, October 1952, October 1954, March 1956.

26. Moore interview; *Annual Report, 1956*, 80–81.

27. Moore interview; Gamarekian, "The Ugly Battle of Orangeburg," 32–33; Gordon, "Boycotts Can Cut Two Ways," 5–10; James Sulton, interview by William C. Hine, July 20, 1994, SCSUA.

28. *Southern School News*, March 1956, April 1956; Moore, "School Desegregation," 55; *Orangeburg Times and Democrat*, April 26, July 19, 1956.

29. Moore interview; Pyatt interview; *Parvenue*, June 2, 1952, Burke High School Library (BHSL); *Pittsburgh Courier*, May 5, 1956.

30. Moore interview; *Columbia State*, April 14, 1956; Office of the President, 2.0, Trustees, 1955–1956, SCSUA; Pyatt interview; Gamarekian, "The Ugly Battle of Orangeburg."

31. R. C. Henderson to B. C. Turner, April 4, 1956, George Bell Timmerman Papers, Colored Normal, Industrial, and Mechanical College (CNIAMC), box 2, 548006, South Carolina State Department of Archives and History (SCDAH).

32. Moore, "School Desegregation," 57; Moore interview; Williams, *Thurgood Marshall*, 105; *Columbia State*, April 11, April 12, April 15, 1956; press release, box 26, Timmerman Papers, 548006, SCDAH; *Pittsburgh Courier*, April 21, 1956; Gamarekian, "The Ugly Battle of Orangeburg," 34; Sulton interview; Pyatt interview.

33. Benner C. Turner to Fred Moore, April 12, 1956, Office of the President, 2.0, Student Council, SCSUA; *Columbia State*, April 15, 1956; Pyatt interview; Moore interview; *New York Post*, April 26, 1956.

34. Pyatt interview; Moore interview; CNIAMC, box 2, Timmerman Papers.

35. Moore interview; Gamarekian, "The Ugly Battle of Orangeburg"; Pyatt interview.

36. Moore interview; CNIAMC, box 2, Timmerman Papers, 548006; Pyatt interview; Potts, *A History of South Carolina State College*, 91; Williams, *Thurgood Marshall*, 109; *New York Times*, June 26, 1956; Hine, "Civil Rights and Campus Wrongs," 320; Quint, *Profile in Black and White*, 123.

37. Benner C. Turner to Ruthie Mae Simmons, no date, Office of the President, 2.0, SCSUA; *Collegian*, March 1956; *Daily Worker*, May 4, 1956; *New York Times*, May 26, 1956; *New York Post*, May 1, 1956; Gamarekian, "The Ugly Battle of Orangeburg," 34; Pyatt interview; Moore interview; Septima Clark to Roy Wilkins, June 6, 1956, Bracey and Meier, eds., *Papers of the NAACP, Part 3: The Campaign for Educational Equality. Series D: Central Office Records, 1956–1965. Group III, Series A, General Office File, Desegregation—Schools, South Carolina*, reel 8; Papers of the NAACP, Part 22: Legal Department Administrative Files, 1956–1965. Group V, series B, *Administrative Files. General Office File-Schools, South Carolina*, reel 20; reel 26, Part 10.

38. Quint, *Profile in Black and White*, 117–23.

39. Application for Entrance Examination to Enter the University of South Carolina, Cornell Franklin and James Jones, February 11, 1958, Sumwalt Papers; W. C. McCall notes, Negroes, 1957–1958, Sumwalt Papers, MDCL.

40. *Columbia State*, January 16, January 17, January 18, 1958; Mat Alston, Thelma McClam, and Christine Thomas to James Hinton, January 17, 1958; J. Arthur Brown, H. P. Sharper, I. D. Newman, Levi Byrd to Mr. Hinton, January 25, 1958; John H. Wrighten to Roy Wilkins, January 22, 1958; James Jones, Thelma McClam, Cornell F. Mitchell, Mary Alston

to Mr. Roy Wilkins, March 18, 1958; Mrs. Andrew Simkins to Mr. Roy Wilkins, March 24, 1958; Mr. Roy Wilkins to Mrs. Simkins, April 3, 1958, Bracey and Meier, eds., *Papers of the NAACP, Part 3: The Campaign for Educational Equality. Series D: Central Office Records, 1956–1965*, reel 8.

41. Tushnet, *Making Civil Rights Law*, 268.

42. Memorandum, Re: Segregation, no date, Robinson Papers; CBSCMB, December 5, December 19, 1960; May 17, June 28, January 18, June 14, 1961; April 14, May 9, June 13, 1962; E. R. Crow to Ernest Hollings, August 22, 1960, Educational Finance Commission Folder, Ernest Hollings Papers, SCDAH.

43. Mildred Perry to George Rogers, October 19, 1954, box 929, OAR, CCSD; CBSCMB, November 3, 1954; Report of Inspection Made by PTA, November 11, 1954, box 929, OAR, CCSD; CBSCMB, January 5, 1955; Rhett School PTA to Robert Gaines, October 22, 1955; Thomas Carrere, Report to Board, January 27, 1956, box 863, OAR, CCSD; Mrs. P. T. Poinsette, Chairman, October 3, 1956, box 863, OAR, CCSD; *Charleston News and Courier*, October 27, 1960; CBSCMB, January 5, 1955; *Charleston News and Courier*, June 19, 1956; CBSCMB, March 13, 1957; Mrs. Peter Poinsette to C. A. Brown, March 27, 1957, box 929, OAR, CCSD.

44. C. A. Brown to Hugh Sinkler, October 8, 1956, box 900, OAR, CCSD; CBSCMB, December 12, 1956; CBSCMB, March 13, March 20, April 15, 1957.

45. *Charleston Evening Post*, May 22, 1957; Roy Wilkins to J. Arthur Brown, June 5, 1957, box II-C-184, NAACP Papers; Robert Gaines to Thomas Waring, May 23, 1957, box 900, OAR, CCSD; CBSCMB, May 22, May 29, 1957.

46. Merriweather interview; Robert Gaines to Thomas Waring, May 23, 1957, box 900, OAR, CCSD; CBSCMB, May 29, 1957; *Charleston Evening Post*, May 22, 1957.

47. *Charleston Evening Post*, May 22, 1957; CBSCMB, May 29, June 11, October 9, July 7, July 2, May 29, August 14, October 9, 1957; January 3, June 11, 1958; Albert Scott and Ervin Dominick to Charleston School Board, box 863, OAR, CCSD; CBSCMB, August 21, 1959; Information for the Board Number 53, July 22, 1959, box 900, OAR, CCSD; Memo of Conference with Delegation from Rhett School PTA, January 16, 1959, box 900, OAR, CCSD; CBSCMB, April 7, April 13, 1960.

48. Marshall interview, 95, 125.

7. Evading *Brown*, 1954–1960

1. Friedman, ed., *Oral Argument*, 413, 414, 423, 428, 430; Kluger, *Simple Justice*, 724.

2. NAACP brief cited in Kluger, *Simple Justice*, 728; Tushnet, *Making Civil Rights Law*, 227; Friedman, ed., *Oral Argument*, 402.

3. *Brown v. Board of Education*, 349 U.S. 294 (1955), in Friedman, ed., *Oral Argument*, 533–34.

4. *Briggs v. Elliott*, 132 F. Supp. 776 (1955) at 777–78.

5. David W. Robinson Papers, 0802–0805, South Carolina State Department of Archives and History (SCDAH); *Southern School News*, August 1956; *Charleston News and Courier*, August 18, 1956.

6. Undated Memo, Legal Memoranda, 1954, Robinson Papers, 0802–0805, SCDAH; Memoranda, Re: Segregation, no date, Robinson Papers, 0802–0805, SCDAH.

7. Jacob Joseph Martin to Registrar, School of Law, June 14, 1950, Smith Papers, University of South Carolina Archives (USCA); *Columbia State*, June 16, 1950; Norman Smith to

Cleveland Stevans, August 19, 1950, Smith Papers, USCA. Other African American applications are contained in the Smith Papers; Minutes of the Board of Trustees of the University of South Carolina, October 24, 1951, Manuscript Department, Caroliniana Library (MDCL), University of South Carolina, Columbia, South Carolina; University of South Carolina *Catalogue*, 1952–1953, 53, 227; U.S. Commission on Civil Rights, *Equal Protection of the Laws*, 151.

8. Minutes of the Board of Trustees, May 29, October 24, 1951; MDCL; Comments on the Recommendations of the Committee on College Testing Program, May 18, 1951, Smith Papers; Sol Blatt Jr. to Donald S. Russell, June 10, 1955, Donald S. Russell Papers, USCA, Henry R. Simms to Dr. John L. Plyer, August 6, 1951, South Carolina College Association, Smith Papers.

9. Lesesne, *A History of the University of South Carolina*, 78.

10. W. C. McCall to Drs. Bowles and Fels, October 23, 1953, Exams and Counseling, Russell Papers; Donald Russell to Dr. R. F. Poole, May 14, 1954, Exams and Counseling, Russell Papers; W. L. Williams to Donald Russell, November 10, 1953, Exams and Counseling, Russell Papers.

11. Lemann, *The Big Test*, 77; Folger, *The Future School and College Enrollments*, 8–9, 27–29; W. L. Williams to Donald Russell, November 10, 1953, Russell Papers.

12. Faculty Minutes, May 27, 1954; Minutes of the Board of Trustees, May 28, 1954, Manuscript Department, Caroliniana Library (MDCL); Travelstead, "I Was There," Travelstead, topical file, USCA; *Charleston News and Courier*, June 9, 1954.

13. Memo to Donald Russell, H.B., no date, Exams and Counseling, Russell Papers; W. C. McCall to Donald Russell, May 28, 1954, Exams and Counseling, Russell Papers; W. C. McCall to Donald Russell, July 13, 1954, Exams and Counseling, Russell Papers; Memo from W. C. McCall, August 13, 1954, Exams and Counseling, Russell Papers; Donald Russell to W. C. McCall, August 15, 1956, Exams and Counseling, Russell Papers; Memo for Mr. Turnball from Edith Huddleston, August 7, 1956, Exams and Counseling, Russell Papers.

14. Donald Russell to General Mark Clark, April 24, 1954, Exams and Counseling, Russell Papers; Donald Russell Memo, no date, Entrance Exams, Russell Papers; Minutes of the Board of Trustees, March 20, March 29, October 24, 1951; March 18, 1952; May 28, 1954, MDCL; Henry R. Simms to Donald Russell, August 21, 1956, Exams and Counseling, Russell Papers; Henry R. Simms to Mr. Wiles, September 7, 1954, Exams and Counseling, Russell Papers; Potts, *A History of South Carolina State College*, 108; Minutes of the South Carolina College Entrance Examination Program Committee, February 6, 1958, Exams and Counseling, Robert L. Sumwalt Papers, USCA; William Turnball to W. C. McCall, August 10, 1956, Exams and Counseling, Russell Papers.

15. Educational Testing Service, *Annual Report, 1955–1956*, 73; Black, *Southern Governors and Civil Rights*, 82.

16. Ashmore, *The Negro and the Schools*, 46; Guy B. Johnson, Racial Integration in Southern Higher Education, Collection number 3826; series 5, subseries 5:10, box 95, folder 1461, 3, 7, 9, Wilson Library, University of North Carolina, Chapel Hill, North Carolina; W. C. McCall to Dr. Richard B. Brooks, May 5, 1956, Exams and Counseling, Russell Papers; Committee on Entrance Examinations, December 6, 1955, Exams and Counseling, Russell Papers; Minutes of Meeting of South Carolina College Entrance Examination Program Committee, February 6, 1958, Exams and Counseling, Sumwalt Papers; *Race Relations Law Reporter* 4 (1959): 82; *Southern School News*, July 1956, October 1958; Karl, *The College Handbook, 1959–61*, 553, 548; Ibid., *1963–65*, xxii; Shabazz, *Advancing Democracy*, 158.

17. *Statistics for the Sixties*, 24. Between 1950 and 1956 the number of "nonwhites" enrolled in college rose from 94,000 to 196,000. See Wise, *They Come for the Best of Reasons*, 13.

18. *New York Times*, March 17, April 3, 1956; January 27, 1957; *Southern School News*, March 1958, October 1958; U.S. Commission on Civil Rights, *Equal Protection of the Laws*, 45–46, 60–64; *Race Relations Law Reporter* 1 (1956): 118; *Booker v. State Board of Education*, 248 F. 2d 689; *Ayers v. Allain*, 893 F.2d 732 (1990) at 735, 737; 674 F. Supp. 1523 (1987) at 1530. Although the NAACP challenged these new admission policies, the courts upheld the right of university officials to "fix admission requirements" and "pass on the qualifications of applicants." See *Hunt v. Arnold*, 172 F. Supp. 847; *Race Relations Law Reporter* 4 (1959): 86.

19. David W. Robinson, Memo, Gressette Committee, May 3, 1983, Robinson Papers, 0802–0805, SCDAH.

20. Memorandum—Re: Segregation, no date, Legal Memoranda, Robinson Papers, SCDAH; Robert Gaines to Thomas Carrere, August 5, 1955, box 900, Office of Archives and Records (OAR), Charleston County School District (CCSD); *Carson v. Warlick*, 238 F. 2d. 724 (1956); *Shuttlesworth v. Birmingham Board of Education*, 162 F. Supp. 372 (1958); *New York Times*, December 30, 1958; H. L. Erckmann to C. A. Brown, August 25, 1955, box 900, OAR, CCSD; [Charleston] Board of School Commissioners, Minute Books (CBSCMB), June 8, 1955; Greenberg, *Crusaders in the Courts*, 251; *Southern School News*, July 1955;

21. Memorandum—Re: Segregation, no date, Legal Memoranda, Robinson Papers, SCDAH; *Southern School News*, February 1956, November 1956, September 1957, October 1961; *Times* (London), July 16, 1963; U. S. Commission on Civil Rights, *Education 1961*, 118–19; *Jones v. School Board of Alexandria*, 179 F. Supp. 280 (1959); McCauley and Ball, eds., *Southern Schools*, 72.

22. Memorandum—Re: Segregation, no date, 0802–0805, Robinson Papers, SCDAH; CBSCMB, July 14, 1954; January 11, November 8, 1956; January 27, February 6, May 8, May 13, August 14, September 11, November 12, November 14, 1957; *Charleston News and Courier*, September 9, 1957; *Charleston Evening Post*, September 21, 1956.

23. Kluger, *Simple Justice*, 320; Bureau of the Census, *Eighteenth Census of the United States*, General Population, Table 78; 13, 16; *Census of Population and Housing, 1960*, 13, 32, 33; Bureau of the Census, *Eighteenth Census of the United States*, General Population, Table 78, 13, 16.

24. CBSCMB, January 27, September 11, 1957.

25. CBSCMB, January 27, 1957; Thomas Waring to Roy Wilkins, April 27, 1959, 23/456–13, Waring Papers.

8. Disorder and Desegregation, 1960–1963

1. Marshall interview, 131, 128–29; Woodward, *The Strange Career of Jim Crow*, 170.

2. Marshall interview, 124.

3. Southern Education Reporting Service, *A Statistical Summary of School Segregation-Desegregation*; *Florida ex. rel. Hawkins v. Board of Control*, 347 U.S. 971 (1954); 350 U.S. 413 (1956); U.S. Commission on Civil Rights, *Equal Protection of the Laws*, 171; *Cooper v Aaron* 358 U.S. 1 (1958).

4. U.S. Commission on Civil Rights, *Equal Protection of the Laws*, 171–273; Halberstam, "A Good City Gone Ugly," 442–43.

5. Sitton, "Negro Sitdowns Stir Fear of Wider Unrest in the South," 433; Chafe, *Civilities and Civil Rights,* 23–24; Morris, *The Origins of The Civil Rights Movement,* 190, 196; Woodward, "*Strange Career* Critics: Long May They Persevere," 865; Dittmer, *Local People,* 75; Bartley, *The New South,* 298.

6. Chafe, *Civilities and Civil Rights,* 23–24, 79, 122, 95, 71.

7. Morris, *The Origins of The Civil Rights Movement,* 199; press release, no date, box II-C-143, NAACP Papers; Oppenheimer, *The Sit-in Movement,* 152, 170–71; Williams, *Thurgood Marshall,* 145; Hine, "Civil Rights and Campus Wrongs," 323; Core Papers, reel 42, 42/411/1137, Microforms Department, Boston Public Library, Boston, Massachusetts.

8. James Blake, interview by author, Charleston, July 17, 1990; *Parvenue,* February 1956, December 1956, November-December 1959, May 1960, June 1960, Burke High School Library (BHSL); *Burke Bulldog,* 1960, BHSL.

9. Voices of the Civil Rights Movement, 197, 218; Blake interview; Graves interview; Hunt interview; Cook interview; *Parvenue,* March 1960, BHSL; Powledge, *Free at Last,* 212, 219, 220.

10. Hunt interview; Graves interview; [Charleston] City Board of School Commissioners, Minute Books (CBSCMB), April 13, 1960.

11. Blake interview; Hunt interview; Graves interview; Burke High School, Commencement Program 1960, Hunt Papers, box 1, Avery Research Center (ARC).

12. Blake interview; Powledge, *Free at Last,* 217, 220; Tushnet, *Making Civil Rights Law,* 310.

13. *Charleston News and Courier,* July 8, November 1, 1961; *United States and Ganaway v. Charleston County School District,* plaintiff's exhibits 1403, 1406, National Archives and Records Center (NARC), Atlanta, Georgia.

14. CBSCMB, October 14, November 11, 1959; May 2, 1960; Voices of the Civil Rights Movement, 110–11; Hutchinson interview; *Charleston News and Courier,* October 3, October 8, October 9, October 13, 1960; CBSCMB, October 21, December 19, 1960; *New York Times,* October 14, 1960; George Stanyard interview.

15. CBSCMB, December 5, December 19, 1960; May 17, June 28, January 18, June 14, December 13, 1961; April 14, May 9, June 13, 1962; *Charleston News and Courier,* October 3, October 13, October 21, 1960; George Stanyard interview.

16. CBSCMB, May 10, July 29, 1961; trial transcript, *Brown v. School District No. 20,* Civil Action 7747, volume 1, 32, National Archives and Records Center, NARC, Atlanta, Georgia; Matthew Perry to J. Arthur Brown, April 24, 1961, J. Arthur Brown Papers, ARC; Gloster Current to J. Arthur Brown, September 26, 1960, box III-C-143, NAACP Papers.

17. Annual Report of the South Carolina Branches of the NAACP, 1960, box III-C-194, NAACP Papers; I. D. Newman to Henry Moon, box III-C-141, NAACP Papers; press release, sit-ins, box III-C-143, NAACP Papers; Roy Wilkins to Gloster Current, October 26, 1959, box II-C-143, NAACP Papers; Matthew Perry to Robert Carter, April 11,1960, box III-A-288, NAACP Papers; "Pickets Fridays and Saturdays," May 26, 1962, Reprisals, South Carolina, unprocessed documents, NAACP Papers; CORE Papers, reel 42, 409/1095, Boston Public Library.

18. Powledge, *Free at Last,* 61, 219–20, 453–56; Constance Baker Motley, interview by Mrs. Walter Gelhorn, March 19, 1977, Butler Library, Columbia University, New York, New York; *New York Times,* June 25, 1961; *Charleston Evening Post,* November 9, 1983; Hunt interview; Graves interview; Frederick Cook interview.

19. Powledge, *Free at Last*, 454; Hunt interview; Motley interview.

20. Tushnet, *Making Civil Rights Law*, 235; Clark, 72; Trillin, *An Education in Georgia;* Hunter-Gault, *In My Place*, 178–79; Pratt, *We Shall Not Be Moved*, 93–94; Dittmer, *Local People*, 140; Cohodas, *The Band Played Dixie;* Doyle, *An American Insurrection;* Branch, 650, 653, 655, 668, 671–72.

21. Powledge, *Free at Last*, 453–57; *Southern School News*, April 1963; Hunt interview; Williams, *Thurgood Marshall*, 180; *Charleston News and Courier*, October 29, 1962; January 24, 1963.

22. Jacoway and Colburn, eds., *Southern Businessmen and School Desegregation*, 7–8; Sproat, "Firm Flexibility: Perspectives on Desegregation in South Carolina"; McMillan, "Integration with Dignity," 16–18.

23. *Journal of the House of Representatives, 1963*, 38; *Charleston News and Courier*, January 24, September 1, 1963; McMillan, "Integration," 18; *Southern School News*, June 1963; *Columbia State*, April 5, 1963.

24. *Greenville News*, January 13, 1963; Motley interview; Powledge, *Free at Last*, 455; R. D. Herbert to W. D. Workman, July 25, 1963, integration file, W. D. Workman Papers, Manuscript Department, Caroliniana Library (MDCL); *New York Times*, October 24, 1963; *Columbia Record*, April 1, 1971.

25. *Charleston Evening Post*, January 24, 1963; Concerned Clemson Alumni, January 1963, Integration file, Workman Papers; *Rebel Underground*, April 1963, Clemson File, W. D. Workman Papers; *Charleston News and Courier*, April 25, 1963.

26. *Southern School News*, September 1963, October 1963; *Columbia State*, April 1, 1971; "The Origins of Desegregation at the University of South Carolina, 1963–1988," University of South Carolina Film Library, Columbia, South Carolina; Lesesne, *A History of the University of South Carolina*, 145–49; Cox, "1963—The Year of Decision," 172; *Gamecock*, February 27, 1989.

27. Journal of the House of Representatives, 1963, 189–90; *Charleston News and Courier*, January 24, 1963; *Southern School News*, September 1962, February 1963.

28. Goldfield, *Black, White, and Southern*, 116.

29. Meier and Rudwick, *CORE*, 90, 217, 356. SNCC activist Reginald Robinson wrote the following in 1963: "In my first report I said the NAACP was the only vocal group here. Mr. J. A. Brown has a big White House with two cars and he is also FAT [emphasis in original]. I meet with NAACP President JAB, who gave me a long talk on NAACP policy. It will be 2063 before the NAACP gets anything done." See Reginald Robinson, SNCC Papers, reel 40, 236:536, Boston Public Library; Fairclough, *Race and Democracy*, xv; Press Release: Sit-Ins, Reprisals, General, 1960–1965, NAACP Papers; Blake interview; Bass and Nelson, *Orangeburg Massacre*.

30. Garrow, *Bearing the Cross*, 249–50; *Southern School News*, June 1963, July 1963; Bloom, *Class, Race, and the Civil Rights Movement*, 175; The Charleston Movement, unprocessed documents, J. Arthur Brown Papers, ARC; *Times* (London), July 16, 1963; *Columbia State*, June 6, 1963; Chafe, *Civilities and Civil Rights*, 107, 109, 119, 120, 157, 160; Morris, *The Origins of The Civil Rights Movement*, 203, 206, 213; Norell, *Reaping the Whirlwind*, 136; Halpern, *On the Limits of the Law*, 18–20; Oppenheimer, *The Sit-in Movement*, 137; Newby, *Black Carolinians*, 315; Cox, "1963—The Year of Decision," 348; Bartley, *The New South*, 337; National Association for the Advancement of Colored People, *Annual Report, 1963*, 43; National Association for the Advancement of Colored People, *Annual*

Report, 1964, 52; *Southern School News*, July 1963; Colburn, *Racial Change and Community Crisis*, 42, 50–51.

31. Charleston Movement, ARC; Blake interview; *Charleston Inquirer*, June 21, 1963; Voices of the Civil Rights Movement, 200, 202, 208; *Charleston Inquirer*, August 9, 1963; Hunt interview; J. Arthur Brown interview; *Charleston News and Courier*, June 24, 1963. Blake interview; Hunt interview.

32. Blake interview; *Charlotte Observer*, July 17, 1963; Eskew, *But for Birmingham*, 230–33.

33. Blake interview; Fraser, *Charleston*, 411; *Columbia State*, July 4, 1963; *City of Charleston v. NAACP*, unprocessed legal documents, NAACP Papers; *Charleston Inquirer*, July 29, 1963; *Charleston News and Courier*, July 24, 1963; O'Neill, "From the Shadow of Slavery"; Report of the Treasurer of the NAACP, unprocessed documents, J. Arthur Brown papers, ARC.

34. *Charleston Inquirer*, July 7, July 19, July 27, 1963; *Columbia State*, July 22, 1963.

35. *City of Charleston v. NAACP*, unprocessed documents, NAACP Papers; *Charleston News and Courier*, July 24, 1963; *Columbia State*, August 2, 1963; *Charleston Inquirer*, August 9, 1963; *New York Times*, July 18, July 22, 1963; NAACP press release, August 3, 1963, box III-C-143, NAACP Papers.

36. Blake interview; NAACP press release, August 3, 1963, box III-C-143, NAACP Papers.

37. Blake interview; *Charleston News and Courier*, August 10, 1963; *Charleston Inquirer*, August 9, 1963.

38. *McNeese Board of Education*, 373 U.S. 668 (1963); Cremin, *American Education*, 261; *Southern School News*, July 1963.

39. Millicent Brown, interviews by author, August 9, November 3, 1989; July 6, July 16, 1990, Charleston; Motion for a Preliminary Injunction, *Brown v. School District Number 20*, May 26, 1962, NARC, Atlanta, Georgia; Complaint, *Brown v. School District 20*, 3, 7, 8; *Brown*, trial transcript, volume 1, 22, 38, NARC, Atlanta, Georgia.

40. Motley interview; *Charleston News and Courier*, June 21, 1964; *Southern School News*, September 1963; *Brown* transcript, volume 3, 1–29, 32, 33, 61, 76; defendants' answer, *Brown v. School District 20*, February 14, 1962; July 9, 1963, NARC, Atlanta, Georgia.

41. *Brown* transcript, volume 3, 38, NARC, Atlanta, Georgia; Motley interview, 350; *Charleston News and Courier*, August 1, 1963.

42. *Charleston News and Courier*, August 8, 1963; *Columbia State*, August 6, August 21, 1963; *United States v. Charleston County School District*, defendant's exhibit, 92, NARC, Atlanta, Georgia; *Brown* transcript, volume 1, 50–53, 28–29, NARC, Atlanta, Georgia; Coleman and others, *Equality of Educational Opportunity*, 120.

43. *Charleston News and Courier*, August 14, 1963.

44. Navasky, *Kennedy Justice*; Hugh Sinkler to Laurence Stoney, August 20, 1963, Thomas Waring Papers, 23–432–23–435, South Carolina Historical Society, Charleston; Schlesinger, *A Thousand Days*, 937.

45. *Brown v. School District Number 20*, 226 F. Supp. 819 (1963) at 819, 826, 827.

46. *Charleston News and Courier*, August 23, September 3, 1963; *Charleston Inquirer*, September 6, 1963; *Charleston News and Courier*, August 23, September 3, 1963; CBSCMB, August 22, August 24, 1963; *Charleston News and Courier*, August 24, 1963; Blake interview; *Southern School News*, October 1963.

47. *Charleston News and Courier*, September 2, September 5, 1963; *New York Times*, September 3, September 4, 1963; CBSCMB, August 28, 1963; *Charleston Evening Post*, August 30, 1963.

9. A New Educational Order, 1963–1972

1. *Columbia State* and *Columbia Record*, August 23, 1964.

2. [Charleston] City Board of School Commissioners, Minute Books (CBSCMB), August 22, September 11, 1963; August 12, 1964; *United States and Ganaway v. Charleston County School District*, plaintiff's exhibit, number 14, National Archives and Records Center (NARC), Atlanta, Georgia.

3. *Charleston News and Courier*, August 30, 1963.

4. *Charleston News and Courier*, September 3, September 4, September 9, September 18, October 25, December 11, 1963.

5. *Charleston News and Courier*, September 7, September 8, September 11, September 12, September 22, 1963.

6. *Charleston News and Courier*, September 10, 1963; September 11, October 25, December 11, 1963; *Columbia State*, December 27, 1964; Annual Report of the County Superintendent, Charleston County, 1963–1964, Sheet A, S 152045, South Carolina State Department of Archives and History (SCDAH); Annual Report of the County Superintendent, Charleston County, 1966–1967, 1967–1968, 1969–1970, Sheet A, S 152045, SCDAH.

7. *Charleston News and Courier*, September 25, October 30, 1963; Robert Rosen, interview by author, Charleston, July 19, 1990; CBSCMB, November 13, 1963.

8. *Charleston News and Courier*, September 5, September 8, September 30, October 7, 1963; October 26, 1967; *Brown v. South Carolina State Board of Education*, 269 F. Supp. 199 (1968); *South Carolina State Board of Education v. Brown*, 393 U.S. 222 (1968); *United States and Ganaway v. Charleston County School District*, plaintiff's exhibit, number 1427, NARC, Atlanta, Georgia; Fuquay, "Civil Rights and the Private School Movement in Mississippi, 1964–1971," 159–80.

9. *United States and Ganaway v. Charleston County School District*, plaintiff's exhibit, number 1426, defendant's exhibit, number 102, NARC, Atlanta, Georgia; Simms interview; George Stanyard interviews; *Charleston News and Courier*, June 17, 1990.

10. David W. Robinson to L. Marion Gressette, December 10, 1963, Robinson Papers, 0802–0805, SCDAH; *United States and Ganaway v. Charleston County School District*, plaintiff's exhibit 927, NARC, Atlanta, Georgia.

11. A Plan in Regard to the Integration Push in the Public Schools of South Carolina, August 22, 1963, Robinson Papers, *Brown* File, SCDAH; Memorandum on Testing as a Method of Achieving Some Measure of Racial Segregation in the Public Schools; Augustus Graydon to John S. Wilson, August 22, 1963, Robinson Papers, *Brown* File, 0802–0805, SCDAH; David W. Robinson to L. Marion Gressette, October 13, 1964, Robinson Papers, 0802–0805, SCDAH.

12. *Brown v. School District 20*, order, April 13, 1964, NARC, Atlanta, Georgia.

13. CBSCMB, January 13, February 10, 1965; Bullock, *A History of Negro Education in the South*, 279.

14. Merriweather interview; CBSCMB, February 20, December 18, 1967; February 12, 1968; George Stanyard interview; Wilkinson, *From Brown to Bakke*, 110, 86; King, "The Case against Tokenism," 11.

15. Voices of the Civil Rights Movement, 93–94; Millicent Brown, interviews by author; *Parvenue*, May 1963; Merriweather interview; unprocessed documents related to the desegregation of Rivers High School, J. Arthur Brown Papers, Avery Research Center (ARC).

16. Solomon Breibart, interview by author, Charleston, September 11, 1991; *Columbia State*, August 23, 1964; Millicent Brown interviews.

17. Solomon Beibart interview; Millicent Brown interviews; Jacqueline Ford, interview by author, Charleston, September 12, 1991; Rosen interview; *Columbia State*, August 23, 1964.

18. Voices of the Civil Rights Movement, 93–96, 98; Brown interviews.

19. Brown interviews; Voices of the Civil Rights Movement, 98; Bradley, "Wearing My Name": Beals, *Warriors Don't Cry.*

20. CBSCMB, September 7, 1966; plaintiff's answers to interrogatories, June 1, 1966, *Brown v. School District 20*, NARC, Atlanta, Georgia.

21. Between 1964 and 1974 the Justice Department and HEW filed 1,100 suits, redefining the meaning of school desegregation. Ravitch, *The Troubled Crusade*, 142, 162; *Green v. School Board of New Kent County*, 391 U.S. 430 (1968) at 437–38.

22. Answers to interrogatories, June 1, June 20, 1966, *Brown v. School District*, NARC, Atlanta, Georgia; *Brown v. School District*, order, March 10, 1967, NARC, Atlanta, Georgia; CBSCMB, September 7, 1966; May 8, 1967; *Charleston News and Courier*, October 2, 1967.

23. *United States and Ganaway v. Charleston County School District*, plaintiff's exhibit, number 1403, NARC, Atlanta, Georgia.

24. CBSCMB, December 18, February 20, 1967; *United States and Ganaway v. Charleston County School District*, plaintiff's exhibit, number 1403, NARC, Atlanta, Georgia.

25. *Brown v. School District*, order, March 10, 1967, NARC, Atlanta, Georgia; Coleman and others, *Equality of Educational Opportunity*, 23.

26. Byrnes, *All in One Lifetime*, 408; CBSCMB, March 15, 1954; January 13, October 12, 1955; December 12, 1956; *Charleston News and Courier*, October 11, 1955.

27. Simms interview; CBSCMB, December 11, February 10, 1963; April 14, May 10, October 13, 1965; December 12, 1966; Information for the Board, October 12, 1965, Office of Archives and Records (OAR), Charleston County School District (CCSD).

28. CBSCMB, February 10, October 13, 1965; March 21, August 11, August 18, April 22, September 9, 1966; Mizell, "School Desegregation in South Carolina," 30; Information for the Board, number 269, February 12, 1968, OAR, CCSD; *United States and Ganaway v. Charleston County School District*, transcript, day 29, 130–34, NARC, Atlanta, Georgia; answer to interrogatories, August 21, 1968, *Brown v. School District*, NARC, Atlanta, Georgia.

29. *United States and Ganaway v. Charleston County School District*, plaintiff's exhibit, number 1403, NARC, Atlanta, Georgia; Merriweather interview; answers to interrogatories, June 1, 1966, *Brown v. School District*, NARC, Atlanta, Georgia; CBSCMB, April 1, 1968; *Charleston News and Courier*, undated clipping, vertical file, Charleston County Public Library (CCPL); *Columbia State*, April 12, April 15, 1987; *Charleston News and Courier*, June 17, 1990; *Charlotte Observer*, May 13, 1984.

30. Answer to interrogatories, August 21, 1968, *Brown v. School District*, NARC, Atlanta, Georgia; CBSCMB, September 30, September 31, 1968; Goldfield, *Black, White, and Southern*, 253.

31. Cecelski, *Along Freedom Road*, 10; *Charleston Chronicle*, January 10, May 25, 1972; Brown, "Civil Rights Activism."

32. *Brown v. Board of Education*, in Friedman, ed., *Oral Argument*, 329.

33. *United States and Ganaway v. Charleston County School District*, transcript, day 10, 9, 41–42, NARC, Atlanta Georgia; *United States and Ganaway v. Charleston County School District*, case number 90–1812, Court of Appeals, dissent, 28, NARC, Atlanta, Georgia.

34. Joseph Darden deposition, *United States and Ganaway v. Charleston County School District*, transcript, day 18, 49; day 19, 36–41, NARC, Atlanta, Georgia.

35. Thomas Carrere, Memo, Major Reservations Concerning the Gibson Bill, box 862, OAR, CCSD; *Charleston Evening Post*, January 23, October 3, 1968; Thomas Carrere to Charleston School Board, January 20, 1967, box 862, OAR, CCSD.

36. *United States and Ganaway v. Charleston County School District*, transcript, day 25, 32–41, NARC, Atlanta, Georgia; *Charleston News and Courier*, March 4, 1967.

37. *United States and Ganaway v. Charleston County School District*, transcript, day 13, 142–43, NARC, Atlanta, Georgia; transcript, day 6, 89, NARC, Atlanta, Georgia; *Charleston News and Courier*, March 4, 1967.

38. *United States and Ganaway v. Charleston County School District*, order, June 5, 1990, NARC, Atlanta, Georgia; *United States and Ganaway v. Charleston County School District*, appellees' brief, 8, 12, NARC, Atlanta, Georgia; *United States v. Charleston County School District*, 738 F. Supp. 1513 (1990) at 1521.

39. For an analysis of African American migration to the suburbs see Taeuber and Taeuber, *Negroes in Cities*; Massey and Denton, *American Apartheid*; Ganaway, order, 58, NARC, Atlanta, Georgia; Bernice Robinson Collection, unprocessed documents, ARC; Lucille Whipper, interview by author, Mt. Pleasant, South Carolina, July 23, 1990; Wigfall interview; *Charleston Chronicle*, February 10, March 3, 1973.

40. *Charleston News and Courier*, June 3, 1975; U.S. Department of Education, Office of Civil Rights, Elementary and Secondary Survey, Elementary and Secondary School, Civil Rights Compliance Report, District Listing Summary, 1968–1994, U.S. Department of Education, Office of Civil Rights, Washington, D.C.

41. Wigfall interview; Senate Select Committee, *Hearings before the Select Committee on Equal Educational Opportunity*; P. R. Morgan and James M. McPartland, "The Extent of Classroom Segregation"; Meier, Stewart, and England, *Race, Class, and Education*; House of Representatives, *Investigation of Schools and Poverty in the District of Columbia*; American Friends Service Committee, *The Status of School Desegregation in the South*; Alabama Council on Human Relations, *It's Not Over in the South*.

42. *United States v. South Carolina*, case files, NARC, Atlanta, Georgia; *United States v. South Carolina*, 445 F. Supp. 1094 (1977); Augustus Graydon to David W. Robinson, August 22, 1963, Robinson Papers, *Brown* File, 0802–0805, SCDAH.

43. Bartley, *The New South*, 380; *Charleston News and Courier*, June 3, 1975; Goldfield, *Black, White, and Southern*, 270; Granovetter, "The Micro-Structure of School Desegregation," 81–110.

44. Bureau of the Census, *Nineteenth Census of the United States, Volume I*, 825–27; *Charleston News and Courier*, June 3, 1975; *Charleston Chronicle*, February 10, March 3, 1973; Chafe, *The Unfinished Journey*, 441; Fordham and Ogbu, "Black Students' School Success," 176–206; Fordham, *Blacked Out*, 22.

45. *Charleston Chronicle*, June 17, 1972; March 17, 1973; *Burke Bulldog*, 1971, Burke High School Library (BHSL); *Parvenue*, November 1974, May 1973; October 1972, BHSL; Simms interview; Whipper interview; Hunt interview; Merriweather interview; Graves interview; Simms interviews; Frederick Cook interview.

46. Wilson, *The Declining Significance of Race*, xi; Freeman, *Black Elite*; Jencks and Riesman, *The Academic Revolution*, 441, 448. The vast literature on school and university desegregation tells us little about class, and we need to know more about the family background characteristics of students who desegregated southern colleges and universities. In South

Carolina the students who crossed the color line came from advantaged backgrounds. Harvey Gantt's father held a skilled job at the Charleston Naval Shipyard. Henrie Monteith was the daughter of a schoolteacher who graduated from St. Francis de Sales School in Virginia; James Solomon was a U.S. Air Force veteran who taught math at Morris College in Sumter, South Carolina. In Georgia, Charlayne Hunter's father was a U.S. Army chaplain, and her mother was a teacher. Hamilton Holmes's father and grandfather were college graduates; see Pratt, *We Shall Not Be Moved*.

47. Williams, *Thurgood Marshall*, 178–86; Powledge, *Free at Last*, 645; Goldfield, *Black, White, and Southern*, 228–29; Bureau of the Census, *Sixteenth Census of the United States: 1940 Population, Volume 2*, 425; Bureau of the Census, *Eighteenth Census of the United States*, General Population, Table 78; Bureau of the Census, *Nineteenth Census of the United States*, 1970 Census of Population, Table 173, 42-556-558.

48. Newby, *Black Carolinians*, 349–56; State College, *Catalogue, 1964–1965*, 237–39; Coleman and others, *Equality of Educational Opportunity*, 368; Hine, "South Carolina State College," 165; Martin, *The Deep South Says "Never,"* 89; Jencks and Riesman, *The Academic Revolution*, 470; Potts, *A History of South Carolina State College*, 150–52; Jaynes and Williams, eds., *A Common Destiny*, 176–79; Hill, *The Traditionally Black Institutions of Higher Education, 1960–1982*; Dent, *Southern Journey*, 94–95; Windham, *Education, Equality, and Income*, 46–47.

49. *Adams v. Richardson*, 356 F. Supp. 92 (1973); *Adams v. Bell*, 711 F.2d 161 (1983); Halpern, *On the Limits of the Law*; Martin, *The Deep South Says "Never,"* 89–106; Potts, *A History of South Carolina State College*, 150–53; Preer, *Lawyers v. Educators*, 189–232; Greenberg, *Crusaders in the Courts*, 395–97.

Epilogue

1. Howard P. Willens and others, Brief Amicus Curiae for Educational Testing Service, *United States of America v. State of South Carolina*, micro: 01/01/1976, Educational Testing Service Archives, Princeton, New Jersey, 8; Educational Testing Service, "Report on a Study of the Use of the National Teachers Examinations by the South Carolina Department of Education, AMP-76–1417, Educational Testing Service Archives, Princeton, New Jersey. In South Carolina the percentage of African American teachers employed fell from 42 percent in 1955 to less than 20 percent in 1987. *Charleston Post-Courier*, May 2, 1987; *United States v. South Carolina*, 1108.

2. National Center for Educational Statistics, *The Condition of Education, 1982*, 66–67; King, "The Limited Presence of African American Teachers," 140; Haney, Madaus, and Krietzer, "Charms Talismanic," 227.

3. *Richardson v. McFadden*, 540 F. 2d 744 (1976) at 744, 750; *Richardson v. McFadden*, case number 73-2512, trial transcript, volume 1, 10, National Archives and Records Center (NARC), Philadelphia, Pennsylvania.

4. *Adams v. Richardson*, 356 F. Supp. 92 (1973); *Adams v. Bell*, 711 F. 2d 161 (1983); Webster, Stockard, and Henson, "Black Student Elite," 287; Lesesne, *A History of the University of South Carolina*, 313.

5. *Hobson v. Hansen*, 269 F. Supp. 401 (1967) at 474; Newby, *Black Carolinians*, 309; U.S. Commission on Civil Rights, "Educational Accountability and High-Stakes in the Carolinas," http://permanent.access.gpo.gov/www.usccr.gov/pubs/eduacct/edac.../ (accessed June 27, 2005).

6. Bond and King, "State High School Graduation Testing," 3.

BIBLIOGRAPHY

Manuscript Sources

Atlanta, Georgia
National Archives and Records Center
  Briggs v. Elliott
  Brown v. School District Number 20
  United States and Ganaway v. Charleston County School District
  United States v. Charleston County School District
  United States v. South Carolina

Boston, Massachusetts
Boston Public Library, Microforms Division
  Congress of Racial Equality Papers
  Schomberg Clipping File
  Student Nonviolent Coordinating Committee Papers

Chapel Hill, North Carolina
University of North Carolina, Wilson Library
  Guy B. Johnson Papers

Charleston, South Carolina
Avery Research Center, College of Charleston
  Black Charleston Collection
  Book Lovers Club Collection
  J. Arthur Brown Collection
  Joyce Ravenel Butler Collection
  Charleston Interracial Committee, 1942–1953
  Complete Transcription of Conference, South Carolina Voices of the Civil Rights
    Movement, November 5–6, 1982
  Cosmopolitan Civic League
  Frank A. DeCosta Collection
  Directory of Charleston County Public Schools
  Mamie Fields Collection
  Eugene Hunt Collection
  Henry Hutchinson Collection
  Anna Kelly Collection
  Charles Mason Collection
  Minutes of the Advisory Committee to Mr. George Rogers
  Miscellaneous Smalls Collection

Peter Poinsette Collection
Angela Polite Documents
Bernice Robinson Collection
Lois Simms Collection
J. Waties Waring Collection
Office of Archives and Records, Charleston County School District
Annual Report of School Superintendent, 1949–1950
Avery Institute, Box 891
Budget Letters, 1949, Box 903
City Board of School Commissioners, Minute Books, 1924–1957
Constituent Board Minutes, District 20, 1956–1981
Improvement of Negro Schools, Box 896
Miscellaneous Documents, Box 862
Miscellaneous Documents, Box 929
National Defense, 1943–1944, Box 863
Negro History, 1958, Box 863
Principals' Reports, Box 900
Principals' Summary, 1950–1951, Box 903
Salaries, 1931–1941, Box 896
Salaries, Comparative, 1938–1943, Box 896
Simonton School, Box 863
Student Records, 1940–1945
Use of School Buildings and Property, 1959
Papers in the Possession of Private Individuals
J. Arthur Brown Papers, Millicent Brown
Ruth Cook, Burke Class of 1945, Graduation memorabilia
Robert Rosen Papers, Robert Rosen
Special Collections, Robert Scott Smalls Library, College of Charleston
Correspondence Relating to Applications by Negroes for Entrance into the College
Septima Poinsette Clark Collection
South Carolina Historical Society
Thomas R. Waring Papers

Columbia, South Carolina

South Carolina Department of Archives and History
Annual Reports of County Superintendent, Charleston County, 1949–1969
Annual Reports of County Superintendent, Clarendon County, 1946–1954
George F. Byrnes Papers
High School Accreditation Reports, 1945–1950
Office of Civil Rights Compliance Reports
David W. Robinson Papers
George Bell Timmerman Papers
Caroliniana Library, University of South Carolina
J. A. DeLaine Papers
John McCray Papers
Hays Mizell Papers
National Association for the Advancement of Colored People, Sumter Branch

    South Carolina Council on Human Relations Papers
    W. D. Workman Papers
University of South Carolina Archives
    Donald S. Russell Presidential Papers
    Norman O. Smith Presidential Papers
    Robert L. Sumwalt Presidential Papers

Los Angeles, California
University of California at Los Angles, Special Collections
    Ralph Bunche Papers

Nashville, Tennessee
Fisk University, Special Collections
    Julius Rosenwald Fund Papers, Mineral Spring School

New Haven, Connecticut
Sterling Library, Yale University
    Richard Kluger Collection

New Market, Tennessee
Highlander Research Center
    Civil Rights—South Carolina

Orangeburg, South Carolina
Miller F. Whittaker Library, South Carolina State University
    Board of Trustees
    William F. Hine Collection
    Law School, 1946–1951
    Nelson Nix Papers
    SAC, 1938–1965
    Scrapbooks
    Benner C. Turner Papers
    Miller F. Whittaker Papers

Philadelphia, Pennsylvania
National Archives and Records Center
    Richardson v. McFadden

Princeton, New Jersey
Educational Testing Service Archives
    Ben D. Wood Papers

Tarrytown, New York
Rockefeller Archive
    General Education Board, State A and M File

Washington, D.C.
Library of Congress, Manuscript Division
    Charleston, South Carolina
    Clarendon County, South Carolina
    Farmville, Virginia

Hearne, Texas
La Grange, Texas
Lumberton, North Carolina
National Association for the Advancement of Colored People Papers
Orangeburg, South Carolina
Arthur Spingarn Papers
Moorland-Spingarn Research Center, Howard University
J. Waties Waring Papers
National Archives
Records of the National Youth Administration
National Council of Negro Women Archives
Charleston, S.C.

Interviews by Author

Blake, James. Interview by author. Charleston, July 17, 1990.

Breibart, Solomon. Interview by author. Charleston, September 11, 1991.

Brockington, Benjamin. Interview by author. Charleston, January 5, 1991.

Brown, Millicent. Interviews by author. Charleston, August 9, November 3, 1989; July 6, July 19, 1990.

Cook, Frederick. Interview by author. Charleston, January 10, 1991.

Cook, Ruth. Interview by author. Charleston, January 15, 1991.

Duvall, Viola (Stewart). Interview by author. Philadelphia, September 4, 1990.

Ford, Jacqueline. Interview by author. Charleston, September 12, 1991.

Graves, J. Michael. Interview by author. Charleston, July 16, 1990.

Hamilton, Lonnie. Interview by author. North Charleston, July 12, 1990.

Hasell, Oliver. Interview by author. Charleston, July 18, 1990.

Heyward, Nevada. Interview by author. Charleston, July 9, 1990.

Holmes, Dorothy. Interview by author. Charleston, July 31, 1990.

Howard, Marjorie. Interview by author. Charleston, January 15, 1991.

Hunt, Eugene. Interview by author. Charleston, July 11, 1990.

Hutchinson, Henry. Interview by author. Charleston, July 18, 1990.

Kelly, Anna. Interview by author. Charleston, July 17, 1991.

Merriweather, William. Interview by author. Charleston, July 19, 1990.

Moore, Fred. Interview by author. Orangeburg, S.C., April 15, 2003.

Poinsette, Peter and Lucille. Interview by author. Charleston, July 11, 1991.

Rosen, Robert. Interview by author. Charleston, July 17, 1990.

Shaw, May. Interview by author. Baltimore, May 5, 1989.

Shokes, Alma. Interview by author. Charleston, July 12, 1990.

Simms, Lois. Interview by author. Charleston, January 6, 10, 1991.

Smalls, Oliver. Interview by author. Charleston, August 10, 1989.

Smith, Malissa (Burkehalter). Interview by author. Atlanta, July 28, 1990.

Stanyard, George. Interview by author. Charleston, July 9, 1990; January 8, 1991.

Stanyard, Hermine. Interview by author. Charleston, July 8, 1990; January 8, 1991.

Thompson, Albert. Interview by author. Charleston, July 6, 1990.

Whaley, Thelma. Interview with author. Charleston, July 9, 1990.

Whipper, Lucille. Interview by author. Mt. Pleasant, S.C., July 23, 1990.

White, Moses. Interview by author. Charleston, January 10, 1991.

Wigfall, Alma. Interview by author. Charleston, January 10, 1991.

Williams, Cecil. Interview by author. Orangeburg, S.C., April 16, 2003.

Interviews by Others

Bennett, L. Howard. Interview by Edmund L. Drago and Eugene C. Hunt. June 23, 1981, Avery Research Center (ARC), College of Charleston.

Briggs, Harry. Interview by Richard Kluger. November 29, 1977, Sterling Library, Yale University.

Brogdon, Julia (Purnell). Interview by Edmund L. Drago. November 13, 1987, ARC, College of Charleston.

Brown, J. Arthur. Interview by Edmund L. Drago and Eugene C. Hunt. August 14, 1981, ARC, College of Charleston.

Clark, Kenneth. Interview by Richard Kluger. November 4, 1971, Sterling Library, Yale University.

Coley, Nell. Interview by William H. Chafe. Perkins Library, Duke University.

Crawford, T. J. Interview by William C. Hine. March 9, 1989, Miller Whittaker Library, South Carolina State University (SCSU).

De Laine, J. A. Interview by Richard Kluger. November 1, 1971, Sterling Library, Yale University.

Elman, Philip. Interview by Richard Kluger. August 19, 1971, Sterling Library, Yale University.

Figg, Robert. Interview by Richard Kluger. October 17, 1971, Sterling Library, Yale University.

Finney, Ernest A. Interview by Charles H. Houston Jr. August 11, 1994, Perkins Library, Duke University.

Fleming, Billie. Interview by Richard Kluger. October 22, 1971, Sterling Library, Yale University.

Kerford, Leo. Interview by Charles H. Houston Jr. August 9, 1994, Perkins Library, Duke University.

Marshall, Thurgood. Interview by Ed Erwin. February 15, 1977, Butler Library, Columbia University.

Moore, Fred. Interview by William C. Hine. July 21, 1994, Miller Whittaker Library, SCSU.

Motley, Constance Baker. Interview by Mrs. Walter Gelhorn. March 19, 1977, Butler Library, Columbia University.

Nance, Maceo M. Interview by William C. Hine. March 14, 1989, Miller Whittaker Library, SCSU.

Perry, Matthew. Interview by William C. Hine. July 21, 1994, Miller Whittaker Library, SCSU.

————. Interview by Grace McFadden. August 18, 1980, University of South Carolina Film Library, University of South Carolina, Columbia, S.C.

Pyatt, Rudolph. Interview by William C. Hine. August 25, 1994, Miller Whittaker Library, SCSU.

Roache, Lewie, C. Interview by William C. Hine. August 16, 1990, Miller Whittaker Library, SCSU.

Sulton, James. Interview by William C. Hine. July 20, 1994, Miller F. Whittaker Library, SCSU.

Waring, J. Waties. Interviews by Harlan B. Phillips and Louis M. Star. 1955–1957, Butler Library, Columbia University.

Whitehead, Matthew. Interview by Richard Kluger. March 18, 1971, Sterling Library, Yale University.

Wrighten, John. Interview by William C. Hine. July 6, 1989, Miller F. Whittaker Library, SCSU.

Legal Cases

Adams v. Richardson, 356 F. Supp. 92 (1973); 711 F. 2d 161 (1983).

Alston v. School Board of the City of Norfolk, 112 F. 2nd 992 (1940).

Ayers v. Allain, 893 F. 2d 732 (1990).

Battle v. Wichita Falls Junior College District, 101 F. Supp. 82 (1951).

Booker v. State Board of Education, 248 F. 2d 689 (1956).

Bradford v. School District, Number 20, 364 F. 2d 185 (1966).

Briggs v. Elliott, 98 F. Supp. 529 (1951); 132 F. Supp. 776 (1955).

Brown v. Board of Education of Topeka, 347 U. S. 483 (1954); 349 U.S. 294 (1955).

Brown v. School District Number 20, 226 F. Supp. 819 (1963).

Brown v. South Carolina State Board of Education, 296 F. Supp. 199 (1968).

Carson v. Warlick, 238 F. 2d 724 (1945).

Constantine v. Southwestern Louisiana Institute, 120 F. Supp 417 (1954).

Cooper v. Aaron, 358 U.S. 1 (1958).

Elmore v. Rice, 72 F. Supp. 516 (1947).

Ex. Parte Banks, 48 So. 2D 35 (1950).

Gantt v. Clemson Agricultural College of South Carolina, 226 F. Supp. 416 (1962); 213 F. Supp. 103 (1962).

Green v. County School Board of New Kent County, 391 U.S. 430 (1968).

Hawkins v. Board of Control, 162 F. Supp. 851 (1958).

Hobson v. Hansen, 269 F. Supp. 401 (1967).

Hunt v. Arnold, 172 F. Supp 847 (1959).

Jones v. School Board of City of Alexandria, 179 F. Supp. 280 (1959).

McDaniel v. Bd. of Public Instruction for Escambia Co., Florida, 39 F. Supp. 638 (1941).

McNeese v. Board of Education, 373 U.S. 668 (1963).

Mills v. Board of Trustees of Anne Arundel County, 30 F. Supp. 245 (1939).

Missouri ex. rel. Gaines v. Canada, 305 U.S. 337 (1938).

Reynolds et. al. v. Board of Public Instruction for Dade County Fla. et. al., 148 F. 2d. 754 (1945).

Richardson v. McFadden, 540 F.2d 744 (1976).

Shuttlesworth v. Birmingham Board of Education, 162 F. Supp. 372 (1958).

Singleton v. Jackson Municipal Separate School District, 372 F. 2d. 729 (1965).

State ex. rel. v. Michael v. Witham, 165 S.W. 2d 378 (1942).

Sweatt v. Painter, 339 U.S. 629 (1950).

Thompson v. Gibbes, 60 F. Supp. 872 (1945).

Turner v. Keefe, 50 F. Supp. 647 (1943).

Tyler v. Vickery, 517 F. 2d 1089 (1975).

United States v. Charleston County School District, 738 F. Supp. 1513 (1990); 960 Fed. 2d. 1227 (1992).

United States v. South Carolina, 445 F. Supp. 1094 (1977).

University of Maryland v. Donald G. Murray, 169 Md. 478 (1936).

Williams v. Zimmerman, 172 Md. 563; 192 A 353 (1937).

Wilson v. City of Paducah, 100 F. Supp 116 (1951).
Wrighten v. Board of Trustees, 72 F. Supp. 948 (1947).

Government Documents

Annual Report of State Superintendent of Education of the State of South Carolina, 1926. Columbia: General Assembly, 1926.

Annual Report of State Superintendent of Education of the State of South Carolina, 1938. Columbia: General Assembly, 1938.

Annual Report of State Superintendent of Education of the State of South Carolina, 1941. Columbia: General Assembly, 1941.

Annual Report of State Superintendent of Education of the State of South Carolina, 1942. Columbia: General Assembly, 1942.

Annual Report of State Superintendent of Education of the State of South Carolina, 1943. Columbia: General Assembly, 1943.

Annual Report of State Superintendent of Education of the State of South Carolina, 1946. Columbia: General Assembly, 1946.

Blose, David T., and Ambrose Caliver. *Statistics on the Education of Negroes.* Washington, D.C.: U.S. Government Printing Office, 1938.

Bureau of the Census. *Census of Population and Housing.* Washington, D.C.: U.S. Government Printing Office, 1933.

———. *Eighteenth Census of the United States.* Washington D.C.: U.S. Government Printing Office, 1963.

———. *Fifteenth Census of the United States.* Washington, D.C.: U.S. Government Printing Office, 1932.

———. *Nineteenth Census of the United States.* Washington D.C.: U.S. Government Printing Office, 1973.

———. *Seventeenth Census of the United States.* Washington D.C.: U.S. Government Printing Office, 1952.

———. *Sixteenth Census of the United States.* Washington, D.C.: U.S. Government Printing Office, 1943.

Caliver, Ambrose. *Availability of Education to Negroes in Rural Communities.* Washington, D.C.: U.S. Government Printing Office, 1936.

———. *A Background Study of Negro College Students.* Washington, D.C.: Government Printing Office, 1933.

———. *Education of Negro Teachers.* Washington D.C.: U.S. Government Printing Office, 1933.

———. *Secondary Education for Negroes.* Washington D.C.: U.S. Government Printing Office, 1933.

———. *Vocational Education and Guidance for Negroes.* Washington, D.C.: U.S. Government Printing Office, 1937.

Coleman, James C., and others. *Equality of Educational Opportunity.* Washington, D.C.: U.S. Government Printing Office, 1966.

Eckelberry, R. J. *The History of Municipal Universities in the United States.* Washington, D.C.: U.S. Government Printing Office, 1932.

Federal Manuscript Census, Edisto Island, South Carolina, 1930.

Federal Manuscript Census, James Island, South Carolina, 1930.

Federal Security Agency, U.S. Office of Education. *Biennial Survey of Education in the United States, 1936–38*. Washington, D.C.: U.S. Government Printing Office, 1942.

———. *Biennial Survey of Education in the United States, 1938–40 and 1940–42*. Washington D.C.: U.S. Government Printing Office, 1947.

———. *Biennial Survey of Education in the United States, 1942–44*. Washington D.C.: U.S. Government Printing Office, 1949.

———. *Biennial Survey of Education in the United States, 1944–46*. Washington, D.C.: U.S. Government Printing Office, 1950.

———. *Biennial Survey of Education in the United States, 1946–48*. Washington, D.C.: U.S. Government Printing Office, 1951.

Hill, Susan T. *The Traditionally Black Institutions of Higher Education, 1960–1982*. Washington, D.C.: National Center for Educational Statistics, 1984.

House of Representatives, Committee on Education and Labor. *Investigation of Schools and Poverty in the District of Columbia*. Washington, D.C.: U.S. Government Printing Office, 1966.

Johnson, Charles S. "The Negro Public Schools: A Social and Educational Survey." In *Louisiana Looks at Its Schools*, edited by Carelton Washburne, 115–247. Baton Rouge: Louisiana Educational Survey Commission, 1942.

Johnson, Palmer O., and Oswald L. Harvey, *The National Youth Administration*. Washington, D.C.: U.S. Government Printing Office, 1938.

Jones, Thomas Jesse. *Negro Education: A Study of the Private and Higher Schools for Negroes in the South*. Washington, D.C.: U.S. Government Printing Office, 1917.

Journal of the House of Representatives, 1963. Columbia: General Assembly, 1963.

Journal of the Senate, 1948. Columbia: General Assembly, 1948.

Klein, Arthur J. *Survey of Negro Colleges and Universities*. Washington, D.C.: U.S. Government Printing Office, 1929.

Lynch, Kenneth M. *Medical Schooling in South Carolina*. Charleston: State Medical College, 1970.

Morgan, P. R., and James M. McPartland. "The Extent of Classroom Segregation." Educational Resources Information Center. Document No. 210 405, 1981.

National Center for Educational Statistics. *The Condition of Education, 1982*. Washington, D.C.: U.S. Government Printing Office.

Report of Special Committee to Investigate Statutory Laws Dealing with Education, February 5, 1941. Columbia: General Assembly, 1941.

School Directory of South Carolina, 1930–1950. Columbia: State Co., 1930–1950.

Senate Select Committee on Equal Educational Opportunity, *Hearings before the Select Committee on Equal Educational Opportunity*. Washington: D.C.: U.S. Government Printing Office, 1971.

South Carolina State Board of Education, *Requirements for Teacher Education and Certification*. Columbia, S.C.: State Co., 1948.

Strohecker, Henry. *Present Day Public Education in the County and City of Charleston*. Charleston: Charleston County Board of Education, 1929.

U.S. Commission on Civil Rights, *Education 1961 Commission on Civil Rights Report*. Washington, D.C.: U.S. Government Printing Office, 1961.

———. *Equal Protection of the Laws in Public Higher Education*. Washington, D.C.: Government Printing Office, 1960.

U.S. Department of Education, Office of Civil Rights. Elementary and Secondary Survey, Elementary and Secondary School Civil Rights Compliance Report, District Listing

Summary, 1968–1994. United States Department of Education, Office of Civil Rights, Washington, D.C.

U.S. Department of Health, Education, and Welfare. *Biennial Survey of Education in the United States, 1948–50*. Washington, D.C.: U.S. Government Printing Office, 1954.

―――. *Biennial Survey of Education in the United States, 1950–52*. Washington D.C.: Government Printing Office, 1957.

―――. *Biennial Survey of Education in the United States, 1952–54*. Washington, D.C.: U.S. Government Printing Office, 1959.

―――. *Guidelines on School Desegregation*. Washington, D.C.: U.S. Government Printing Office, 1965.

U.S. National Emergency Council. "South Carolina, State and National Reports, 1933–1938." Washington, D.C.: Statistical Division, 1938.

U.S. Office of Education. *National Survey of the Higher Education of Negroes*. Washington, D.C.: U.S. Government Printing Office, 1942.

Wilkerson, Doxey A. *Special Problems of Negro Education*. Washington, D.C.: U.S. Government Printing Office, 1939.

Newspapers

Charleston Chronicle
Charleston Evening Post
Charleston News and Courier
Collegian (State College)
Columbia State
Lighthouse and Informer (Columbia)
New York Post
New York Times
Parvenue (Burke Industrial School)
Pittsburgh Courier
Race Relations Law Reporter (Nashville)
Southern School News (Nashville)

Books and Articles

Abernathy, Ralph David. *And the Walls Came Tumbling Down: An Autobiography*. New York: Harper and Row, 1989.

Alabama Council on Human Relations. *It's Not Over in the South: School Desegregation in Forty-three Southern Cities Eighteen Years after "Brown."* Washington, D.C.: Research Press, 1972.

American Friends Service Committee. *The Status of School Desegregation in the South*. Washington, D.C.: Lawyers Constitutional Committee, 1972.

Anderson, James D. *The Education of Blacks in the South, 1860–1935*. Chapel Hill: University of North Carolina Press, 1988.

Armor, David J. *Forced Justice: School Desegregation and the Law*. New York: Oxford University Press, 1995.

Ashmore, Henry S. *The Negro and the Schools*. Chapel Hill: University of North Carolina Press, 1954.

Atkins, James A. "Negro Educational Institutions and the Veterans' Educational Facilities Program." *Journal of Negro Education* 17 (Spring 1948): 141–53.

Auerbach, Jerold S. *Unequal Justice: Lawyers and Social Change in Modern America*. New York: Oxford University Press, 1976.

Badger, Anthony J. *The New Deal: The Depression Years*. New York: Noonday Press, 1989.

Bagnell, Robert. "Lights and Shadows in the South." *Crisis* 39 (April 1932): 124–25.

Bagwell, William. *School Desegregation in the Carolinas: Two Case Studies*. Columbia: University of South Carolina Press, 1972.

Baker, Scott. "Testing Equality: The National Teacher Examination and the NAACP's Legal Campaign to Equalize Teachers' Salaries, 1936–1963." *History of Education Quarterly* 35 (Spring 1995): 49–64.

Ball, W. W. "Improvement in Race Relations in South Carolina: The Cause." *South Atlantic Quarterly* 39 (October 1940): 385–90.

Bartley, Numan V. *The New South, 1945–1980*. Baton Rouge: Louisiana State University Press, 1995.

———. *The Rise of Massive Resistance: Race and Politics in the South during the 1950s*. Baton Rouge: Louisiana State University Press, 1969.

Bass, Jack, and Jack Nelson. *Orangeburg Massacre*. Macon: Mercer University Press, 1999.

Beals, Melba Pattillo. *Warriors Don't Cry: A Searing Memoir of the Battle to Integrate Little Rock's Central High*. New York: Pocket Books, 1995.

Beam, Lura. *He Called Them by Lightning*. Indianapolis: Bobbs-Merrill, 1967.

Beezer, Bruce. "Black Teacher's Salaries and the Federal Courts before *Brown v. Board of Education*: One Beginning for Equity." *Journal of Negro Education* 55 (1986): 200–213.

Bell, Derrick. *And We Are Not Saved: The Elusive Quest for Racial Justice*. New York: Basic Books, 1987.

———. *Faces at the Bottom of the Well: The Permanence of Racism*. New York: Basic Books, 1992.

———. *Silent Covenants: "Brown v. Board of Education" and the Unfulfilled Hopes for Racial Reform*. New York: Oxford University Press, 2004.

Bender, Jay. "One Week That Changed the State." *South Carolina Lawyer* 11 (November–December 1999): 33–37.

Benson, Arthur L. "Problems of Evaluating Test Scores of White and Negro Teachers. *Proceedings of the Southern Association of Colleges and Secondary Schools* 59 (1955): 168–74.

Bethune, Mary McLeod. "My Secret Talks with FDR." In *The Negro in Depression and War: Prelude to Revolution, 1930–1945*, edited by Bernard Sternsher, 53–65. Chicago: Quadrangle, 1969.

Black, Earl. *Southern Governors and Civil Rights: Racial Segregation as a Campaign Issue in the Second Reconstruction*. Cambridge, Mass.: Harvard University Press, 1976.

Bloom, Jack. *Class, Race, and the Civil Rights Movement*. Bloomington: Indiana University Press, 1987.

Bolton, Charles C. "Mississippi's School Equalization Program, 1945–1954: 'A Last Gasp to Try to Maintain a Segregated Educational System.'" *Journal of Southern History* 66 (November 2000): 781–804.

Bond, Horace Mann. *Black American Scholars: A Study of Their Beginnings*. Detroit: Belamp Publishing, 1972.

———. *The Education of the Negro in the American Social Order*. New York: Prentice-Hall, 1934.

Bond, Linda A., and Diane King. *State High School Graduation Testing: Status and Recommendations*. Oak Brook, Ill.: North Central Regional Educational Lab, 1995.

Bracey, John H., and August Meier, eds. *Papers of the NAACP.* Bethesda, Md.: University Publications of America, 1995.

Braddock, Jomills, Robert Crain, and James McPartland. "A Long Term View of School Desegregation: Some Recent Studies of Graduates as Adults." *Phi Delta Kappan* 66 (December 1984): 250–64.

Branch, Taylor. *Parting the Waters: America in the King Years, 1954–63.* New York: Simon & Schuster, 1988.

Brewton, John. *Excellent Schools, Their Characteristics.* Columbia: Steering Committee of the Investigation of Educational Qualifications of Teachers in South Carolina, 1944.

Brown, Cynthia Stokes. *Ready from Within.* Navarro, Calif.: Wild Tree Press, 1986.

Brownlee, Fred Lee. *A New Day Ascending.* New York: Pilgrim Press, 1946.

Byrnes, James F. *All in One Lifetime.* New York: Harper, 1958.

Bullock, Henry Allen. *A History of Negro Education in the South from 1619 to the Present.* Cambridge, Mass.: Harvard University Press, 1967.

Bunche, Ralph J. *The Political Status of the Negro in the Age of FDR.* Chicago: University of Chicago Press, 1973.

Burke, W. Lewis, and Willam C. Hine, "The South Carolina State College Law School." In *Matthew J. Perry: The Man, His Times, and His Legacy,* edited by Burke and Belinda F. Gergel, 17–60. Columbia: University of South Carolina Press, 2004.

Caliver, Ambrose. "Certain Significant Developments in the Education of Negroes during the Past Generation." *Journal of Negro History* 35 (April 1950): 111–34.

Callahan, John. "American Culture Is of a Whole." *New Republic* 20 (March 1, 1999): 34–48.

Carter, Dan T. *The Politics of Rage: George Wallace, the Origins of the New Conservatism and the Transformation of American Politics.* Baton Rouge: Louisiana State University Press, 1995.

Cecelski, David S. *Along Freedom Road: Hyde County, North Carolina, and the Fate of Black Schools in the South.* Chapel Hill: University of North Carolina Press, 1994.

Cell, John W. *The Highest Stage of White Supremacy: The Origins of Segregation in South Africa and the American South.* New York: Cambridge University Press, 1982.

Chafe, William H. *Civilities and Civil Rights: Greensboro, North Carolina, and the Black Struggle for Freedom.* New York: Oxford University Press, 1980.

———. *The Unfinished Journey.* New York: Oxford University Press, 1995.

"Charleston Snobbish Aristocracy 'Passing' Out of Existence." *Ebony* 1 (October 1946): 17.

Clark, E. Culpepper. *The Schoolhouse Door: Segregation's Last Stand at the University of Alabama.* New York: Oxford University Press, 1993.

Clark, Septima. *Echo in My Soul.* New York: Dutton, 1962.

Cohodas, Nadine. *The Band Played Dixie: Race and the Liberal Conscience at Ole Miss.* New York: Free Press, 1997.

Colburn, David R. *Racial Change and Community Crisis, St. Augustine, Florida, 1877–1980.* Gainesville: University of Florida Press, 1991.

Coles, Robert. *Farewell to the South.* Boston: Little, Brown, 1972.

Comer, James. P. *Maggie's American Dream.* New York: New American Library, 1988.

Conant, James Bryant. *The Education of American Teachers.* New York: McGraw-Hill, 1963.

Cook, Blanche Wiesen. *Eleanor Roosevelt.* Vol. 2, *1933–1938.* New York: Viking, 1999.

Couch, William, Jr., "Rural Education in Mississippi." *Journal of Negro Education* 21 (Winter 1952): 226–28.

Crawford, Vicki L., Jacqueline Anne Rouse, and Barbara Woods, eds. *Women in the Civil Rights Movement: Trailblazers and Torchbearers, 1941–1965.* New York: Carlson, 1990.

Cremin, Lawrence A. *American Education: The Metropolitan Experience, 1876–1980.* New York: Harper & Row, 1988.

Cruse, Harold. *Plural But Equal: A Critical Study of Blacks and Minorities and America's Plural Society.* New York: Morrow, 1987.

Dailey, Jane, Glenda Elizabeth Gilmore, and Bryant Simon, eds. *Jumpin' Jim Crow: Southern Politics from Civil War to Civil Rights.* Princeton: Princeton University Press, 2000.

Daniel, J. McT. *Excellent Teachers.* Columbia: R. L. Bryan, 1944.

Daniel, Pete. "Going among Strangers: Southern Reactions to World War II." *Journal of American History* 77 (December 1990): 886–91.

Daniel, Walter G. "The Availability of Education for Negroes in the Secondary School." *Journal of Negro Education* 16 (Summer 1947): 450–58.

Davenport, Roy K. "A Background Study of a Negro College Freshman Population." *Journal of Negro Education* 8 (April 1939): 186–97.

Davis, Allison, and John Dollard. *Children of Bondage: The Personality Development of Negro Youth in the Urban South.* Washington D.C.: American Council on Education, 1940.

Davis, Thomas E. "A Study of Fisk University Freshman." *Journal of Negro Education* 2 (July 1933): 477–83.

DeCosta, Frank A. "The Education of Negroes in South Carolina." *Journal of Negro Education* 16 (1947): 405–16.

———. "Negro Higher and Professional Education in South Carolina." *Journal of Negro Education* 17 (1948): 350–60.

Dent, Tom. *Southern Journey: A Return to the Civil Rights Movement.* New York: Morrow, 1997.

Dewitt, Franklin R. *School of Law: South Carolina State College.* Orangeburg: By the author, 2002.

Diggs, Louise. *It All Started on Winters Lane: A History of the Black Community in Catonsville, Maryland.* Baltimore: By the author, 1995.

Dilworth, Mary. *Teacher's Totter: A Report on Teacher Certification Issues.* Washington, D.C.: Institute for the Study of Educational Policy, 1984.

Dittmer, John. *Local People: The Struggle for Civil Rights in Mississippi.* Urbana: University of Illinois Press, 1994.

Division of Surveys and Field Services. *Public Higher Education in South Carolina.* Nashville: George Peabody College for Teachers, Vanderbilt University, 1946.

———. *Public Schools of Charleston, South Carolina.* Nashville: George Peabody College for Teachers, Vanderbilt University, 1949.

Dollard, John. *Caste and Class in a Southern Town.* 3rd ed. Garden City, N.Y.: Doubleday, 1957.

Douglas, Davison M. *Reading, Writing, and Race: The Desegregation of the Charlotte Schools.* Chapel Hill: University of North Carolina Press, 1995.

Downey, Matthew T. *Ben D. Wood: Educational Reformer.* Princeton: Educational Testing Service, 1965.

Doyle, William. *An American Insurrection: The Battle of Oxford, Mississippi, 1962.* New York: Doubleday, 2001.

Drago, Edmund L. *Initiative, Paternalism, and Race Relations: Charleston's Avery Normal Institute.* Athens: University of Georgia Press, 1990.

Du Bois, W. E. B. *Dusk of Dawn.* New York: Harcourt Brace, 1940.

———. "A Negro Nation within the Nation." In *W. E. B. Du Bois Speaks: Speeches and Addresses, 1920–1960,* edited by Philip S. Foner. New York: Pathfinder Press, 1970.

DuBose, Louise Jones. *South Carolina Lives*. Hopkinsville, Ky.: Historical Record Association, 1963.

Duke, Daniel L. *The School That Refused to Die: Continuity and Change at Thomas Jefferson High School*. Albany: State University of New York Press, 1995.

Edgar, Walter B. *South Carolina: A History*. Columbia: University of South Carolina Press, 1998.

———, ed. *South Carolina: The W.P.A. Guide to the Palmetto State*. Columbia: University of South Carolina Press, 1988.

Educational Testing Service. *Annual Report, 1953–1954*. Princeton: Educational Testing Service, 1954.

———. *Annual Report, 1954–1955*. Princeton: Educational Testing Service, 1955.

———. *Annual Report, 1955–1956*. Princeton: Educational Testing Service, 1956.

———. *Annual Report, 1959–1960*. Princeton: Educational Testing Service, 1960.

Edwards, G. Franklin. *The Negro Professional Class*. New York: Free Press, 1959.

Egerton, John. *Speak Now against the Day: The Generation before the Civil Rights Movement in the South*. New York: Knopf, 1994.

Ellison, Ralph. *Invisible Man*. New York: Random House, 1952.

Embree, Edwin R., and Julia Waxman. *Investment in People*. New York: Harper, 1949.

Eskew, Glenn T. *But for Birmingham: The Local and National Movements in the Civil Rights Struggle*. Chapel Hill: University of North Carolina Press, 1997.

Estill, Harry F. *The Beginners History of Our Country*. Dallas: Southern Publishing, 1919.

Fairclough, Adam. "'Being in the Field of Education and Also Being a Negro . . . Seems . . . Tragic': Black Teachers in the Jim Crow South." *Journal of American History* 87 (June 2000): 65–91.

———. *A Better Day Coming: Blacks and Equality, 1890–2000*. New York: Viking, 2001.

———. "The Costs of *Brown*: Black Teachers and School Integration." *Journal of American History* 91 (June 2004): 43–55.

———. *Race and Democracy: The Civil Rights Struggle in Louisiana, 1915–1972*. Athens: University of Georgia Press, 1995.

———. *Teaching Equality: Black Schools in the Age of Jim Crow*. Athens: University of Georgia Press, 2001.

Fass, Paula S. *Outside In: Minorities and the Transformation of American Education*. New York: Oxford University Press, 1989.

Ferriss, Abbott. *Indicators of Trends in American Education*. New York: Russell Sage Foundation, 1969.

Fields, Mamie, with Karen Fields. *Lemon Swamp and Other Places: A Carolina Memoir*. New York: Free Press, 1983.

Fitchett, E. Horace. "The New Program for the Recertification of Teachers in South Carolina." *Journal of Negro Education* 15 (Autumn 1946): 703–16.

———. "The Role of Claflin College in Negro Life in South Carolina." *Journal of Negro Education* 12 (Winter 1943): 42–68.

Fleming, Jacqueline. *Blacks in College*. London: Jossey-Bass, 1988.

Folger, J. K. *The Future of College Enrollments in the Southern Region*. Atlanta: Southern Regional Education Board, 1954.

Fordham, Signithia. *Blacked Out: Dilemmas of Race, Identity, and Success at Capital High*. Chicago: University of Chicago Press, 1996.

Fordham, Signithia, and John U. Ogbu. "Black Students' School Success: Coping with the Burden of 'Acting White.'" *Urban Review* 18 (1986): 176–206.

Foucault, Michael. *Discipline and Punish: The Birth of the Modern Prison.* New York: Pantheon, 1977.

Fraser, Walter J., Jr. *Charleston! Charleston! The History of a Southern City.* Columbia: University of South Carolina Press, 1989.

Frazier, E. Franklin. *Black Bourgeoisie: The Rise of a New Middle Class in the United States.* New York: Free Press, 1957.

————. *Negro Youth at the Crossways.* Washington, D.C.: American Council on Education, 1940.

Fredrickson, George M. *White Supremacy: A Comparative Study in American and South African History.* New York: Oxford University Press, 1981.

Freeman, Richard B. *Black Elite: The New Market for Highly Educated Black Americans.* New York: McGraw-Hill, 1976.

Freyer, Tony. *The Little Rock Crisis.* Westport, Conn.: Greenwood Press, 1984.

Frick, H. L. *A Proposed Plan for the Certification of Teachers in South Carolina.* Columbia: State Co., 1944.

Friedman, Leon, ed. *Argument: The Oral Argument before the Supreme Court in Brown v. Board of Education of Topeka, 1952–55.* New York: Chelsea House, 1983.

Fultz, Michael. "The Displacement of Black Educators Post-*Brown:* An Overview and Analysis." *History of Education Quarterly* 41 (Spring 2004): 11–45.

Fuquay, Michael W. "Civil Rights and the Private School Movement in Mississippi, 1964–1971." *History of Education Quarterly* 42 (Summer 2002): 159–80.

Gaillard, Frye. *The Dream Long Deferred.* Chapel Hill: University of North Carolina Press, 1988.

Gaines, Kevin. "Whose Integration Was It? An Introduction." *Journal of American History* 91 (June 2004): 19–25.

Gamarekian, Edward. "The Ugly Battle of Orangeburg." *Reporter* 16 (January 25, 1957): 32–34.

Gardner, Howard. *The Disciplined Mind: What All Students Should Understand.* New York: Simon & Schuster, 1999.

Gardner, Sarah E. Foreword to *Teaching Equality: Black Schools in the Age of Jim Crow,* by Adam Fairclough. Athens: University of Georgia Press, 2001.

Garrow, David J., ed. *Atlanta, Georgia, 1960–1961.* New York: Carlson, 1981.

————. *Bearing the Cross: Martin Luther King, Jr., and the Southern Christian Leadership Conference.* New York: Morrow, 1986.

"General Discussion." *Quarterly Review of Higher Education among Negroes* 6 (October 1938): 254.

Genovese, Eugene D. *Roll Jordan Roll: The World the Slaves Made.* New York: Random House, 1972.

Gibson, Charles. *Industrial Education Survey.* Charleston: Walker, Evans & Cogswell, 1920.

Giddings, Paula. *When and Where I Enter: The Impact of Black Women on Race and Sex in America.* New York: Bantam, 1985.

Gilmore, Glenda Elizabeth. *Gender and Jim Crow: Women and the Politics of White Supremacy in North Carolina, 1896–1920.* Chapel Hill: University of North Carolina Press, 1986.

Ginsberg, Eli. *The Negro Potential.* New York: Columbia University Press, 1956.

Glen, John M. *Highlander: No Ordinary School, 1932–1962.* Lexington: University Press of Kentucky, 1988.

Goldfield, David R. *Black, White, and Southern: Race Relations and Southern Culture, 1940 to the Present*. Baton Rouge: Louisiana University Press, 1990.

Goodson, Martia G., ed. *Chronicles of Faith: The Autobiography of Frederick D. Patterson*. Tuscaloosa: University of Alabama Press, 1991.

Gordon, Asa H. *Sketches of Negro Life and History in South Carolina*. Columbia: University of South Carolina Press, 1971.

———. "South Carolina Negro Common Schools." *Crisis* 34 (December 1927): 330–32.

Gordon, William. "Boycotts Can Cut Two Ways." *New South* (April 1956): 5–10.

Granovetter, Mark. "The Micro-Structure of School Desegregation." In *School Desegregation Research*, edited by Jeffrey Prager, Douglas Longshore, and Melvin Seeman, 81–110. New York: Plenum Press, 1986.

Grant, Gerald. *The World We Created at Hamilton High*. Cambridge, Mass.: Harvard University Press, 1989.

Green, Constance McLaughlin. *The Secret City: A History of Race Relations in the Nation's Capital*. Princeton: Princeton University Press, 1967.

Greenberg, Jack. *Crusaders in the Courts: How a Dedicated Band of Lawyers Fought for the Civil Rights Revolution*. New York: Basic Books, 1994.

Greene, Harry W. *Holders of Doctorates among Negroes*. Boston: Meador, 1946.

Greer, William M. "The High School of Charleston: Ninety Eight Years of Service." *Southern Association Quarterly* 1 (November 1937): 1–4.

Halberstam, David. "A Good City Gone Ugly." In *Reporting Civil Rights*, 1:440–46. New York: Library of America, 2003.

Halpern, Stephen C. *On the Limits of the Law: The Ironic Legacy of Title VI of the 1964 Civil Rights Act*. Baltimore: Johns Hopkins University Press, 1995.

Haney, Walter, George Madaus, and Amelia Kreitzer. "Charms Talismanic: Testing Teachers for the Improvement of American Education." In *Review of Research in Education*, edited by Ernest Z. Rothkopf, 169–238. Washington, D.C.: American Educational Research Association, 1987.

Harlan, Louis R. *Separate and Unequal: Public School Campaigns and Racism in the Southern Seaboard States, 1901–1915*. New York: Atheneum, 1969.

Harvey, Gordon E. *A Question of Justice: New South Governors and Education, 1968–1976*. Tuscaloosa: University of Alabama Press, 2002.

Herskovits, Melville J. *Myth of the Negro Past*. New York: Harper and Brothers, 1941.

Hine, Darlene Clark, ed. *The State of Afro-American History: Past, Present, and Future*. Baton Rouge: Louisiana State University Press, 1986.

Hine, William C. "Civil Rights and Campus Wrongs: South Carolina State College Students Protest, 1955–1968." *South Carolina Historical Magazine* 97 (October 1996): 310–33.

———. "South Carolina State College: A Legacy of Education and Public Service." *Agricultural History* 65 (1991): 149–67.

———. "South Carolina's Challenge to Civil Rights: The Case of South Carolina State College, 1945–1954." *Agriculture and Human Values* 9 (Winter 1992): 38–50.

Hoffman, Erwin D. "The Genesis of the Modern Movement for Equal Rights in South Carolina, 1930–1939." In *The Negro in Depression and War: Prelude to Revolution, 1930–1945*, edited by Bernard Sternsher, 193–214. Chicago: Quadrangle, 1969.

Holt, Thomas. *Black over White: Negro Political Leadership in South Carolina during Reconstruction*. Chicago: University of Illinois Press, 1979.

Houston, Charles. "A Challenge to Negro College Youth." *Crisis* 45 (January 1938): 14–15.

———. "Cracking Closed University Doors." *Crisis* 43 (March 1936): 364–72.

———. "Educational Inequalities Must Go!" *Crisis* 42 (October 1935): 300–316.

———. "Enrollment in Negro Colleges and Universities." *School and Society* 50 (July 29, 1939): 141.

———. "How to Fight for Better Schools." *Crisis* 43 (February 1936): 52–59.

Hunter, E. C. *Education of Teachers.* Columbia: University of South Carolina Press, 1944.

Hunter-Gault, Charlayne. Foreword to *Maggie's American Dream,* by James P. Comer. New York: New American Library, 1988.

———. *In My Place.* New York: Farrar Straus Giroux, 1992.

Irons, Peter. *Jim Crow's Children: The Broken Promise of the Brown Decision.* New York: Viking, 2002.

Irvine, Jordan Jacqueline, and Michele Foster, eds. *Growing Up African-American in Catholic Schools.* New York: Teachers College Press, 1996.

Jackson, Reid E. "Financial Aid Given by Southern States to Negroes for Out-of-State-Study." *Journal of Negro Education* 13 (Winter 1944): 30–39.

Jacoway, Elizabeth, and R. David Colburn. *Southern Businessmen and Desegregation.* Baton Rouge: Louisiana State University Press, 1982.

Janken, Robert Kenneth. *White: The Biography of Walter White, Mr. NAACP.* New York: New Press, 2003.

Jaynes, Gerald David, and Robin M. Williams, eds. *A Common Destiny: Blacks and American Society.* Washington, D.C.: National Academy Press, 1989.

Jencks, Christopher, and David Riesman. *The Academic Revolution.* Garden City, N.Y.: Doubleday, 1968.

Jenkins, Martin D. "The Availability of Higher Education for Negroes in Southern States." *Journal of Negro Education* 16 (Summer 1947): 459–73.

Johnson, Charles S. *Growing Up in the Black Belt: Negro Youth in the Rural South.* Washington, D.C.: American Council on Education, 1941.

———. *The Negro College Graduate.* Chapel Hill: University of North Carolina Press, 1938.

———. *The Negro in American Civilization.* New York: Holt, 1930.

———. "Present Trends in the Employment of Negro Labor." *Opportunity* 7 (April 1929): 146–48.

———. *Shadow of the Plantation.* Chicago: University of Chicago Press, 1934.

Johnson, Daniel M., and Rex R. Campbell, *Black Migration in America: A Social and Demographic History.* Durham: Duke University Press, 1981.

Johnson, Guy B. "A Letter from Guy Johnson." *Crisis* 46 (September 1939): 271.

Jones, Faustine C. *A Traditional Model of Educational Excellence: Dunbar High School of Little Rock, Arkansas.* Washington, D.C.: Howard University Press, 1981.

Jones-Jackson, Patricia. *When Roots Die: Endangered Traditions on the Sea Islands.* Athens: University of Georgia Press, 1987.

Joyner, Charles. Foreword to *When Roots Die,* by Patricia Jones-Jackson. Athens: University of Georgia Press, 1987.

Kaestle, Carl F., and others. *Literacy in the United States: Readers and Reading since 1880.* New Haven, Conn.: Yale University Press, 1991.

Kantrowitz, Stephen. *Ben Tillman and the Reconstruction of White Supremacy.* Chapel Hill: University of North Carolina Press, 2000.

Karl, Donald S. *The College Handbook.* New York: College Entrance Examination Board, 1959–1961.

———. *The College Handbook.* New York: College Entrance Examination Board, 1963–1965.

Katznelson, Ira, and Margaret S. Weir. *Schooling For All: Class, Race, and the Decline of the Democratic Ideal.* New York: Basic Books, 1985.

Keller, William H. *Make Haste Slowly.* College Station: Texas A & M Press, 1999.

Kelley, Robin D. G. "We Are Not What We Seem: Rethinking Black Working-Class Opposition in the Jim Crow South." *Journal of American History* 80 (June 1993): 75–112.

Key, V. O., Jr. *Southern Politics in State and Nation.* New York: Random House, 1949.

King, Martin Luther, Jr. "The Case against Tokenism." *New York Times Magazine,* August 5, 1962, 11.

King, Sabrina Hope. "The Limited Presence of African American Teachers." *Review of Educational Research* 63 (Summer 1993): 115–49.

Kiser, Clyde Vernon. *Sea Island to City: A Study of St. Helena Islanders in Harlem and Other Urban Centers.* New York: Atheneum, 1969.

Klarman, Michael J. *From Jim Crow to Civil Rights: The Supreme Court and the Struggle for Racial Equality.* New York: Oxford University Press, 2004.

———. "How *Brown* Changed Race Relations: The Backlash Thesis." *Journal of American History* 81 (June 1994): 81–118.

Kluger, Richard. *Simple Justice: The History of Brown v. Board of Education and Black America's Struggle for Equality.* New York: Knopf, 1975.

Kousser, J. Morgan. *The Shaping of Southern Politics: Suffrage Restriction and the Establishment of the One-Party South, 1880–1910.* New Haven, Conn.: Yale University Press, 1974.

Ladino, Robyn D. *Desegregating Texas Schools.* Austin: University of Texas Press, 1996.

Lagemann, Ellen Condliffe. *An Elusive Science: The Troubling History of Education Research.* Chicago: University of Chicago Press, 2000.

———. *Private Power for the Public Good: A History of the Carnegie Foundation for the Advancement of Teaching.* Middletown, Conn.: Wesleyan University Press, 1983.

Lassiter, Matthew B., and Andrew B. Lewis, eds. *The Moderates' Dilemma.* Charlottesville: University Press of Virginia, 1998.

Lawson, Stephen F. *Black Ballots: Voting Rights in the South.* New York: Cambridge University Press, 1976.

Leidholdt, Alexander. *Standing before a Shouting Mob.* Tuscaloosa: University of Alabama Press, 1997.

Leloudis, James L. *Schooling the New South: Pedagogy, Self, and Society in North Carolina, 1880–1920.* Chapel Hill: University of North Carolina Press, 1996.

Lemann, Nicholas. *The Big Test: The Secret History of the American Meritocracy.* New York: Farrar, Straus & Giroux, 1999.

Lesesne, Henry H. *A History of the University of South Carolina, 1940–2000.* Columbia: University of South Carolina Press, 2001.

Levine, David O. *The American College and the Culture of Aspiration, 1915–1940.* Ithaca, N.Y.: Cornell University Press, 1986.

———. "Discrimination in College Admissions." In *The History of Higher Education,* edited by Lester F. Goodchild and Harold S. Wechsler, 510–27. Needham Heights, Mass.: Simon & Schuster, 1997.

Levine, Lawrence. *Black Culture and Consciousness: Afro-American Thought from Slavery to Freedom*. New York: Oxford University Press, 1977.

Lewis, David L. "The Origins and Causes of the Civil Rights Movement." In *The Civil Rights Movement in America*, edited by Charles W. Eagles, 3–17. Jackson: University of Mississippi Press, 1986.

Lewis, Earl. *In Their Own Interests: Race, Class, and Power in Twentieth-Century Norfolk, Virginia*. Berkeley: University of California Press, 1991.

Lewis, John, with Michael D'Orso. *Walking with the Wind: A Memoir of the Movement*. New York: Simon & Schuster, 1998.

Lindley, Betty, and Earnest K. *A New Deal for Youth*. New York: Viking Press, 1938.

Lomotey, Kofi, ed. *Going to School: The African-American Experience*. Albany: State University of New York Press, 1990.

Lucas, J. Anthony. *Common Ground: A Turbulent Decade in the Lives of Three American Families*. New York: Vintage, 1986.

Manegold, Catherine S. *In Glory's Shadow: Shannon Faulkner, the Citadel, and a Changing America*. New York: Knopf, 2000.

Margo, Robert A. *Race and Schooling in the South, 1880–1950: An Economic History*. Chicago: University of Chicago Press, 1990.

Marshall, Thurgood. "An Evaluation of Recent Efforts to Achieve Racial Integration in Education through Resort to the Courts." *Journal of Negro Education* 21 (Summer 1952): 316–27.

———. "The Legal Battle." *NAACP Branch Bulletin* 1 (April 1943): 1.

Martin, Frank C., II, and others. *South Carolina State University*. Charleston: Arcadia, 2000.

Martin, John Bartlow. *The Deep South Says "Never."* New York: Ballantine, 1957.

Massey, Douglas S., and Nancy A. Denton, *American Apartheid: Segregation and the Making of the Underclass*. Cambridge, Mass.: Harvard University Press, 1993.

Mays, Benjamin E. *Born to Rebel: An Autobiography*. New York: Scribners, 1971.

McAdam, Doug. *Political Process and the Development of Black Insurgency, 1930–1970*. Chicago: University of Chicago Press, 1982.

McCauley, Patrick, and Edward Ball, eds. *Southern Schools: Progress and Problems*. Nashville: Southern Education Reporting Service, 1959.

McCuistion, Fred. *The South's Negro Teaching Force*. Nashville: Julius Rosenwald Fund, 1931.

McMillan, George. "Integration with Dignity." *Saturday Evening Post* 236 (March 16, 1963): 16–21.

McMillan, Lewis. *Negro Higher Education in the State of South Carolina*. Orangeburg, S.C.: By the author, 1952.

McMillen, Neil R. *Dark Journey: Black Mississippians in the Age of Jim Crow*. Chicago: University of Illinois Press, 1989.

McNeil, Genna Rea. "Community Initiative in the Desegregation of the District of Columbia Schools, 1947–1954." *Howard Law Journal* 23 (1980): 25–41.

———. *Groundwork: Charles Hamilton Houston and the Struggle for Civil Rights*. Philadelphia: University of Pennsylvania Press, 1983.

McNeil, Jim. *Charleston's Naval Yard*. Charleston, S.C.: Naval Civilian Administration Association, 1985.

McNeil, Linda M. *Contradictions of School Reform: The Educational Costs of Standardzied Testing*. New York: Routledge, 2000.

McPherson, James M. *The Abolitionist Legacy: From Reconstruction to the NAACP*. Princeton: Princeton University Press, 1975.

Meffert, John, Sherman Pyatt, and the Avery Research Center. *Charleston, South Carolina.* Charleston: Arcadia Publishing, 2000.

Meier, August, and Elliott Rudwick. *Along the Color Line: Explorations in the Black Experience.* Urbana: University of Illinois Press, 1976.

———. *CORE.* New York: Oxford University Press, 1973.

Meier, Kenneth J., Joseph Stewart Jr., and Robert E. England. *Race, Class, and Education: The Politics of Second-Generation Discrimination.* Madison: University of Wisconsin Press, 1989.

Minchin, Timothy J. *Hiring the Black Worker: Racial Integration in the Southern Textile Industry, 1960–1980.* Chapel Hill: University of North Carolina Press, 1999.

Mizell, Hays. "School Desegregation in South Carolina." *Integrated Education* 4 (December/January 1966/1967): 30.

Mohr, Clarence L., and Joseph E. Gordan. *Tulane: The Emergence of a Modern University, 1945–1980.* Baton Rouge: Louisiana State University Press, 2001.

Monti, Daniel J. *A Semblance of Justice: St. Louis School Desegregation and Order in Urban America.* Columbia: University of Missouri Press, 1985.

Moore, F. Henderson. "School Desegregation." In *The Angry Black South*, edited by Glenford E. Mitchell and William H. Peace, 51–72. New York: Corinth Books, 1962.

Morris, Aldon D. *The Origins of the Civil Rights Movement: Black Communities Organizing for Change.* New York: Free Press, 1984.

Murray, Florence. *The Negro Handbook.* New York: Current Reference Publications, 1947.

Myrdal, Gunnar. *An American Dilemma: The Negro Problem and Modern Democracy.* New York: Harper and Row, 1944.

Naipaul, V. S. *A Turn in the South.* New York: Knopf, 1989.

Navasky, Victor. *Kennedy Justice.* New York: Atheneum, 1971.

Nieman, Donald G. *Promises to Keep: African Americans and the Constitutional Order, 1796 to the Present.* New York: Oxford University Press, 1991.

Nelson, Stephen. *Charleston Looks at Its Services for Negroes.* Charleston: Charleston Welfare Council, 1947.

Newbold, N. C. "The Public Education of Negroes and the Current Depression." *Journal of Negro Education* 2 (January 1933): 5–15.

Newby, I. A. *Black Carolinians: A History of Blacks in South Carolina from 1895 to 1968.* Columbia: University of South Carolina Press, 1973.

Norrell, Robert J. *Reaping the Whirlwind: The Civil Rights Movement in Tuskegee.* New York: Random House, 1985.

Olsen, Keith W. *The G.I. Bill, the Veterans, and the Colleges.* Lexington: University Press of Kentucky, 1973.

Oppenheimer, Martin. *The Sit-in Movement.* New York: Carlson, 1990.

Orazem, Peter F. "Black-White Differences in Schooling Investment and Human Capital Production in Segregated Schools." *American Economic Review* 77 (September 1987): 714–23.

Orfield, Gary, and Susan E. Eaton. *Dismantling Desegregation: The Quiet Reversal of Brown v. Board of Education.* New York: New Press, 1996.

Orser, W. Edward. "Neither Separate or Equal: Foreshadowing *Brown* in Baltimore County, 1935–1937." *Maryland Historical Magazine* 92 (Spring 1997): 5–35.

Paddock, George. "Avery Institute." *American Missionary* 79 (May 1925): 64–65.

Patterson, James T. *Brown v. Board of Education: A Civil Rights Milestone and Its Troubled Legacy.* New York: Oxford University Press, 2001.

Perman, Michael. *Struggle for Mastery: Disenfranchisement in the South, 1880–1908.* Chapel Hill: University of North Carolina Press, 2001.

Peters, William. "A Southern Success Story." *Redbook* 115 (June 1960): 41–105.

Peterson, Paul E. *The Politics of School Reform, 1870–1940.* Chicago: University of Chicago Press, 1985.

Pierce, Truman M., and others. *White and Negro Schools in the South.* Englewood Cliffs, N.J.: Prentice-Hall, 1955.

Pilley, John G. "The National Teacher Examination Service." *School Review* 49 (March 1941): 180.

Potts, John. *A History of South Carolina State College.* Orangeburg: South Carolina State College, 1978.

Powdermaker, Hotense. *After Freedom: A Cultural Study of the Deep South.* New York: Viking Press, 1939.

Powledge, Fred. *Free at Last? The Civil Rights Movement and the People Who Made It.* Boston: Little, Brown, 1991.

Pratt, Robert A. *The Color of Their Skin: Education and Race in Richmond, Virginia, 1954–89.* Charlottesville: University Press of Virginia, 1992.

———. *We Shall Not Be Moved: The Desegregation of the University of Georgia.* Athens: University of Georgia Press, 2002.

Preer, Jean L. *Lawyers v. Educators: Black Colleges and Desegregation in Public Higher Education.* Westport, Conn.: Greenwood Press, 1982.

Pride, Richard A., and J. David Woodward. *The Burden of Busing: The Politics of Desegregation in Nashville, Tennessee.* Knoxville: University of Tennessee Press, 1985.

Quint, Howard. *Profile in Black and White: A Frank Portrait of South Carolina.* Washington, D.C.: Public Affairs Press, 1958.

Ransom, Leon. "Education and the Law." *Journal of Negro Education* 11 (October 1942): 568–70.

Raper, Arthur F. *Preface to Peasantry: A Tale of Two Black Belt Counties.* Chapel Hill: University of North Carolina Press, 1936.

Ravitch, Diane. *Left Back: A Century of Failed School Reforms.* New York: Simon & Schuster, 2000.

———. *The Troubled Crusade: American Education, 1945–1980.* New York: Basic Books, 1983.

Reed, Merl E. *Seedtime for the Modern Civil Rights Movement: The President's Committee on Fair Employment Practice, 1941–1946.* Baton Rouge: Louisiana State University Press, 1991.

Reid, Ira De A. "Lily-White Labor." *Opportunity* 7 (June 1930): 170–73.

Reporting Civil Rights. Part 1, *American Journalism, 1941–1963.* New York: Library of America, 2003.

Robinson, Armstead L., and Patricia Sullivan, eds. *New Directions in Civil Rights Studies.* Charlottesville: University Press of Virginia, 1991.

Robinson, Dorothy Redus. *Bell Rings at Four: A Black Teacher's Chronicle of Change.* Austin, Tex.: Madronna Press, 1987.

Robinson, Jo Ann Gibson. *The Montgomery Bus Boycott and the Women Who Started It.* Knoxville: University of Tennessee Press, 1987.

Roche, Jeff. *Restructured Resistance: The Silbey Commission and the Politics of Desegregation in Georgia.* Athens: University of Georgia Press, 1998.

Rogers, Frederick A. *The Black High School and Its Community.* Lexington, Mass.: D. C. Heath, 1975.

Rogers, George C., Jr. *Generations of Lawyers: A History of the South Carolina Bar.* Columbia: South Carolina Bar Foundation, 1992.

Rosenberg, Gerald N. *The Hollow Hope: Can Courts Bring About Social Change?* Chicago: University of Chicago, 1991.

Rousseve, Charles Barthelemy. *The Negro in Louisiana.* New Orleans: Xavier University Press, 1937.

Rowan, Carl T. *Dream Makers, Dream Breakers: The World of Justice Thurgood Marshall.* Boston: Little, Brown, 1993.

———. *South of Freedom.* New York: Knopf, 1952.

Sass, Herbert Ravenel. *Charleston Grows: An Economic, Social, and Cultural Portrait of an Old Community in the New South.* Charleston: Carolina Art Association, 1949.

Schlesinger, Arthur, M., Jr. *The Politics of Upheaval.* Boston: Houghton Mifflin, 1960.

———. *A Thousand Days: John F. Kennedy in the White House.* Boston: Houghton Mifflin, 1965.

Shabazz, Amilcar. *Advancing Democracy: African Americans and the Struggle for Access and Equity in Higher Education in Texas.* Chapel Hill: University of North Carolina Press, 2004.

Shaw, Stephanie J. *What a Woman Ought to Do: Black Professional Women Workers during the Jim Crow Era.* Chicago: University of Chicago Press, 1996.

Sherwood, Grace. *The Oblates: One Hundred and One Years.* New York: Macmillan, 1931.

Shoemaker, Don, ed. *With All Deliberate Speed: Segregation-Desegregation in Southern Schools.* New York: Harper, 1957.

Simms, Lois Averetta. *A Chalk and Chalkboard Career in Carolina.* New York: Vantage, 1995.

Sitkoff, Harvard. *A New Deal for Blacks: The Emergence of Civil Rights as a National Issue.* Vol. 1, *The Depression Decade.* New York: Oxford University Press, 1978.

———. *The Struggle for Black Equality, 1954–1980.* New York: Hill & Wang, 1981.

Sitton, Claude. "Negro Sitdowns Stir Fear of Wider Unrest in the South." In *Reporting Civil Rights,* 1:433–39. New York: Library of America, 2003.

Smith, Bob. *They Closed Their Schools: Prince Edward County, Virginia, 1951–1964.* Chapel Hill: University of North Carolina Press, 1965.

Smith, James P. "Race and Human Capital: A Reply." *American Economic Review* 76 (December 1976): 1225–29.

"South Carolina Fights Illiteracy." *National Negro Digest* (circa 1940): 12–52.

Southern Education Reporting Service. *A Statistical Summary of School Segregation-Desegregation.* Nashville: Southern Education Reporting Service, 1965.

Sowell, Thomas. "Black Excellence—the Case of Dunbar High School." *Public Interest* 35 (1974): 3–21.

Sproat, John G. "Firm Flexibility: Perspectives on Desegregation in South Carolina." In *New Perspectives on Race and Slavery in America: Essays in Honor of Kenneth Stampp,* edited by Robert Abzug and Stephen Maizlish, 164–84. Lexington: University of Kentucky Press, 1986.

Statistics for the Sixties: Higher Education in the South. Atlanta: Southern Regional Education Board, 1963.

Stein, Judith. *The World of Marcus Garvey: Race, Class and Modern Society.* Baton Rouge: Louisiana State University Press, 1986.

Sterner, Richard. *The Negro's Share: A Study of Income, Consumption, Housing, and Public Assistance.* New York: Harper and Brothers, 1943.

Sternsher, Bernard, ed. *The Negro in Depression and War.* Chicago: Quadrangle, 1969.

Stevens, Robert B. *Law School: Legal Education in America from the 1850s to the 1980s.* Chapel Hill: University of North Carolina Press, 1983.

Stoltz, Robert. *Emerging Patterns for Teacher Education and Certification in the South.* Atlanta: South Regional Educational Board, 1981.

Sullivan, Patricia. *Days of Hope: Race and Democracy in the New Deal Era.* Chapel Hill: University of North Carolina Press, 1996.

Swanson, Christopher B. "Sketching a Portrait of Public High School Graduation: Who Graduates and Who Doesn't." In *Droupouts in America,* edited by Gary Orfield, 13–40. Cambridge, Mass.: Harvard Educational Press, 2004.

Synnott, Marcia G. "Desegregation in South Carolina, 1950–1963: Sometime between 'Now' and 'Never.'" In *Looking South: Chapters in the Story of an American Region,* edited by Winfred B. Moore Jr. and Joseph F. Tripp, 51–64. New York: Greenwood Press, 1989.

Taeuber, Karl E., and Alma F. Tauber. *Negroes in Cities: Residential Segregation and Neighborhood Change.* New York: Atheneum, 1969.

Thomas, William B. "Black Intellectuals, Intelligence Testing in the 1930s, and the Sociology of Knowledge." *Teachers College Record* 85 (1984): 496–531.

Thompson, Charles H. "Current Events of Importance in Negro Education: The Effect of the Depression upon Educational Activities among Negroes." *Journal of Negro Education* 2 (January 1933): 117–18.

———. "Editorial Note." *Journal of Negro Education* 4 (July 1935): 289–92.

———. "Editorial Note: Negro Higher and Professional Education in the United States." *Journal of Negro Education* 17 (Summer 1948): 221–23.

Tindall, George B. *The Emergence of the New South, 1913–1945.* Baton Rouge: Louisiana University Press, 1967.

———. *South Carolina Negroes: 1877–1900.* Columbia: University of South Carolina Press, 1952.

Trillin, Calvin. *An Education in Georgia: Charlayne Hunter, Hamilton Holmes, and the Integration of the University of Georgia.* Athens: University of Georgia, 1991.

Turner, Lorenzo D. *Africanisms in the Gullah Dialect.* Chicago: University of Chicago Press, 1949.

Tushnet, Mark V. *Making Civil Rights Law: Thurgood Marshall and the Supreme Court, 1936–1961.* New York: Oxford University Press, 1994.

———. *The NAACP's Legal Strategy against Segregated Education, 1925–1950.* Chapel Hill: University of North Carolina Press, 1987.

Twig, Edward. "Charleston: The Great Myth." *Forum and Century* 103 (January 1940): 7.

Twining, Mary A., and Keith E. Baird. *Sea Island Roots: African Presence in the Carolinas and Georgia.* Trenton, N.J.: Africa World Press, 1991.

Tyack, David, Elizabeth Hansot, and Robert Lowe. *Public Schools in Hard Times: The Great Depression and Recent Years.* Cambridge, Mass.: Harvard University Press, 1984.

Vance, Rupert C. *All These People: The Nation's Human Resources in the South.* Chapel Hill: University of North Carolina Press, 1945.

Wadelington, Charles W., and Richard F. Knapp, *Charlotte Hawkins Brown and Palmer Memorial Institute.* Chapel Hill: University of North Carolina Press, 1999.

Walker, Vanessa Siddle. *Their Highest Potential: An African American School Community in the Segregated South.* Chapel Hill: University of North Carolina Press, 1996.

Warren, Earl. *The Memoirs of Earl Warren*. Garden City, N.Y.: Doubleday, 1977.

Washington, Harold R. "Comment: History and Role of Black Law Schools." *Howard Law Journal* 18 (1974): 385–421.

Webster, David S., Russell L. Stockard, and James W. Henson. "Black Student Elite: Enrollment Shifts of High-Achieving, High Socio-Economic Status Black Students from Black to White Colleges during the 1970s." *College and University* 56 (Spring 1981): 283–91.

Weiss, Nancy J. *Farewell to the Party of Lincoln: Black Politics in the Age of FDR*. Princeton: Princeton University Press, 1983.

Wells, Amy Stuart, and Robert L. Crain. *Stepping over the Color Line: African American Students in White Suburban Schools*. New Haven, Conn.: Yale University Press, 1997.

Westbrook, Robert B. *John Dewey and American Democracy*. Ithaca, N.Y.: Cornell University Press, 1991.

Wilkinson, J. Harvie. *From Brown to Bakke: The Supreme Court and School Integration, 1954–1978*. New York: Oxford University Press, 1979.

Williams, Cecil J. *Freedom and Justice: Four Decades of Civil Rights Struggle as Seen by a Black Photographer of the Deep South*. Macon: Mercer University Press, 1995.

Williams, Juan. *Thurgood Marshall: American Revolutionary*. New York: Times Books, 1998.

Wilson, William Julius. *The Declining Significance of Race: Blacks and Changing American Institutions*. Chicago: Chicago University Press, 1978.

———. *The Truly Disadvantaged: The Inner City, the Underclass, and Public Policy*. Chicago: University of Chicago Press, 1987.

Windham, Douglas M. *Education, Equality, and Income*. Lexington, Mass.: Heath Lexington Books, 1970.

Wise, W. Max. *They Come for the Best of Reasons: College Students Today*. Washington, D.C.: American Council on Education, 1958.

Wolf, Eleanor P. *Trial and Error: The Detroit School Segregation Case*. Detroit: Wayne State University Press, 1981.

Wolters, Raymond. *The Burden of Brown: Thirty Years of School Desegregation*. Knoxville: University of Tennessee Press, 1984.

Wood, Ben D. *An Announcement of a Teacher Examination Service*. New York: National Committee on Teacher Examinations of the American Council on Education, 1939.

———. "Dr. Wood's Statement." *Progressive Education* 17 (March 1940): 155–56.

———. "Making Use of the Objective Examination as a Phase of Teacher Selection." *Harvard Educational Review* 10 (May 1940): 278.

Wood, Ben D., and F. S. Beers. "Knowledge versus Thinking?" *Teachers College Record* 37 (March 1936): 487–99.

Woodson, Carter G. *The Mis-Education of the Negro*. Washington, D.C.: Associated Publishers, 1969.

Woodward, C. Vann. "*Strange Career* Critics: Long May They Persevere." *Journal of American History* 75 (December 1988): 857–68.

———. *The Strange Career of Jim Crow*. New York: Oxford University Press, 1957.

Woolfolk, George R. *Prairie View: A Study in Public Conscience, 1878–1946*. New York: Pageant Press, 1982.

Wright, Richard. *Black Boy*. New York: Harper, 1945.

Yarbrough, Tinsley E. *A Passion For Justice: J. Waties Waring and Civil Rights*. New York: Oxford University Press, 1987.

Dissertations, Theses, and Unpublished Works

Aba-Mecha, Barbara. "Black Woman Activist in Twentieth Century South Carolina: Modjeska Monteith Simkins." Ph.D. diss., Emory University, 1978.

Bradley, Josephine Ophelia Boyd. "Wearing My Name: School Desegregation, Greensboro, North Carolina, 1954–1958." Ph.D. diss., Emory University, 1995.

Brown, Aaron. "An Evaluation of the Accredited Secondary Schools for Negroes in the South." Ph.D. diss., University of Chicago, 1944.

Brown, Millicent E. "Civil Rights Activism in Charleston, South Carolina, 1940–1970." Ph.D. diss., Florida State University, 1997.

Brown, Titus. "African American Education in Central Georgia: Ballard Normal School." Ph.D. diss., Florida State University, 1995.

Cann, Marvin. "Burnett Maybank and the New Deal in South Carolina, 1931–1941." Ph.D. diss., University of South Carolina, 1967.

Carrere, Thomas. "A Study of the Power Structure of a Selected S.C. County." Ph.D. diss., University of South Carolina, 1972.

Cox, Maxie Myron. "1963—The Year of Decision: Desegregation in South Carolina." Ph.D. diss., University of South Carolina, 1996.

Duffy, Joseph. "Charleston Politics in the Progressive Era." Ph.D. diss., University of South Carolina, 1963.

Hamer, Fritz P. "A Southern City Enters the Twentieth Century: Charleston, Its Navy Yard, and World War II, 1940–1948." Ph.D. diss., University of South Carolina, 1998.

Hayes, Jack. "South Carolina and the New Deal." Ph.D. diss., University of South Carolina, 1972.

Hemenway, Theodore. "Beneath the Yoke of Bondage." Ph.D. diss., University of South Carolina, 1976.

Holland, Davis Rutledge. "A History of the Desegregation Moment in the South Carolina Public Schools during the Period 1954–1976." Ph.D. diss., Florida State University, 1978.

Jones, Butler Alfo. "Law and Social Change: A Study of the Impact of New Legal Requirements Affecting Equality of Educational Opportunities for Negroes." Ph.D. diss., New York University, 1955.

Lochbaum, Julie M. "The World Made Flesh: The Desegregation Leadership of the Rev. J. A. DeLaine." Ph.D. diss., University of South Carolina, 1993.

Lowe, Stephen H. "The Magnificent Fight: Civil Rights Litigation in South Carolina Federal Courts, 1940–1970." Ph.D. diss., Michigan State University, 1999.

Moore, Burchill Richardson. "A History of Negro Public Schools of Charleston, South Carolina, 1867–1942." Master's thesis, University of South Carolina, 1942.

O'Neill, Stephen. "From the Shadow of Slavery: The Civil Rights Years in Charleston." Ph.D. diss., University of Virginia, 1994.

Seacrest, Andrew. "In Black and White: Press Opinion and Race Relations in South Carolina, 1954–1964." Ph.D. diss., Duke University, 1972.

Simmons, J. Andrew. "Professional and Cultural Background of the Teachers in South Carolina High Schools for Negroes." Master's thesis, Columbia University, 1934.

Synnott, Marcia. "Desegregation in South Carolina, 1950–1963." Paper presented at the Fifth Citadel Conference on the South, the Citadel, Charleston, S.C., April 10, 1987.

Terry, Robert Lewis. "J. Waties Waring, Spokesman for Racial Justice in the New South." Ph.D. diss., University of Utah, 1970.

Warlick, Kenneth Ray. "Practical Education and the Negro College in North Carolina, 1880–1930." Ph.D. diss., University of North Carolina, 1980.

Wilson, Ann E. Jarvella. "Knowledge for Teachers: The National Teacher Examination Program, 1940 to 1970." Ph.D. diss., University of Wisconsin, 1984.

INDEX

University of Mississippi, 135, 139–40,
   147–48
University of Missouri: law school, 31–33;
   journalism school, 70
University of North Carolina, 33
University of Pennsylvania, 40, 65
University of South Carolina, xxi, xxii, 56,
   175; African American applications for
   admission in the 1950s, 121, 123, 130;
   African American enrollment in 1970,
   149; enrollment in 1940s and 1950s,
   130, 133; desegregation of, 139, 149,
   176; law school, 31–32, 53, 62, 63–4, 76,
   78–85, 95; Scholastic Aptitude Scores of
   students in 1970, 179
University of Virginia, 24

Van den Haag, Ernest, 155
Vanderbilt University, survey of South
   Carolina State College, 73–74
Veal, Frank, 123
Vinson, Frederick Moore, 83
Virginia, xxii, 30, 31; college entrance
   requirements in 134; desegregation of
   higher-education in, 140; NAACP challenges to segregation in, 94; opposition
   to desegregation in, 127; salary-equalization campaign in, 46–48, 54; segregation
   committee in, 94

Walker, Vanessa Siddle, 7
Wallace, George, xv
Wallace, O. T., 69
Waring, J. Waties, xvii; biography of, 54–55;
   higher education rulings, 78–79, 82; role
   in *Briggs v. Elliott* (1951), 93, 95, 97–99;
   teacher equalization rulings, 54–55, 57
Waring, Thomas R., 102, 110, 138; accep-
   tance of desegregation, 147; on desegre-
   gation of University of South Carolina,
   132; opposition to desegregation in
   Charleston, 159–61; support for Citi-
   zens' Councils, 111–12; support for pri-
   vate schools in Charleston, 159–61
Warlick, Kenneth R., 71
Washington, D.C., 20, 29, 87, 136
Welch, Aubrey, 1
Wells, Reverdy, 92
West Virginia, 31, 62; diploma privilege in,
   84

Whipper, Lucille, xiii, 172, 175
White, Mary Lou, 142–43
White, Walter, 1, 46, 48, 54, 61, 114
white flight, 90, 159–61, 166
white supremacy, xv, xvii, xxiii, 22, 23, 36,
   39; new system of white supremacy, 51
Whitehead, Matthew, 96,
Whittaker, Miller F., 32, 72–74, 80
Wigfall, Alma, 172–73
Wilkerson, Doxey, 17, 45
Wilkerson High School, 141
Wilkins, Roy, 34, 114, 119, 122–26; sup-
   port for sit-ins and demonstrations in
   Charleston, 146, 150–53
Williams, Cecil J., xiii
Williams, James L., 149
Williams, W. L., 131
Wilmington, Delaware, 136
Wilson, William Julius, 175
Winthrop College, 56
Wood, Ben D., 44; early life and education,
   48; marketing the National Teacher
   Examination in the South, 49–50; in
   South Carolina, 51–52, 56–58, 61
Woodward, C. Vann, 139–40
Woolfolk, George R., 117
Workman, W. D., 98, 102, 109, 149
World War II, xxi, 35, 73, 82; African
   American veterans, 66, 77, 98; campaign
   for Double V, 36, 42; economic impact
   on African Americans, 88–89; GI Bill, 63,
   72
Wrighten, John H.: application to Uni-
   versity of South Carolina Law School,
   76–77; campaign to desegregate the College of Charleston, 66–70; early life and
   education, 63–66; as law student at
   South Carolina State, 82–83; legal advisor to Charleston branch of the NAACP,
   85, 110, 143; relationship with NAACP
   lawyers, 80–82; as student at South
   Carolina State College, 71, 75–76
Wrighten v. Board of Trustees, 78

Xavier, 76

Yarbrough, Tinsley E., 55
Young, Clinton, 105

ABOUT THE AUTHOR

R. SCOTT BAKER is an associate professor of education at Wake Forest University. A former high school teacher and literacy coordinator, he lives in Lewisville, North Carolina.

CPSIA information can be obtained at www.ICGtesting.com
Printed in the USA
LVOW05*0755041213

363774LV00005B/10/P